WORKSHOPS IN COMPUTING
Series edited by C. J. van Rijsbergen

Also in this series

Women into Computing: Selected Papers 1988–1990
Gillian Lovegrove and Barbara Segal (Eds.)

3rd Refinement Workshop (organised by BCS-FACS, and sponsored by IBM UK Laboratories, Hursley Park and the Programming Research Group, University of Oxford), Hursley Park, 9–11 January 1990
Carroll Morgan and J. C. P. Woodcock (Eds.)

Designing Correct Circuits, Workshop jointly organised by the Universities of Oxford and Glasgow, Oxford, 26–28 September 1990
Geraint Jones and Mary Sheeran (Eds.)

Functional Programming, Glasgow 1990, Proceedings of the 1990 Glasgow Workshop on Functional Programming, Ullapool, Scotland, 13–15 August 1990
Simon L. Peyton Jones, Graham Hutton and Carsten Kehler Holst (Eds.)

4th Refinement Workshop, Proceedings of the 4th Refinement Workshop, organised by BCS-FACS, Cambridge, 9–11 January 1991
Joseph M. Morris and Roger C. Shaw (Eds.)

AI and Cognitive Science '90, University of Ulster at Jordanstown, 20–21 September 1990
Michael F. McTear and Norman Creaney (Eds.)

Software Re-use, Utrecht 1989, Proceedings of the Software Re-use Workshop, Utrecht, The Netherlands, 23–24 November 1989
Liesbeth Dusink and Patrick Hall (Eds.)

Z User Workshop, 1990, Proceedings of the Fifth Annual Z User Meeting, Oxford, 17–18 December 1990
J.E. Nicholls (Ed.)

IV Higher Order Workshop, Banff 1990
Proceedings of the IV Higher Order Workshop, Banff, Alberta, Canada, 10–14 September 1990
Graham Birtwistle (Ed.)

ALPUK 91 Proceedings of the 3rd UK Annual Conference on Logic Programming, Edinburgh, 10–12 April 1991
Geraint A. Wiggins, Chris Mellish and Tim Duncan (Eds.)

Specifications of Database Systems, International Workshop on Specifications of Database Systems, Glasgow, 3–5 July 1991
David J. Harper and Moira C. Norrie (Eds.)

7th UK Computer and Telecommunications Performance Engineering Workshop, Edinburgh, 22–23 July 1991
J Hillston, P.J.B. King and R.J. Pooley (Eds.)

continued on back page...

T.P. Clement and K.-K. Lau (Eds.)

Logic Program Synthesis and Transformation

Proceedings of LOPSTR 91, International Workshop on Logic Program Synthesis and Transformation, University of Manchester, 4–5 July 1991

Sponsored by the Association for Logic Programming and ALPUK

Published in collaboration with the British Computer Society

Springer-Verlag
London Berlin Heidelberg New York
Paris Tokyo Hong Kong
Barcelona Budapest

Timothy Paul Clement, MA, DPhil
Department of Computer Science
University of Manchester
Oxford Road
Manchester M13 9PL, UK

Kung-Kiu Lau, BSc, PhD
Department of Computer Science
University of Manchester
Oxford Road
Manchester M13 9PL, UK

ISBN 3-540-19742-7 Springer-Verlag Berlin Heidelberg New York
ISBN 0-387-19742-7 Springer-Verlag New York Berlin Heidelberg

British Library Cataloguing in Publication Data
LOPSTR '91 (University of Manchester)
Logic program synthesis and transformation. – (Workshops in computing)
I. Title II. Clement, Tim III. Lau, Kung-Kiu IV. Series
005.1
ISBN 3-540-19742-7

Library of Congress Data available

34/3830-543210 Printed on acid-free paper

Foreword

Program synthesis and transformation have, for a long time, attracted people from Logic, Computer Science, Artificial Intelligence and Software Engineering, because they are challenging topics where mathematical rigour is expected to contribute to software production. People in Logic Programming, keenly aware of its affinity with these two topics, have also explored the possibilities opened up by the notion of logic programs.

Logic programs are broadly definable as logical formulae which are executable one way or another. They all depend on the choice of the logic and execution mechanism. But no matter what they are, their declarative character distinguishes them from, say, imperative programs. Since, for example, programs and specification are both logical formulae and can be manipulated by a deductive system, it is usual that the soundness of synthesized programs is established without much difficulty. Also, the freedom of procedural interpretation of logic programs together with their abstractness allows us to develop various types of programs including concurrent ones.

Leaving declarative aspects on one side, however, we have to note other aspects, which more often than not turn out to be vital in actual logic program development. They include side effects, transformation strategies, implementation of meta-programming and so on. This is especially true for partial evaluation.

In order to discuss theoretical and practical problems concerning logic program synthesis and transformation, LOPSTR 91 was held at the University of Manchester, 4–5 July, 1991. It was the first workshop exclusively directed towards logic program synthesis and transformation and 24 papers were presented. It is hoped that the proceedings will provide a comprehensive view of the current activities in these areas and material for future research.

Ibaraki
July 1991

Taisuke Sato

Preface

The aim of LOPSTR 91 is to fill a gap in the existing range of Logic Programming workshops, namely the absence of a workshop dedicated to 'program synthesis' and its close relation 'program transformation'. Judging by the success of LOPSTR 91, we have not only confirmed the presence of this gap, but hopefully also made a small contribution to remedying the situation. Our thanks to all the contributors who made LOPSTR 91 the success that it is.

These proceedings provide a complete record of the workshop. All the talks presented at the workshop are included, in the form of full papers or extended abstracts. Extended abstracts represent either work in its infancy or work that has been published in full elsewhere. We are most grateful to all the referees for their work.

We thank the Association for Logic Programming for supporting student travel to the workshop, and ALPUK for sponsoring the workshop.

Last, but not least, we would also like to thank Lynn Howarth for her help with the organisation of the workshop.

Here's to LOPSTR 92!

Manchester
September 1991

Tim Clement and Kung-Kiu Lau

Contents

Program Equivalence, Program Development and Integrity Checking

Jonathan M. Lever
Department of Computing, Imperial College
London, UK

Abstract

This paper is concerned with the analysis of equivalence in logic program development. Different formulations of program equivalence are discussed and it is demonstrated that the perfect model semantics provides a measure that is of appropriate strength for the analysis of equivalence in program development. The development of a logic program is compared with the evolution of a deductive database, and it is shown that the notion of integrity constraints on a deductive database can be applied to a developing logic program to give conditions for the perfect equivalence of successive versions of the program. This results in a method which allows program equivalence to be analysed retrospectively without placing restrictions on the manner in which one version of a program can be derived from another.

1 Introduction

The relation of equivalence between programs is of central importance in program development, and apart from an important paper by Maher [8] has received little attention in the logic programming literature. Previously, proof that a step of program development respected program equivalence has only been possible when that step was achieved by the application of a general purpose technique for program transformation known to give a program equivalent to the original. While such transformations have their place in program development, it is likely that they can only expect to account for a small proportion of the changes made to a program under development [4]. In contrast, the method for analysis of equivalence presented in this paper is general purpose and offers a retrospective analysis of equivalence in program development which places no restrictions on the nature of changes that may take place between successive generations of the program.

A method to determine program equivalence can be applied to prove the correctness of a program by showing it to be equivalent to previous versions whose correctness may be easier to grasp, as is frequently found in the derivation of a more computationally orientated program from a naive version. A second application is to the case of a change in the way data is represented in a program, where one wishes to show that other relations which draw on the data have been preserved. Thirdly, when a large scale program is being assembled using code drawn from a variety of sources it is useful to have a way of determining the equivalence of certain common relations which may receive different definitions according to different sources.

In [8], Maher compares different notions of equivalence associated with various different semantics that have been defined for definite clause logic programs. These different notions are of different strengths in the sense that two programs that are equivalent under a relatively weak notion of equivalence (such as equivalence of success sets) may fail to be equivalent under some stronger notion (such as full logical equivalence). It is shown that a fairly weak formulation of equivalence is most appropriate for the analysis of program development as strong a notion of equivalence greatly restricts the scope for interesting and computationally significant differences between equivalent definitions of relations. A more liberal notion accepts such differences whilst ensuring that the two programs still share some significant aspects: the bottom line is probably equivalence of success sets.

The discussion of Maher is extended to take into account recent developments in the semantics of logic programs. In particular, the perfect model semantics proposed by Przymusinski [10] is shown to provide a notion of equivalence which is of appropriate strength for the analysis of program development. Since the perfect model semantics is defined for the class of locally stratified logic programs, the results of the paper are in general applicable to this wide class of programs.

An analogy is drawn between the development of a logic program and the evolution of a deductive database. It is shown that notion of integrity constraints on a database can be applied to a developing logic program, and a theorem is proved which enables perfect equivalence to be evaluated by proving constraint satisfaction under the perfect model semantics. A technique for proving satisfaction of program properties and integrity constraints under the perfect model semantics has been developed elsewhere [7].

2 Program Equivalence in Program Development

The different semantics that have been proposed for logic programs give rise to different notions of program equivalence [8]. These different equivalences are of different strengths: an equivalence $\sim_1$ is (strictly) stronger than an equivalence $\sim_2$ if for all programs P and Q, whenever P $\sim_1$ Q then P $\sim_2$ Q (and $\sim_2$ is not stronger than $\sim_1$). For the analysis of equivalence in program development it is important to employ a notion of equivalence of an appropriate strength. If the notion of equivalence is too strong, it may be impossible to make any significant changes to a program whilst respecting program equivalence. This issue is best investigated through consideration of some simple examples.

Example 2.1

Program 1: $p \leftarrow q$
$q \leftarrow r$

Program 2: $p \leftarrow r$
$q \leftarrow r$

Here, Program 2 is obtained from Program 1 by a simple step of partial evaluation. It is easy to imagine such a step being made in program development.

However, according to the notion of program equivalence formulated as identity of T_P functions (the strongest of the equivalences considered by Maher in [8]), the above two program are not equivalent, since for Program 1, $T_P(\{r\}) = \{q\}$, while for Program 2, $T_P(\{r\}) = \{p, q\}$.

Similarly, the programs are not equivalent according to identity of their respective $(T_P + Id)$ functions [8] since for Program 1, $(T_P + Id)(\{r\}) = \{q, r\}$, while for program P, $(T_P + Id)(\{r\}) = \{p, q, r\}$. Nor are Programs 1 and 2 logically equivalent, since Program 2 has a model in which q is true and p is false, whereas Program 1 has no such model. These notions of equivalence are therefore too strong for the analysis of equivalence in program development as equivalence would be destroyed by a simple step of partial evaluation as in this example.

There are two types of equivalence are defined using Clark's completion [8]:

(i) logical equivalence of completions: $E \models P1{*} \leftrightarrow P2{*}$ where E denotes Clark's Equality Theory and $P{*}$ the completed definitions of the clauses in P.

(ii) Herbrand equivalence of completions: $\models_{HU} P1{*} \leftrightarrow P2{*}$, where $\models_{HU}$ denotes consequence in Herbrand models only.

It is shown by Maher that logical equivalence of completions implies equality of the finite failure sets and of the ground finite failure sets of the two programs, while Herbrand equality of completions implies equality of ground finite failure sets only. It follows that development of a program which results in an increase in either the finite failure set or the ground finite failure set (and consequently improves termination properties of the program) will not preserve logical equivalence of completions. Similarly, an increase in the ground finite failure set does not preserve Herbrand equivalence of completions. The completions of the following two programs are neither logically equivalent nor Herbrand equivalent:

Example 2.2

Program 1: p ← q
q ← q

Program 2: p ← q

The appropriateness of classifying the above two programs as 'equivalent' is perhaps more controversial than in the case of the two programs of Example 2.1, but can be argued for as follows:

(i) The modification of Program 1 to Program 2 clearly represents a 'good' step of program development as the termination characteristics of the program are improved[1].

(ii) Although the programs differ with respect to termination, they are by no means completely different — in particular, they have the same success set.

[1]Although this is a somewhat artificial example, a similar situation could arise in the elimination of a loop in the development of a path-finding program, say.

The above example suggests that a notion of equivalence that is sensitive to changes in termination behaviour of the developing program is too strong to provide a base-line for the analysis of equivalence in program development. Ideally, termination could be monitored through some secondary technique while program equivalence is investigated with respect to some measure weaker than equivalence or Herbrand equivalence of completions.

From the different strengths of equivalence considered by Maher, there remains only the relatively weak equivalence given by equivalence of success sets. This formulation of program equivalence allows for considerable variation between two equivalent programs, with the consequence that creative and computationally significant changes can be made to a program under development while still respecting program equivalence.

For definite clause programs, equivalence of success sets can also be thought of as equivalence of least Herbrand models. However, a notion of equivalence which restricts attention to Herbrand models can give counter-intuitive results which arise from the emphasis placed on the language in which the programs are considered to be written. Restricting attention to a language with a fixed supply of constants and function symbols as is usually implied by a Herbrand semantics means that adding a definition of a new predicate which mentions some constant or function symbol outside the language to two previously equivalent programs can result in two programs which are non- equivalent[2]. Consider the following example.

Example 2.3

Program 1: p(x)
q(a)

Program 2: p(a)
q(a)

These programs have equivalent least Herbrand models given by p(a), q(a) if the language of the program is taken to be that containing the single constant 'a' and no function symbols. However, if the fact 'r(b)' is added to both programs, the two Programs 1^+ and 2^+ obtained no longer have equivalent least Herbrand models as the least Herbrand model of Program 1^+ is {p(a), p(b), q(a), r(b)} while that of Program 2^+ is {p(a), q(a), r(b)}.

This aspect of equivalence according to the least Herbrand model is undesirable for the analysis of program development, in which addition of new relations to a program may well create conditions similar to those in the above example. Some authors have suggested an extension of the semantics given by the least Herbrand model of a definite clause program to that given by the class MIN(P) of all minimal models of the program P which are also models of the axioms of Clark's Equality Theory for P [11]. This extension provides a notion of equivalence which is comparable in strength to that given by equivalence of least Herbrand models while at the same time avoiding the problems associated with a Herbrand notion of equivalence indicated above.

For these reasons, equivalence according to the class of minimal models MIN(P) is the most appropriate measure for the analysis of equivalence in the development of a definite clause logic program.

[2]See also Kunen's remarks reported in [13] p.44.

The perfect model semantics proposed by Przymusinski [10] coincides with the minimal model semantics for definite clause programs and is applicable to the wider class of locally stratified logic programs. It permits the discussion of program equivalence to be extended to this class of programs through a notion of 'perfect equivalence' — two programs being perfect equivalent if they have the same perfect models.

The perfect model semantics is one of a number of recent developments in the area of semantics of logic programs which have arisen out of a growing dissatisfaction with the semantics provided by the completion (see, for example, [6]). Other such semantics are the stable model semantics [2], the well-founded semantics [14] and the semantics given by the iterated least fixpoint model [1]. While these semantics differ considerably in the manner in which they are defined, and most significantly in whether non-Herbrand models are considered, there are many convergences which have been shown for the classes of stratified and locally stratified programs. Thus, for stratified programs the iterated least fixpoint model is identical to the unique Herbrand perfect model, and for locally stratified programs the well-founded semantics coincides with the perfect model semantics whilst the unique stable model is identical to the unique Herbrand perfect model (most of these results are given in [2]). It follows that perfect equivalence is sufficient to imply equivalence according to each of the other semantics listed above.

A final point for discussion in relation to the semantics of program equivalence is how to formulate equivalence of programs which are written in different languages in the sense that there are constants, function symbols or predicates used in one of the programs which do not appear in the other. The approach outlined by Maher [8] is to compare the two programs with respect to some common sub-language. As Maher points out, this approach makes sense where a predicate is defined in terms of different auxiliary predicates, for when comparing, say, the programs for naive reverse and tail-recursive reverse, it is not significant that one program has a definition of 'append' while the other does not.

Maher acknowledges that using the common sub-language produces counter-intuitive results in situations in which the programs use different sets of constant or function symbols — in the extreme case, any two programs written in disjoint languages would be equivalent. However, this problem does not arise in connection with the notion of perfect equivalence adopted here as consideration is not restricted to Herbrand models. When evaluating perfect equivalence of programs, the sets of constants and of function symbols of the language in which the comparison is made are implicitly taken as containing the respective sets from both programs. The only assumption in force comes from the fact that perfect models satisfy the axioms of Clark's Equality Theory, with the result that for the purposes of the comparison, the constants and function symbols of the two programs together receive their free interpretation. In particular, constants that appear in one program but not in the other are considered to denote objects different to those denoted by the constants of the other program.

3 Program Equivalence and Integrity Checking

In this section, an analogy is drawn between the development of a logic program and the evolution of a deductive database. The evolution of a database is typically not equivalence preserving as it must reflect changes in the world represented by the database, but the distinction between the statements of the database and the integrity constraints is of relevance for the development of logic programs. Both are logical sentences that are true of the world represented by the database (provided that integrity is not violated), but the statements of the database are used for computation while the integrity constraints are not. In developing a logic program, the statements of an old version of a program remain true of the relations defined in a new version but are no longer used in computing these relations and can be therefore be viewed as integrity constraints on the new program.

To obtain equivalence of the old and new programs rather than subsumption of the old program by the new, the perspective must be reversed so that integrity constraints on the old program defined by the clauses of the new program are also considered. It will be shown that perfect equivalence of two locally stratified program can be evaluated by taking the clauses of each program as integrity constraint on the other program and showing constraint satisfaction under the perfect model semantics.

Before proving this result some background concerning the perfect model semantics must be established — in particular the concept of a 'preference relation' between models. For the sake of simplicity of presentation only the class of stratified programs, for which this preference relation is derived from a priority relation between predicate symbols, is considered. The results extend to the class of locally stratified programs, where the preference relation is derived from a priority relation defined over the set of ground atoms [9].

The priority relation, $<$, between predicate symbols is defined by Przymusinski so that for each clause of the program

(i) Negative premises have higher priority than the head

(ii) Positive premises have priority higher than or equal to the head

More formal definitions and motivation can be found in [10]. The preference relation between models, $\prec$, is derived from the priority relation between predicates in such a way as to minimise extensions of high priority predicates — again, the reader is refered to [10] for the precise definition. N $\preceq$ M denotes that the model N is either preferable to or equal to M. Finally, a model is perfect iff there are no models preferable to it. As an example, for the program consisting of the single clause

$$p \leftarrow \text{not } q$$

the predicate q has a higher priority than p. The program has the single perfect (Herbrand) model p, which is preferable to the model q.

The set of perfect models of a program P is denoted by PERF(P), while the expression PERF(P) $\models$ W states that the formula W is true in all perfect models of the program P.

The following result of [10] is needed as a lemma:

Lemma (Przymusinski)
For every model N of a locally stratified program P there is a Perfect model M with $M \preceq N$.

A condition that the preference relations of the two programs are identical is required in the statement of the theorem, written $\prec_{P1} \equiv \prec_{P2}$. The preference relations $\prec_{P1}$ and $\prec_{P2}$ of two programs P1 and P2 are defined to be identical if and only if for any two models N and M of both P1 and P2, $N \prec_{P1} M$ iff $N \prec_{P2} M$. Identity of the priority relations defined by two programs is a necessary condition for identity of their preference relations and can be determined syntactically. It is not however a sufficient condition. For example, the programs

Program 1: p ← not q
p

Program 2: p ← q
p

define different priority relations. However, both programs have the same (Herbrand) models — p and p, q — and the preference relations of both programs agree in preferring p to p, q. Nor is identity of preference relations a necessary condition for perfect equivalence — one can construct an example in which for two models N and M of both programs, $N \prec_{P1} M$ and $M \prec_{P2} N$, but where there exists a third model of both programs S such that $S \prec_{P1} N$ and $S \prec_{P2} M$. Neither N nor M is a perfect model for either of the programs and the difference in the preference relations is not reflected in a difference in the selection of perfect models.

The condition on the identity of preference relations is therefore stronger than would be liked, especially when determined by identity of priority relations, as it excludes comparison of certain pairs of programs which may nonetheless be perfect equivalent. However, the issue of whether a difference in preference relations is of significance is in general extremely difficult to determine.

Theorem
Let P1 and P2 be locally stratified logic programs with $\prec_{P1} \equiv \prec_{P2}$.
Then PERF(P1) $\models$ P2 and PERF(P2) $\models$ P1 iff PERF(P1) = PERF(P2).

Proof
If PERF(P1) = PERF(P2) then trivially PERF(P1) $\models$ P2 and PERF(P2) $\models$ P1.

The proof that PERF(P1) $\models$ P2 and PERF(P2) $\models$ P1 implies PERF(P1) = PERF(P2) is by contradiction.

Suppose not i.e. that PERF(P1) $\models$ P2, PERF(P2) $\models$ P1 and without loss of generality that there exists a model M $\in$ PERF(P1) such that M $\notin$ PERF(P2).

Since PERF(P1) $\models$ P2, M is a model of P2.

Since M $\notin$ PERF(P2), M is not a perfect model of P2 and by the lemma there exists a perfect model M$'$ of P2 with M$' \preceq_{P2}$ M. Since M$' \neq$ M, M$' \prec_{P2}$ M.

Since PERF(P2) $\models$ P1, M$'$ is a model of P1, and since M$' \prec_{P2}$ M and $\prec_{P1} \equiv \prec_{P2}$, M$' \prec_{P1}$ M.

Therefore M is not a perfect model of P1, giving a contradiction. □

4 Evaluating Constraints to show Perfect Equivalence

In order to show the perfect equivalence of two programs using the theorem of Section 3, a method for showing constraint satisfaction under the perfect model semantics is required, that is, a method for showing that an integrity constraint is true in all perfect models of a program. In logic programming, integrity constraints are commonly written as denials [12], and in [7] , a suitable technique for proving satisfaction of constraints expressed in this way that was developed in the context of proving program properties is described. The technique is based on SLS-resolution, the procedural counterpart of the perfect model semantics.

SLS-Resolution is similar to SLDNF-Resolution but replaces the finite failure of SLDNF by a notion of infinite failure under which an SLS-tree is failed if all its branches are either finite and failed or are infinite [11]. SLS-Resolution is sound with respect to the perfect model semantics — in particular, if a query '$\leftarrow$ Q(x)' has a failed SLS-tree using a program P, where Q(x) is some conjunction with free variables x, then PERF(P) $\models \neg\exists$ xQ(x) i.e. PERF(P) $\models\leftarrow$ Q(x). Constraint satisfaction can therefore be proved by treating each constraint as a query to be evaluated from the relevant program (together with the definitions of any predicates local to the other program) and showing the existence of a *failed* SLS-tree for this query. This is straightforward when the constraint has an SLS-tree which is finite and failed, while the technique presented in [7] allows the existence of an infinite failed SLS-tree to be deduced from consideration of a finite sub-tree and thereby gives some practical significance to the theoretical notion of infinite failure.

When checking equivalence in this way, if any constraint succeeds then the two programs are non-equivalent. Further, the computed answer substitution gives information about which instances of a predicate are provable from one program but not from the other. This information may then be used in debugging.

While the generation of infinite computations during constraint evaluation is ultimately dependant on the behaviour of the individual programs in that respect, if the programs are comparatively 'well-behaved' — successful queries are fully instantiated by their computed answer substitutions and ground queries terminate — then it is only in the case of constraints derived from the definitions of relations defined recursively *in both programs* that infinite computations are generated.

The combination of formulation of conditions for program equivalence as integrity constraints and a resolution-based approach to evaluating constraint satisfaction also allows work on deriving database updates which preserve constraint satisfaction such as [3] to be applied to program development. From an incomplete definition of the new program further definitions can be synthesised in such a way as to satisfy the constraints arising from the old program, which is achieved by asserting definitions which cause the SLS-trees for the evaluation of the constraints to be failed.

5 Examples

The first example concerns the development of a program representing a 'blocks world' and is adapted from [5] p.212. In Program 1 the state of the world is represented through the relations 'on(x, y)' and 'clear(x)'. In Program 2 it is represented by means of the single relation 'state(z)' through the use of a function symbol '*on*'. While the second program is less natural than the first, it offers the advantage that changes in the state of the world can be carried out more easily. Also, the integrity constraint '← on(x, y), clear(y)' can be shown to be satisfied by Program 2 independently of the definition of 'state(z)' i.e. independently of the state of the world, which is not the case for the representation used in Program 1. The intricacies of Program 2 are necessary to ensure safe handling of negated subgoals.

Example 4.1

```
Program 1: on(a, b)
           on(b, c)
           on(c, table)
           on(d, table)

           clear(a)
           clear(d)

Program 2: on(x, y) ← state(z), member(on(x, y) z)
           clear(y) ← state(z), member(on(y, x) z), not something_on(y, z)

           something_on(y, z) ← member(on(x, y) z)

           member(x, x.y)
           member(x, u.y) ← member(x, y)

           state(on(a, b).on(b, c).on(c, table).on(d, table).nil)
```

It is desired to prove that the change of representation has been accomplished correctly, that is, to show the equivalence of the programs for the relations 'on(x, y)' and 'clear(x)' which are defined by both programs. In a context such as this it is plainly unnecessary to consider equivalence with respect to predicates such as 'member(x, y)' which are local to one or other of the programs.

Conditions for the equivalence of Program 1 and Program 2 with respect to the relations 'on(x, y)' and 'clear(x)' are formulated by taking the clauses defining each of these relations in one program as integrity constraints on the other program (augmented by definitions of local predicates from the first program as necessary). The integrity constraints are written as denials by negating the head of each clause and transferring it to the body.

Constraints on Program 2

← not on(a ,b)
← not on(b, c)
← not on(c, table)
← not on (d, table)
← not clear(a)
← not clear(d)

Constraints on Program 1 + Definitions of predicates local to Program 2

← state(z), member(*on*(x, y) z), not on(x ,y)
← state(z), member(*on*(x, y) z), not something_on(y, z), not clear(y)

The above constraints all fail finitely when evaluated using SLS-resolution — for the reader unfamiliar with SLS-resolution, finite failed SLS-trees are identical to finite failed SLDNF- trees. From the soundness of SLS-resolution it follows that

PERF(Program 2) ⊨ Program 1
and PERF(Program 1 ∪ Local Predicates) ⊨ Program 2

Applying the theorem of Section 4 gives the equivalence of Programs 1 and 2 with respect to their common relations.

Example 4.2

The following two program both define predicates 'even(x)' and 'odd(x)'.

Program 1: even(0)
even(s(s(x))) ← even(x)
odd(s(x)) ← even(x)

Program 2: even(x) ← odd(s(x))
odd(s(0))
odd(s(s(x))) ← odd(x)

The conditions that the two programs are equivalent are given by satisfaction of the following sets of constraints:

Constraints on Program 2

← not even(0)
← even(x), not even(s(s(x)))
← even(x), not odd(s(x))

Constraints on Program 1

$\leftarrow$ odd(s(x)), not even(x)
$\leftarrow$ not odd(s(0))
$\leftarrow$ odd(x), not odd(s(s(x)))

The constraints all have failed SLS-trees. The technique presented in [7] is able to show the satisfaction of those constraints that generate infinite failed SLS-trees. Hence the two programs are perfect equivalent.

6 Conclusions

The notion of integrity constraints on a database can be applied to a developing logic program to give conditions for the equivalence of successive versions of the program. Perfect equivalence has been shown to be of appropriate strength for the analysis of equivalence in program development and can be evaluated, subject to a condition on the use of negation in the two programs, by showing constraint satisfaction under the perfect model semantics. The method contributes to the development of logic programs by permitting program equivalence to be established retrospectively, without placing restrictions on the way in which a programmer may derive one version of a program from another.

Acknowledgements
Thanks to Chris Hogger for many useful discussions and comments on draft versions of this paper. This research was carried out as part of the ESPRIT Basic Research Action COMPULOG.

References

[1] K. R. Apt, H. A. Blair, and A. Walker. Towards a theory of declarative knowledge. In J. Minker, editor, *Foundations of Deductive Databases and Logic Programming*, pages 89–148. Morgan Kaufman, 1988.

[2] M. Gelfond and V. Lifschitz. The stable model semantics for logic programming. In R. A. Kowalski, editor, *Proceedings of the Fifth Logic Programming Symposium*, pages 1070–1080, Seatle,Washington, 1988. MIT Press.

[3] A. Guessom and J. W. Lloyd. Updating knowledge bases. *New Generation Computing*, 8(1):77–89, 1990.

[4] C. J. Hogger. Programming environments. Invited talk, ECAI 88, 1988.

[5] R. A. Kowalski. *Logic for Problem Solving.* North Holland, Amsterdam, 1979.

[6] K. Kunen. Some remarks on the completed database. In *Proceedings of the Fith Logic Programming Symposium*, pages 978–992. MIT Press, 1988.

[7] J. M. Lever. Proving program properties by means of SLS-resolution. In *Proceedings of the Eighth Int. Conference on Logic Programming*, pages 614–628. MIT Press, 1991.

[8] M. J. Maher. Equivalences of logic programs. In J. Minker, editor, *Foundations of Deductive Databases*, pages 627–658. Morgan Kaufmann, 1988.

[9] T. C. Przymusinski. On the declarative semantics of deductive databases and logic programs. In J. Minker, editor, *Foundations of Deductive Databases and Logic Programming*, pages 193–216. Morgan Kaufman, 1988.

[10] T. C. Przymusinski. Perfect model semantics. In R. A. Kowalski, editor, *Proceedings of the Fifth Logic Programming Symposium*, pages 1081–1096, Seatle,Washington, 1988. MIT Press.

[11] T. C. Przymusinski. On the declarative and procedural semantics of logic programs. *Journal of Automated Reasoning*, 5:167–205, 1989.

[12] F. Sadri and R. A. Kowalski. A theorem proving approach to database integrity. In J. Minker, editor, *Foundations of Deductive Databases*, pages 313–362. Morgan Kaufmann, 1988.

[13] J. C. Shepherdson. Negation in logic programming. In J. Minker, editor, *Foundations of Deductive Databases and Logic Programming*, pages 19–88. Morgan Kaufman, 1988.

[14] A. Van Gelder, K. Ross, and J. Sclipf. Unfounded sets and well-founded semantics for general logic programs. In *Proceedings of the Seventh Symposium on Principles of Database Systems*, pages 221–230, 1988.

Program Specification and Synthesis in Constructive Formal Systems

Pierangelo Miglioli, Ugo Moscato, Mario Ornaghi
Dipartimento di Scienze dell'Informazione
Universita' degli Studi di Milano
Via Comelico 39
20135 Milano, Italy

Abstract

Constructive mathematics has been proposed by many authors as a theoretical basis for program synthesis, and various implementations of this idea have been developed. However, the main problem in implementation is how to build a real environment for software development. In this paper, we present the main features of a logical system we are studying which provides specification tools and a deductive system for deriving programs from their specifications. Our aim is to use this system as a starting point for a real programming environment.

1 Introduction

It is well known that within suitable constructive systems proofs can be interpreted as "programs" (e.g. [MO, Sat, BC, MaL, Goa]); also various implementations inspired by this paradigm have been developed (e.g. [BSW, CAB, HN, Got, Hen]). We have partially implemented a system named PAP (Proofs As Programs) [BrMMO, MMO0] for program synthesis, based on a superintuitionistic first order logic where both classical and constructive semantics can be used in a consistent way.

In our experience with PAP we encountered some problems related to an attempt at building up a real programming environment, i.e. one which has at least the following features:

- it contains a *formal specification language* with an abstract but *natural* declarative semantics;
- it contains an appropriate set of derivation rules to derive correct programs from formal specifications such that derivations are *natural* and short;
- the set of programs derivable from a specification should cover *all* the possible algorithms which satisfy the specification.

Such a programming system is not easy to achieve whilst maintaining a sound theoretical basis. In the following sections we describe the present state of our research.

In Section 2 we introduce the specification formalism for PAP, which is based on a semantics which combines realizability [Kl] and uniform solvability [Med].

In Section 3 we present the associated derivation rules. These rules give rise to a constructive logical system which is stronger than the intuitionistic one and is classically consistent; in Appendix we list the logical rules and define their computational meaning.

Finally in Section 4 we make some final remarks and we discuss the possibility of mixing different kinds of reasoning, in particular classical and constructive reasoning.

2 The Specification Formalism

From an informal point of view, a specification of a program characterizes a class of equivalent programs; generally it also contains some characterization of the data on which these programs work.

Formalizing this notion depends on the general framework in which it is carried out. Often there is no substantial distinction between data and programs, e.g. in an algebraic approach a specification is an equational theory which defines at the same time data and operations in an abstract way. Also, it may happen that the specifications and the programs are not distinguished in a clean way, e.g., in PROLOG, the axioms (clauses) characterizing a relation to be computed are also the program to compute it.

In our approach, we distinguish between all the above aspects: a program specification is a *specification sequent* interpreted in a class of models in a *context*; a *context* contains the definition of the data on which the program works and is axiomatized by a first order theory; a *program* is a *proof* of a (program) specification.

In Section 2.1 we explain the interpretation of sequents as program specifications and in Section 2.2 we show how a context can be specified by first order axioms.

2.1 Program Specifications and their Semantics

When specifying a program P one starts from some initial knowledge of the problem motivating the construction of P; we call this knowledge a *context*, a triple of the form:

$$C = (L, M, NT) \tag{1}$$

where L is a first order language built up from a many sorted signature; M is a class of models for L; and NT is a set of normal (or canonical) terms (e.g. in arithmetic, the numerals $0, succ(0), \ldots$).

A program specification in a context C is a *specification sequent* of the form:

$$\textsf{from } A(\underline{x}) \textsf{ give } \underline{z} : B(\underline{x}, \underline{z}) \tag{2}$$

where A, B are formulas of L, the free variables of A are contained in $\underline{x}$ and the free variables of B are contained in $\underline{x}$,$\underline{z}$ ($\underline{x}$, $\underline{z}$ may be empty); we call $\underline{x}$ the *free variables*, A the *input formula*, $\underline{z}$ the *output variables* and B the *output formula* of the sequent.

The definition of the meaning of a specification sequent is based on the notion of a *truth evaluation*. Intuitively, a truth evaluation represents the *knowledge* which is needed to explain *why a formula is true*, starting from the truth of its subformulas. For example, the truth of the formula $happy(John) \vee \neg happy(John)$ has two possible explanations: (a) it is true because $happy(John)$ is true; (b) it is true because $happy(John)$ is false. A formal semantics based on truth evaluations is given in Section 2.1.1; here we explain the meaning of specifications sequents in an intuitive way.

The free variables are considered as input variables. For every input substitution $\underline{x}/\underline{t}$ (by *normal terms* $\underline{t}$), the instance

$$\text{from } A(\underline{t}) \text{ give } \underline{z} : B(\underline{t}, \underline{z}) \tag{3}$$

is interpreted as follows:

- from $A(\underline{t})$ states that we may give any truth evaluation E_A of $A(\underline{t})$ as an input which explains why $A(\underline{t})$ is true in some model m of M we have in mind;
- give $\underline{z} : B(\underline{t}, \underline{z})$ indicates that we get an output substitution $\underline{z}/\underline{t}'$ (by *normal terms* $\underline{t}'$) and an output evaluation E_B, which explains why $B(\underline{t}, \underline{t}')$ is true in m;
- we require that the output data depends only on the input data.

For instance, let us consider the following specification sequent:

$$\text{from } beautiful(x) \vee \neg beautiful(x) \text{ give } likes(Mary, x) \vee \neg likes(Mary, x) \tag{4}$$

in the context characterized by the relations *beautiful* and *likes*, the constant symbols *John*, *Mary*, *Phil* (which are the normal terms) and the class M of the models satisfying the axiom

$$\forall x : (likes(Mary, x) \leftrightarrow beautiful(x)) \ . \tag{5}$$

Let $x/John$ be an input substitution; then an input evaluation of $beautiful(John) \vee \neg beautiful(John)$ is needed. If the input evaluation is $beutiful(John)$, the correct answer is $likes(Mary, John)$; if it is $\neg beautiful(John)$, the correct answer is $\neg likes(Mary, John)$.

In general (4) specifies the input-output relation which, for every constant K, associates the output $likes(Mary, K)$ to the input $(x/K, beautiful(K))$ and the output $\neg likes(Mary, K)$ to the input $(x/K, \neg beautiful(K))$. Therefore, for every model m of the context, if the input is true in m, then the corresponding output is true in m.

In this example the outputs depend only on the inputs, as required. This requirement seems to be obvious, but it has an interesting consequence, namely that the underlying logic cannot be classical logic. For instance, let us consider (in the context of (4)) the sequent

$$\text{from give } likes(Mary, x) \vee \neg likes(Mary, x) \tag{6}$$

and the input substitution $x/John$; $likes(Mary, John) \vee \neg likes(Mary, John)$ is true in any model; but this sequent has no input formula and so no input evaluation can be given; therefore we do not have sufficient knowledge to evaluate the output formula, i.e. to state whether $likes(Mary, John)$ is true or not.

This is related to the knowledge needed to solve a problem and, in our semantics, it is linked to the following notion of uniformity. We say that a formula A is *uniformly valid* in a class M of models iff there is a truth evaluation E_A which is true in all the models of M (i.e. the explanation of the truth of A does not depend on the model). We also say that a specification

$$\text{from } A(\underline{x}) \text{ give } \underline{z} : \; B(\underline{x}, \underline{z}) \tag{7}$$

is *uniformly solvable* in M iff, for every instance

$$\text{from } A(\underline{t}) \text{ give } \underline{z} : \; B(\underline{t}, \underline{z}) \tag{8}$$

and for every evaluation E_A of $A(\underline{t})$ there is an output substitution $\underline{z}/\underline{t}'$ and an output evaluation E_B of $B(\underline{t}, \underline{t}')$ such that, if E_A is true in a model m of M, then E_B is true in m.

Now since we want to specify programs, we require that truth evaluations are represented in some data structure and that the functions involved are recursive; this is captured, in our semantics, by a notion of *recursive realizability*.

Let us consider, for example, the sequent

$$\text{from give } Z : \; y + Z = x \vee \neg \exists Z : y + Z = x \tag{9}$$

in the context of Peano Arithmetic it specifies the problem of finding, for every input substitution x/n, y/m an output substitution Z/d such that $d = x - y$ or to state that such a Z/d does not exist.[1] This specification is solvable since there is an algorithm to compute d or to state that d does not exist; but in arithmetic there are specifications of this kind such that the existence domain is not recursive, so that the corresponding specification sequent is not solvable.

A final example is related to the notion of an oracle. Let us consider the sequent:

$$\text{from } \forall x : \; (r(x) \vee \neg r(x)) \text{ give } Z : \; U(Z) \tag{10}$$

a truth evaluation of the input formula is a function F such that, for every x, $F(x)$ is an explanation of the truth of $r(x) \vee \neg r(x)$. For every model m of the context we have a function $F_m(x)$ evaluating the truth of $r(x)$ according to the interpretation of r in m; we call this function an *oracle* which is true in m. The meaning of the sequent is that a program solving the specified task can 'call the oracle F' as a routine. In PAP oracles are realized by an interaction with the user.

In the next section we explain some elements of a formal semantics corresponding to the above intuitive explanation.

2.1.1 Constructive Semantics of Program Specifications

For the sake of conciseness, we codify evaluations by natural numbers (Gödel numbers) and we call the code for an evaluation *a realization*. Our codification has the following features, where $\mathcal{N}$ is the set of the natural numbers:

[1] n, m, d are normal terms, i.e. numerals.

- We indicate by $\langle x_1, \ldots, x_n \rangle$ the Gödel number of an n-tuple $x_1, .., x_n$ of natural numbers.
- We indicate by $\lceil t \rceil$ the Gödel number of a term t.
- We have a denumerable set O of functions from $\mathcal{N}$ into $\mathcal{N}$, which are the 'oracles', and the denumerable set $F = \{f_0, f_1, f_2, \ldots\}$ of the partial functions from $\mathcal{N}$ into $\mathcal{N}$ recursive in O.

Realizations and their truth in a model m are defined according to the following definition of $m \models_O r : H$ (this is to be read as 'the information codified by r is true in m for the closed formula H with respect to the oracles O'):

Definition 2.1

$m \models_O r : P$ iff $r = 0$ and $m \models_c P$

$m \models_O r : A \wedge B$ iff $r = \langle a, b \rangle$ and $m \models_O a : A$ and $m \models_O b : B$

$m \models_O r : A \vee B$ iff ($r = \langle 1, a \rangle$ and $m \models_O a : A$) or ($r = \langle 2, b \rangle$ and $m \models_O b : B$)

$m \models_O r : \exists x : A(x)$ iff $r = \langle \lceil t \rceil, a \rangle$, $t \in NT$ and $m \models_O a : A(t)$

$m \models_O r : A \rightarrow B$ iff $m \models_c A \rightarrow B$ and, for every a, $m \models_O a : A$ implies $m \models_O f_r(a) : B$

$m \models_O r : \forall x : A(x)$ iff $m \models_c \forall x : A(x)$ and for every $t \in NT$, $m \models_O f_r(\lceil t \rceil) : A(t)$

where P represents an atomic formula or $P = \neg A$ (A is any closed formula); and $m \models_c H$ means that H is true in the model m, according to the usual definitions of classical model theory.

We remark that in the clauses related to $\rightarrow$ and $\forall$ we also require that the O-realized formula is true in m; this requirement allows us to prove the following property:

Property 2.1 If $m \models_O r : A$ then $m \models_c A$.

If we consider $\exists$-reachable models, i.e. models such that for every true closed formula $\exists x : A(x)$ there is a term t of NT such that $A(t)$ is true, we can also prove the following proposition:

Proposition 2.1 For every $\exists$-reachable model m there is a choice of the set O of oracles such that, for every closed formula A, the following property holds: if $m \models_c A$, then there is a realization r such that $m \models_O r :\ A$.

By **Property 2.1** and **Proposition 2.1**, the truth of a formula in a model m is strictly related to the truth of some realization of it.

As we have explained in the informal treatment, we are interested in a notion of uniform validity and of uniform solvability in a class of models; now we give a formal definition of uniform solvability.

Definition 2.2 Let M be a class of models and H a closed formula. We say that $M \models h : H$ iff, for every O and for every $m \in M$, $m \models_O h : H$. We say that H is *uniformly valid* in M, iff there is a realization h such that $M \models h : H$; we also say that H is uniformly valid iff it is valid in the class M_L of all the models for the language L in question. We say that a sequent from $A(\underline{x})$ give $\underline{z} : B(\underline{x}, \underline{z})$ is *uniformly solvable* in M iff, for every input $(\underline{x}/\underline{t}, r)$ there is an output $(\underline{z}/\underline{t}', r')$ such that, for every O and for every $m \in M$, $m \models_O r : A(\underline{t})$ implies $m \models_O r' : B(\underline{t}, \underline{t}')$.

The above definitions are only a starting point from which different semantics could be developed, but here we are not interested in a more detailed treatment.

We conclude this section by remarking that $0 : \neg\neg A$ is uniformly valid in a class M iff A is classically valid in M. Hence, $\neg\neg A$ could be used to represent classical semantics. To reflect this, we introduce the following definition:

$$true(A) =_{def} \neg\neg A \tag{11}$$

2.2 Data Specification

In the previous sections we have defined the meaning of solvable specification sequents. To make this notion effective, we need some method to prove solvability. The proof system described in Section 3 gives such a method in the case where the class of the models considered is the class of all the models of the language. But, if we consider a particular context, we need to characterize our context by logical axioms to be used to prove solvability in that context. Such axioms should be adequate from a constructive point of view, as we shall explain below.

In PAP data types are defined using the following definition of a first order theory T axiomatizing an intended model:

Definition 2.3 We say that a model i is *isoinitial* [BMM, BMMO] in a class M of models iff, for every model $m \in M$, there is a unique isomorphic embedding from i into m. A first order theory T *axiomatizes* an abstract data type (ADT) dt iff dt is a reachable model of T and it is isoinitial in the class of the models of T.

The analogy with the initial algebra approach [GTW] is evident (we use isomorphic embeddings instead of homomorphisms). An ADT axiomatized by a first order theory T has the following nice properties:

- the ground term model constructed in the usual way (the carrier is given by the equivalence classes defined according to provability in T) is an isoinitial model of T and it is isomorphic to any other isoinitial model;
- the ground term model is recursive;
- the following characterization holds: a first order theory T axiomatizes an ADT iff T has a reachable model and T is atomically complete, i.e. for every ground atomic formula A one has $T \vdash A$ or $T \vdash \neg A$.

There are many examples of theories axiomatizing an isoinitial ADT. For example, the completion $Comp(P)$ of a set P of Horn clauses (as defined in Lloyd ([Llo])) axiomatizes an ADT if negation as failure corresponds to falsity in the minimum model, which is (in this case) an isoinitial model.

In PAP constructively adequate axiomatizations of isoinitial ADT's are considered, i.e. axiomatizations such that for every axiom there is a realization of it which is true in all the models which satisfy the axioms; in this way, we can use the realizations of the axioms to realize the provable formulas. Interesting adequate axioms are the formulas of the form $true(H)$ and induction schemas, as we will discuss in Section 3.

Since obtaining good specifications of data types and proving their relevant properties requires a great effort, reusability of proofs becomes very important. Hence, whilst redesigning PAP we have started a study of parametric and loose specifications (in a sense similar to OBJ3 for example).

The general idea is that a loose ADT-specification is a set of axioms T which does not axiomatize an ADT, but which is such that every larger and consistent set of axioms T' axiomatizes an ADT iff suitable constraint formulas are provable in T'.

Reusability comes from the following property of loose specifications. A provable specification sequent in a loose specification T is not solvable in T (T is too weak), but it becomes solvable in every expansion T' of T satisfying the constraint formulas; then we can prove solvability directly in the loose specification T. We have already meaningful results with respect to the kind of constraint formulas that are needed. [2]

We remark that, while the notion of an isoinitial model can be given in a quite classical setting, here the use of a constructive logic becomes an essential point. Indeed, constraint formulas are often computability constraints such as $\forall x : (A(x) \vee \neg A(x))$ (which constrains $A(x)$ to be decidable only in a constructive system). Now we have to study the problem of consistency; our aim is to find meaningful enrichment tools which preserve consistency.

3 The Calculus

The logical part of the calculus to prove solvability is given in the Appendix. It is a valid calculus with respect to the above notion of uniform solvability (i.e. a provable sequent is also uniformly solvable); but we don't have a completeness result. From the deductive point of view, the calculus is equivalent to the intuitionistic predicate calculus enriched by the following axioms:

$Kuroda : \forall x : \neg\neg A(x) \rightarrow \neg\neg\forall x : A(x)$

$at.\ rule :\ \neg\neg A \rightarrow\ A$ with A **atomic.**

The main features of the calculus are the following.

3.1 The Rules and the Proof Editor

The calculus is a goal directed sequent calculus and a proof has the general form shown in the following example of the AND inference rule:

[2] These results are based on a study on first order constructive systems [MMO1, MMO2].

$$\begin{array}{ll}
\textsf{from } A \textsf{ give } \underline{z} : B \textsf{ by AND} & \text{if } A \Rightarrow \underline{u}_k : A_k \text{ for } 1 \leq k \leq n, \\
\quad \textsf{from } A_1 \textsf{ give } \underline{w}_1 : B_1 & (B_1 \wedge \ldots \wedge B_n) \Rightarrow \underline{z} : B \\
\quad \ldots & \text{and } \underline{w}_i \cap \underline{w}_j = \Phi, \text{ for } i \neq j \\
\quad \textsf{from } A_n \textsf{ give } \underline{w}_n : B_n & \\
\textsf{end} &
\end{array}$$

from A give $\underline{z} : B$ is the *main sequent*, which represents the goal to be proved; the meaning of the rule is that, to prove the main sequent, we may prove $n \geq 1$ *subsequents* (i.e. from A_1 give $\underline{w}_1 : B_1$ .... from A_n give $\underline{w}_n : B_n$) which must satisfy the conditions listed on the right hand side, we call the applicability conditions (A.C.).

In the A. C. the variables $\underline{u}_k$ are free in the k-th subsequent, but not in the main sequent; we say that $\underline{u}_k$ are *local* to the subsequent, while we call *global* the variables which are free in the main sequent. The A. C. are automatically checked by a proof editor and the condition $A \Rightarrow \underline{u}_k : A_k$ means that the sequent from A give $\Rightarrow \underline{u}_k : A_k$ can be automatically proved by the proof editor, which incorporates a suitable theorem prover.

If the A. C. hold, the proof editor accepts the subsequents. In this way, a proof is given in a top-down style, under the control of the proof editor.

Another characteristic of the proof editor we are studying is *modularity*. Every proof is carried out in an *environment* containing a signature, axioms and a library of proved theorems; in particular, an environment may contain the proof that a function is computable or the proof that the relation defined by some formula is decidable. This allows incremental definition of abstract data types. Moreover, we are studying the implementation of parametric environments, in order to allow reusability of theorems proved in loose and parametric theories (see also Section 2.3).

3.2 Computational Meaning of Proofs

Every inference rule also has a computational meaning, so that a proof can be interpreted as a high level program. To execute a proof as a program, we have to instantiate the global variables by an input substitution and to give an input realization; then the computation goes on choosing suitable subsequents, instantiating their local variables, passing them the input realization and executing them. In the Appendix we define the computational meaning of proofs by a structured operational semantics in a style *a la* Plotkin.

We have also defined an intermediate programming language PL, in order to simplify the translation of proofs into programs; the constructs of PL reflect the computational meaning of the inference rules described in the Appendix.

For PL we are studying an operational semantics where the evaluation mechanism is based on rewriting. Starting from the operational semantics, we are studying correct program transformations which allow us to optimize programs. We have a simplification algorithm based on partial evaluation; it simplifies every program P corresponding to the rules of the first group of the Appendix into a case control structure. In this fact one can recognize a version of Herbrandt's theorem. Now we are studying the possibility of giving optimizations related to implication, universal quantification, induction and descending chain (see Section 3.3 below).

3.3 Using Context Axioms

In order to use the axioms specifying a particular context, it is possible to introduce an axiom A by the rule:

$$\text{from give } A \text{ by axiom} \tag{12}$$

but this rule is constructively adequate only if A has a realization which is uniformly valid in the context considered (i.e. not every axiomatization is acceptable from a constructive point of view). We have two interesting cases of constructively adequate axioms:

- axioms of the form $true(A)$ which have the unique realization 0 (since $M_A \vdash 0 : true(A)$ in the class M_A of the classical models of A, we can write down any classical theory using $true$);

- induction schemas, which can be realized by recursion.

An induction schema is better represented in the form of an inference rule, which has a computational meaning in terms of recursion. Then induction rules are the way to synthesize recursive programs and become very important. We are studying different kinds of induction rules, in order to enlarge the class of the synthesizable programs. With respect to this goal, we have also studied how to capture iteration by a corresponding inference rule. This rule is the following descending chain principle linked to a well founded relation rel:

$$\begin{array}{ll} \text{from } H(\underline{a}) \text{ give } K \text{ by DC}(\underline{X}\ rel\ \underline{x}) & \text{if } \underline{X},\ \underline{x} \text{ not free in } K \\ \quad \text{from } H(\underline{x}) \text{ give } \underline{X} : (H(\underline{X}) \wedge \underline{X}\ rel\ \underline{x}) \vee K & \end{array}$$

For the sake of simplicity, we suppose that the only free variables of the main sequent are $\underline{a}$. The computational meaning is the following: we start with an input substitution $\underline{a}/\underline{t}_0$ and an input realization h_0; then we assign the variables $\underline{x}$ of the subproof by $\underline{t}_0$ and we get, e.g. an output substitution $\underline{X}/\underline{t}_1$ and a realization $\langle 1, \langle h_1, 0\rangle\rangle$; in this case we restart the execution of the subproof by $\underline{x}/\underline{t}_1$ and h_1; this process is iterated until the output realization is of the form $\langle 2, k\rangle$; at this point we have a realization k of K, which is our final result.

By this principle we can synthesize every program P for which there is a Hoare like proof of total correctness, say PH, in the following sense: PH can be translated into a corresponding proof PC of our system, in such a way that the execution sequences of PC are equivalent to the ones of P.

4 On Classical and Constructive Reasoning

The class of the synthesizable programs can be enlarged in three ways: by powerful induction principles; by constructive logical principles giving rise to logics stronger than the intuitionistic one; by allowing classical reasoning in particular cases. Classical reasoning can be introduced in proofs of our calculus by the rule ELEM (see the Appendix).

The possibility of mixing classical and constructive reasoning is useful for various reasons.

First of all, it allows us to choose two different levels of analysis of logical formulas; the classical analysis, which is related to truth and not to computations and the constructive analysis, which implies computability. Let us suppose, for example, that we want to compute some input-output relation expressed by some complex formula $F(x,z)$; if we are not interested in the constructive analysis of the whole formula, we can express our problem as follows: from... give $z : trueF(x,z)$ and we can use classical logic in the subproofs dealing with the elementary formula $trueF(x,z)$

Another important aspect is related to the relationships between the meaning of formulas and that of programs. We have two extreme choices:

1) the meaning of a formula is given by the 'programs solving it', so that there are strict relationships between the meaning of formulas and the meaning of programs;

2) the semantics of formulas is independent from that of programs and the relation between them is based on some notion of correctness.

The first choice is related to the application of some kind of type theory, where a formula is a type and the proofs of a formula are the elements of its type (i.e. the 'programs solving it'). An example of the second one is given by Hoare's correctness calculi, where assertions are interpreted in terms of classical truth, while program constructs are treated in a completely separate way.

We think that it is possible to have an approach combining 1) and 2); our proposal can be seen as an attempt at doing so. We give a double interpretation of formulas. On the one hand, we have the classical notion of a model and of truth of a formula in a model; on the other hand, a formula defines the class of the possible evaluations of its truth. Also evaluations can be true or false in a model and the truth of evaluations is related to the truth of formulas by the following property: if there is a true evaluation of a formula F, then F is true. Evaluations are the data on which our programs work and the link between the semantics of formulas and that of programs is given by the following notion of correctness: a program is correct iff its computations preserve the truth of evaluations.

A final remark is the following: while a 'purist' attitude (reducing everything to a few central principles) may be useful from the point of view of mathematical foundations, it is not acceptable if one tries to deal with programming. As a matter of fact, in programming there are so many aspects that any restricted choice becomes a limitation; one needs robust systems, open to the possibility of incorporating various kinds of reasoning. So it seems that some kind of eclecticism and genericity is needed; but some ultimate criterion related to the problem of correctness is also needed.

We think that such a criterion could be based on classical reasoning; but this is not mandatory. For example, in our approach we might have a situation where models are Kripke models of some modal system, realizations are defined as before, but the satisfaction relation for classical models is substituted by the forcing relation for Kripke models. We have studied from a logical point of view the possibility of defining forcings on the realizations, but we have not yet considered the possible applications of this study in program synthesis; perhaps, an application might be related to data bases.

Appendix: The Logical Rules

Part I: The Inference Rules

Here we list the inference rules, in the formalism explained in Section 3.1. For the sake of simplicity we don't underline the variables; by x, y, z, ... we indicate (possibly empty) tuples of variables.

Rules working on $\wedge$, $\vee$, $\exists$, $\neg$:

from A give $z: B$ by BINCL	if $A \Rightarrow z: B$

from A give $z: B$ by AND
    from A_1 give $w_1: B_1$
    ...
    from A_n give $w_n: B_n$
end
	if $A \Rightarrow u_k: A_k$ for $1 \leq k \leq n$,
	$B_1 \wedge \ldots \wedge B_n \Rightarrow z: B$
	and $w_i \cap w_j = \Phi$, for $i \neq j$

from A give $z: B$ by OR
    from A_1 give $w_1: B_1$
    ...
    from A_n give $w_n: B_n$
end
	if $A \Rightarrow u: A_1 \vee \ldots \vee A_n$
	and $B_k \Rightarrow z: B$ for $1 \leq k \leq n$

from A give $z: B$ by SEQ
    from A_1 give $w_1: B_1$
    ...
    from A_n give $w_n: B_n$
end
	if $A \Rightarrow u_1: A_1$, $B_{k-1} \Rightarrow u_k: A_k$
	for $1 < k \leq n$ and $B_n \Rightarrow z: B$

from A give P by ELEM(...)	if $A \vdash P$ is classically proved by theorem (...) in the environment and P is atomic or of the form $\neg A$ or $true(A)$

Rules working on $\rightarrow, \forall$

from $H \rightarrow K, A$ give $z: B$ *by* CALL$\rightarrow$ from K_1 give B_1	if $A \Rightarrow H$, $A \wedge K \Rightarrow u: K_1$, $B_1 \Rightarrow z: B$
from $\forall x: H(x), A$ give $z: B$ *by* CALL$\forall(t)$ from A_1 give B_1	if $H(t) \wedge A \Rightarrow u_1: A_1$, $B_1 \Rightarrow z: B$
from A give $H \rightarrow K$ *by* IMP(...)	if $A, H \vdash K$ proved by theorem (...) of the environment
from A give $\forall x: H$ *by* ANY(...)	if $A \vdash H(p)$ proved by theorem (...) of the environment and p not free in A

Identity rules

from A give $t = t$ by ID1	
from A give $B(t_2)$ by ID2(...) from A_1 give $B(t_1)$	if $A \Rightarrow u: A_1$ and $A \vdash t_1 = t_2$ proved by theorems (...) in the environment

Environment TEST rule

$$\begin{array}{ll} \text{from } A \text{ give } z:\ B\ by\ \text{TEST(P)} & \text{if P is } decidable \text{ in the environment} \\ \quad \text{from } P, A_1 \text{ give } w_1:\ B_1 & \text{and } A \Rightarrow u_i : A_i \text{ and } B_i \Rightarrow z : B, \\ \quad \text{from } \neg P, A_2 \text{ give } w_2:\ B_2 & \text{for } 1 \leq i \leq 2 \end{array}$$

TEST is the (derived) rule to use the decidability lemmas of the environment. If we omit the decidability requirement, we obtain classical logic.

Part II: Computational Meaning of the Rules

The operational semantics is given in a style a la Plotkin. The notation

$$(s, R_A) \text{ from } A(x) \text{ give } z : B(x,z)\ \ (d, R_B)$$

means that the couple $\langle (s, R_A)\ ,\ (d, R_B)\rangle$ belongs to the input-output relation computed by the proof or subproof with main sequent from $A(x)$ give z : $B(x, z)$, where: $s = x/t$ is the input substitution, r_A is the input realization, d is the union $x/t \cup z/t'$ of the input and of the output substitution and d_B is the output realization.

$$\frac{(s, R_A)\ A \Rightarrow z : B\ (e, R_B) \qquad \text{(basic operation)}}{(s, R_A) \text{ from } A \text{ give } z:\ B \text{ by BINCL } (e, R_B)}$$

$$\frac{\begin{array}{l}(s, R_A)\ A \Rightarrow u_i : A_i\ (d_i, R_{A_i}), \text{ for } 1 \leq i \leq n, \\ (d_i, R_{A_i}) \text{ from } A_i \text{ give } w_i:\ B_i\ (e_i, R_{B_i}), \text{ for } 1 \leq i \leq n, \\ (e_1 \cup \ldots \cup e_n, \langle R_{B_1}, \ldots, R_{B_n}\rangle)\ B_1 \wedge \ldots \wedge B_n \Rightarrow z : B\ (e, R_B)\end{array}}{(s, R_A) \text{ from } A \text{ give } z:\ B \text{ by AND } (e, R_B)}$$

$$\frac{\begin{array}{l}(s, R_A)\ A \Rightarrow u : (A_1 \vee \ldots \vee A_n)\ (d, \langle i, R_{A_i}\rangle) \\ (d, R_{A_i}) \text{ from } A_i \text{ give } w_i:\ B_i\ (e_i, R_{B_i}) \\ (e_i, R_{B_i})\ B_i \Rightarrow z : B\ (e, R_B)\end{array}}{(s, R_A) \text{ from } A \text{ give } z:\ B \text{ by OR } (e, R_B)}$$

$$\frac{\begin{array}{l}(s, R_A)\ A \Rightarrow u_1 : A_1\ (d_1, R_{A_1}), \\ (e_{i-1}, R_{B_{i-1}})\ B_{i-1} \Rightarrow u_i : A_i\ (d_i, R_{A_i}), \text{ for } 2 \leq i \leq n, \\ (d_i, R_{A_i}) \text{ from } A_i \text{ give } w_i : B_i\ (e_i, R_{B_i}), \text{ for } 1 \leq i \leq n, \\ (e_n, R_{B_n})\ B_n \Rightarrow z : B\ (e, R_B)\end{array}}{(s, R_A) \text{ from } A \text{ give } z:\ B \text{ by SEQ } (e, R_B)}$$

$$\frac{\begin{array}{l}(s, R_A)\ A \Rightarrow H\ (s, R_H), \\ (s, R_H)\ prog(R_{H \to K})\ (s, R_K), \\ (s, \langle R_A, R_K\rangle))\ (A \wedge K) \Rightarrow u : K_1\ (d, R_{K_1}), \\ (d, R_{K_1}) \text{ from } K_1 \text{ give } B_1\ (g, R_{B_1}), \\ (g, R_{B_1})\ B_1 \Rightarrow z : B\ (e, R_B)\end{array}}{(s, \langle R_{H \to K}, R_A\rangle) \text{ from } H \to K, A \text{ give } z:\ B\ by\ \text{CALL}\!\to\ (e, R_B)}$$

$$\frac{\begin{array}{l}(t)\ prog(R_{\forall x:H})\ (s, R_{H(t)}), \\ (s, \langle R_{H(t)}, R_A\rangle)\ H(t) \wedge A \Rightarrow u : A_1\ (d, R_{A_1}) \\ (d, R_{A_1}) \text{ from } A_1 \text{ give } B_1\ (g, R_{B_1}), \\ (g, R_{B_1})\ B_1 \Rightarrow z : B\ (e, R_B)\end{array}}{(s, \langle R_{\forall x:H}, R_A\rangle) \text{ from } \forall x : H(x), A \text{ give } z:\ B\ by\ \text{CALL}\forall(t)\ (e, R_B)}$$

(s, R_A) from A give $H \rightarrow K$ *by* IMP(thj) $(s, index[(imp((s, R_A), thj)])$

(s, R_A) from A give $\forall x : H$ *by* ANY(thj) $(s, index[(any((s, R_A), thj)])$

(s, R_A) from A give P *by* ELEM(...) $(s, 0)$

(s, R_A) from A give $t = t$ *by* ID1 $(s, 0)$

$$\frac{(s, R_A)A \Rightarrow u : A_1\ (d, R_{A_1}),\quad (d, R_{A_1}) \text{ from } A_1 \text{ give } B(t_1)\ (e, R_B)}{(s, R_A) \text{ from } A \text{ give } B(t_2) \text{ by ID2}(\ldots)\ (e, R_B)}$$

where $index[(imp((s, R_A), thj)]$ is the index of the program $R_{H \rightarrow K}$ to be used in a corresponding CALL→; $prog(R_{H \rightarrow K})$ indicates such a program; analogously for $(s, index[(any((s, R_A), thj)])$ and $prog(R_{\forall x:H})$.

Acknowledgments

The authors are indebted to the editors of this book Kung-Kiu Lau and Tim Clement for their help in improving some parts of this paper and for forcing (read 'obliging') the authors to learn and to use LaTeX. The work has been done in the framework of the project 'Logica matematica e sue applicazioni' of Italian Ministero della Universita' e della Ricerca Scientifica e Tecnologica.

References

[BC] Bates J., Constable R., Proofs as programs, *ACM Transaction on Programming Languages and Systems* **7**(1), 1985, 113-136.

[BMM] Bertoni A., Mauri G., Miglioli P., On the power of model theory to specify abstract data types and to capture their recursiveness, *Fundamenta Informaticae* **IV**.2, 1983, 127-170.

[BMMO] Bertoni A., Mauri G., Miglioli P., Ornaghi M., Abstract data types and their extension within a constructive logic, in Kahn G., MacQueen D.B., Plotkin G. (eds), *Semantics of data types* (Sophia-Antipolis, 1984), *Lecture Notes in Computer Science* **173**, Springer-Verlag, Berlin, 1984, 177-195.

[BrMMO] Bresciani P., Miglioli P., Moscato U., Ornaghi M., PAP: Proofs as Programs - (abstract), *Journal of Symbolic Logic* **51** (3), 1986, 852-853.

[BSW] Bundy A., Smaill A., Wiggins G., The synthesis of logic programs from inductive proofs, in Lloyd J. (ed), *Computational logic*, Springer-Verlag, 1990, 135-149.

[CAB] Constable R., Allen S., Bromley H. et al., *Implementing Mathematics with the Nuprl Development System*, Prentice-Hall, 1986.

[Goa] Goad C., Computational uses of the manipulation of formal proofs, Rep. STAN-CS-80-819, Stanford University, 1980.

[GTW] Goguen J.A., Thatcher J.W., Wagner E.G., An initial algebra approach to the specification, correctness and implementation of abstract data types, IBM Res. Rep. RC6487, Yorktown Heights, 1976.

[Got] Goto S., Program synthesis from natural deduction proofs, International Joint Conference on Artificial Intelligence, Tokyo, 1979, 339-341.

[Hen] Henson M., Realizability models for program construction, in J. van de Snepscheut, *Mathematics of program construction, Lecture Notes in Computer Science* **375**, Springer-Verlag, Berlin, 1989.

[HN] Hiyashi S., Nakano H., *PX: A computational logic*, MIT Press, Cambridge, 1988.

[Kl] Kleene S., *Introduction to metamathematics*, North Holland, Amsterdam, 1952.

[Llo] Lloyd J., *Foundations of logic programming*, Springer-Verlag, 1987.

[MaL] Martin-Löf P., Constructive Mathematics and Computer Programming, in L. Cohen, J. Los, H. Pfeiffer, K. Podewski (eds), *VI International Congress for Logic, Methodology and Philosophy of Science*, North-Holland, Amsterdam, 1982, 153-179.

[Med] Medvedev T., Finite problems, *Sov. Math. Dok.* 3, 1962.

[MMO0] P. Miglioli, U. Moscato, M. Ornaghi, PAP: a logic programming system based on a constructive logic, *Lecture Notes in Computer Science* **306**, Springer-Verlag, 1988.

[MMO1] Miglioli P., Moscato U., Ornaghi M., Constructive theories with abstract data types for program synthesis, in Skordev D.G. (ed), *Mathematical Logic and its Applications*, Plenum Press, New York, 1988, 293-302.

[MMO2] Miglioli P., Moscato U., Ornaghi M., Semi-constructive formal systems and axiomatization of abstract data types, in Diaz J., Orejas F. (eds), *TAPSOFT '89, Lecture Notes in Computer Science* **351**, Springer-Verlag, Berlin, 1989, 337-351.

[MO] Miglioli P., Ornaghi M., A logically justified model of computation I,II, *Fundamenta Informaticae* **IV**.1,2, 1981.

[Sat] Sato M., Towards a mathematical theory of program synthesis, *International Joint Conference on Artificial Intelligence*, Tokyo, 1979, 757-762.

Synthesis and Transformation of Logic Programs from Constructive, Inductive Proof

Geraint Wiggins
geraint@ed.ac.uk

Alan Bundy
bundy@ed.ac.uk

Ina Kraan
inak@ai.ed.ac.uk

Jane Hesketh
jane@ai.ed.ac.uk

DReAM Group
Department of Artificial Intelligence
University of Edinburgh
80 South Bridge
Edinburgh EH1 1HN
Scotland

Abstract

We discuss a technique which allows synthesis of logic programs in the "proofs-as-programs" paradigm [Constable 82]. Constructive, inductive proof is used to show that the specification of a program is realisable; elaboration of a proof gives rise to the synthesis of a program which realises it. We present an update on earlier ideas, and give examples of and justification for them. The work is presented as foundation for further work in *proof planning*, where we aim to synthesise not only programs, but *good* programs.

1 Introduction

In this paper, we present further developments in work on a method for the synthesis of logic programs originally presented in [Bundy *et al* 90a]. The method uses the constructive, inductive proof of conjectures which specify the desired programs' input/output behaviour, coupled with simultaneous automatic extraction of the computational content of the proofs. The method has been implemented as a user-directed proof development system which provides a rich environment for the elaboration of synthesis proofs. The implementation, the *Whelk* system, has been designed to be amenable to application of existing ideas and further developments in the technique of *proof planning*, in which inductive proofs are developed automatically [Bundy 88, Bundy *et al* 91, Wiggins 90].

In Section 2 we present a brief background summary of the ideas of [Bundy *et al* 90a]. In Section 3, we discuss issues arising from the attempt to synthesise logic programs in our chosen paradigm and style. Section 4 gives an example of program synthesis and transformation within our technique, and Section 5 summarises the ideas presented and suggests some directions for future work.

2 The Basic Technique

Whelk is based on the "proofs-as-programs" paradigm of [Constable 82]. In order to adapt this approach, intended for the synthesis of *functional* programs, to that of *logic* programs, we view logic programs, in the "all ground" mode, as functions onto a valued Boolean-valued type. We can then in principle perform synthesis of programs by the constructive proof of conjectures of the following general form (though we explain below why this form is not precisely ideal for our purposes):

$$\vdash \forall \overline{\imath}{:}\overline{\tau}.\exists b{:}boole.spec(\overline{\imath}) \leftrightarrow b$$

We will call a conjecture which specifies the behaviour of a program to be synthesised a *specification conjecture*. The conjecture states that, for all vectors of input values ($\overline{\imath}$) of the correct type(s) ($\overline{\tau}$) [1], there is some Boolean value (b), such that $spec(\overline{\imath})$ is logically equivalent to that value. We define the Boolean type to contain only the constants true and false, so it is not possible merely to instantiate b with $spec(\overline{\imath})$ to prove the conjecture. Therefore, one might think of the proof process as proving the decidability of the spec. See [Bundy *et al* 90a] for more detail.

The approach differs from the conventional functional proofs-as-programs approach, and from some other attempts to adapt it to logic programming (*eg* [Fribourg 90]) in that it allows us to synthesise programs which are partial, many-valued relations (as logic programs often are) rather than (strict) functions.

Now, in order to prove a conjecture *constructively*, we must show not just that there *is* a value of b in boole for each possible combination of inputs, $\overline{\imath}$ — rather, we must show that we can *construct* that Boolean value. Showing that we *can* construct the value involves showing *how* to construct it. Therefore,

[1] *ie* a vector of input value/type pairs

the proof must contain (in some maybe abstruse form) instructions for such a construction.

In the event that $\overrightarrow{\iota:\tau}$ is empty, we can supply either *true* or *false* as the witness for our Boolean variable b, simply by introduction on the existential — this then becomes the body of our synthesised program. If $\overrightarrow{\iota:\tau}$ is not empty (so there are universally quantified, typed variables in our specification conjecture) then the Boolean witness may depend on the values of those variables. Our proof will therefore consist of nested case-splits[2], dividing the types of the variables into sub-types for which a single Boolean value may be computed. These case splits, conjoined with the values of the various b's associated with them, will constitute the main body of the synthesised program.

3 Whelk: The Current Implementation

3.1 Whelk

Whelk has been implemented within a proof development system originally designed for the Oyster system [Horn 88, Bundy *et al* 90c]. The Martin-Löf Constructive Type Theory of Oyster has been replaced in Whelk by a much simpler typed first-order logic. This design decision has raised some questions about how the synthesis-proof approach actually works, which we discuss in this section.

Whelk provides a rich environment for the user guided development of proofs (synthesis proofs or otherwise). It includes a tactic language which allows the construction of more complicated compound rules from the atomic ones which define the proof system; this mechanism will allow the application of automatically planned proof steps in future work.

A fundamentally important feature in the program synthesis application is that each rule of inference in the proof system corresponds one-to-one with a rule of construction for a structure called the *extraction* from the proof. This correspondence is so arranged that the extraction from a proof of a specification conjecture (as above) constitutes a logic program which fulfils the spec for all input where spec is true, and which fails for all input where spec is false. This will become clearer in the examples below.

[2] except in the trivial case where the synthesised program is always true or always false

3.2 The Form of The Specification Conjecture

Before we can use *Whelk* for program synthesis, we must motivate our chosen form of specification conjecture. It is important to understand in advance that there are several options open, and that we do not suggest that any one is in any absolute sense better than any other. We feel, however, that the option we have chosen offers the best insight into the operation of the synthesis system from the point of view of the user.

3.2.1 Existential Quantifier and Logical Equivalence

To recapitulate: in [Bundy *et al* 90a], we loosely outlined an approach where we proved a conjecture of the form

$$\vdash \forall \vec{\iota}{:}\vec{\tau}.\exists b{:}\mathsf{boole}.spec(\vec{\iota}) \leftrightarrow b$$

to show that, for all well-typed input there is some truth value (true or false, here) to which the specification $spec(\vec{\iota})$ is logically equivalent. Because our proof system is constructive, we have to show not only that some such value exists, but that we can generate it. This is equivalent to saying that $spec(\vec{\iota})$ is decidable. Also, the extraction may be thought of as a witness for b.

Closer inspection, however, shows that this approach is flawed. The logic of our proof system is a typed first-order logic. However, the existentially quantified variable b in the specification conjecture above is (assuming the usual interpretation of $\leftrightarrow$) a variable over formulae, and not over terms. Thus, the existential quantifier is second-order, which we do not want.

In fact, the original intention was that the right hand side of the equivalence should be notated in a different language from the left (or at least in a disjoint subset of the same language). By arranging the categories of the various expressions carefully, we could overcome the apparent syntactic ill-formation. This, indeed, will be the approach we follow later in this discussion, but with this form of synthesis conjecture, we suggest that the mixture of languages is inelegant and potentially confusing.

An alternative solution to the problem would be simply to allow the second-order quantifier *in this circumstance only* (first-order existentials frequently arise in the body of spec); however, this approach is unsatisfying because of its rather *ad hoc* flavour — the necessary restriction on quantifier order is hard to justify in the larger context of the proof system.

3.2.2 Meta-Variable and Logical Equivalence

A better version of essentially the same idea is to allow the proof system to support uninstantiated meta-variables, and to prove a conjecture of the form

$$\vdash \forall \overline{\iota}{:}\overline{\tau}.\mathrm{spec}(\overline{\iota}) \leftrightarrow \mathcal{M}$$

where $\mathcal{M}$ is a meta-variable over formulæ. In this approach, the construction of the extraction is much more explicit than in the others presented here, as it actually constitutes the (partially instantiated) value of the variable $\mathcal{M}$ as the proof proceeds. This technique, however, would involve significant changes to the operation of the Oyster/Whelk environment, and thus is not ideal for our purposes here. Further, recent work by Ina Kraan on using the meta-variable approach to give a semantics for synthesis involving the form of conjecture we do use (see 3.2.5) suggests that though there are some difficult logical problems associated with its use as a semantics, it is in itself a potentially useful technique for program synthesis. One advantage over the Whelk system is that all the rules required are derivable directly from a standard Sequent Calculus, and thus are known *a priori* to be sound. We intend to pursue this approach in parallel with the Whelk system, in order to be able to compare the two.

This technique might be viewed as deductive synthesis, as, for example, in [Bibel & Hörning 84].

3.2.3 Lifting with Functional Specification

Another meta-flavoured approach would be to change the form of our synthesis conjecture to

$$\vdash \forall \overline{\iota}{:}\overline{\tau}.\exists b{:}\mathrm{boole}.\mathrm{spec}(\overline{\iota}) =_{\mathrm{boole}} b$$

In this formula, we have lifted the original spec to the meta-level, and are actually reasoning about the term which names it under a bijective naming function. Thus, all of the connectives and predicates permissible in the logic must have a functional equivalent. For example, the "and" connective, $\wedge$: formula $\times$ formula $\mapsto$ formula, must correspond with a function $\wedge'$: boole $\times$ boole $\mapsto$ boole. This is to an extent inconvenient, because the system must maintain the distinction (in terms of the constructed program, $\wedge$ and $\wedge'$ are *significantly* different) — and it is in the nature of logic systems that such a distinction must be explicit in the inference rules. Thus, the user has to worry about a distinction which is largely irrelevant to the production of the proof (NB as opposed to the program) s/he must elaborate, which complicates the system unnecessarily. Oddly, it turns out to be undesirable to remove the source of this problem in the formal sense (see 3.2.4) — but we can nevertheless protect the user from its most irritating effects, as we explain in 3.2.5.

3.2.4 Decidability Proof

Perhaps the most obvious route to the construction of the program we need is a specification conjecture of the form

$$\vdash \forall \overline{\iota}{:}\overline{\tau}.\mathrm{spec}(\overline{\iota}) \vee \neg \mathrm{spec}(\overline{\iota})$$

In this approach, we are showing that there is some truth value for the spec, in much the same way as in 3.2.1, and relying on the constructive nature of our proof system to give us an executable extraction. However, there is a significant difference here, because there is no existential quantifier, and no explicit truth value associated with the spec for any given value(s) of $\overline{\iota}$. In removing the truth value, we remove the basis of the problem arising in the sections above, which is clearly one related to self-reference; all the way along, we have been attempting to reason about the truth values of a logical expression in a(n object-level, first-order) system *within* that system, which is not straightforwardly possible.

Unfortunately, this apparent step forward brings with it a disadvantage. In the approach of 3.2.1, above, we were able in some degree to motivate our use of that form of synthesis conjecture by saying that the logic program we would eventually synthesise would be a witness for the existentially quantified Boolean variable, b. Now, though, we have thrown our variable away, and there is no equivalent intuitive foothold on which to base a semantics for our proof system. We also lose the useful notion that we are trying to show the existence of some (logical) output for all possible input, which is the fundamental tenet of the proofs-as-programs approach.

3.2.5 Existential Quantifier and Realisation Operator

On this basis, therefore, we must take a step back, and attempt to compromise on a system which is logically correct and transparent (like 3.2.4), but also easily motivated as an instance of our chosen paradigm (like 3.2.1, 3.2.2 and 3.2.3). Ideally, the system should not introduce needless complication for the user (as does 3.2.3), and it should definitely not mix meta- and object-levels in an unmotivated, and, indeed, syntactically ill-formed, way (as does 3.2.1).

The solution, then, is a compromise between user-friendliness, logical correctness, and intuitive transparency. It involves the addition of a new operator in our logic which will allow us correctly to mix formulæ and terms in the way suggested by 3.2.1. We will also restrict our type boole to contain only the values true and false, which will give us the effect of enforcing the proof of decidability, as in 3.2.4. The scope of our new operator also gives us a motivated way to separate the two different kinds of operator (the distinction between the connectives and the functions in 3.2.3) without bothering the user.

The operator we use to do all this is read as "realises", written

$$\hookrightarrow: \mathsf{formula} \times \mathsf{term} \mapsto \mathsf{formula}$$

and its meaning is defined by:

$$\vdash \mathsf{formula} \hookrightarrow \mathsf{b} \qquad \textit{iff} \qquad \begin{cases} \vdash \mathsf{formula} \leftrightarrow (\mathsf{b} =_{\mathsf{boole}} \mathsf{true}) \\ \vdash \neg\mathsf{formula} \leftrightarrow (\mathsf{b} =_{\mathsf{boole}} \mathsf{false}) \end{cases}$$

where formula is an object level formula in our logic and b is in boole. $=_{\mathsf{boole}}$ denotes equality in boole.

Since our specification formula is now within the scope of the realisation operator, we have a straightforward syntactic distinction between (*eg*) the $\wedge$ and $\wedge'$ of section 3.2.3, which makes little difference from the point of view of the user applying inference rules (indeed, it allows him/her to *ignore* the difference, which is desirable), but allows the proof system to detect unambiguously which way any given connective should be treated.

The semantics above gives us a connection between the formula of the spec itself and some Boolean value(s); we must now give a semantics for the extraction system which will supply the synthesised logic program required to produce these values for any given well-typed input.

3.3 Semantics of Whelk Extractions

3.3.1 The Languages $\mathcal{L}_{\mathcal{E}}$ and $\mathcal{L}_{\mathcal{I}}$

The semantics of our extraction system is fairly complicated, and will be reported in detail elsewhere. There follows enough of a sketch to allow the reader to understand the example in Section 4.

First, we have in the logic of our proof system the usual first-order connectives, $\neg$, $\rightarrow$, $\vee$, $\wedge$, $\forall$ and $\exists$, with the addition of $\leftarrow$ and $\leftrightarrow$ for convenience. We have the realisation operator $\hookrightarrow$, as above, and $\oplus$ (exclusive or) which will allow us to make certain optimisations as part of the proof process. We also have the operator : for sort/type membership, sorts, boole = { true false }, nat = { 0 s(0) s(s(0)) ... }, and the parametric type of lists: α list = { [] $[h_0]$ $[h_0, h_1]$ ... } where $h_i{:}\alpha$. Finally, formulæ may consist of literals (*ie* predicates, often applied to argument terms), statements of equality within a type (written $=_\tau$), combinations of these made with the connectives, or contradiction (written $\{\}$). Terms may consist of literals (*ie* functions, often applied to argument terms). We will call this language the *external* logic, $\mathcal{L}_\mathcal{E}$, on the grounds that it is what the user sees as s/he elaborates proofs.

In order to motivate our extraction system, we also need an *internal* logic, $\mathcal{L}_\mathcal{I}$, which is mostly invisible to the user of Whelk. It is almost identical with $\mathcal{L}_\mathcal{E}$, and maps to it, through a function we call the *interpretation*. The elements of the $\mathcal{L}_\mathcal{I}$ correspond one-to-one with the syntactically identical elements of $\mathcal{L}_\mathcal{E}$, *except* in the following cases.

The Boolean terms true and false of $\mathcal{L}_\mathcal{E}$ correspond with *predicates* true and false respectively in $\mathcal{L}_\mathcal{I}$.

Only type/sort constructor functions are allowed in $\mathcal{L}_\mathcal{I}$; non-constructor functions have no correspondent in $\mathcal{L}_\mathcal{I}$.

The $\hookrightarrow$ operator has no correspondent in $\mathcal{L}_\mathcal{I}$.

We write formula* to denote the expression in $\mathcal{L}_\mathcal{I}$ which corresponds with formula in $\mathcal{L}_\mathcal{E}$ under the interpretation.

3.3.2 Realisation Semantics

Recall first that the semantics of $\hookrightarrow$ is defined thus:

$$\vdash \mathsf{formula} \hookrightarrow \mathsf{b} \qquad \textit{iff} \qquad \begin{cases} \vdash \mathsf{formula} \leftrightarrow (\mathsf{b} =_{\mathsf{boole}} \mathsf{true}) \\ \vdash \neg\mathsf{formula} \leftrightarrow (\mathsf{b} =_{\mathsf{boole}} \mathsf{false}) \end{cases}$$

where formula is a closed object level formula in $\mathcal{L}_\mathcal{E}$ and b is in boole.

Note that, while formula may contain quantifiers, the expression as a whole is unquantified, which makes the semantics simpler — b is simply either true or false. If we add in universal quantification of the entire formula, to represent arguments to our synthesised predicate, we have a more complicated semantics for the realisation, which can be written thus, in terms of a composition of sub-proofs (the universally quantified input vector $\overline{x{:}\tau}$ has been introduced as a hypothesis):

$$\overline{x{:}\tau}, \mathsf{condition}_1 \vdash \mathsf{formula} \hookrightarrow \mathsf{b}_1$$

$$\vdots$$

$$\overline{x{:}\tau}, \mathsf{condition}_n. \vdash \mathsf{formula} \hookrightarrow \mathsf{b}_n$$

where $\mathrm{condition}_i$ is a (possibly empty) conjunction of conditions (either sets of equations – *ie* unifiers – or references to axiomatic predicates) free in (some of the) $\overline{x}$. It is important to note that the $\mathrm{condition}_i$ must together select all the elements of the product type $\prod_t t \in \overline{\tau}$, so that the predicate is defined for all well-typed input. Whelk ensures this during construction of the proof.

The corresponding *pure logic procedure* (see definition in [Bundy *et al* 90a]), constructed automatically as a side-effect of the elaboration in Whelk of the proof, is then defined thus:

$$\mathrm{extract}(\overline{x{:}\tau}) \quad \longleftrightarrow \quad \bigvee_{1 \leq i \leq n} (\mathrm{condition}_i{}^* \wedge b_i{}^*)$$

In fact, it turns out that some sub-terms of the $\mathrm{condition}_i$ are irrelevant and/or tautologous, and will not appear in the extracted construction.

3.3.3 Example: zero/*1*

For an initial very simple example, let us consider the predicate **zero/1**, which is true if its argument is the natural number 0 and false otherwise. Our synthesis conjecture is:

$$\vdash \forall x{:}\mathrm{nat}.\exists b{:}\mathrm{boole}.x =_{nat} 0 \hookrightarrow b$$

The proof runs as follows. (Note that though this is a Gentzen Sequent Calculus derivation, it is presented backwards, in refinement style. Thus "introduction" steps actually make operators disappear.) First, we introduce the universal quantifier, to give:

$x{:}\mathrm{nat}$
$\vdash \exists b{:}\mathrm{boole}.x =_{nat} 0 \hookrightarrow b$

Then, we import a lemma about the decidability of equality in the naturals, giving

$x{:}\mathrm{nat}$
$\forall x{:}\mathrm{nat}.\forall y{:}\mathrm{nat}.x =_{nat} y \oplus \neg x =_{nat} y$
$\vdash \exists b{:}\mathrm{boole}.x =_{nat} 0 \hookrightarrow b$

We eliminate the universals in the hypothesis with the values x and 0, giving:

$x{:}\mathrm{nat}$
$\forall x{:}\mathrm{nat}.\forall y{:}\mathrm{nat}.x =_{nat} y \oplus \neg x =_{nat} y$
$x =_{nat} 0 \oplus \neg x =_{nat} 0$
$\vdash \exists b{:}\mathrm{boole}.x =_{nat} 0 \hookrightarrow b$

We can now eliminate disjunction, to give two subconjecture (in the context of the above hypotheses):

$x =_{nat} 0$ $\vdash \exists b{:}boole.x =_{nat} 0 \hookrightarrow b$	$\neg x =_{nat} 0$ $\vdash \exists b{:}boole.x =_{nat} 0 \hookrightarrow b$

Next, we proceed by supplying witnesses for the Boolean, b — true and false respectively:

$x =_{nat} 0$ $\vdash x =_{nat} 0 \hookrightarrow \mathrm{true}$	$\neg x =_{nat} 0$ $\vdash x =_{nat} 0 \hookrightarrow \mathrm{false}$

The introduction rules for the $\hookrightarrow$ operator are defined so that we can make the following step:

$x =_{nat} 0$ $\vdash x =_{nat} 0$	$\neg x =_{nat} 0$ $\vdash \neg x =_{nat} 0$

And finally, both branches can now be terminated by tautology, since each subconjecture appears in its own hypotheses.

The *pure logic procedure* synthesised from this proof, and written in $\mathcal{L}_{\mathcal{I}}$, is as follows:

$$\mathrm{zero}(x{:}nat) \longleftrightarrow (x =_{nat} 0 \wedge \mathrm{true}) \vee (\neg x =_{nat} 0 \wedge \mathrm{false})$$

which corresponds with the semantic scheme given above in the following way. Labelling the left branch of the proof as 0, and the right branch as 1, we are looking for a b_0, a b_1, a $\mathrm{condition}_0$ and a $\mathrm{condition}_1$. The two b's were supplied by the existential introduction: true and false respectively, in $\mathcal{L}_{\mathcal{E}}$, mapped to their predicative correspondents in $\mathcal{L}_{\mathcal{I}}$ by *. $\mathrm{condition}_0$ is then $x =_{nat} 0$ and $\mathrm{condition}_1$ is $\neg x =_{nat} 0$, which map to their syntactic identities under *.

The program may be trivially partially evaluated to give

$$\mathrm{zero}(x{:}nat) \longleftrightarrow x =_{nat} 0$$

and converted (automatically, by Whelk) to the Gödel module (Natural Zero is the Gödel constant we have chosen, to be distinct from the integer 0):

```
MODULE Zero.

IMPORT Naturals.

PREDICATE Zero:  Natural.

Zero(x) <- x = Zero.
```

Various other construction steps are hidden within the proof; the only points of any major significance are that the initial universal introduction gives rise to the argument of the synthesised predicate, and that the lemma does not appear in the extraction. This latter is achieved because hypotheses (*ie* the $\mathrm{condition}_i$ of the semantic scheme) are only built into the construction when they are actually used to show that a conjecture is an axiom.

3.3.4 Inductive Realisation Semantics

For any program synthesis system to have a reasonable coverage, it must be able to synthesise recursive programs — this applies even more to logic and functional program synthesis than to synthesis of other kinds of programs. In order to introduce recursion into programs synthesised by Whelk, we take advantages of the close relationship between recursion and induction. Indeed, recursion is necessarily intimately linked with induction throughout the "proofs-as-programs" literature (*eg* [Constable 82]); without this duality synthesis of recursive programs. In the Constructive Type Theory of the Oyster system, for example, each recursive data-type has its own explicit *induction term.*

In a constructive logic, inductive proofs are always of a form in which it is shown that, given an existing *construction*, one can *construct* a further value (*cf* classical logic, where pure existence proof is acceptable). Choice of an induction scheme in the proof corresponds with choice of (class of) algorithm in program construction — for example, given the usual specification of list sorting,

$$\mathrm{perm}(X, Y), \mathrm{ord}(Y)$$

one can derive either bubble sort (*via* structural induction on the input type) or quicksort (*via*, for example, a divide-and-conquer form of course-of-values induction). The choice of induction schemes to generate "good" programs is an interesting and difficult question, which will be a central topic of our future research, to be implemented in extensions of the existing CLAM proof planner [Bundy *et al* 91]. This work will be linked with existing work at Edinburgh on transformation of functional synthesis proofs to give more efficient extracted programs [Madden 91].

The use of inductive proof to construct recursive programs requires a small extension to the semantics presented above. Until now, we have excluded the instantiation of Boolean variables by anything other than ground terms in boole. Now, in order to allow recursion, we must admit instantiation by a restricted class of Boolean-valued expressions — namely, atoms defined themselves during the proof as pure logic procedures. The general form of the pure logic procedure is now

$$\mathsf{extract}_m(\overrightarrow{x_m{:}\tau_m}) \longleftrightarrow \bigvee_{1\leq i\leq n_m} (\mathsf{condition}_{(m,i)}{}^* \wedge b_{(m,i)}{}^*)$$

where $b_{(m,i)} \in \{\ \mathsf{true}\ \ \mathsf{false}\ \ \mathsf{extract}_1(\overrightarrow{y_1{:}\sigma_1})\ldots\mathsf{extract}_r(\overrightarrow{y_r{:}\sigma_r})\ \}$, and $m{:}\mathsf{nat}, r{:}\mathsf{nat}$.

It is important to understand that this less restrictive régime is only admitted in the *internal* logic, $\mathcal{L}_\mathcal{I}$ — thus, the original idea of forcing a proof, in $\mathcal{L}_\mathcal{E}$, of decidability is preserved.

The introduction of recursive calls in the Whelk system is handled by the association of specific program components with hypotheses. In the case of the substitutions in the example above, the computational content associated with the hypothesis was simply the hypothesis itself; in the case of the induction hypothesis, that content is a recursive call to the predicate being defined, with the appropriate substitution of arguments. This will become clear in the example of Section 4.

3.4 "Real" Logic Programs

Given a pure logic procedure it is a near-trivial task to convert to languages such as Prolog and Gödel. One of the advantages of this technique is that information contained in the proof can help in detecting significant factors in the execution of the finished program — for example, in general, it is advisable to include a Gödel `DELAY` declaration for inductively constructed predicates, so they they are only unfolded when the induction variable is ground, thus helping prevent unbounded recursion. The elicitation of the information necessary to do this from a program can be difficult; from an inductive proof, it is often trivial.

4 An Example of Program Construction

Regrettably there is only space for one example here. However, synthesis of the `notmember`/2 predicate is a good example of how the Whelk system may be used for synthesis, or to produce partial evaluations of existing programs. `notmember`/2, predictably, succeeds if and only if its first argument, a natural number, is not a member of the list of naturals which constitutes its second argument. We use a pure logic procedure exactly equivalent to the conventional `member`/2 definition as a lemma, which motivates one of our case splits.

Negation, as defined in the proof system, gives us the rest of the mechanism we need.

We start with the following synthesis conjecture. (In the proof below, for lack of space, we will omit repeated hypotheses and assume an incremental context unless otherwise stated.)

$$\vdash \forall x{:}nat.\forall y{:}nat\ list.\exists b{:}boole.\neg member(x, y) \hookrightarrow b$$

First, we introduce both the universal quantifiers:

$$\begin{array}{l} x{:}nat \\ y{:}nat\ list \\ \vdash \exists b{:}boole.\neg member(x, y) \hookrightarrow b \end{array}$$

and then apply primitive induction on y. The base case of the induction runs fairly simply as follows:

$$\vdash \exists b{:}boole.\neg member(x, []) \hookrightarrow b$$

We introduce true on the Boolean existential:

$$\vdash \neg member(x, []) \hookrightarrow true$$

We will need a lemma about membership of empty lists to prove this:

$$\begin{array}{l} \forall z{:}nat.\neg member(z, []) \\ \vdash \neg member(x, []) \hookrightarrow true \end{array}$$

and we must make the appropriate substitution in the lemma:

$$\begin{array}{l} \neg member(x, []) \\ \vdash \neg member(x, []) \hookrightarrow true \end{array}$$

We can now introduce $\hookrightarrow$, as in the earlier example, to give:

$$\begin{array}{l} \neg member(x, []) \\ \vdash \neg member(x, []) \end{array}$$

which is a tautology. We are now left with half a pure logic procedure, the ellipsis "..." being the part as yet unconstructed. The sub-procedure, $notmember_1$ is constructed as a result of the application of induction.

$$\begin{array}{l} notmember(x{:}nat, y{:}nat\ list) \longleftrightarrow \\ \qquad notmember_1(x{:}nat, y{:}nat\ list) \end{array}$$

$$\begin{array}{l} notmember_1(x{:}nat, y{:}nat\ list) \longleftrightarrow \\ \qquad y =_{nat\ list} [] \wedge true \wedge true \vee \\ \qquad \exists v1{:}nat\ list.\exists v0{:}nat.y =_{nat\ list} [v0 \mid v1] \wedge \ldots \end{array}$$

In terms of the semantic scheme, in subproof l of the proof, branch 0 gives us (in $\mathcal{L}_{\mathcal{I}}$)

$$\begin{array}{lll} \mathsf{condition}_{\langle 1,0\rangle} & \text{is} & y =_{\mathsf{nat\ list}} [\,] \\ b_{\langle 1,0\rangle} & \text{is} & \mathsf{true} \end{array}$$

The step case of the proof proceeds as follows. Initially, we have two new variables, to define the non-empty list for the induction, and the induction hypothesis. Note that the extraction component associated with this hypothesis in *Whelk* is

$$\mathsf{notmember}_1(x{:}\mathsf{nat}, v1{:}\mathsf{nat\ list})$$

the witness for this assumption being, of course, the proof of the base case.

$$\begin{array}{l} v0{:}\mathsf{nat} \\ v1{:}\mathsf{nat\ list} \\ \exists b{:}\mathsf{boole}.\neg\mathsf{member}(x, v1) \hookrightarrow b \\ \vdash \exists b{:}\mathsf{boole}.\neg\mathsf{member}(x, [v0 \mid v1]) \hookrightarrow b \end{array}$$

The first thing we do is rewrite the member reference according to the definition lemma (which is the usual definition of `member/2`).

$$\begin{array}{l} \vdash \forall z{:}\mathsf{nat}. \\ \quad\quad \forall v0{:}\mathsf{nat}. \\ \quad\quad\quad\quad \forall v1{:}\mathsf{nat\ list}. \\ \quad\quad\quad\quad\quad\quad \mathsf{member}(z, [v0 \mid v1]) \leftrightarrow z =_{\mathsf{nat}} v0 \vee \mathsf{member}(z, v1) \end{array}$$

After the appropriate substitutions in the conjecture above, we have:

$$\vdash \exists b{:}\mathsf{boole}.\neg(x =_{\mathsf{nat}} v0 \vee \mathsf{member}(x, v1)) \hookrightarrow b$$

As in the `zero/1` example, earlier, we now need to decide on the equality subterm, so we introduce an appropriate lemma, and substitute inside it, giving:

$$\begin{array}{l} x =_{\mathsf{nat}} v0 \oplus \neg x =_{\mathsf{nat}} v0 \\ \vdash \exists b{:}\mathsf{boole}.\neg(x =_{\mathsf{nat}} v0 \vee \mathsf{member}(x, v1)) \hookrightarrow b \end{array}$$

As before, we eliminate the $\oplus$, giving two branches of the proof, which we will consider separately here. First, the positive equality case:

$$\begin{array}{l} x =_{\mathsf{nat}} v0 \\ \vdash \exists b{:}\mathsf{boole}.\neg(x =_{\mathsf{nat}} v0 \vee \mathsf{member}(x, v1)) \hookrightarrow b \end{array}$$

The formula here is clearly false, because the left disjunct inside the negation is true by tautology, so we can introduce false on the Boolean, to give:

$$\begin{array}{l} x =_{\mathsf{nat}} v0 \\ \vdash \neg(x =_{\mathsf{nat}} v0 \vee \mathsf{member}(x, v1)) \hookrightarrow \mathsf{false} \end{array}$$

Introducing $\hookrightarrow$ then yields:

$$x =_{nat} \nu 0$$
$$\vdash \neg\neg(x =_{nat} \nu 0 \lor member(x, \nu 1))$$

which is proven in the following steps, ending with tautology:

$$x =_{nat} \nu 0$$
$$\neg(x =_{nat} \nu 0 \lor member(x, \nu 1))$$
$$\vdash \{\}$$

$$x =_{nat} \nu 0$$
$$\vdash x =_{nat} \nu 0 \lor member(x, \nu 1)$$

$$x =_{nat} \nu 0$$
$$\vdash x =_{nat} \nu 0$$

Our pure logic procedure now looks like this:

$$notmember(x{:}nat, y{:}nat\ list) \longleftrightarrow$$
$$notmember_l(x{:}nat, y{:}nat\ list)$$

$$notmember_l(x{:}nat, y{:}nat\ list) \longleftrightarrow$$
$$y =_{nat\ list} [] \land true \land true \lor$$
$$\exists \nu 1{:}nat\ list.\exists \nu 0{:}nat.$$
$$y =_{nat\ list} [\nu 0 \mid \nu 1] \land ((x =_{nat} \nu 0 \land false) \lor \ldots)$$

so in our semantic scheme $condition_{\langle l,1 \rangle}$ is $x =_{nat} \nu 0$ and $b_{\langle l,1 \rangle}$ is $false$.

Finally, we have the case of inequality between x and $\nu 0$:

$$\neg x =_{nat} \nu 0$$
$$\vdash \exists b{:}boole.\neg(x =_{nat} \nu 0 \lor member(x, \nu 1)) \hookrightarrow b$$

Rewriting this according to the familiar de Morgan Law (one of those which are constructively valid), and introducing on the disjunction inside the $\hookrightarrow$ gives us two branches, the first being trivially provable by introduction of $true$ and tautology:

$$\neg x =_{nat} \nu 0$$
$$\vdash \exists b{:}boole.\neg x =_{nat} \nu 0 \land \neg member(x, \nu 1) \hookrightarrow b$$

Left branch (branch 2):

$$\neg x =_{nat} \nu 0$$
$$\vdash \exists b{:}boole.\neg x =_{nat} \nu 0 \hookrightarrow b$$

$$\neg x =_{nat} \nu 0$$
$$\vdash \neg x =_{nat} \nu 0 \hookrightarrow true$$

$$\neg x =_{nat} \nu 0$$
$$\vdash \neg x =_{nat} \nu 0$$

The right branch (branch 3) is a copy of our induction hypothesis so we immediately have a tautology. Remember that the construction associated with this step is the recursive call.

$$\exists b{:}boole.\neg member(x, v1) \hookrightarrow b$$
$$\vdash \exists b{:}boole.\neg member(x, v1) \hookrightarrow b$$

Finally, then, we have our pure logic program:

$$notmember(x{:}nat, y{:}nat\ list) \longleftrightarrow notmember_l(x{:}nat, y{:}nat\ list)$$

$$\begin{aligned}
&notmember_l(x{:}nat, y{:}nat\ list) \longleftrightarrow \\
&\quad y =_{nat\ list} [\,] \wedge true \wedge true \vee \\
&\quad \exists v1{:}nat\ list.\exists v0{:}nat. \\
&\qquad y =_{nat\ list} [v0 \mid v1] \wedge \\
&\qquad\quad ((x =_{nat} v0 \wedge false) \vee \\
&\qquad\quad (\neg x =_{nat} v0 \wedge notmember_l(x{:}nat, v1{:}nat\ list)))
\end{aligned}$$

as we would wish. Our semantic scheme has now been instantiated thus:

$condition_{\langle l,2\rangle}$	is	$y =_{nat\ list} [v0 \mid v1] \wedge x =_{nat} v0$
$b_{\langle l,2\rangle}$	is	$false$
$condition_{\langle l,3\rangle}$	is	$y =_{nat\ list} [v0 \mid v1] \wedge \neg x =_{nat} v0$
$b_{\langle l,3\rangle}$	is	$notmember_l(x{:}nat, v1{:}nat\ list)$

In Gödel, the program comes out (automatically) as:

```
MODULE Notmember.

IMPORT Lists.
IMPORT Numbers.

PREDICATE Notmember :  Number * List( Number ).

Notmember(x,y) <-
        Notmember_1(x,y).

PREDICATE Notmember_1 :  Number * List( Number ).

Notmember_1(x,y) <-
        y = [] \/
        Some [v1]
            Some [v0]
                ( y = [v0|v1] &
                    (~ x = v0 &
                        Notmember_1(x,v1))).
```

5 Conclusion and Future Work

In this paper, we have given an overview of the operation of the *Whelk* program synthesis system. We have outlined the semantics which will allow us to demonstrate that the programs synthesised by the system always fulfil the specification in the conjecture proven during the synthesis process. We suggest that the examples here show that the scope of our synthesis system is quite wide. In particular, it is not restricted to certain special classes of program (*eg* stratified, or locally stratified) as are many comparable synthesis/transformation systems.

Much work yet remains to be done. In particular, we have yet to use our semantics to verify all our inference rules; this verification will be carried out in parallel with development of a system using the meta-level approach mentioned in Section 3.2.2. We also wish to increase the choice of induction schemes available to the system, so that (*eg*) divide-and-conquer and course-of-values algorithms are available to the *Whelk* user.

All this, however, is just the starting point for research in automation of the construction of the synthesis proofs themselves. This work will begin forthwith, based on the existing success of the "rippling" paradigm for proof planning [Bundy *et al* 90b, Bundy *et al* ng]. Rippling allows us drastically to reduce the search for correct proofs of synthesis (and other) conjectures by characterising the symbolic behaviour of inductive proofs in a very precise way. The technique can reduce the search space by as many as 33 orders of magnitude (see [Bundy *et al* 88] for more detail). All of the manipulations carried out in the examples in this paper may be motivated in terms of rippling, and thus the proofs may be planned and applied automatically. Also, we have not yet considered how to use the technique to produce *good* programs — this will be a central topic of work in the short term future.

References

[Bibel & Hörning 84] W. Bibel and K.M. Hörning. Lops — a system based on a strategical approach to program synthesis. In A. Biermann, G. Guiho, and Y. Kodratoff, editors, *Automatic Program Construction Techniques*, pages 69–90. MacMillan, 1984.

[Bundy 88] A. Bundy. The use of explicit plans to guide inductive proofs. In R. Lusk and R. Overbeek, editors, *9th*

Conference on Automated Deduction, pages 111–120. Springer-Verlag, 1988. Longer version available from Edinburgh as Research Paper No. 349.

[Bundy *et al* 88] A. Bundy, F. van Harmelen, J. Hesketh, and A. Smaill. Experiments with proof plans for induction. Research Paper 413, Dept. of Artificial Intelligence, Edinburgh, 1988. To appear in JAR.

[Bundy *et al* 90a] A. Bundy, A. Smaill, and G. Wiggins. The synthesis of logic programs from inductive proofs. In J. Lloyd, editor, *Computational Logic*, pages 135–149. Springer-Verlag, 1990. Esprit Basic Research Series. Also available from Edinburgh as DAI Research Paper 501.

[Bundy *et al* 90b] A. Bundy, F. van Harmelen, A. Smaill, and A. Ireland. Extensions to the rippling-out tactic for guiding inductive proofs. In M.E. Stickel, editor, *10th International Conference on Automated Deduction*, pages 132–146. Springer-Verlag, 1990. Lecture Notes in Artificial Intelligence No. 449.

[Bundy *et al* 90c] A. Bundy, van Harmelen. F., C. Horn, and A. Smaill. The Oyster-Clam system. In M.E. Stickel, editor, *10th International Conference on Automated Deduction*, pages 647–648. Springer-Verlag, 1990. Lecture Notes in Artificial Intelligence No. 449.

[Bundy *et al* 91] A. Bundy, F. van Harmelen, J. Hesketh, and A. Smaill. Experiments with proof plans for induction. *Journal of Automated Reasoning*, 1991. In press. Earlier version available from Edinburgh as Research Paper No 413.

[Bundy *et al* ng] A. Bundy, A. Stevens, F. van Harmelen, A. Ireland, and A. Smaill. Rippling: A heuristic for guiding inductive proofs. Research paper, Dept. of Artificial Intelligence, Edinburgh, forthcoming.

[Constable 82] R.L. Constable. Programs as proofs. Technical Report TR 82-532, Dept. of Computer Science, Cornell University, November 1982.

[Fribourg 90] L. Fribourg. Extracting logic programs from proofs that use extended prolog execution and induction. In *Proceedings of Eighth International Conference on Logic Programming*, pages 685 – 699. MIT Press, June 1990.

[Horn 88] C. Horn. The Nurprl proof development system. Working paper 214, Dept. of Artificial Intelligence, Edinburgh, 1988. The Edinburgh version of Nurprl has been renamed Oyster.

[Madden 91] P. Madden. *Automated Program Transformation Through Proof Transformation*. Unpublished PhD thesis, University of Edinburgh, 1991.

[Wiggins 90] G. Wiggins. The improvement of prolog program efficiency by compiling control: A proof-theoretic view. In *Proceedings of the Second International Workshop on Meta-programming in Logic*, Leuven, Beglium, April 1990. Also available from Edinburgh as DAI Research Paper No. 455.

Towards Stepwise, Schema-Guided Synthesis of Logic Programs

Pierre Flener
Institut d'Informatique, Université de Namur
Rue Grandgagnage 21, 5000 Namur, Belgium

Yves Deville
Unité d'Informatique, Université Catholique de Louvain
Place Ste Barbe 2, 1380 Louvain-la-Neuve, Belgium

Abstract

We present a general strategy for stepwise, sound and progressive synthesis of logic programs from specifications by examples and properties. We particularize this to schema-guided synthesis, and state a generic synthesis theorem. We justify some design choices for the development of a particular synthesis mechanism that is guided by a Divide-and-Conquer schema, is inductive and deductive, is interactive, and features a non-incremental presentation of examples. Some crucial steps of this mechanism are explained, and illustrated by a sample synthesis. We draw some conclusions on our results so far, state some related work, and outline future research directions.

1 Introduction

Program synthesis research (see [1]) aims at automating the passage from specifications to programs, as opposed to traditional, manual programming techniques. The key question here is: "what is a specification?". Today, an emerging consensus is that one may speak of "*synthesis*" when the specification does not explicitly reveal recursion or iteration. Otherwise, the technique could be classified as "*transformation*". In this introductory section, we define the starting point and the result of synthesis from examples and properties in a logic programming framework.

Definition 1 A *specification by examples and properties* of a procedure r consists of:

- a set $E(r)$ of ground (input/output) examples of the behavior of r;
- a set $P(r)$ of properties (first-order logic statements) of r.

Let $\Re$ be the relation one has in mind when elaborating such a specification of r. We shall call $\Re$ the "*intended relation*", in contrast to the relation actually specified, called the "*specified relation*". This distinction is very important to software engineering in general, but crucial with incomplete specifications, where one deliberately admits a gap between the two.

The motivation for this specification format will be given in Section 3.1. Usually, *E(r)* is empty, or non-empty only for illustrative purposes. Sometimes, *P(r)* is empty, and the resulting specification by examples is (often) incomplete. Until Section 3, we shall just assume that at least one of *E(r)* and *P(r)* is non-empty.

We are actually only interested in synthesizing *algorithms*, rather than full-fledged programs in an existing programming language. Indeed, algorithm design in itself is already very hard, and we do not want to encumber ourselves with the additional burdens of algorithm optimization, transformation and implementation, that are all well-researched topics anyway (see [2], and some papers in this volume). Algorithms expressed in a logic formalism are here called "*logic descriptions*" (see [2]).

Definition 2 A *logic description* of a procedure *r*, denoted by *LD(r)*, consists of a formula of the form: $r(X,Y) \Leftrightarrow Def[X,Y]$, where *Def* is a first-order logic statement[1,2].

Executable Prolog programs can easily be derived from such logic descriptions [2].

The rest of this paper is organized as follows. In Section 2, we present a general strategy for stepwise, sound and progressive synthesis of logic descriptions from specifications by examples and properties. We particularize this to schema-guided synthesis, and state a generic synthesis theorem. In Section 3, we justify some design choices for the development of a particular synthesis mechanism. Some crucial steps of this mechanism are explained, and illustrated by a sample synthesis. In Section 4, we draw some conclusions on our results so far, state some related work, and outline future research directions.

2 A General Strategy for Stepwise Synthesis

In this section, we outline a general strategy for logic description synthesis. We focus on stepwise synthesis, i.e. there is a series of refinements towards a correct logic description:

$$LD_1(r), LD_2(r), \ldots, LD_i(r), \ldots, LD_f(r).$$

At each step, we want to measure the current logic description against the intended relation: in Section 2.1, we introduce logic description correctness criteria useful for characterizing soundness of synthesis. Across several steps, we want to measure the progression of the synthesized logic descriptions towards the intended relation: in Section 2.2, we introduce logic description comparison criteria useful for characterizing progression of syn-

1. The variables *X* and *Y* are assumed to be universally quantified over *LD(r)*.
2. *F[X,Y]* denotes a formula *F* whose free variables are *X* and *Y*; *F[a,b]* denotes *F[X,Y]* where the free occurrences of *X* and *Y* have been replaced by *a* and *b*, respectively.

thesis. In Section 2.3, we present a strategy for stepwise, sound and progressive synthesis of logic descriptions. In Section 2.4, we particularize this strategy for schema-guided synthesis. In Section 2.5, we state a generic synthesis theorem.

2.1 Correctness Criteria of Logic Descriptions

It is important to measure a logic description against its intended relation. Since we are only concerned with the declarative semantics of logic descriptions, we shall assume model-theoretic criteria for doing so, rather than proof-theoretic ones.

A logic description $LD(r)$ is (totally) correct wrt $\Re$ iff:

$$LD(r) \models r(a,b) \text{ iff } \langle a,b \rangle \in \Re$$

$$LD(r) \models \sim r(a,b) \text{ iff } \langle a,b \rangle \notin \Re$$

i.e. iff the predicate r is interpreted as the relation $\Re$ in all (Herbrand) models of $LD(r)$.

With logic description design by structural induction on some parameter, one only has to focus on a single (Herbrand) interpretation (because the truth value of a ground atom $r(a,b)$ will be the same in all (Herbrand) models of $LD(r)$, see [2]).

Let thus $\Im$ be a Herbrand interpretation such that:

- $r(a,b)$ is true in $\Im$ iff $\Re(a,b)$
- $\Im$ is a model of all primitive predicates (such as "=")
- $\Im$ is a model of all predicates used in the property set $P(r)$.

In the sequel, all logic formulas will be interpreted in $\Im$.

Let $LD(r)$ be: $r(X,Y) \Leftrightarrow Def[X,Y]$.

There are three layers of correctness criteria. The (total) correctness of a logic description wrt its intended relation $\Re$ can now be redefined as follows:

Definition 3 *$LD(r)$ is (totally) correct wrt $\Re$* iff $r(X,Y) \Leftrightarrow Def[X,Y]$ is true in $\Im$.

(Total) correctness can be decomposed into *partial correctness* (the relation defined by $LD(r)$ is included in $\Re$) and *completeness* ($\Re$ is included in the relation defined by $LD(r)$):

Definition 4 *$LD(r)$ is partially correct wrt $\Re$* iff $r(X,Y) \Leftarrow Def[X,Y]$ is true in $\Im$.

Definition 5 *$LD(r)$ is complete wrt $\Re$* iff $r(X,Y) \Rightarrow Def[X,Y]$ is true in $\Im$.

Next comes completeness of a logic description wrt an example set $E(r)$:

Definition 6 *$LD(r)$ is complete wrt $E(r)$* iff $Def[a,b]$ is true in $\Im$, for every example $r(a,b)$ of $E(r)$.

Note that partial correctness of $LD(r)$ wrt $E(r)$ is an irrelevant concept, because we are not interested in logic descriptions that do not cover all the examples of $E(r)$.

Finally, there is consistency of examples and properties wrt the intended relation $\Re$:

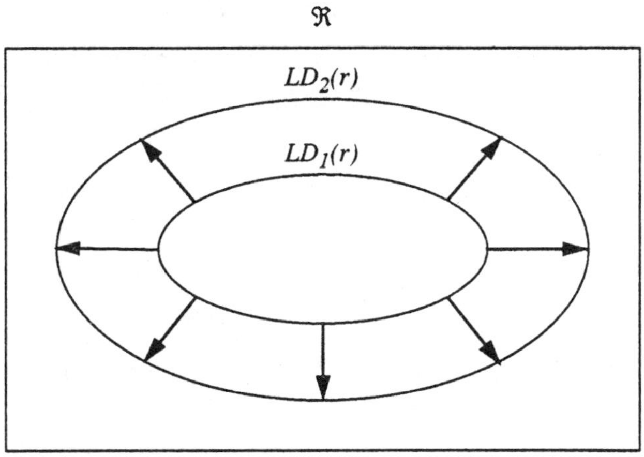

Figure 1 Partial Correctness Preserving (Upward) Progression

Definition 7 *E(r) is consistent with* $\mathfrak{R}$ iff every example of *E(r)* is true in $\mathfrak{I}$.

Definition 8 *P(r) is consistent with* $\mathfrak{R}$ iff every property of *P(r)* is true in $\mathfrak{I}$.

The specified relation of a consistent specification is a subset of the intended relation.

There is obviously no formal definition of the intended relation $\mathfrak{R}$, so some correctness criteria cannot be applied in a formal way. But these correctness criteria can be used to state features and heuristics of the synthesis process.

2.2 Comparison Criteria of Logic Descriptions

It is also important to compare logic descriptions of the same predicate. Let:

- $LD_1(r)$: $r(X,Y) \Leftrightarrow Def_1[X,Y]$
- $LD_2(r)$: $r(X,Y) \Leftrightarrow Def_2[X,Y]$

be two logic descriptions. Intuitively, $LD_1(r)$ is more general than $LD_2(r)$ iff Def_1 is "more often" true than Def_2. More formally:

Definition 9 *$LD_1(r)$ is more general than $LD_2(r)$* iff $Def_2 \Rightarrow Def_1$ is true in $\mathfrak{I}$.

This is denoted by $LD_1(r) \geq LD_2(r)$. The fact of being "*less general*" ($\leq$) is defined dually. The set of logic descriptions of a given predicate is partially ordered under "$\leq$" and "$\geq$". Two logic descriptions, each more general than the other, are "*equivalent*" ($\equiv$).

Let's give a criterion for upward (or partial-correctness preserving) progression:

Definition 10 If (see Figure 1):

- $LD_2(r) \geq LD_1(r)$
- $LD_2(r)$ is partially correct wrt $\mathfrak{R}$

then $LD_2(r)$ is a *better (partially correct) approximation* of $\mathfrak{R}$ than $LD_1(r)$.

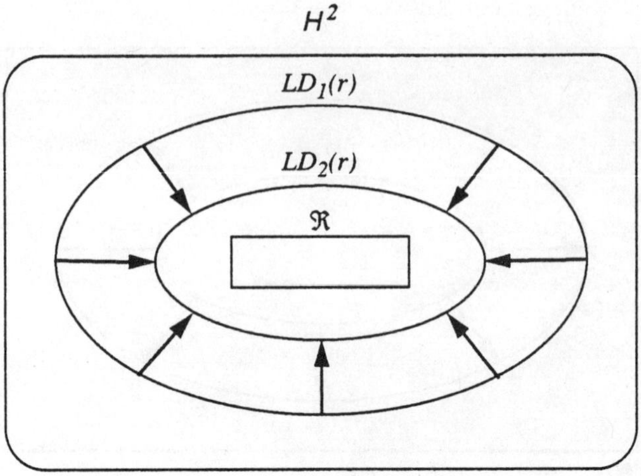

Figure 2 Completeness Preserving (Downward) Progression

Dually, there is a criterion for downward (or completeness preserving) progression:

Definition 11 If (see Figure 2, where H stands for the Herbrand universe):

- $LD_2(r) \leq LD_1(r)$
- $LD_2(r)$ is complete wrt $\Re$

then $LD_2(r)$ is a *better (complete) approximation* of $\Re$ than $LD_1(r)$.

2.3 A Strategy for Stepwise, Sound and Progressive Synthesis

We now have the terminology for defining a strategy for stepwise, sound and progressive synthesis. The first question is to determine in which direction we want to progress: upwards, or downwards? A natural choice seems to be upward progression.

A First Strategy

The first formulation of a strategy of f steps thus reads as follows.

At **Step *1***, "create" $LD_1(r)$ such that:

- $LD_1(r)$ is partially correct wrt $\Re$.

At **Step *i*** ($1<i\leq f$), transform $LD_{i-1}(r)$ into $LD_i(r)$ such that:

- $LD_i(r)$ is a better (partially correct) approximation of $\Re$ than $LD_{i-1}(r)$.

Our particular synthesis mechanism (see Section 3) even has the following feature:

- $LD_i(r)$ is complete wrt $E(r)$, ($1\leq i\leq f$).

The Completeness Issue

An objection arises: what about the completeness of the synthesized logic descriptions? We must remember that synthesis is here example-based, i.e. that constants from $E(r)$ will inevitably appear in the synthesized logic descriptions, thus destroying all possible completeness. We are thus forced to raise the completeness issue. We do it by allowing simultaneous downward progression of the series of logic descriptions that progresses upwards.

Definition 12 Let γ be a total function in the set of logic descriptions, such that $\gamma(LD(r))$ is $LD(r)$ without its equality atoms involving constants introduced from $E(r)$.

It can be shown that γ is a generalization function, i.e. $\gamma(LD(r)) \geq LD(r)$.

Example Let $LD_3(compress)$ be:

```
compress(L,CL) ⇔
     L=[]          ∧ L=[] ∧ CL=[]
   ∨ L=[HL|TL]     ∧ L=[a] ∧ CL=[<a,1>]
                   ∧ HL=a ∧ TL=[]
   ∨ L=[HL|TL]     ∧ L=[b,b] ∧ CL=[<b,2>]
                   ∧ HL=b ∧ TL=[b]
   ∨ L=[HL|TL]     ∧ L=[c,d] ∧ CL=[<c,1>,<d,1>]
                   ∧ HL=c ∧ TL=[d]
```

where the **bold** atoms are synthesized atoms, and the other atoms stem from examples E_1 to E_4 of Figure 4 below. Thus, $\gamma(LD_3(compress))$ is:

```
compress(L,CL) ⇔
     L=[]
   ∨ L=[HL|TL]
```

We shall use this function γ to enhance our strategy.

An Enhanced Strategy

The strategy now reads:

At **Step** 1, "create" $LD_1(r)$ such that:

- $LD_1(r)$ is partially correct wrt $\Re$
- $\gamma(LD_1(r))$ is complete wrt $\Re$.

At **Step** i ($1<i\leq f$), transform $LD_{i-1}(r)$ into $LD_i(r)$ such that:

- $LD_i(r)$ is a better (partially correct) approximation of $\Re$ than $LD_{i-1}(r)$
- $\gamma(LD_i(r))$ is a better (complete) approximation of $\Re$ than $\gamma(LD_{i-1}(r))$.

At **Step** f, "obtain" $LD_f(r)$ such that:

- $LD_f(r) \equiv \gamma(LD_f(r))$.

Thus, the relation defined by $LD_f(r)$ is the intended relation $\Re$, hence $LD_f(r)$ is correct wrt $\Re$. Convergence of the synthesis process is thus achieved. Since there will usually be a gap between the intended relation $\Re$ and the specified one, the given strategy cannot be fully automated, but should serve as a guideline for interactive synthesis.

$$
\begin{array}{lll}
\mathtt{R(X,Y)} \Leftrightarrow & \mathtt{Minimal(X)} & \wedge\ \mathtt{Solve(X,Y)} \\
\quad \vee\ \vee_{1\le k\le c} & \mathtt{NonMinimal(X)} & \wedge\ \mathtt{Decompose(X,\mathbf{HX},\mathbf{TX})} \\
 & & \wedge\ \mathtt{Discriminate}_k\mathtt{(\mathbf{HX},\mathbf{TX},Y)} \\
 & & \wedge\ \mathtt{R(\mathbf{TX},\mathbf{TY})} \\
 & & \wedge\ \mathtt{Process}_k\mathtt{(\mathbf{HX},\mathbf{HY})} \\
 & & \wedge\ \mathtt{Compose}_k\mathtt{(\mathbf{HY},\mathbf{TY},Y)}
\end{array}
$$

Figure 3 The Divide-and-Conquer Logic Description Schema

2.4 Schema-Guided Synthesis

Algorithm schemata are an old idea of computer science (see an early survey in [3]). They are template algorithms with fixed control flows. They embody the essence of algorithm design strategies (e.g. Divide-and-Conquer, Generate-and-Test, Global Search, ...) and are thus an invaluable knowledge source for guiding (semi-)automated algorithm design.

Example Loosely speaking, a *Divide-and-Conquer algorithm* for a binary predicate r over parameters X and Y works as follows. Let X be the induction parameter. If X is minimal, then Y is (usually) easily found by directly solving the problem. Otherwise, i.e. if X is non-minimal, we decompose X into a series $\boldsymbol{HX}$ of heads of X and a series $\boldsymbol{TX}$ of tails of X, the latter being of the same type as X, as well as smaller than X according to some well-founded relation. The tails $\boldsymbol{TX}$ recursively yield tails $\boldsymbol{TY}$ of Y. The heads $\boldsymbol{HX}$ are processed into a series of heads $\boldsymbol{HY}$ of Y. Finally, Y is composed from its heads $\boldsymbol{HY}$ and tails $\boldsymbol{TY}$. But it may happen that different process and compose patterns emerge for the non-minimal form of X: we have to discriminate between them according to the values of $\boldsymbol{HX}$, $\boldsymbol{TX}$ and Y, unless non-determinism requires such alternatives.

Logic description schemata can be expressed as second-order logic descriptions. For instance, logic descriptions designed by a Divide-and-Conquer strategy, and having one single minimal case and one single non-minimal case, will fit the schema of Figure 3.

A Refined Strategy

We can now further refine the above strategy of logic description synthesis:

At **Step** $\boldsymbol{i}$ ($1<i\le f$):

- synthesize instantiation(s) of some predicate variable(s) of the schema
- introduce some "trailing" equality atoms involving constants from $E(r)$.

2.5 A Generic Synthesis Theorem

We now state a generic synthesis theorem explaining how synthesis step i can achieve sound and progressive synthesis.

Theorem 1 *Generic Synthesis Theorem*

Let $LD_{i-1}(r)$ be: $r(X,Y) \Leftrightarrow \vee_{1 \le j \le m} A_j \wedge E_j$

and $LD_i(r)$ be: $r(X,Y) \Leftrightarrow \vee_{1 \le j \le m} A_j \wedge B_j \wedge E_j \wedge F_j$

where A_j, B_j are formulas without equality atoms involving constants introduced from $E(r)$, and E_j, F_j are conjunctions of equality atoms with constants introduced from $E(r)$.

Thus $\gamma(LD_{i-1}(r))$ is: $r(X,Y) \Leftrightarrow \vee_{1 \le j \le m} A_j$

and $\gamma(LD_i(r))$ is: $r(X,Y) \Leftrightarrow \vee_{1 \le j \le m} A_j \wedge B_j$.

The following assertions hold:

(1.1) If $LD_{i-1}(r)$ is partially correct wrt $\Re$
and $A_j \wedge E_j \Rightarrow B_j \wedge F_j$ $(1 \le j \le m)$
then $LD_i(r)$ is a *better (partially correct) approximation* of $\Re$ than $LD_{i-1}(r)$.

(1.2) If $\gamma(LD_{i-1}(r))$ is complete wrt $\Re$
and $\Re(X,Y) \wedge A_j \Rightarrow B_j$ $(1 \le j \le m)$
then $\gamma(LD_i(r))$ is a *better (complete) approximation* of $\Re$ than $\gamma(LD_{i-1}(r))$.

Proof 1 The proof is straightforward (see [4]).

The second condition of assertion (1.1) ensures that the atoms introduced by Step i are redundant with the already existing ones: in other words, we actually have $LD_i(r) \cong LD_{i-1}(r)$. This is not a disaster, because strict progression is achieved by the generalizations. The second condition of assertion (1.2) ensures that the atoms introduced by Step i are "redundant" with the intended relation.

For a specific synthesis mechanism whose steps 2 to $f\text{-}1$ fit into the framework of this theorem, it thus suffices to prove that the method of each step ensures its particular instantiations of the conditions of both assertions. The first conditions of both assertions actually need not be proved, because Step 1 establishes them, and Theorem 1 preserves them.

3 A Particular Synthesis Mechanism

In this section, we present a particular synthesis mechanism. In Section 3.1, we explain the design decisions taken while instantiating the parameters of the framework of Section 2. In Section 3.2 to Section 3.5, the steps of the synthesis mechanism are detailed. Let's first present a running example for this section:

Example *Data compression*. The *compress(L,CL)* procedure succeeds on facts such as:

compress([a, a, a, b, b, a, c, c, c, c], [<a, 3>, <b, 2>, <a, 1>, <c, 4>]).

Compression is performed without forward checking, i.e. each plateau is compressed regardless of whether another plateau of the same character occurs later in the list *L*.

3.1 Decisions

A series of decisions have to be taken before producing a specific synthesis mechanism within the framework of Section 2.

Which Schema?

We adopt the Divide-and-Conquer schema of Figure 3 for guiding synthesis. Indeed, the class of algorithms that can be designed by this strategy is fairly large and important. There will be eight steps to our mechanism:

- Step 1: Creation of a first approximation
- Step 2: Synthesis of *Minimal* and *NonMinimal*
- Step 3: Synthesis of *Decompose*
- Step 4: Synthesis of the recursive atoms
- Step 5: Synthesis of *Solve*
- Step 6: Synthesis of *Process* and *Compose*
- Step 7: Synthesis of *Discriminate*
- Step 8: Generalization

There are two phases: an "*expansion phase*" (Steps 1 to 4), where equality atoms involving constants introduced from *E(r)* are added, and a "*reduction phase*" (Steps 5 to 8), where the actual synthesis takes place. In this paper, we shall focus on the reduction phase.

Note that the schema is not an input to the synthesis mechanism. It is rather a convenient way of explaining how synthesis works.

Which Language for Specifications?

Examples are a very appealing means of conveying information about a relation: they are easy to elaborate/understand, and they implicitly reveal structural manipulations of the parameters. Our plan is thus to use non-empty example sets in specifications. However, examples alone are an incomplete information source, and they cannot explicitly convey semantic operations/tests on parameters. We believe the specifier knows these additional details, and ought thus to be able to provide them, rather than have the synthesis mechanism guess them! We depart thus from traditional example-based synthesis and add a non-empty property set to our specifications. But we would like to give properties the same appeal as examples. It turns out that non-recursive Horn clauses, plus negation, are a very convenient choice. Since synthesis should start from a non-recursive specification, we must disallow recursive properties.

```
E(compress)={ compress([],[])                                   (E1)
              compress([a],[<a,1>])                             (E2)
              compress([b,b],[<b,2>])                           (E3)
              compress([c,d],[<c,1>,<d,1>])                     (E4)
              compress([e,e,e],[<e,3>])                         (E5)
              compress([f,f,g],[<f,2>,<g,1>])                   (E6)
              compress([h,i,i],[<h,1>,<i,2>])                   (E7)
              compress([j,k,l],[<j,1>,<k,1>,<l,1>])}            (E8)
P(compress)={ compress([X],[<X,1>])                             (P1)
              compress([X,Y],[<X,2>]) ⇐ X=Y                     (P2)
              compress([X,Y],[<X,1>,<Y,1>]) ⇐ X≠Y}              (P3)
```

Figure 4 Sample versions of *E(compress)* and *P(compress)*

Example Figure 4 gives sample versions of *E(compress)* and *P(compress)*. Note that properties P_1 to P_3 generalize examples E_2 to E_4, respectively. They also make explicit why examples E_3 and E_4 behave differently: equality/disequality of the first two elements, rather than any other criterion.

Our properties turn out to be an incomplete specification source, too. It is thus important that we do not strive for completely automated synthesis, but rather for interactive synthesis, so as to cope with incompleteness.

Examples give rise to inductive synthesis (generalization [5], [6], [7], learning [8], [9]), whereas axiomatic specifications (and thus properties) give rise to deductive synthesis (proofs-as-programs [10], [11], [12], rewriting [13], [14], [15]). Since we have both specification types, we want to avoid using only one kind of inference, and thus degrading the non-used information source into validation information. We shall therefore strive for inductive **and** deductive synthesis, using whichever inference type is best suited at each step. This approach of course precludes synthesis whenever only examples or only properties are given. It also gives a constructive role to each information type.

How to Present the Examples?

There are two extreme ways of presenting examples: *"one-by-one"* (*"incrementally"*), or *"all-at-once"*. The former approach, advocated in [8] and by the machine learning school of thought, has some nice convergence properties. But we shall adhere to the school of thought advocated in [7], where the examples are presented all-at-once, so that a maximum of information is available at each step.

```
compress(L,CL) ⇔
      L=[]              ∧ CL=[]
    ∨ L=[H1]            ∧ CL=[<H1,1>]
    ∨ L=[H1,H2|TL] ∧ H1=H2
                        ∧ compress([H2|TL],[<H2,M>|T])
                        ∧ add(M,1,N)  ∧ CL=[<H1,N>|T]
    ∨ L=[H1,H2|TL] ∧ H1≠H2
                        ∧ compress([H2|TL],TCL)
                        ∧ CL=[<H1,1>|TCL])
```

Figure 5 A sample version of *LD(compress)*

Which Language for Logic Descriptions?

Since the Divide-and-Conquer schema has a definition part in disjunctive normal form, we shall stick to such logic descriptions at all steps of synthesis.

Example To give a preliminary glimpse of what the synthesis mechanism is supposed to produce, Figure 5 gives a sample version of *LD(compress)*, constructed by the methodology of [2].

Let's now see how the eight synthesis steps identified above can produce an equivalent logic description from the specification by examples and properties of Figure 4.

3.2 The Expansion Phase of Synthesis (Steps 1 - 4)

During the *expansion phase*, the following steps are performed:

- creation of a first approximation (Step 1), via re-expression of the example set as a logic description. In order to ensure applicability of Theorem 1 for Steps 2 - 7, we must assume that *E(r)* and *P(r)* are consistent wrt the intended relation;
- synthesis of *Minimal* and *NonMinimal* (Step 2), from a set of predefined, type-specific, parameterized instantiations;
- synthesis of *Decompose* (Step 3), from a set of predefined, type-specific, parameterized instantiations;
- synthesis of the recursive atoms (Step 4), via deductive and/or analogical reasoning.

Steps 1 to 3 are quite straightforward, but Step 4 isn't (see the results in [4]).

Example Figure 6 shows $LD_4(compress)$, where disjunct D_i corresponds to example E_i. Note that there is one minimal case (disjunct D_1), and one non-minimal case (disjuncts D_2 to D_8). Also note that $\gamma(LD_4(compress))$ is:

```
compress(L,CL) ⇔
      L=[]          ∧ L=[] ∧ CL=[]                                    (D1)
    ∨ L=[HL|TL] ∧ compress(TL,TCL)
                    ∧ L=[a] ∧ CL=[<a,1>]
                    ∧ HL=a ∧ TL=[] ∧ TCL=[]                           (D2)
    ∨ L=[HL|TL] ∧ compress(TL,TCL)
                    ∧ L=[b,b] ∧ CL=[<b,2>]
                    ∧ HL=b ∧ TL=[b] ∧ TCL=[<b,1>]                     (D3)
    ∨ L=[HL|TL] ∧ compress(TL,TCL)
                    ∧ L=[c,d] ∧ CL=[<c,1>,<d,1>]
                    ∧ HL=c ∧ TL=[d] ∧ TCL=[<d,1>]                     (D4)
    ∨ L=[HL|TL] ∧ compress(TL,TCL)
                    ∧ L=[e,e,e] ∧ CL=[<e,3>]
                    ∧ HL=e ∧ TL=[e,e] ∧ TCL=[<e,2>]                   (D5)
    ∨ L=[HL|TL] ∧ compress(TL,TCL)
                    ∧ L=[f,f,g] ∧ CL=[<f,2>,<g,1>]
                    ∧ HL=f ∧ TL=[f,g]
                    ∧ TCL=[<f,1>,<g,1>]                               (D6)
    ∨ L=[HL|TL] ∧ compress(TL,TCL)
                    ∧ L=[h,i,i] ∧ CL=[<h,1>,<i,2>]
                    ∧ HL=h ∧ TL=[i,i] ∧ TCL=[<i,2>]                   (D7)
    ∨ L=[HL|TL] ∧ compress(TL,TCL)
                    ∧ L=[j,k,l] ∧ CL=[<j,1>,<k,1>,<l,1>]
                    ∧ HL=j ∧ TL=[k,l]
                    ∧ TCL=[<k,1>,<l,1>]                               (D8)
```

Figure 6 *LD_4(compress)*

```
compress(L,CL) ⇔
      L=[]
    ∨ L=[HL|TL] ∧ compress(TL,TCL) .
```

Let's now have a close look at the steps of the *reduction phase*.

3.3 Synthesis of *Solve*, *Compose* and *Process* (Steps 5 - 6)

At Step 5, the synthesis of *Solve* for the minimal case is similar to what happens at Steps 6 and 7 for the non-minimal case, and we shall thus not delve into details. Just consider that *CL=L* is synthesized as an instance of *Solve(L,CL)*.

At Step 6, the aim is to transform $LD_5(r)$ into $LD_6(r)$ which fits the following schema:

```
r(X,Y) ⇔ minimal(X)       ∧ solve(X,Y)
                          ∧ ∨_{1≤i≤b} X=x_i ∧ Y=y_i
  ∨ ∨_{1≤k≤C} nonMinimal(X) ∧ decompose(X,HX,TX)
                          ∧ r(TX,TY)
                          ∧ Process_k(HX,HY) ∧ Compose_k(HY,TY,Y)
                          ∧ ∨_{i∈|k|}  X=x_i ∧ Y=y_i
                                    ∧ HX=hx_i ∧ TX=tx_i
                                    ∧ HY=hy_i ∧ TY=ty_i
```

i.e. we want to partition the non-minimal disjuncts into C equivalence classes $/1/, \ldots, /C/$ whose members have equal instantiations of *Process* and *Compose*.

For *Process*, we take the following approach:

- first assume that "=" is a suitable instantiation of *Process*, and synthesize a partition. Note that this assumption is also successful when "=" is actually not a suitable instantiation of *Process*, but the latter can be (loop-)merged with *Compose*;
- otherwise assume that the synthesis of *Process* requires other techniques (not mentioned here), and synthesize a partition, leaving *Process* uninstantiated.

We have two methods to synthesize a partition, and thus an instantiation of *Compose*:

- computation of most specific generalizations: this *MSG Method* will be successful if *Compose* can be expressed as a conjunction of equality atoms;
- synthesis from an inferred specification by examples and properties: this *Synthesis Method* applies when *Compose* itself needs a full-fledged recursive logic description. We shall not explain here when to apply this method, nor how a specification for *Compose* can be inferred from the current logic description (see [4] for details).

The MSG Method fulfills the conditions of Theorem 1. Since the Synthesis Method eventually boils down to using the MSG Method, it is, by induction, sound and progressive as well, provided the specification inference is sound.

Example Assuming *Process* is "=", the MSG Method synthesizes the disjunct partition:

$$\{ \{D_2, D_4, D_7, D_8\}, \{D_3, D_5, D_6\} \}$$

- for the first class, we have the following instances of *<HCL, TCL, CL>*:

```
<a, [],                 [<a,1>]>                    (D2)
<c, [<d,1>],            [<c,1>,<d,1>]>              (D4)
<h, [<i,2>],            [<h,1>,<i,2>]>              (D7)
<j, [<k,1>,<l,1>], [<j,1>,<k,1>,<l,1>]>             (D8)
```

Hence the MSG: *<H,T,[<H,1>|T]>*.

And $Compose_1(HCL,TCL,CL)$ is thus: *CL=[<HCL, 1>|TCL]*

```
compress(L,CL) ⇔
     L=[]         ∧ CL=L
                  ∧ L=[] ∧ CL=[]
   ∨ L=[HL|TL]  ∧ compress(TL,TCL)
                  ∧ CL=[<HL,1>|TCL]
                  ∧ HL=a ∧ TL=[] ∧ TCL=[] ∧ ...
                    ∨ HL=c ∧ TL=[d] ∧ TCL=[<d,1>] ∧ ...
                    ∨ HL=h ∧ TL=[i,i] ∧ TCL=[<i,2>] ∧ ...
                    ∨ HL=j ∧ TL=[k,l] ∧ TCL=[<k,1>,<l,1>] ∧ ...
   ∨ L=[HL|TL]  ∧ compress(TL,TCL)
                  ∧ TCL=[<HL,M>|TTCL] ∧ CL=[<HL,s(M)>|TTCL]
                  ∧ HL=b ∧ TL=[b] ∧ TCL=[<b,1>] ∧ ...
                    ∨ HL=e ∧ TL=[e,e] ∧ TCL=[<e,2>] ∧ ...
                    ∨ HL=f ∧ TL=[f,g] ∧ TCL=[<f,1>,<g,1>] ∧ ...
```

Figure 7 LD_6(compress)

- similarly, for the second class, $Compose_2(HCL,TCL,CL)$ is:

$$TCL=[<HCL, M>|TTCL] \wedge CL=[<HCL, s(M)>|TTCL].$$

Hence $LD_6(compress)$ looks as depicted in Figure 7. Note that the assumption that *Process* is "=" works because *Process* and *Compose* could be merged.

3.4 Synthesis of *Discriminate* (Step 7)

At Step 7, the aim is to transform $LD_6(r)$ into $LD_7(r)$ which fits the following schema:

```
r(X,Y) ⇔ minimal(X)      ∧ solve(X,Y)
                          ∧ ∨1≤i<b X=xi ∧ Y=yi
   ∨ ∨1≤k≤c nonMinimal(X) ∧ decompose(X,HX,TX)
                          ∧ Discriminatek(HX,TX,Y)
                          ∧ r(TX,TY)
                          ∧ processk(HX,HY) ∧ composek(HY,TY,Y)
                          ∧ ∨i∈|k| X=xi ∧ Y=yi
                                   ∧ HX=hxi ∧ TX=txi
                                   ∧ HY=hyi ∧ TY=tyi
```

This objective is achieved by two consecutive tasks:

- synthesis of specialized instantiations of the $Discriminate_k$
- generalization of these specialized instantiations of the $Discriminate_k$.

```
compress(L,CL) ⇔
    L=[]        ∧ CL=L
                ∧ L=[] ∧ Cl=[]
  ∨ L=[HL|TL] ∧ (TL=[]) ∨ (TL=[HTL|TTL] ∧ HL≠HTL)
                ∧ compress(TL,TCL)
                ∧ CL=[<HL,1>|TCL]
                ∧HL=a ∧ TL=[] ∧ TCL=[] ∧ ...
                  ∨ HL=c ∧ TL=[d] ∧ TCL=[<d,1>] ∧ ...
                  ∨ HL=h ∧ TL=[i,i] ∧ TCL=[<i,2>] ∧ ...
                  ∨ HL=j ∧ TL=[k,l] ∧ TCL=[<k,1>,<l,1>] ∧ ...
  ∨ L=[HL|TL] ∧ TL=[HTL|TTL] ∧ HL=HTL
                ∧ compress(TL,TCL)
                ∧ TCL=[<HL,M>|TTCL] ∧ CL=[<HL,s(M)>|TTCL]
                ∧ HL=b ∧ TL=[b] ∧ TCL=[<b,1>] ∧ ...
                  ∨ HL=e ∧ TL=[e,e] ∧ TCL=[<e,2>] ∧ ...
                  ∨ HL=f ∧ TL=[f,g] ∧ TCL=[<f,1>,<g,1>] ∧ ...
```

Figure 8 $LD_7(compress)$

The first task is done using a *Proofs-as-Programs Method* (see [10], [11], [12]): instantiations of the $Discriminate_k$ are extracted from the proof that:

$$\gamma(LD_6(r)) \vdash P(r)\ .$$

The second task is heuristic-driven, i.e. after applying some generalization heuristics, we postulate that the resulting discriminators are the intended ones.

Some theoretical aspects of this step are further detailed in [4].

Example For our *compress* procedure:

- the proof of P_1 reveals a partial, specialized discriminator for the first class:

$$discriminate_1(HL,\ [],\ [<HL,1>]).$$

- the proof of P_3 reveals another partial, specialized discriminator for the first class:

$$discriminate_1(HL,\ [HTL],\ [<HL,1>,\ <HTL,1>]) \Leftarrow HL \neq HTL.$$

We join both, generalize *TL*, eliminate the *CL=*... atoms, and "postulate":

$$discriminate_1(HL,\ TL,\ CL) \Leftrightarrow TL=[] \lor (TL=[HTL/TTL] \land HL \neq HTL).$$

- the proof of P_2 reveals a specialized discriminator for the second class:

$$discriminate_2(HL,\ [HTL],\ [<HL,2>]) \Leftarrow HL=HTL.$$

We generalize *TL*, eliminate the *CL=*... atom, and "postulate":

$$discriminate_2(HL,\ TL,\ CL) \Leftrightarrow TL=[HTL/TTL] \land HL=HTL.$$

Hence $LD_7(compress)$ looks as depicted in Figure 8.

```
compress(L,CL) ⇔
      L=[]         ∧ CL=L
    ∨ L=[HL|TL]    ∧ TL=[]
                   ∧ compress(TL,TCL)
                   ∧ CL=[<HL,1>|TCL]
    ∨ L=[HL|TL]    ∧ TL=[HTL|TTL]  ∧ HL≠HTL
                   ∧ compress(TL,TCL)
                   ∧ CL=[<HL,1>|TCL]
    ∨ L=[HL|TL]    ∧ TL=[HTL|TTL]  ∧ HL=HTL
                   ∧ compress(TL,TCL)
                   ∧ TCL=[<HL,M>|TTCL]  ∧ CL=[<HL,s(M)>|TTCL]
```

Figure 9 $LD_8(compress)$

3.5 Generalization (Step 8)

At Step 8, the aim is to transform $LD_7(r)$ into $LD_8(r)$ which looks like:

```
r(X,Y) ⇔ minimal(X)         ∧ solve(X,Y)
    ∨ ∨1≤k≤c nonMinimal(X) ∧ decompose(X,HX,TX)
                            ∧ discriminatek(HX,TX,Y)
                            ∧ r(TX,TY)
                            ∧ processk(HX,HY) ∧ composek(HY,TY,Y)
```

This is simply achieved by postulating that $LD_8(r)$ is $\gamma(LD_7(r))$.

Example $LD_8(compress)$ looks as depicted in Figure 9. Note that this logic description can be proven to be equivalent to the one given in Figure 5.

4 Conclusions

We have shown how to perform a stepwise, schema-guided, inductive and deductive, non-incremental synthesis of logic descriptions from examples and properties. Most steps are non-deterministic. In this last section, we shall present the framework, results and contributions of this research, and mention some related research, as well as future research.

4.1 Framework, Results and Contributions

This research is led within the framework of the FOLON research project (Université de Namur, Belgium) whose objective is twofold. First, it aims at elaborating a methodology of logic program development, such as described in [2]. Second, it aims at designing an integrated set of tools supporting this methodology. Our research tackles the aspects of logic program synthesis from examples and properties.

The main results of our work on logic program synthesis so far are the definition of a synthesis calculus, the identification of a particular synthesis mechanism, and the development of methods for each of its steps. The descriptions of Steps 5 to 7 in this paper are only target scenarios,a complete survey of all results can be found in [4].

One of the originalities of our approach is the combination of examples with properties, so as to cope with some classical problems of example-based synthesis.

4.2 Related Research

Pointers to related research in program synthesis have been given throughout the text, and we have already stressed in detail how our approach differs from the state of the art. The use of schemata is also advocated in [16], [17], [18], [9] (Divide-and-Conquer), [19] (Global Search), and others, although sometimes in different contexts (e.g. programming tutors/assistants). An early study of the concept of "most specific generalization" is [20].

4.3 Future Research

In the future, we plan to pursue research on the following aspects:

- development of a "proof-of-concept" implementation (in Prolog) of the synthesis mechanism. This should allow the identification of points of interaction with the specifier so that we can cope with incompleteness: wherever inductive reasoning is used, the specifier should be able to give his feedback. It is important to keep this dialogue easy, i.e. a question/answer method asking for the classification of ground atoms as examples/counter-examples seems to be an appropriate choice;
- incorporation of counter-examples in the specifications, the general synthesis strategy, and the synthesis mechanism. Indeed, negative information is quite useful in avoiding over-generalization during inductive reasoning;
- formulation of a choice methodology for examples and properties: it is important to guide the specifier towards choosing relevant examples and properties. This reduces interaction with the specifier, and results thus in highly automated synthesis.

Acknowledgments

The authors gratefully acknowledge many insightful discussions with B. Le Charlier (Université de Namur, Belgium). Parts of the results presented here were found while the first author was on leave at Duke University (NC, USA): many thanks to Prof. A. W. Biermann and Prof. D. W. Loveland for their interest in our research. The first author and the FOLON project are supported by the Belgian National Incentive Program for Fundamental Research in AI.

References

[1] Biermann AW. *Automatic Programming*. In: Encyclopedia of Artificial Intelligence. John Wiley & Sons, 1987, pp 18-35. (A second, extended version is in print).

[2] Deville Y. *Logic Programming - Systematic Program Development*. Addison Wesley, Reading (MA, USA), 1990.

[3] Manna Z. *Mathematical Theory of Computation*. McGraw-Hill, New York (NY, USA), 1974.

[4] Flener P. *Towards Programming by Examples and Properties*. Research Report CS-1991-09, Duke University, Durham (NC, USA), 1991.

[5] Biermann AW. *Dealing with Search*. In: Biermann AW, Guiho G and Kodratoff Y (eds) *Automatic Program Construction Techniques*. Macmillan Publishing Company, New York (NY, USA), 1984, pp 375-392.

[6] Biermann AW and Smith DR. *A Production Rule Mechanism for Generating LISP Code*. IEEE Transactions on Systems, Man and Cybernetics 1979; 5:260-276.

[7] Summers P. *A Methodology for LISP Program Construction from Examples*. Journal of the ACM 1977; 1:161-175.

[8] Shapiro E. *Algorithmic Program Debugging*. PhD thesis. MIT Press, Cambridge (MA, USA), 1982.

[9] Tinkham NL. *Induction of Schemata for Program Synthesis*. PhD thesis, Research Report CS-1990-14, Duke University, Durham (NC, USA), 1990.

[10] Bundy A, Smaill A and Wiggins G. *The Synthesis of Logic Programs from Inductive Proofs*. In: Lloyd JW (ed) *Computational Logic*. Springer Verlag, 1990, pp 135-149.

[11] Fribourg L. *Extracting Logic Programs from Proofs that Use Extended Prolog Execution and Induction*. In: Proceedings of ICLP-90, MIT Press, Cambridge (MA, USA), 1990, pp 685-699.

[12] Manna Z and Waldinger R. *Synthesis: Dreams ⇒ Programs*. IEEE Transactions on Software Engineering 1979; 4:294-328.

[13] Clark KL. *The Synthesis and Verification of Logic Programs*. Research Report DOC 81/36, Imperial College, London (UK), 1981.

[14] Hansson Å. *A Formal Development of Programs*. PhD thesis, University of Stockholm (Sweden), 1980.

[15] Hogger CJ. *Derivation of Logic Programs*. Journal of the ACM 1981; 2:372-392.

[16] Burnay J and Deville Y. *Generalization and Program Schemata*. In: Proceedings of NACLP-89, MIT Press, Cambridge (MA, USA), 1989, pp 409-425.

[17] Gegg-Harrison TS. *Basic Prolog Schemata*. Research Report CS-1989-20, Duke University, Durham (NC, USA), 1989.

[18] Smith DR. *Top-Down Synthesis of Divide-and-Conquer Algorithms*. Artificial Intelligence 1985, 27:43-96.

[19] Smith DR. *The Structure and Design of Global Search Algorithms*. Technical Report KES.U.87.12, Kestrel Institute, Palo Alto (CA, USA), 1988.

[20] Plotkin GD. *A Note on Inductive Generalization*. Machine Intelligence 1970; 5:153-163, Edinburgh University Press (Scotland), 1970.

Inductive Synthesis of Rewrite Rules as Program Synthesis

Klaus P. Jantke and Ulf Goldammer
FB Mathematik & Informatik
Technische Hochschule Leipzig
Postfach 66, 7030 Leipzig
Germany

— Extended Abstract —

1 Introduction

It is rather unrealistic to expect newly designed software specifications to be always complete. Naturally, there are several forms of incompleteness. We are not concerned with explicitly known incompleteness during an unfinished design process. Instead, the present approach is focussed on specifications which are either a little incomplete by mistake or intentionally incomplete as descriptions by examples are. Completing given specifications to an operationally complete form may be understood as program synthesis.

The aim of the investigations presented is to provide new techniques and tools for automatically completing a large number of equational software specifications.

This research work is firmly based on the mathematical theory of inductive inference. This theory may be understood as a mathematical approach to machine learning from possibly incomplete information. It comprises a considerable amount of results ranging from basic theorems about learnability and non-learnability to effective algorithms and implementations. The present paper cannot give a sufficiently complete introduction into the rich area of inductive inference. The interested reader should consult [AnSm] or [KlWi] in this regard. An also very easy introduction into principles and problems of inductive inference has recently been given by the first author in [Jant]. [Gold] is the seminal paper of inductive inference research.

The reader should notice that inductive inference research is the main concern of the first author's research group at Technische Hochschule Leipzig. One of the main developments is to tune inductive inference research to applied areas both for directing theoretical research and for achieving remarkably new applied results. To date results from the theory of inductive inference have not been exploited in software development applications, although this is a very promising area. In fact, we are dealt with a certain way of applying artificial intelligence ideas to software development.

2 The Approach

Currently, the crucial problem is to develop appropriate learning techniques. The application of those techniques, if they have been developed, is an independent question, to some extent. A first approach of the type reported here may be found in [ThJa]. In [Lang] and [LaJa] there have been developed inference rules for automatically completing certain equational specifications.

The Knuth-Bendix completion procedure (cf. [KnBe]) is a tool for algorithmically completing term rewriting systems which are operationally incomplete in the sense that the uniqueness of normal forms is not guaranteed. As the problem of operational completeness is undecidable, one may only expect a technique applicable to an enumerable number of cases. [EhMa], [HuOp], and [KnBe] provide the mathematical background of our approach to algebraic software specification and completion. [[Herm] investigates structurally useful properties allowing automated completion. The approach presented here is distinguished from our former approaches by the weaker goal to synthesize only ground confluent rewrite rule systems. Ground confluence is sufficient for program synthesis, whereas usual Knuth-Bendix completion (cf. the references mentioned) is aimed at synthesizing canonical, i.e. terminating and confluent, rewrite rule systems. In an algebraic framework, a program is a terminating and ground confluent rewrite rule system.

The Knuth-Bendix completion procedure may fail either by generating a critical pair which can not be oriented to form a new rewrite rule or by generating an infinite sequence of critical pairs to be introduced as new rewrite rules. The latter case is investigated. The basic idea is to invoke inductive inference techniques for abbreviating infinitely long sequences of rules by finitely many other rules. If simple syntactic generalization does not do, there will be automatically generated auxiliary operators. This is the key idea of the this paper. The present extended abstract contains only an example invoking inference rules for generalization and operator synthesis investigated in [LaJa].

3 A Standard Example

Assume some almost trivial basic specification

$$\begin{array}{lrcl} (B1) & 0+X & \rightarrow & X \\ (B2) & s(X+Y) & \rightarrow & s(X+Y) \end{array}$$

The following three introductory rules define a desired new procedure operationally incomplete.

$$\begin{array}{lrcl} (I1) & d(0,X) & \rightarrow & 0 \\ (I2) & d(X,0) & \rightarrow & X \\ (I3) & d(Y+X,Y) & \rightarrow & X \end{array}$$

One may easily ckeck that Knuth-Bendix completion applied to the five rules above diverges. Our technique invoking the rules from [LaJa] generates an auxiliary operator called h together with properties expressed as rewrite rules as follows:

$$
\begin{array}{llcl}
(G1) & d(s(X), s(V)) & \rightarrow & h(0, W, V) \\
(G2) & h(Z, s(W), s(V)) & \rightarrow & h(s(Z), W, V) \\
(G3) & h(Z, Y, 0) & \rightarrow & Y \\
(G4) & h(Z, X + Y, X) & \rightarrow & Y
\end{array}
$$

All the axioms above constitute the program synthesized which allows to compute the value of the target function denoted by d for any input data. Generating the rules $(G1), \ldots, (G4)$ from the basic knowledge $(B1), (B2)$ and the introductory rules $(I1), (I2), (I3)$ is completely automatic.

References

[AnSm] D. Angluin and C.H. Smith, Inductive Inference: Theory and Methods, *Computing Surveys* **15** (3), 1983, 237-269.

[EhMa] H. Ehrig and B. Mahr, Fundamentals of Algebraic Specifications 1, *EATCS Monographs on Theoretical Computer Science* **6**, Springer-Verlag, 1985.

[Gold] E. M. Gold, Language Identification in the Limit, *Inform. and Control* **14**, 1967, 447-474.

[[Herm] M. Hermann, Chain Properties of Rule Closures, *Proc. 6th STACS*, Paderborn, 1989, Springer-Verlag, *Lecture Notes in Computer Science* **349**, 1989, 339-347.

[HuOp] G. Huet and D. Oppen, Equations and Rewrite Rules: a Survey, in R. Book (ed), *Formal Language Theory: Perspectives and Open Problems*, Academic Press, New York, 1980, 349-405.

[Jant] K.P. Jantke, Algorithmic Learning from Incomplete Information: Principles and Problems, in J. Dassow and J. Kelemen (eds), *Machines, Languages, and Complexity, Lecture Notes in Computer Science* **381**, Springer-Verlag, 1989, 188-207.

[KlWi] R. Klette and R. Wiehagen, Research in the Theory of Inductive Inference by GDR Mathematicians – A Survey, *Inform. Sciences* **22**, 1980, 149-169.

[KnBe] D.E. Knuth and P.B. Bendix, Simple Word Problems in Universal Algebra, in J. Leach (ed), *Computational Algebra*, Pergamon Press, 1970, 263-297.

[Lang] S. Lange, Towards a Set of Inference Rules for Solving Divergence in Knuth-Bendix Completion, in *Proc. AII'89, Analogical and Inductive Inference, Lecture Notes in Artificial Intelligence* **397**, Springer-Verlag, 1989, 304-316.

[LaJa] S. Lange and K.P. Jantke, Inductive Completion for Transformation of Equational Specifications, in *Proc. Recent Trends in Abstract Data Type Specification, Lecture Notes in Computer Science* **534**, Springer-Verlag, 1991.

[ThJa] M. Thomas and K.P. Jantke, Inductive Inference for Solving Divergence in Knuth- Bendix Completion, in *Proc. AII'89, Analogical and Inductive Inference, Lecture Notes in Artificial Intelligence* **397**, Springer-Verlag, 1989, 288-303.

Formal Program Development in Modular Prolog : A Case Study

M. G. Read
E. A. Kazmierczak*
Department of Computer Science, University of Edinburgh
Edinburgh, United Kingdom

Abstract

In this paper we present a case study in which we specify and *formally* develop a modular PROLOG program from its specification. The modular PROLOG which we use is that proposed in [SW87] which is based on the module system of Standard ML [HMT90, MT90]. We give a specification language for writing specifications of modular PROLOG programs and also a methodology, based on that of Extended ML, for the *stepwise* construction of a program from its specification. The case study is intended to examine the Extended ML methodology applied to formal development of PROLOG programs. We also assess the feasibility and outline the potential difficulties of doing so.

1 Introduction

In this paper we present a *model* oriented approach to formally developing PROLOG programs. The approach is based upon that of the Extended ML wide-spectrum language [ST89, San89, ST91]. In the Extended ML approach a specification denotes a class of models or possible programs. The final program must be a member of this class. This program is not given in a single implementation step but is *constructed* from the original specification via a number of smaller *program development* steps. At each step some design choices are made, for example, choosing the modular structure of the final program or giving an actual algorithm to realize some aspect of the specification. To guarantee that each step results in a *correct* refinement of the original specification proof obligations are associated with each step and must be *formally* discharged.

This style of program development is independent of the particular logic and programming language used and only depends upon a definition of what it means for a program module to satisfy its specification (written in the specification logic in question). The question that we ask is if this style of program development is suited to other programming languages, for example, PROLOG.

*Supported by SERC grant GR/E 78463

The purpose of this paper is to describe a case study showing just how program development using the Extended ML approach may be put into practice in developing modular PROLOG programs. We begin by describing a modular version of PROLOG and a language for specifying modular PROLOG programs. We then present our case study which is the formal development of a program to test confluence of rewrite rules [HO80, Klo87].

The reason for choosing PROLOG is that it, like Standard ML [HMT90, MT90], has a semantics which can be formalized [Llo84]. This is required for the kind of formal development which is presented here because of the requirement that proof obligations need to be formally discharged. Formally discharging a proof obligation means knowing exactly when a program satisfies (or, is a model of) a specification.

The reason for choosing the term rewriting example is so that the example is sufficiently large to naturally lead to a modular PROLOG program via several program development steps. Consequently it is a good test for the development methodology. It was also chosen because of its relevance to other work on decomposing term rewriting systems into modules, for example, [Les89, Les90].

The remainder of this paper is organized as follows. Section 2 describes the module language and program development methodology in more detail. In section 3 we present the major results about term rewriting which we use and in section 4 our requirements specification and one program development step are presented. We conclude in section 5.

2 Specifying Modular PROLOG Programs

2.1 PROLOG with Modules

The target language which we use is PROLOG enhanced with module constructs similar to those of Standard ML [SW87]. The modules system which we use consists of three components: ***structures***, ***signatures*** and ***functors***. Structures are program modules and program clauses in a structure are "executable". They consist of a two basic elements: (1) data declarations and (2) predicate and function definitions.

An example of a structure is given in figure 1. The data declaration in figure 1 is given by:

```
fun zero : 0
fun suc  : 1
```

which declares two function constants `zero` with arity 0 and `suc` with arity 1. Predicates may also be declared as follows:

```
pred le : 2
```

```
structure Elements =
  struct
     fun zero : 0
     fun suc  : 1

     le(zero,X).
     le(suc(X),suc(Y)) :- le(X,Y).
  end.
```

Figure 1:

but this is always used in signatures for the purpose of making some predicates visible while hiding others. Function declarations introduce the language which is available for constructing terms while predicate and function declarations introduce the language for constructing (atomic) formulae. In the structure `Elements` the predicate `le` uses terms built up only from the function constants `zero` and `suc`. Another example is the structure in figure 2 which provides a sorting predicate based upon a substructure `Elem`.

```
structure Sort =
  struct
     structure Elem = Elements

     insert(X,[],[X]).
     insert(X,[Y|Z],[X,Y|Z]) :- Elem/le(X,Y).
     insert(X,[Y|Z],[Y|W]) :- not(Elem/le(X,Y)),
                              insert(X,Z,W).

     sort([],[]).
     sort([X],[X]).
     sort([X|Y],Z) :- sort(Y,W),
                      insert(X,W,Z).
  end.
```

Figure 2:

Signatures are interfaces to structures. They specify which components of the structure are externally visible but hide the details of the code. An example is given in figure 3. The structure `Elements` *matches* the signature `ELEM` precisely because it contains a predicate definition `le` and function constants `zero` and `suc` as required by the signature. If the signature `ELEM` in 3 is ascribed to the structure **Elements** then this is written as:

```
structure Elements : ELEM =
  struct
    fun zero : 0
    fun suc : 1

    le(zero,X).
    le(suc(X),suc(Y)) :- le(X,Y).
  end.
```

Signatures may also specify substructures. Any structure matching the signature **SORT** in figure 4 must also contain a substructure **Elem** with the signature **ELEM**. The structure **Sort** of figure 2 matches the signature **SORT** because it contains a predicate **sort** of arity 2 and a substructure **Elem** which will match the signature **ELEM**. Note that the predicate **insert** is hidden by the signature **SORT**.

```
signature ELEM =
  sig
    fun zero : 0
    fun suc  : 1

    pred le : 2
  end.
```

Figure 3:

Functors are parameterized modules. They accept structures as arguments and return structures as results. For example, in figure 2 the substructure **Elem** is assigned to **Elements** but if we wish to have a generic sorting structure which will sort elements from any structure which includes a **le** predicate then we may use a functor as in figure 5.

```
signature SORT =
  sig
    structure Elem : ELEM
    pred sort : 2
  end.
```

Figure 4:

```
functor Sort(X:ELEM):SORT =
  struct
    structure Elem = X

    . . .

  end.
```

Figure 5:

2.2 Specifying Structures and Functors

In practice PROLOG programs use many extra logical features such as cut. Also the ordering of clauses in a program is important for termination. Here we assume only pure PROLOG with negation and no extra-logical features or cut as the language in which programs will be written.

To specify pure PROLOG programs we make the following additions, along the same lines as Extended ML [San89, ST89], to the language outlined above.

1. Axioms, written in First Order Predicate logic, are allowed in signatures and structures. This means that the same module constructs are used to structure both PROLOG programs and their specifications. Axioms are written using the following notation: `&` (conjunction), `|` (disjunction), `->` (implication), `not` (negation) and `<->` (equivalence).

2. Signatures must be ascribed to every interface of a structure or functor. This was not necessary in our examples of 2.1 but in specification interfaces provide the description of the behaviour of modules from which they to be developed.

3. Requirements specifications are given by adding a `?` in place of actual structure or functor bodies.

Signatures with axioms specify classes of PROLOG structures, for example, consider the signature in figure 6. The class of structures which will now match the signature `ELEM` will be all those with at least two function constants, `zero` and `suc`, and a predicate `le` which is a pre-order. The structure in figure 2 certainly matches this signature.

As well as just the *flat* specifications like the pre-order in figure 6 specifications may exhibit internal structure. Substructures and *local* or auxiliary predicates and axioms can be used in specifications. The signature in figure 7 uses both the substructure `Elem` and three auxiliary predicates, `member`, `permutation` and `ordered` to specify sorting.

```
signature ELEM =
  sig
    fun zero : 0
    fun suc  : 1

    pred le : 2

    axiom forall x => le(x,x)
    axiom forall x => forall y => forall z =>
          le(x,y) & le(y,z) -> le(x,z)
  end;
```

Figure 6: A signature specifying a pre-order

A statement of the programming task can now be given as in figure 8. This is the *requirements specification* from which further program development takes place. What is required in this case is a parameterized module which accepts any structure with a predicate `le` and function constants `zero` and `suc` and returns a sorting module for lists of that data. The phrase `include SORT` includes all the axioms and definitions in the signature `SORT`. The phrase `sharing X = Elements` introduces a *sharing constraint*. Sharing constraints are part of the module language for PROLOG [SW87] and impose the constraint that two structures be built up in exactly the same way. In specifications like the requirements specification of figure 8 a sharing constraint expresses the fact that the result *depends* upon the input[1].

In figure 8 for example, the sharing constraint specifies that the predicate `Elements/le` in `SORT` is the same as the predicate `X/le` in the (actual) parameter. Without this sharing constraint the predicate `Elements/le` need not be the same as that of the parameter `X`, and so the requirements specification would not explicitly require us to sort lists of data from the module `X`.

2.3 Stepwise Development of PROLOG Programs

One proceeds from a requirements specification to a program by a series of development steps. Each development step results in a program which is *correct* (in the sense described below) with respect to the results of the previous development step if all the proof obligations associated with that step are *formally* discharged. We may think of each development step as filling in some detail left open in the previous step, for example, providing a predicate definition for some predicate which hitherto has only been specified using axioms. Once

[1] This is a form of dependent type. See for example [ST91].

```
signature SORT =
  sig
    structure Elements : ELEM

    pred sort : 2

    local

      pred member : 2

      axiom forall x => not(member(x,[]))
      axiom forall x,y => forall l =>
            member(x,[x|l])
      axiom forall x,y => forall l =>
            member(x,l) -> member(x,[y,l])

      pred permutation : 2

      axiom forall l => forall l' =>
            permutation(l,l') <->
            (forall x =>
             member(x,l) <-> member(x,l'))

      pred ordered : 1

      axiom ordered([])
      axiom forall a => ordered([a])
      axiom forall a => forall b => forall l =>
            Elem/le(a,b) & ordered([b|l]) -> ordered([a,b|l])
    in
      axiom forall l,l' =>
            permutation(l,l') & ordered(l')
            <-> sort(l,l')
    end
  end;
```

Figure 7: A signature with substructures and hidden functions

```
functor Sort(X:ELEM):sig
                      include SORT
                      sharing X = Elements
                    end = ?
```

Figure 8: Specification of a Sorting Functor

the results of a development step includes no axioms and all the predicates are defined by PROLOG predicate definitions then the development process is complete. If all the proof obligations have been discharged then this final program satisfies the original requirements specification by *construction*.
There are three possible kinds of development steps in the Extended ML methodology which we also use to stepwise refine our modular PROLOG programs [San89].

Functor Decomposition
Intuitively functor decomposition is used to break a task into subtasks. Suppose we are given the following specification:

$$functor\ F(X:\Sigma):\Sigma' = ?$$

The first of the development steps allows us to define the functor `F` in terms of the composition of a number of other functors, for example, in the simple case of two new functors `G` and `H` we have:

$$functor\ F(X:\Sigma):\Sigma' = G(H(X))$$

where

$$functor\ G(Y:\Sigma_G):\Sigma'_G = ?$$
$$functor\ H(Z:\Sigma_H):\Sigma'_H = ?$$

and Σ_H, Σ'_H, Σ_G and Σ'_G are all appropriately defined signatures. The task of finding a solution to `F` has been broken up into the subtasks of finding solutions to `G` and `H`. This decomposition is *correct* if:

1. all structures matching the parameter signature of `F` also match the parameter signature of `H`, that is, $\Sigma \models \Sigma_H$[2];
2. all structures matching the result signature of `H` can be used as an argument for `G`, that is, $\Sigma'_H \models \Sigma_G$;

[2]The notation $\Sigma \models \Sigma_H$ is to be read as Σ "matches" Σ_H and is defined in section 2.4

3. all structures matching the result signature of G also match the result signature of F, that is, $\Sigma'_G \models \Sigma'$.

The development of the functors H and G may now proceed separately.

Coding
Given a specification of the form:

$$structure\ A : \Sigma\ = ?$$

or

$$functor\ F(X : \Sigma) : \Sigma'\ = ?$$

coding is used to replace the ? by an actual structure body to give

$$structure\ A : \Sigma\ =\ strexp$$

or in the case of functors

$$functor\ F(X : \Sigma) : \Sigma'\ =\ strexp$$

A *coding* development step is *correct* if

$$strexp \models \Sigma$$

in the case of structures and

$$\Sigma \cup strexp \models \Sigma'$$

in the case of functors. A structure body need not be all PROLOG code. Indeed the possibility of fixing only some design details exists since axioms are allowed within structure bodies. An example is the functor in figure 9 which could be one stage in the development of the sorting functor of figure 8.

Refinement Refinement is the third kind of development step used to fill in design choices left open by a coding step or by another refinement step. Given a functor of the form:

$$functor\ F(X : \Sigma) : \Sigma'\ =\ strexp$$

we can replace *strexp* by *strexp'* in a refinement step to give:

$$functor\ F(X : \Sigma) : \Sigma'\ =\ strexp'$$

A refinement step is *correct* if

$$\Sigma \cup strexp' \models strexp$$

The rules for coding structures are similar.

```
functor Sort(X:ELEM):sig
                       include SORT
                       sharing X = Elements
                     end =
  struct
    structure Elem = X

    pred insert : 2

    axiom insert(x,[],[x])
      and forall x,y => forall l =>
          Elem/le(x,y) -> insert(x,[y|l],[x,y|l])
      and forall x,y,z => forall l =>
          not(Elem/le(x,y)) & insert(x,l,z) -> insert(x,[y|l],[y|z]).

    sort([],[]).
    sort([X],[X]).
    sort([X|Y],Z) :- sort(Y,W),
                     insert(X,W,Z).
  end.
```

Figure 9:

2.4 Matching

So far we have not explicitly defined *matching* in the sense of a structure matching a signature. For the purposes of "matching" PROLOG programs are considered to be equivalent to their *predicate completions* [Cla78].

Let *strexp* be a structure and *sigexp* be a signature. The rules for matching, written *strexp* $\models$ *sigexp*, are defined as follows:

1. the set of function constants in *strexp* must be equal to the set of function constants in *sigexp* and the arity of each function constant in *strexp* must be the same as the corresponding function constant in *sigexp*;

2. the predicate symbols of *sigexp* must be a subset of the predicate symbols in *strexp*;

3. the axioms, including the predicate completions of any programs, of *strexp* must entail the axioms of *sigexp*.

The rules for matching signatures $sigexp_1 \models sigexp_2$ are identical.

The restriction on sets of function constants in point 1. above is necessary because quantifiers range over the terms defined by function constants and these need to be identical in both *strexp* and *sigexp*. This is important for proofs involving existential quantifiers.

3 Term Rewriting and the Knuth Bendix Theorem

The subject of our case study is the formal development of a module to test the confluence of sets of rewrite rules and so below we review some of the important definitions of term rewriting.

Let Σ be a (universal algebra) signature, X a set of variables, $T_\Sigma(X)$ the set of all terms which can be constructed using the operator symbols in Σ and the variables in X and σ and ρ be two terms in $T_\Sigma(X)$. A *rewrite rule* [Bun83, HO80, Klo87] is an ordered pair of terms, which we write $\sigma \rightarrow \rho$ (σ "rewrites to" ρ), such that the variables of ρ are a subset of the variables of σ. The following is now taken from [HO80, Klo87].

Definition 3.1 *Let B be a set of rewrite rules and $\phi : X \rightarrow T_\Sigma(Y)$ be any substitution. The* one step rewriting relation $\rightarrow_B$ *defined by B is inductively defined as follows:*

1. *if $\sigma \rightarrow \rho \in B$ then $\phi(\sigma) \rightarrow_B \phi(\rho)$ where by abuse of notation we assume that ϕ is extended to Σ terms;*

2. *if $\phi_1(x) = t_1$, $\phi_2(x) = t_2$ and $\forall y.\, y \neq x \Rightarrow \phi_1(y) = \phi_2(y) = y$ and $t_1 \rightarrow_B t_2$ then for any term t, $\phi_1(t) \rightarrow_B \phi_2(t)$;*

3. if $t_1 \rightarrow_B t_2$ *then* $\phi(t_1) \rightarrow_B \phi(t_2)$.

The reflexive and transitive closure of $\rightarrow_B$ is written $\rightarrow_B^*$.

Definition 3.2 $\rightarrow_B^*$ *is* confluent *if*

$$\forall t \in T_\Sigma(X). \quad t \rightarrow_B^* t_1 \wedge t \rightarrow_B^* t_2 \Rightarrow \exists t'.t_1 \rightarrow_B^* t' \wedge t_2 \rightarrow_B^* t'$$

The Newman theorem [New42] is often used to reduce the problem of testing a set of rewrite rules for confluence to the problem of testing the set of rules for *local confluence* and *termination.*

Definition 3.3 *A set of rewrite rules is* locally confluent *if*

$$\forall t \in T_\Sigma(X). \quad t \rightarrow_B t_1 \wedge t \rightarrow_B t_2 \Rightarrow \exists t'.t_1 \rightarrow_B^* t' \wedge t_2 \rightarrow_B^* t'$$

Definition 3.4 *A set of rewrite rules is* terminating *if for no term* $t \in T_\Sigma(X)$ *there exists an infinite string of one step reductions*

$$t \rightarrow_B t_1 \rightarrow_B t_2 \rightarrow_B \ldots$$

Theorem 3.5 (Newman) *A set of rewrite rules is confluent if and only if it is terminating and locally confluent.*

One procedure for testing local confluence relies on finding *critical pairs* [KB70, HO80, Bun83].

Definition 3.6 *If* $\sigma_1 \rightarrow \rho_1$ *and* $\sigma_2 \rightarrow \rho_2$ *are two rewrite rules such that there exists a unifier* ϕ *of* σ_2 *and some subterm* μ *of* σ_1 *then a* critical pair *for* $\sigma_1 \rightarrow \rho_1$ *and* $\sigma_2 \rightarrow \rho_2$ *is defined to be*

$$\langle \phi(\sigma_1)[\mu \leftarrow \phi(\rho_2)], \phi(\rho_1) \rangle$$

We use the notation $\sigma[\mu \leftarrow \rho]$ to mean the term σ with the subterm μ replaced by ρ. The Knuth-Bendix theorem now gives a means for testing local confluence of set of rewrite rules under the assumption that the rewrite rules are terminating.

Theorem 3.7 (Knuth-Bendix) *Let* B *be a set of rewrite rules. If for all critical pairs* $\langle P, Q \rangle$ *in* B *there exists a term* R *such that* $P \rightarrow^* R$ *and* $Q \rightarrow R^*$ *then* B *is locally confluent.*

Testing the termination property is not as straightforward. The basic technique which we assume is based on the concept of a *termination* ordering [Der82, Klo87]. The basic idea is to define an ordering on terms in the language such that if $t \rightarrow t'$ then $t' \leq t$. If for every rewrite rule in a set of rewrite rules the left hand side is greater than the right hand side and the ordering on terms is well founded and satisfies some additional closure properties then the set of rewrite rules is terminating.

```
functor Confluence(R:REWRITES):
            sig
              include CONFLUENCE
              sharing R = Rewrites
            end = ?
```

Figure 10:

4 A Case Study: Testing the Confluence of a Set of Rewrite Rules

We wish to now give a requirements specification for a program that will test a set of rewrite rules for confluence. Rather than starting with the specification of confluence as

$$\forall t, t_1, t_2 . t \rightarrow_B^* t_1 \wedge t \rightarrow_B^* t_2 \Rightarrow \exists t' . t_1 \rightarrow_B^* t' \wedge t_2 \rightarrow_B^* t'$$

we begin with the simpler problem testing for the confluence of a set of rewrite rules by using the Newman theorem 3.5.

4.1 The Requirements Specification

The requirements specification is given in figure 10 while the signatures for the requirements specification are given in appendix A.

The parameter to this functor is a structure which manipulates Σ terms with the predicates in the signature `REWRITES`. Intuitively the predicates do the following:

isrule(r,rs) succeeds if `r` is a rewrite rule in the set `rs` of rewrite rules;

lhs : 2 returns the left hand side of a rule;

rhs : 2 returns the right hand side of a rule;

subexp(e,e') succeeds if `e` is a subexpression of `e'`;

unify:3 unifies two terms and returns the most general unifier;

replsubexp(e1,e2,e3,e4) replaces the subexpression `e2` in `e1` by `e3` returning `e4`;

apply:3 applies a substitution to a term;

rewrite(e,e',rs) performs a 1 step rewrite of `e` to `e'` using one of the rules in `rs`.

```
functor Confluence(R:REWRITES):
          sig
            include CONFLUENCE
            sharing R = Rewrites
          end =
    Local(Noetherian(R))
```

Figure 11:

The signature `REWRITES` also contains a number of auxiliary predicates, for example, `member:2`, `modify:4` and `subst:4`.

The result signature is given in appendix A.2. The only predicate definition which is returned by the functor `Confluence` is `confluent` and the substructure `Rewrites`.

The sharing constraints expresses that the substructure `Rewrites` must be the same as the actual parameter and so also states that the axioms and predicates in the result signature are *dependent* on the actual parameter. The programming task is now to provide a functor body which gives a program to implement `confluent`.

4.2 A Program Development Step

We now wish to construct a PROLOG program from the requirements specification in figure 10 by using the methodology outlined in section 2.3. Indeed there are only two choices of program development step to apply to the functor in figure 10, that is, functor decomposition or coding. We choose a functor decomposition as in figure 11 where the requirements specifications for the functors `Local` and `Noetherian` are given in figure 12. The signature `NOETHERIAN` specifies termination in terms of a termination ordering `po`.

This decomposition gives rise to only one non-trivial proof obligation:

$$LOCAL\_CONFLUENCE \models CONFLUENCE$$

What needs to be shown is that the axioms for the predicate `noetherian` in `LOCAL_CONFLUENCE` are sufficient to prove the properties of `noetherian` in `CONFLUENCE`. We have only given an informal argument for the correctness of this decomposition step [Rea] and it remains to give a formal proof of it. At this point we have used only first order logic in our specifications and so formally discharging this proof obligation would require a proof system for first order predicate logic.

Much harder is showing that parts of the PROLOG code satisfy their specification. In this case we would require two additional features in the proof system:

```
functor Local(N:NOETHERIAN) :
        sig
          include LOCAL_CONFLUENCE
          sharing N/Rewrites = Rewrites
        end = ?

functor Noetherian(R:REWRITES):
        sig
          include NOETHERIAN
          sharing R = Rewrites
        end = ?
```

Figure 12:

1. reasoning with negation and the order of clauses in a logic program;
2. induction rules for reasoning about data inductively defined by function constants.

A means of meeting the second requirement is to augment a proof system for the first order predicate calculus by the appropriate inductive rules for data types, for example, for lists we have:

$$\frac{P(nil/x) \quad \forall a \forall l.P(l/x) \Rightarrow P([a|l]/x)}{\forall t.P(t)}$$

for any predicate P.

5 Conclusions and Further Work

In this paper we have presented a language for structuring PROLOG programs, a language for specifying structured PROLOG programs, a methodology for *formally* deriving programs from specifications of modular programs and briefly outlined a case study in the use of the specification language and the program development methodology.

This case study has shown up at least two areas in which further work is required:

1. the area of proof systems for discharging proof obligations and especially for rules dealing with negation and ordering of axioms (see for example [And89] where some work has been done on the latter topic);
2. a formal definition of the specification language is required to establish exactly the class of programs which can be models of a specification.

More generally in the area of discharging proof obligations is the problem of proving theorems in structured specifications [FC89]. A definition of the language would need to specify precisely what program modules denote and what it means for them to satisfy a specification.

The benefits to be gained by adopting this approach are precisely those that can be gained by using a modular approach to program design. Also once a program module has been constructed from its requirements specification it can be re-used. All that is known about a module is given in the interfaces and the details of the code are hidden from the user.

To make the approach feasible and practical for specifying and constructing PROLOG programs from specifications the major hurdle appears to be in discharging proof obligations. With the advent of the proper tools and proof systems this burden ought to be eased and this is one of the goals of research into Extended ML. If this can be done then this approach gives a simple method of constructing PROLOG programs to meet specifications with all the benefits of a modular specification and target language.

Acknowledgements

We would like to thank Don Sannella for reading over earlier drafts of this paper as well as Terry Stroup, Stefan Kahrs and James Harland for their useful comments. Also our thanks to anonymous referees for thier suggestions.

References

[And89] J. H. Andrews. Proof-theoretic characterisations of logic programming. Technical Report ECS-LFCS-89-77, University of Edinburgh, 1989.

[Bun83] A. Bundy. *The computer modelling of mathematical reasoning.* Academic Press, 1983.

[Cla78] K. L. Clark. Negation as failure. In H Gallaire and J Minker, editors, *Logic and Databases*, pages 293–322. Plenum Press, New York, 1978.

[Der82] N. Dershowitz. Orderings for term rewriting systems. *Theoretical Computer Science*, 17:279 – 301, 1982.

[FC89] J. Farrés-Casals. Proving Correctness of Constructor Implementations. In *1989 Symp. on Mathematical Foundations of Computer Science, LNCS 379*, pages 225 – 235. Springer-Verlag, 1989.

[HMT90] R. Harper, R. Milner, and M. Tofte. *The Definition of Standard ML.* MIT Press, 1990.

[HO80] G. P. Huet and D. C. Oppen. Equations and Rewrite Rules. In Ronald V. Book, editor, *Formal Language Theory: Perspectives and Open Problems*, pages 349 – 405. Academic Press, 1980.

[KB70] D. E. Knuth and P. B. Bendix. Simple problems in universal algebra. In J. Leech, editor, *Computational Problems in Abstract Algebra*, pages 203 – 297. Pergammon Press, 1970.

[Klo87] J.W. Klop. Term Rewriting Systems : A Tutorial. *Bulletin of the EATCS*, pages 144 – 192, June 1987.

[Les89] Pierre Lescanne. Implementation of Completion by Transition Rules + Control: ORME. In *TAPSOFT'89, LNCS 351*, pages 262 – 269. Springer - Verlag, 1989.

[Les90] P. Lescanne. Completion Procedures as Transition Rules + Control. In *Algebraic and Logic Programming, Springer LNCS 463*, pages 28 – 41. Springer - Verlag, 1990.

[Llo84] J. Lloyd. *Foundations of Logic Programming.* Springer Verlag, 1984.

[MT90] R. Milner and M. Tofte. *Commentary on Standard ML.* MIT Press, 1990.

[New42] M. H. A. Newman. On theories with a combinatorial definition of equivalence. *Annals of Mathematics*, 43(2), April 1942.

[Rea] M. G. Read. Formal Development of Prolog Programs. 4th year project report, University of Edinburgh, May 1991.

[San89] D. Sannella. Formal Program Development in Extended ML for the Working Programmer. Technical Monograph ECS-LFCS-89-102, Laboratory for the Foundations of Computer Science, December 1989.

[ST89] D. Sannella and A. Tarlecki. Toward Formal Development of ML Programs: Foundations and Methodology - Extended Abstract. In *Proceedings of the Colloquium on Current Issues in Programming Languages, LNCS 352*, pages 375 – 389. Springer Verlag, 1989.

[ST91] D. Sannella and A. Tarlecki. A Kernel Specification Formalism with Higher Order Parameterization. In *7th Workshop on Specification of Abstract Data Types.* Lecture Notes in Computer Science, to appear. Springer Verlag, 1991.

[SW87] D. T. Sannella and L. A. Wallen. A Calculus for the Construction of Modular Prolog Programs. In *IEEE 4th Symp. on logic programming*, 1987.

A Signatures for the Requirements Specification

A.1 The Signature REWRITES

```
signature REWRITES =
  sig
    pred isrule:2, lhs:2, rhs:2, subexp:2
    pred unify:3, apply:3, rewrite : 3
    pred replsubexp : 4

    fun var : 1
    fun rule : 2, op : 2

    local
      pred member : 2

      axiom forall x => not(member(x,[]))
      axiom forall x => forall l => member(x,[x|l])
      axiom forall x,y => forall l =>
            member(x,l) -> member(x,[y|l])

      pred modify : 4

      axiom forall e1,e2 => modify([],e1,e2,[])
      axiom forall e,e1,e2 => forall l =>
            e \== e1 -> modify([e|l],e1,e2,[e|l])
      axiom forall e,e1,e2 => forall l =>
            e == e1 -> modify([e|l],e1,e2,[e2|l])

      pred subst : 4

      axiom forall v,x,y =>
            v \== x -> subst(var(x),v,y,var(x))
      axiom forall v,x,t =>
            v == x -> subst(var(v),v,t,t)
      axiom forall v,x,t => forall l,l' =>
            subst(op(x,[]),v,t,op(x,[]))
      axiom forall e,e',v,x,t => forall l,l' =>
            subst(e,v,t,e') &
            subst(op(x,l),v,t,op(x,l')) ->
                  subst(op(x,[e|l]),v,t,op(x,[e'|l']))

      pred FV : 2
```

```
  axiom forall x => FV(var(x),[var(x)])
  axiom forall x => FV(op(x,[]),[])
  axiom forall x => forall t => forall terms =>
        FV(t,l1) & FV(terms,l2) & append(l1,l2,l) ->
        FV(op(x,[t|terms]),l)

  pred dom : 2

  axiom dom([],[])
  axiom forall l,l' => forall v => forall t =>
        dom(l,l') -> dom([(v,t)|l],[v|l'])

  pred disjoint : 2

  axiom forall l,l' => forall x =>
        disjoint(l,l') <->
        member(x,l) -> not(member(x,l'))

in

  axiom forall r,rs =>
        member(r,rs) -> isrule(r,rs)

  axiom forall e => lhs(rule(e,_),e)
  axiom forall e => rhs(rule(_,e),e)

  axiom forall e => subexp(e,e)
  axiom forall e,e' => forall l =>
        subexp(e,e') & member(e',l) ->
               subexp(e,op(_,l))

  axiom forall e,e' => replsubexp(e,e,e',e')
  axiom forall e,e' => forall l,l' =>
        (exists e1,e2 =>
           member(e1,l) &
           replsubexp(e1,e,e',e2) &
           modify(l,e1,e2,l'))
        -> replsubexp(op(x,l),e,e',op(x,l'))

  axiom forall e => apply([],e,e)
  axiom forall e,e' => forall v,t => forall l =>
        forall fv => forall s,s' =>
        FV(t,fv) &
        dom([(v,t)|s],s') &
```

```
          disjoint(fv,s') &
          subst(e,v,t,e') &
          apply(s,e',e'')  ->
                 apply([(v,t)|z],e,e'')

    axiom forall e,e',t => forall u =>
          apply(u,e,t) &
          apply(u,e',t) ->
                 unify(e,e',u)

    axiom forall e,e' => forall rs =>
          (exists r,lr,rr,rr' => exists e'' =>
           exists phi =>
           lhs(r,lr)
           & subexp(e'',e)
           & apply(phi,lr,e'')
           & rhs(r,rr)
           & apply(phi,rr,rr')
           & replsubexp(e,e'',rr',e'))
             -> rewrite(e,e',rs)
   end
 end
```

A.2 The Signature CONFLUENCE

```
signature CONFLUENT =
  sig
    pred confluent:1

    structure Rewrites : REWRITES

    local

      pred normal_form : 2

      axiom forall e => forall rs =>
            normal_form(e,rs) <->
            not(exists t => Rewrites/rewrite(e,t,rs))

      pred critical_pair : 3

      axiom forall p,q,rs =>
            exists theta =>
            exists r1,r2,lhs1,lhs2,rhs1,rhs2 =>
```

```
        exists sub1,sub1',lhs1',lhs2' =>
            Rewrites/isrule(r1,rs) &
            Rewrites/isrule(r2,rs) &
            Rewrites/lhs(r1,lhs1) &
            Rewrites/lhs(r2,lhs2) &
            Rewrites/rhs(r1,rhs1) &
            Rewrites/rhs(r2,rhs2) &
            Rewrites/subexp(sub1,lhs1) &
            Rewrites/unify(sub1,lhs2,theta) &
            Rewrites/apply(theta,lhs1,lhs1') &
            Rewrites/apply(theta,lhs2,lhs2') &
            Rewrites/apply(theta,sub1,sub1') &
            Rewrites/apply(theta,rhs1,p) &
            Rewrites/replsubexp(lhs1',sub1',rhs2',p) ->
                    critical_pair(p,q,rs)

pred reduces : 3

axiom forall e => reduces(e,e)
axiom forall rs => forall e,e' =>
      (exists e'' =>
       exists r   =>
             Rewrites/isrule(r,rs) &
             Rewrites/rewrite(e,e'',r) &
             reduces(e'',e',rs)) ->
                reduces(e,e',rs)

pred locally_confluent : 1

axiom forall rs =>
      (forall p,q =>
       critical_pair(p,q,rs) ->
        (exists e =>
         reduces(p,e,rs) & reduces(q,e,rs)) )
      -> locally_confluent(rs)

pred noetherian : 1

axiom forall rs =>
      ( forall e =>
        exists e' =>
          reduces(e,e',rs) & normal_form(e',rs) )
      -> noetherian(rs)
```

```
in

   axiom forall rs  =>
         noetherian(rs) &
         locally_confluent(rs) ->
           confluent(rs)

  end
end
```

B The Signatures for the Program Development Steps

B.1 The Signature LOCAL_CONFLUENCE

```
signature LOCAL_CONFLUENCE =
  sig
    pred locally_confluent : 1, confluent : 1
    pred reduces : 3

    structure Noetherian : NOETHERIAN

    local

      pred critical_pair : 3

      axiom forall p,q,rs =>
            exists theta =>
            exists r1,r2,lhs1,lhs2,rhs1,rhs2 =>
            exists sub1,sub1',lhs1',lhs2' =>
                Rewrites/isrule(r1,rs) &
                Rewrites/isrule(r2,rs) &
                Rewrites/lhs(r1,lhs1) &
                Rewrites/lhs(r2,lhs2) &
                Rewrites/rhs(r1,rhs1) &
                Rewrites/rhs(r2,rhs2) &
                Rewrites/subexp(sub1,lhs1) &
                Rewrites/unify(sub1,lhs2,theta) &
                Rewrites/apply(theta,lhs1,lhs1') &
                Rewrites/apply(theta,lhs2,lhs2') &
                Rewrites/apply(theta,sub1,sub1') &
                Rewrites/apply(theta,rhs1,p) &
                Rewrites/replsubexp(lhs1',sub1',rhs2',p) ->
                        critical_pair(p,q,rs)

      pred reduces : 3

      axiom forall e => reduces(e,e)
      axiom forall rs => forall e,e' =>
            (exists e'' =>
             exists r   =>
                   Rewrites/isrule(r,rs) &
                   Rewrites/rewrite(e,e'',r) &
```

```
                    reduces(e'',e',rs)) ->
                       reduces(e,e',rs)

  in
    axiom forall rs =>
        (forall p,q => critical_pair(p,q,rs) ->
          (exists r => reduces(p,r,rs) & reduces(q,r,rs)) )
         -> locally_confluent(rs)

    axiom forall rs =>
         Noetherian/noetherian(rs) & locally_confluent(rs)
         -> confluent(rs)
  end
end
```

B.2 The Signature NOETHERIAN

```
signature NOETHERIAN =
  sig
    pred noetherian : 1

    structure Rewrites : REWRITES

    local

      pred po : 2

      axiom forall x => po(x,x)

      axiom forall x,y,z =>
            po(x,y) & po(y,z) -> po(x,z)

      axiom exists x => forall y => po(x,y)

      axiom forall e, e' => forall rs =>
            Rewrites/reduces(e,e',rs) <-> po(e,e')

      axiom forall e,e' => forall t,t' =>
            po(e,e') &
            Rewrites/subexp(e,t) &
            Rewrites/subexp(e',t') ->
              po(t,t')

      axiom forall theta => forall t,t' =>
```

```
            forall e,e' =>
            po(t,t') &
            Rewrites/apply(theta,t,e) &
            Rewrites/apply(theta,t',e') ->
              po(e,e')
  in

    axiom forall rs => forall r => forall lr,rr =>
            Rewrites/isrule(r,rs) &
            Rewrites/lhs(r,lr) &
            Rewrites/rhs(r,rr) &
            po(rr,lr)
            -> noetherian(rs)
  end
end
```

Towards Synthesis of Nearly Pure Prolog Programs

Luboš Popelinský*
Dept. of Computer Science
Masaryk University of Brno and
Brno Machine Learning Group
Burešova 20, 601 77 Brno
Czechoslovakia
E-mail: popel@cspuni12.bitnet

— Extended Abstract —

1 Shapiro's IDS

In [4] the Interactive Debugging System (IDS), a system for debugging pure Prolog programs, is decsribed. In IDS, a program being debugged, an example (either positive or negative), and metaknowledge about procedures are used as input. A refinement operator then uses breadth first search beginning with the most general clause. IDS can also build new clauses by inductive inference. The following operators for generalization/specialization are used: adding/removing subgoals, instantiating variables and unifying two terms.

IDS detects three types of error:[1] *inconsistence* – goal suceeds although a failure is expected; *incompleteness* – goal fails although a success is expected; and *nontermination*. In the case of either inconsistence or nontermination, the user is asked about the success/failure of subgoals. After an incorrect clause is found the user is asked to select one of the following actions: to remove the clause, to add a new clause, or to modify an incorrect clause. If a modification is chosen, then an incorrrect clause is specialized. If incompletness is detected, the user can add a new clause into an incomplete procedure, or alternatively IDS modifies a procedure to be more general.

2 Oracle

IDS depends on an *oracle* (e.g. the user) for information necessary for a correct program synthesis. Before starting a synthesis the oracle has to provide input/output examples of program behaviour and metaknowledge about a predicate being synthesised – its arity, predicates on the right side of its rules and the type declarations of its arguments (input or output arguments, lists etc.).

---

*The author would like to thank ALP and the organising commitee of LOPSTR 91, namely Kung-Kiu Lau and Tim Clement, for the opportunity to take part in this wonderful workshop, and all the participants for their help and patience.

[1] A goal is a ground term.

The type of a procedure can be declared. A procedure is *determinate* if it has at most one solution for any goal. It is *total* if it has at least one solution for any goal in its domain.

During the process of debugging, the oracle is asked to determine the success/failure of some subgoals. However it is very unpleasant for a human oracle to answer a lot of questions. In [4] simple ways of mechanizing the oracle is described. The user's answers to queries are remembered within and between sessions and a query procedure is modified in such a way that information in a database about an input/output behaviour of the new procedure is consulted first. In [1] and [2] additional improvements of oracle mechanization are introduced.

3 mE

The mE program[3], based on the IDS approach, is proposed to make programming of some subclasses of Prolog programs – namely rule-based systems – easier. The main idea is to give a programmer the possibility to control an inductive inference from a program. In mE, the user can choose another node in the refinement tree as the initial one and give information for pruning a search tree as well.

Besides improvements to the oracle described above, mE offers additional tools for mechanizing the oracle. A database of examples can contain nonground terms, example generators, which can be used for selectiing the most promising initial node in a refinement tree.

If a procedure is declared to be `impure`, mE tries to synthesize a procedure containing `not` and `ifthenelse` predicates. If mE doesn't succeed, the user is informed about the failure and his or her assistance is expected.

Only predicates declared to be `asserted` and `retracted` can be asserted or retracted respectively. Then if a procedure is declared to contain for instance `assert`, only predicates declared as `asserted` can be used as arguments in the body of a synthesized procedure.

Predicates `assert` and `retract` are replaced by list processing predicates `append` and `remove` respectively and a metainterpreter is modified.

Procedures which are declared to be `correct`, are not metainterpreted. They are processed in the same way as built-in predicates. If a predicate X is `askable`, the user is asked about the goal X and information is added to the set of examples in order to use it for synthesising that undefined procedure in future.

There are two ways to use mE. The programmer can incorporate knowledge about a program into the program itself, for instance declaration of procedures or additional examples. For beginners it is better to use an integrated environment.

References

[1] Huntbach M. *An improved version of Shapiro's model inference system.* Proc. 3rd Int.Conf. on Logic Programming London 1986, LNCS 225, pp. 180-187.

[2] Nadjm-Tehrani S. *Contributions to the Declarative Approach to Debugging Prolog Programs.* Linkoeping Studies in Science and Technology, Thesis No. 187, Dept. of Computer and Information Science, Linkoeping University, 1989.

[3] Popelinský L. *Inductive Inference of Nearly Pure Prolog Programs.* Technical report, Dept. of Comp. Sci., Masaryk University of Brno, 1991.

[4] Shapiro, E.: *Algorithmic Program Debugging.* The MIT Press, 1982.

Formal validation of transformation schemata

Mattias Waldau
Computing Science Department
Uppsala University
Box 520, 751 20 Uppsala
Sweden
mattias@csd.uu.se

Abstract

We present a first-order theory Γ, which is used to validate transformation schemata. The theory Γ consists of two kinds of axioms. Δ is the subset of the axioms Γ which can be executed using a SLD-resolution like inference system, and Γ-Δ contains first-order programs, as defined by T. Sato [Sat90], and induction axioms. Induction is essential if we want to prove correctness of more elaborate transformation schemata, e.g., a scheme which makes a program tail-recursive.

We show how to prove the correctness of transformation schemata using an ordinary proof system for intuitionistic first-order logic. Let ϑ be a transformation scheme which is proved correct. If we apply the scheme ϑ to a (first-order) program, the resulting program *computes* the same set of solutions as the original one.

We exemplify the method by proving the correctness of unfold/fold transformation, and of a scheme, which replaces recursion by tail-recursion.

1 Introduction

Transformation schemata have been proven correct in many ways, e.g., by informal reasoning, by looking at the refutation tree, by looking at some fixpoint operator, or by using three-valued logic. We propose that transformation schemata should be proved correct using formal proofs. A *formal proof* is a proof which can be proof checked, i.e., it has a well-defined syntax and well-defined inference rules.

We present a theory where a standard intuitionistic first-order proof system is used to prove correctness of transformation schemata. The theory includes descriptions of data structures (including induction axioms), programs, and first-order programs. The programs are equivalences, not, as usual, Horn clauses, but we show that this doesn't affect the execution. We can execute the programs using a SLD-resolution like proof system. First-order programs are defined by almost arbitrary first-order formulas, and cannot be executed.

Let Γ be a first-order theory not including a definition of the predicate P. Let $\forall x\{P(x) \Leftrightarrow \varphi[x]\}$ be the a (first-order) program. We apply a transformation on P and the result is the program $\forall x\{P(x) \Leftrightarrow \psi[x]\}$. The transformation is correct if

$$\forall x\{P(x) \Leftrightarrow \varphi[x]\} \Leftrightarrow \forall x\{P(x) \Leftrightarrow \psi[x]\}$$

is provable from Γ. We will show that the truth of the statement above means that both programs compute the same set of solutions, and this holds even if we used induction and first-order programs when proving the correctness of the transformation.

2 An intuitionistic stratified theory

2.1 Preliminaries

Predicate symbols are capitalized and terms are in lower-case, constants and function symbols in the beginning of the alphabet (c, f, g), terms in the middle (t, r), and variables at the end (x, y, z). On many places where a term occurs, it may be replaced by a tuple of terms. An *arity* is associated with each function symbol and predicate symbol. Variables range over all terms. Lower-case Greek symbols are used for formulas (φ, ψ, σ) and upper-case for set of axioms (Γ, Δ). We use "$(\cdot)$" to make the arguments of a function or of a predicate explicit and we use "$[\cdot]$" to make the free variables of a formula explicit. Let x be tuple of variables and φ a formula, then the expression $\varphi[x]$ is a formula whose free variables form a subset of x. Note that we will not require that $\varphi[x]$ has any free variables. The result of substituting the (tuple) term t for (the tuple) x in the formula $\varphi[x]$ is denoted by the formula $\varphi[t]$. Normally, the fact that the terms and variables may be tuples can be ignored. It is only needed to extend the results from unary and binary predicates to predicates with higher arity.

The logical constants are $\exists$, $\forall$, $\neg$, $\wedge$, $\vee$, $\Rightarrow$, $\Leftrightarrow$. The constants $\exists$, $\forall$, $\neg$ bind strongest, followed by $\wedge$, then $\vee$, and lastly $\Rightarrow$, $\Leftrightarrow$. Free variables are implicitly universally quantified. $\varphi \Leftrightarrow \psi$ is short for $(\varphi \Rightarrow \psi) \wedge (\psi \Rightarrow \varphi)$, and $t \neq r$ is short for $\neg(t=r)$.

EXAMPLE 1. For example, $P(x,0)$ and $\exists y\, Q(y,x) \wedge R(x)$ are two instances of $\varphi[x]$, and then $P(s(0),0)$ and $\exists y\, Q(y,s(0)) \wedge R(s(0))$ are the respective instances of $\varphi[s(0)]$. The formula $\exists y \exists z\, P(y,z,0)$ is an instance of $\exists x\, \varphi[x]$, since x may be the tuple $<y,z>$. □

A theory Γ is *consistent* if there exists no formula φ such that both $\Gamma \vdash \varphi$ and $\Gamma \vdash \neg\varphi$. If we have proved $\Gamma \vdash \exists x\, \varphi[x]$, then a term t such that $\Gamma \vdash \varphi[t]$ is a *witness* for x. If such a witness t always exists, we say that the theory has got *existence property*.

2.2 The theory

There are three kinds of user defined axioms: equality axioms, axioms for ordinary predicates and axioms for inductive predicates. After these axioms are defined, we define when a set of axioms form an intuitionistic stratified theory (IST).

We give each predicate symbol a level. The idea of level is, if the level of the predicate P is smaller than the level of the predicate Q, then P is defined before Q. If the levels of P and Q are equal, then P and Q are defined simultaneously, for example, they are mutually recursive. We require that predicates used negatively in the body are already defined.

DEFINITION 1. A natural number, called *level* is associated with each predicate symbol. The predicate = has level 0. The level of a formula is the level of the predicate symbol occurring in it with the highest level.

DEFINITION 2. A formula φ is *stratified* for level l if

i. $level(\varphi) \leq l$,

ii. for each occurrence of $\psi \Rightarrow \sigma$ and $\neg\psi$ in φ there exists a level k, such that $k<l$, and ψ is stratified for level k.

EXAMPLE 2. Let the levels of =, P, Q, and R be 0, 1, 1, 2, respectively. Then $level(P \Rightarrow Q)=1$, $level(P \Rightarrow P)=1$, and $level(x=y \Rightarrow R)=2$. Neither formula is stratified for level 1 but all are stratified for levels greater than 1. □

Equality

We have a free interpretation of the terms, i.e., only closed syntactically equal terms are equal.

DEFINITION 3. Each function symbol f has an arity n. For each function symbol f, we may add the following axiom. (The $\Leftarrow$ direction follows from the general equality axioms.)

$$f(x_1, x_2, \ldots, x_n)=f(y_1, y_2, \ldots, y_n) \Rightarrow x_1=y_1 \wedge x_2=y_2 \wedge \ldots \wedge x_n=y_n$$

If f and g are syntactically distinct symbols with arity m and n, respectively, the following axiom may be added to the theory.

$$f(x_1, x_2, \ldots, x_m)\neq g(y_1, y_2, \ldots, y_n)$$

EXAMPLE 3 (Natural numbers and lists). Natural numbers are defined by the function symbols 0 and s. Two numbers are equal if their successors are equal, and every number greater than 0 is unequal to 0.

$$s(x)=s(y) \Rightarrow x=y \qquad\qquad s(t)\neq 0$$

Lists can be represented by the function symbols *cons* and *nil*, with arity 2 and 0.

$$cons(x_1, x_2)=cons(y_1, y_2) \Rightarrow x_1=y_1 \wedge x_2=y_2 \qquad\qquad cons(x_1, x_2)\neq nil$$

Natural numbers and lists are disjoint.

$$cons(x_1, x_2)\neq 0 \qquad\qquad cons(x_1, x_2)\neq s(y)$$

$$0\neq nil \qquad\qquad s(x)\neq nil$$

□

Note that we are allowed to add these equality axioms, not forced. For example, if we do not state that the constants 0 and *nil* are unequal, we can never prove that they are equal, neither can we prove that they are unequal, we just do not know. If we introduce these axioms for every constant and function symbol we get Clark's equality theory [Cla78], except for the axiom $t[x]\neq x$. This axiom is not generally true in the theory, only typed instances are provable using induction, e.g., $Nat(x) \Rightarrow t[x]\neq x$.

Ordinary predicates

Most of the programs are written using ordinary predicates.

DEFINITION 4. An *ordinary predicate* P is defined by one axiom $\forall x\{P(x) \Leftrightarrow \varphi[x]\}$ where φ is an arbitrary first-order formula such that φ is stratified w.r.t. *level*(P).

An *typed ordinary predicate* P is defined by one axiom $\forall x\{\psi[x] \Rightarrow (P(x) \Leftrightarrow \varphi[x])\}$. Both φ and ψ are arbitrary first-order formulas such that φ is stratified w.r.t. *level*(P) and ψ is stratified w.r.t. a level less than *level*(P).

The formula $\psi[x]$ is called the *type* of a predicate, $P(x)$ is the *head* and $\varphi[x]$ is the *body*.

A (typed) *first-order program predicate* is a (typed) ordinary predicate.

EXAMPLE 4. *Zeroes*(l) is true if l is a list of zeroes.

$$List(l) \Rightarrow [x \in y \Leftrightarrow \exists x'\exists y'\{y{=}cons(x',y') \wedge (x{=}x' \vee x \in y')\}]$$

$$List(l) \Rightarrow [Zeroes(l) \Leftrightarrow \forall x\{x \in l \Rightarrow x{=}0\}]$$

The *level* of the predicate symbols must satisfy the following restrictions: $level(\in) \geq level(=)$, $level(\in) > level(List)$, $level(Zeroes) > level(\in)$, $level(Zeroes) \geq \text{level}(=)$, and $level(Zeroes) > level(List)$. One such assignment is $level(Zeroes){=}2$, $level(\in){=}1$, $level(List){=}0$. (We will soon state the reasons for the level of *List*.) □

Recursive data structures

We want to define inductive data structures and get an induction scheme for each data structure. Note that since we have many types each induction scheme must be typed. Nonrecursive data structures, like persons in a database, Boolean values, and records (in the meaning of Pascal) are easiest to define using ordinary predicates.

EXAMPLE 5 (Natural numbers). The following axioms allows us to construct natural numbers and prove properties with induction over natural numbers.

$$Nat(0)$$

$$Nat(x) \Rightarrow Nat(s(x))$$

$$Nat(x) \wedge \varphi[0] \wedge \forall y\{Nat(y) \wedge \varphi[y] \Rightarrow \varphi[s(y)]\} \Rightarrow \varphi[x]$$ □

EXAMPLE 6 (Ordered lists). We need an auxiliary predicate *Lessall*(v,r), which is true if v is smaller than all the elements in the list r. It can be defined as

$$List(r) \Rightarrow \{Lessall(v,r) \Leftrightarrow \forall x\{x \in r \Rightarrow x > v\}$$

We do not need to make ordered lists and unordered lists disjoint, therefore, we can use the function symbols *cons* and *nil* in both data types. Thus, all ordered lists are lists.

$$Olist(nil)$$

$$Olist(x) \wedge Lessall(y,x) \Rightarrow Olist(cons(y,x))$$

$$Olist(z) \wedge \varphi[nil] \wedge \forall x\{Olist(x) \wedge \varphi[x] \wedge Lessall(y,x) \Rightarrow \varphi[cons(y,x)]\} \Rightarrow \varphi[z]$$ □

The definitions of natural number and ordered lists are special cases of the following definition.

DEFINITION 5. An *inductive predicate* is a predicate symbol T (not defined anywhere else), and a set of terms $t_1[x_1], t_2[x_2], \ldots t_n[x_n]$. There may be an atomic formula $P_i[x_i]$ associated with each term $t_i[x_i]$. The *level* of each predicate symbol P_i is less than or equal to the *level* of T. Each tuple of arguments x_i consists of two (possible empty) disjoint parts, z and $y_1, y_2, \ldots, y_m$, where all arguments except z are recursive arguments. The following axioms define the inductive predicate T:

For each term $t_i[z,y_1,y_2,\ldots y_m]$ and associated, atomic formula $P_i[z,y_1,y_2,\ldots y_m]$ we have an introduction axiom:

$$T(x_1) \land T(x_2) \land \ldots \land T(x_m) \land P_i[y,x_1,x_2,\ldots x_m] \Rightarrow T(t_i[y,x_1,x_2,\ldots x_m])$$

The induction axiom is constructed as follows:

$$T(x) \land \ldots \text{ Premises } \ldots \Rightarrow \varphi[x]$$

where for each term $t_i[z,y_1,y_2,\ldots y_m]$ and associated formula $P_i[z,y_1,y_2,\ldots y_m]$ the following formula is among the premises

$$\forall y_1\ldots\forall y_m\forall z\{T(y_1) \land \varphi[y_1] \land \ldots \land T(y_m) \land \varphi[y_m] \land P_i[z,y_1,\ldots y_m]$$
$$\Rightarrow \varphi[t_i[z,y_1,\ldots y_m]]\}$$

An intuitionistic stratified theory

We have now defined the set of axioms which are included in an IST.

DEFINITION 6. A set of axioms Γ is an *intuitionistic stratified theory* (IST) if a level assignment exists for the predicate symbols such that every axiom of Γ belongs to one of the following categories:

i. axioms for the logical constants of intuitionistic first-order logic,
ii. equality axioms (definition 3),
iii. axioms for ordinary predicates (definition 4),
iv. axioms for inductive predicates (definition 5).

We try to keep the number of axioms as low as possible. Many useful formulas used as axioms by other researchers in this area are theorems in the theory and need to be proved true. The following statements are examples of such theorems: A natural number is either 0 or the successor of a natural number. An ordered list is not a natural number, and vice versa. All ordered lists are lists. Identity over natural numbers is a total relation. Complete induction. Additionally, by a meta argument, we can prove computational induction over programs correct.

2.3 Programs and goals

We identify a subset of the first-order theory which can be executed efficiently, using a sound and complete proof procedure. This subset is called programs. We use equivalences as programs. The programs are similar to completed programs [Cla78].

DEFINITION 7. An *open goal* is an arbitrary formula built using $\land$, $\lor$, $\forall$, $\exists$, $=$, and program predicates. A *goal* is a closed open goal.

A predicate is a *program predicate* if it is defined as an ordinary predicate in the form $\forall x\{P(x) \Leftrightarrow \varphi[x]\}$ where $\varphi[x]$ is an open goal.

A *typed program predicate* is an typed ordinary predicate in the form $\forall x\{\psi[x] \Rightarrow (P(x) \Leftrightarrow \varphi[x])\}$ where $\varphi[x]$ and $\psi[x]$ are open goals.

An inductive predicate is a program predicate if the associated predicates are program predicates.

We have chosen to define the program by natural deduction inference rules, since the inference rules also reveal how a goal is proved. In the appendix we show how to execute the programs, using an execution mechanism similar to SLD-resolution.

DEFINITION 8. A *program* Δ is the following set of inference rules: P is a program predicate defined by $\forall x\{P(x) \Leftrightarrow \varphi[x]\}$ or $\forall x\{\psi[x] \Rightarrow (P(x) \Leftrightarrow \varphi[x])\}$. Then, we have the following inference rule, respectively:

$$\frac{\varphi[t]}{P(t)}P\text{-I} \qquad\qquad \frac{\varphi[t] \quad \psi[t]}{P(t)}P\text{-I}$$

T is an inductive program predicate. For each axiom
$\forall y \forall x_1 \ldots \forall x_m\{T(x_1) \wedge \ldots \wedge T(x_m) \wedge P_i[y,x_1,x_2,\ldots x_m] \Rightarrow T(t_i[y,x_1,x_2,\ldots x_m])\}$:
we have the following inference rule:

$$\frac{T(r_1) \quad T(r_2) \quad \ldots \quad T(r_m) \quad P_i[s,r_1,r_2,\ldots r_m]}{T(t_i[s,r_1,r_2,\ldots r_m])}T\text{-I}$$

We also add inference rules for the logical constants.

$$\frac{\varphi \quad \psi}{\varphi \wedge \psi}\wedge\text{I} \qquad \frac{\varphi}{\varphi \vee \psi}\vee\text{I} \qquad \frac{\psi}{\varphi \vee \psi}\vee\text{I}$$

$$\frac{\varphi[x]}{\forall x\, \varphi[x]}\forall\text{I} \qquad \frac{\varphi[t]}{\exists x\, \varphi[x]}\exists\text{I} \qquad \frac{}{t=t}=\text{I}$$

A program which contains no typed predicates is called a *untyped program*.

DEFINITION 9. A goal is *well-typed* if the types of the typed programs predicates, used in a successful execution of the goal, are respected.

EXAMPLE 7. *Plus*(x,y,z) is true if z is the sum of x and y. The following three definitions of *Plus* are all programs (actually, the first one is incorrect).

i. $Plus(x,y,z) \Leftrightarrow x=0 \wedge y=z \vee \exists x'\exists z'(x=s(x') \wedge z=s(z') \wedge Plus(x',y,z'))$

ii. $Plus(x,y,z) \Leftrightarrow$

$$Nat(x) \wedge Nat(y) \wedge Nat(z) \wedge [x=0 \wedge y=z \vee \exists y'\exists z'(x=s(x') \wedge z=s(z') \wedge Plus(x',y,z'))]$$

iii. $Nat(x) \wedge Nat(y) \wedge Nat(z) \Rightarrow$

$$\{Plus(x,y,z) \Leftrightarrow x=0 \wedge y=z \vee \exists x'\exists z'(x=s(x') \wedge z=s(z') \wedge Plus(x',y,z'))\}$$

The goal $\exists x\, Plus(s(0),s(s(0)),x)$ corresponds to the question: what is the sum of 1 and 2? The last program is a typed program. The difference between the second and third definition is that using the second definition we can prove $\neg Plus(nil, nil, nil)$ from Γ, whereas this does not follow from the third one. All goals $Plus(t_1, t_2, t_3)$ such that either t_2 or t_3 is a natural number are well-typed w.r.t. the typed program for *Plus*. □

We will from now on ignore untyped programs, since they always can be seen as a special case of typed programs.

2.4 Properties of the intuitionistic stratified theory

The following theorems are proved in [Wal91]. We first map all axioms to inference rules and prove that all proofs have a normal form. Then, the theorems below are proved by investigating the structure of normal proofs.

Let Γ be an IST, and Δ the program of Γ.

THEOREM 1 (Consistency). Γ is consistent.

THEOREM 2 (Existence Property). If $\Gamma \vdash \exists x\ \varphi[x]$, then $\Gamma \vdash \varphi[t]$ for some term t.

If all goals derivable from Γ are derivable from the program Δ alone, we will show that formal proofs can be used to validate transformation schemata. We say that the specification Γ is a conservative extension of the program Δ w.r.t. goals if this property holds. Thus, even if we use nonprogram axioms to transform a program, they are unnecessary when it comes to proving a specific goal.

DEFINITION 10. Let Γ and Δ be two sets of axioms, and Ξ a set of formulas. The theory Γ is a *conservative extension* of Δ w.r.t. Ξ if for all φ in Ξ, $\Gamma \vdash \varphi$ iff $\Delta \vdash \varphi$.

The following two theorems justify the choice of programs and goals. A more accurate version of it proves the soundness and completeness of the execution procedure described in definition 14.

THEOREM 3. Let Ξ be a set of goals (see definition 8). Then, Γ is a conservative extension of Δ w.r.t. Ξ.

The following corollary essentially says that if we prove a goal $P[t]$, we only need to consider the predicates which are used directly or indirectly in the definition of P.

COROLLARY 4. Let φ be a goal, and Δ' the program axioms of Γ with level less than or equal to $level(\varphi)$. Then, $\Gamma \vdash \varphi$ iff $\Delta' \vdash \varphi$.

3 Correctness of transformation schemata

Two programs are equal if the sets of computable solutions are equivalent.

DEFINITION 11. Assume that P is defined by $\forall x\{\psi[x] \Rightarrow (P(x) \Leftrightarrow \varphi[x])\}$, and let t be a term such that $\Gamma \vdash \psi[t]$.

i. The term t is a *specified solution* if $P(t)$ is provable, i.e., $\Gamma \vdash P(t)$.
ii. The term t is a *computed solution* if $P(t)$ is provable from the program, i.e., $\Delta \vdash P(t)$.

If the term $t[x]$ contains the free variable x and $\Gamma \vdash \forall x\ \psi[t[x]]$, then $t[x]$ is a specified solution if $\forall x\ P(t[x])$ is provable, and $t[x]$ is a computed solution if $\forall x\ P(t[x])$ is provable from the program.

DEFINITION 12 (Equivalence of two definitions of the same program predicate). Let Γ_1 and Γ_2 be equal, except that they have different definitions of the predicate P. The two definitions of the program P are *equal*, if for all terms t, t is a specified solution of P in Γ_1 iff t is a computed solution of P in Γ_2.

In the following two theorems we assume that $\forall x\{\psi[x] \Rightarrow [P(x) \Leftrightarrow \varphi_1[x]]\}$ is a (first-order) program, that $\forall x\{\psi[x] \Rightarrow [P(x) \Leftrightarrow \varphi_2[x]]\}$ is a program, and that $\Gamma \cup \{\forall x\{\psi[x] \Rightarrow [P(x) \Leftrightarrow \varphi_2[x]]\}\}$ is a conservative extension w.r.t. goals of $\Delta \cup \{\forall x\{\psi[x] \Rightarrow [P(x) \Leftrightarrow \varphi_2[x]]\}\}$.

THEOREM 5 (Verification sentence for equivalence of two definitions of the same program predicate). The two definitions of P are equal if
$\Gamma \vdash \forall x\{\psi[x] \Rightarrow [P(x) \Leftrightarrow \varphi_1[x]]\} \Leftrightarrow \forall x\{\psi[x] \Rightarrow [P(x) \Leftrightarrow \varphi_2[x]]\}$.

PROOF. Let t be any term, such that $\Gamma \vdash \psi[t]$. We must show that
$\Gamma \cup \{\forall x\{\psi[x] \Rightarrow [P(x) \Leftrightarrow \varphi_1[x]]\}\} \vdash P(t)$ iff $\Delta \cup \{\forall x\{\psi[x] \Rightarrow [P(x) \Leftrightarrow \varphi_2[x]]\}\} \vdash P(t)$
Note that by corollary 4 the definition of P is not needed when we prove $\psi[t]$.

($\Rightarrow$)

i. Suppose $\Gamma \cup \{\forall x\{\psi[x] \Rightarrow [P(x) \Leftrightarrow \varphi_1[x]]\}\} \vdash P(t)$.

ii. By the hypothesis
$\Gamma \vdash \forall x\{\psi[x] \Rightarrow [P(x) \Leftrightarrow \varphi_1[x]]\} \Leftrightarrow \forall x\{\psi[x] \Rightarrow [P(x) \Leftrightarrow \varphi_2[x]]\}$, the deduction theorem, and the replacement theorem we get
$\Gamma \cup \{\forall x\{\psi[x] \Rightarrow [P(x) \Leftrightarrow \varphi_2[x]]\}\} \vdash P(t)$.

iii. Thus, since $\Gamma \cup \{\forall x\{\psi[x] \Rightarrow [P(x) \Leftrightarrow \varphi_2[x]]\}\}$ is a conservative extension w.r.t. goals of $\Delta \cup \{\forall x\{\psi[x] \Rightarrow [P(x) \Leftrightarrow \varphi_2[x]]\}\}$,
$\Delta \cup \{\forall x\{\psi[x] \Rightarrow [P(x) \Leftrightarrow \varphi_2[x]]\}\} \vdash P(t)$ holds.

($\Leftarrow$) Analogously. ∎

It is rather clumsy to use the theorem directly, and the following corollary captures a common case. Assume that there is a well-ordering $\prec$ over the arguments of P. If we only use the definitions of P for (in a given context!) smaller arguments, it is enough to prove that the bodies of the definitions of P are equal. (Note that proving $\sigma[c]$ is the same as proving $\forall x\ \sigma[x]$, if c is a unique constant not occurring anywhere else.)

COROLLARY 6. The two definitions of P are equivalent if
$\Gamma \cup \forall y\{y \prec c \Rightarrow \{\psi[y] \Rightarrow [P(y) \Leftrightarrow \varphi_1[y]]\}\}$
$\quad \cup \forall y\{y \prec c \Rightarrow \{\psi[y] \Rightarrow [P(y) \Leftrightarrow \varphi_2[y]]\}\}$
$\vdash \varphi_1[c] \Leftrightarrow \varphi_2[c]$
(c is a unique constant not occurring anywhere else).

PROOF. $\Gamma \vdash \forall x\{\forall y\{y \prec x \Rightarrow \{\psi[y] \Rightarrow [P(y) \Leftrightarrow \varphi_1[y]]\} \wedge \{\psi[y] \Rightarrow [P(y) \Leftrightarrow \varphi_2[y]]\}$
$\quad \Rightarrow \{\varphi_1[x] \Leftrightarrow \varphi_2[x]\}\}$
$\quad \Rightarrow \forall x\{\psi[x] \Rightarrow [P(x) \Leftrightarrow \varphi_1[x]]\} \Leftrightarrow \forall x\{\psi[x] \Rightarrow [P(x) \Leftrightarrow \varphi_2[x]]\}$
holds, thus by theorem 5 both definitions are equal. ∎

The well-ordering is used to prevent that $\forall x\{P(x) \Leftrightarrow \varphi[x]\}$ is transformed into $\forall x\{P(x) \Leftrightarrow P[x]\}$. We may use several different well-orderings during a transformation by splitting up the transformation in different phases.

The definition of equal programs also ensures correctness for existentially quantified goals. Assume that $\Gamma \cup \{\forall x\{\psi[x] \Rightarrow [P(x) \Leftrightarrow \varphi_1[x]]\} \vdash \exists x\, P(t[x])$ for some term $t[x]$. By the existence property we know that there exists a term r such that $\Gamma \cup \{\forall x\{\psi[x] \Rightarrow [P(x) \Leftrightarrow \varphi_1[x]]\} \vdash P(r)$. If the programs are equal, then $\Delta \cup \{\forall x\{\psi[x] \Rightarrow [P(x) \Leftrightarrow \varphi_2[x]]\} \vdash P(r)$. Generalize the term r in t by the existentially quantified variable x and we have $\Delta \cup \{\forall x\{\psi[x] \Rightarrow [P(x) \Leftrightarrow \varphi_2[x]]\} \vdash \exists x\, P(t[x])$.

Application 1: Unfold/fold transformations

We use the following syntax to write *transformation rules* and *conditional transformation rules*, respectively:

$$\psi_1[t] \longrightarrow \psi_2[t] \qquad\qquad \varphi[t] \mid \psi_1[t] \longrightarrow \psi_2[t]$$

The rules means that if we have a formula, which contains the subformula $\psi_1[t]$ for any term t and the optional condition φ holds in the context of the subformula, then we may replace $\psi_1[t]$ by $\psi_2[t]$.

DEFINITION 13. Let Γ be a first-order program, and $\forall x\{\psi[x] \Rightarrow [P(x) \Leftrightarrow \varphi_1[x]]\}$ the predicate we want to transform. The program predicate symbol P is not defined in Γ, but it may be used in Γ. Substitute the variable x in the body $\varphi[x]$ for a unique parameter c, where c is called the original argument. Let $\prec$ be a well-ordering defined for the type of c. Then the following transformation rules can be used to transform $\varphi[c]$,

i. Unfolding: $t \prec c \mid P(t) \longrightarrow \varphi_1[t]$
ii. Folding: $t \prec c \mid \varphi_1[t] \longrightarrow P(t)$
iii. Replacement:
If $\Gamma \vdash \sigma_3 \Rightarrow [\sigma_1 \Leftrightarrow \sigma_2]$, then $\sigma_3 \mid \sigma_1 \longrightarrow \sigma_2$ and $\sigma_3 \mid \sigma_2 \longrightarrow \sigma_1$.

We denote the result of applying a sequence of transformation rules to $\varphi_1[c]$ by $\varphi_2[c]$. The resulting program is $\forall x\{\psi[x] \Rightarrow [P(x) \Leftrightarrow \varphi_2[x]]\}$.

THEOREM 7 (Correctness of Unfold/Fold transformations). If we apply the unfold/fold rules and replacement to $\varphi_1[x]$ and obtain $\varphi_2[x]$, then program $\forall x\{\psi[x] \Rightarrow [P(x) \Leftrightarrow \varphi_1[x]]\}$ is equivalent to the program $\forall x\{\psi[x] \Rightarrow [P(x) \Leftrightarrow \varphi_2[x]]\}$.

The theorem follows immediately from corollary 6.

EXAMPLE 8. We have the following first-order program (together with axioms describing lists).

a. $List(l) \Rightarrow [Zeroes(l) \Leftrightarrow \forall x\{x \in l \Rightarrow x{=}0\}]$
b. $List(l) \Rightarrow [x \in y \Leftrightarrow \exists x'\exists y'\{y{=}cons(x',y') \wedge (x{=}x' \vee x \in y')\}]$

We will transform Zeroes to the following program.

c. $List(l) \Rightarrow [Zeroes(l) \Leftrightarrow l{=}nil \vee \exists x'\exists y'\{y{=}cons(x',y') \wedge (x'{=}0 \wedge Zeroes(y')\}]$

The transformation goes as follows: (Note that throughout the transformation we may use the assumption $List(l)$)

1. Initial body,
$\forall x\{\underline{x \in l} \Rightarrow x=0\}$
2. Unfolding the definition of $\in$,
gives $\forall x\{\underline{\exists x'\exists y'}\{l=cons(x',y') \wedge (x=x' \vee x \in y')\} \Rightarrow x=0\}$
3. $(\exists y\, \varphi[y]) \Rightarrow \psi \longrightarrow \forall y(\varphi[y] \Rightarrow \psi)$,
gives $\underline{\forall x}\forall x'\forall y'\{l=cons(x',y')\underline{\wedge}(x=x' \vee x \in y') \Rightarrow x=0\}$
4. $\forall x\forall y\, \varphi[x,y] \longrightarrow \forall y\forall x\, \varphi[x,y]$,
$\varphi \wedge \psi \Rightarrow \sigma \longrightarrow \varphi \Rightarrow (\psi \Rightarrow \sigma)$,
$\forall x[\varphi \Rightarrow (\psi[x] \Rightarrow \sigma)] \longrightarrow \varphi \Rightarrow \forall x(\psi[x] \Rightarrow \sigma)$
gives $\forall x'\forall y'\{l=cons(x',y') \Rightarrow \forall x[\underline{(x=x' \vee x \in y') \Rightarrow x=0}]\}$
5. $\varphi \vee \psi \Rightarrow \sigma \longrightarrow (\varphi \Rightarrow \sigma) \wedge (\psi \Rightarrow \sigma)$,
$\forall x(\varphi[x] \wedge \psi[x]) \longrightarrow \forall x\, \varphi[x] \wedge \forall x\, \psi[x]$,
gives $\forall x'\forall y'\{l=cons(x',y') \Rightarrow \{\underline{\forall x[x=x' \Rightarrow x=0]} \wedge \underline{\forall x[x \in y' \Rightarrow x=0]}\}\}$
6. $\forall x(x=y \Rightarrow \varphi[x]) \longrightarrow \varphi[y]$,
fold since $y' \prec l$,
gives $\underline{\forall x'\forall y'\{l=cons(x',y') \Rightarrow \{x'=0 \wedge Zeroes(y')\}\}}$
7. $List(l) \mid \forall x\forall y[l=cons(x,y) \Rightarrow \varphi[x,y]] \longrightarrow l=nil \vee \exists x\exists y[l=cons(x,y) \wedge \varphi[x,y]]$
gives $l=nil \vee \exists x'\exists y'\{y=cons(x',y') \wedge x'=0 \wedge Zeroes(y')\}$

By corollary 7, a) and c) programs are equivalent. □

Application 2: Transforming recursion into tail recursion

The correctness of unfold/fold transformations is rather obvious and therefore we prove the correctness of a more complicated transformation. We have chosen the transformation of recursive programs into tail recursive programs.

Assume that a program can be rewritten to the following form (we have chosen the convenient syntax of Prolog)

```
f(X, Y) :- b(X), u(Y).
f(X, Y) :- r(X, E, X2), f(X2, Y2), a(E, Y2, Y).
```

by introducing auxiliary predicates. Also assume that the predicate *a* describes an associative and partial function with the identity described by the predicate *u* and that the argument *X2* of *r* is always smaller than *X* for some wfo $\prec$. Then the program above can be transformed into the following tail recursive program.

```
f(X, Y) :- u(V), g(V, X, Y).
g(V, X, V) :- b(X).
g(V, X, Y) :- r(X, E, X2), a(V, E, V2), g(V2, X2, Y).
```

EXAMPLE 9. Naive reverse and factorial are examples of programs that can be optimized using this scheme. We first rewrite the program

```
reverse([], []).
reverse([H|T], Y) :- reverse(T, T2), append(T2, [H], Y).
```

so that it matches the transformation scheme.

```
reverse(X, Y) :- b(X), u(Y).
reverse(X, Y) :- r(X, E, X2), reverse(X2, Y2), a(E, Y2, Y).
b([]).
u([]).
r([H|T], [H], T).
a(E, Y2, Y) :- append(Y2, E, Y).
```

Now we may transform the program using the rule, since append is an associative function with identity *nil*, and get

```
reverse(X, Y) :- u(V), g(V, X, Y).
g(V, X, V) :- b(X).
g(V, X, Y) :- r(X, E, X2), a(V, E, V2), g(V2, X2, Y).
```

By unfolding the *b*, *u*, *r*, *a* and *append* predicates we get the ordinary tail recursive reverse program.

```
reverse(X, Y) :- g([], X, Y).
g(V, [], V).
g(V, [H|T], Y) :- g([H|V], T, Y).
```

□

THEOREM 8 (Linear recursion to tail recursion). Assume that we have a program in the form

a. $\forall x \forall y \{F(x,y) \Leftrightarrow B(x) \wedge U(y) \vee \exists e \exists x' \exists y' (R(x,e,x') \wedge F(x',y') \wedge A(e,y',y))\}$

and that the following sentences are provable.

b. $\forall x \forall y \forall z \forall z' \{A(x,y,z) \wedge A(x,y,z') \Rightarrow z{=}z'\}$: The predicate A is a partial function from its first two arguments into the last.

c. $\forall x \forall y \forall z \forall o \{\exists v(A(x,y,v) \wedge A(v,z,o)) \Leftrightarrow \exists w(A(x,w,o) \wedge A(y,z,w))\}$: The predicate A is associative.

d. $\forall x \forall y \forall z \{U(x) \Rightarrow (A(x,y,z) \Leftrightarrow y{=}z)\}$: Every term t such that $U(t)$ is a left identity for the predicate A.

e. $\forall x \forall y \forall z \{U(x) \Rightarrow (A(y,x,z) \Leftrightarrow y{=}z)\}$: Every term t such that $U(t)$ is a right identity for the predicate A.

f. $\forall x \forall y \forall z \{R(x,y,z) \Rightarrow z \prec x\}$: The third argument of R is smaller than the first.

Then the linear recursive program F can be replaced by the equivalent tail-recursive program F

g. $\forall x \forall y \{F(x,y) \Leftrightarrow \exists v \{U(v) \wedge G(v,x,y)\}\}$

h. $\forall x \forall y \forall v \{G(v,x,y) \Leftrightarrow$
$B(x) \wedge v{=}y \vee \exists e \exists x' \exists v' \{R(x,e,x') \wedge A(v,e,v') \wedge G(v',x',y)\}\}$

PROOF. Let cx, cy be unique constants. The theorem is proved by deriving
$B(cx) \wedge U(cy) \vee \exists e \exists x' \exists y'(R(cx,e,x') \wedge F(x',y') \wedge A(e,y',cy)) \Leftrightarrow \exists v\{U(v) \wedge G(v,cx,cy)\}$
from b)-f), h),
$\forall x \forall y \{x \prec cx \Rightarrow \{F(x,y) \Leftrightarrow B(x) \wedge U(y) \vee \exists e \exists x' \exists y'(R(x,e,x') \wedge F(x',y') \wedge A(e,y',y))\}\}$, and
$\forall x \forall y \{x \prec cx \Rightarrow \{F(x,y) \Leftrightarrow \exists v \{U(v) \wedge G(v,x,y)\}\}\}$.
The correctness of the transformation scheme then follows from corollary 6. The full proof can be obtained from the author. ∎

4 Related Work

Unfold/fold transformation was introduced into logic programming by T. Sato and H. Tamaki [Tam84] and it was proved that it preserves the success set. Their results have been extended for SLDNF-resolution by M. J. Maher [Mah87] and H. Seki [Sek89]. Recently, T. Sato has defined a unfold/fold system for first-order programs [Sat90]. His system differs from the one presented here in three ways: T. Sato allows call-consistent program which is a proper superset of stratified programs, but instead we allow induction axioms. T. Sato uses the notion of *foldable* in order not to obtain the tautology $\forall x\{P(x) \Leftrightarrow P(x)\}$ during folding, whereas we need a well-ordering.

R.M. Burstall and J. Darlington [Bur77] showed how to transform recursive equations to tail-recursive equations using Eureka definitions, and their work has been applied to logic programming by many researchers. We have used the method given by K. Futamura [Fut86] and adapted it to relations. Transformation schemata, which rewrite recursive logic programs into tail-recursive program, have also been given by D. R. Brough and C. J. Hogger [Bro87]. Schemata for Prolog programs have been given by R. O'Keefe [O90] and T. Gegg-Harrison [Geg89].

Stratified theories were introduced into logic programming to enable some completeness results for SLDNF-resolution [Llo87].

There are intuitionistic extensions of Horn clauses which include some negation and implication and still have a complete execution procedure, e.g., the clausal intuitionistic logic of L. T. McCarty [McC88] and language of Dale Miller [Mil89]. Currently, these theories lack induction. Implications in the body of a program and induction schemata do not coexist well. We have given induction prority over implications. For example, if we would allow arbitrary implications in bodys in an IST, the following formula

$$Nat(x) \wedge Nat(y) \wedge Nat(z) \Rightarrow (Plus(x,y,z) \Leftrightarrow Plus(y,x,z)),$$

which states that *Plus* is commutative in its first two arguments, would be a goal. It is provable from Γ, but not from Δ. Thus, an efficient SLD-resolution like inference system cannot prove that goal, we need a complete first-order theorem prover.

An IST is a special case of the iterative inductive definitions as defined by Per Martin-Löf [Mar71]. Essentially, we have introduced the following two restrictions: We have replaced the very general proof system of iterative inductive definitions with a traditional first-order proof system, and we have a free interpretation of the terms. Previously, M. Hagiya and T. Sakurai have applied iterative inductive definitions to logic programming [Hag84]. The main difference between their work and ours is that our programs are equivalences, whereas they have retained the more powerful production rules of iterated inductive definitions.

5 Conclusion

We have presented a method where transformation schemata can be proved correct using a standard proof system for first-order intuitionistic logic. However, the method will not be really usable until good semi-automatic theorem provers are available. The problem is that formal proofs tend to become unwieldingly long and incomprehensible. Topics for future research: extend the results to classical first-order logic, extend the programs to include negation and/or implication.

References

[Bro87] Brough, D.R. and Hogger, C.J. Compiling Associativity into Logic Programs. Tech. Rept. 87/2, Imperial College, London, 1987.

[Bur77] Burstall, R.M. and Darlington, J. A transformation System for Developing Recursive Programs. *JACM 24*, 1 (1977), 44–67.

[Cla78] Clark, K.L. Negation as failure. In *Logic and data bases*. Plenum Press, Gallaire, H. and Minker, J., pp. 293–322, New York, 1978.

[Fut86] Futamura, Y. *Recursion Reduction: A Technique for Designing Efficient Recursive Programs*. 1986, Lecture Notes, Uppsala.

[Geg89] Gegg-Harrison, T.S. Basic Prolog Schemata. Tech. Rept. CS-1989-20, Dept of Computer Science, Duke University, Durham, North Carolina, 1989.

[Hag84] Hagiya, M. and Sakurai, T. Foundation of logic programming based on inductive definition. *New Generation Computing 2*, 2 (1984), 59–77.

[Llo87] Lloyd, J.W. *Foundations of logic programming,* Springer-Verlag , 2(1987).

[Mah87] Maher, M.J. Correctness of a Logic Program Transformation System. Tech. Rept. , IBM T.J. Watson Research Center, 1987.

[Mar71] Martin-Löf, P. Hauptsatz for the intuitionistic theory of iterated inductive definitions. In *Proceedings of the Second Scandinavian Logic Symposium,* Fenstad, J.E., North-Holland, 1971.

[McC88] McCarty, L.T. Clausal intuitionistic logic. *JLP 5*, 1 (1988).

[Mil89] Miller, D. A logical analysis of modules in logic programming. *JLP* (1989), 79–108.

[O90] O'Keefe, R. *The craft of Prolog,* MIT press (1990).

[Sat90] Sato, T. A First Order Unfold/Fold System. Tech. Rept. 90-17, Electrotechnical Laboratory, Umezono, Tsukuba, Ibaraki, Japan 305, 1990.

[Sek89] Seki, H. Unfold/Fold Transformation of Stratified Programs. In *6th ICLP,* 1989, pp. 554–568.

[Tam84] Tamaki, H. and Sato, T. Unfold/Fold transformations of logic programs. In *Proceedings of the 2nd ICLP,* 1984.

[Wal91] Waldau, M., *Verification of logic programs using verification sentences,* Computing Science Dept, Uppsala University, Sweden, 1991, .

Appendix: Execution of programs

The programs are a natural extension of Horn clauses and, accordingly, we can use an execution mechanism similar to SLD-resolution. The programs can be executed using the following procedure, which is complete. N.B.: Completeness does not refer to completeness w.r.t. models, but completeness w.r.t. intuitionistic provability.

DEFINITION 14 (How to compute a goal). Input: A program Δ and a goal φ. Output: The witnesses for the existential variables in the goal.

execute(φ) is defined by case analysis on the structure of φ:

φ is $r=t$: r and t are identical.

φ is $\psi \wedge \sigma$: *execute*(ψ) and *execute*(σ).

φ is $\psi \vee \sigma$: *execute*(ψ) or *execute*(σ).

φ is $\forall x\ \psi[x]$: *execute*($\psi[c]$) for a new parameter c.

φ is $\exists x\ \psi[x]$: *execute*($\psi[t]$) for some term t.

φ is $P(t)$ where P is a untyped predicate with definition $\forall x\{P(x) \Leftrightarrow \psi[x]\}$: *execute*($\psi[t]$).

φ is $P(t)$ where P is a typed predicate with definition $\forall x\{\sigma[x] \Rightarrow (P(x) \Leftrightarrow \psi[x])\}$: *execute*($\psi[t]$) and *execute*($\sigma[t]$).

φ is $T(t)$ where T is an inductive predicate with definition $\forall x\{\psi[x] \Rightarrow T(t_i[x])\}$: There exists an instantiation r of x, such that t and $t_i[r]$ are identical, *execute*($\psi[t_i[r]]$).

We emulate the linear structure of SLD-resolution by allowing that, when executing a conjunction $\psi \wedge \sigma$, we do not need to complete *execute*(ψ) before we start with *execute*(σ). It is easy to generalize the definition to the non ground case, i.e., SLD-resolution, just introduce substitutions and change the = case, $\exists$ case, and inductive predicate case accordingly.

There are two minor problems. The witness is not allowed to contain parameters of universal quantifiers introduced later on. Secondly, what does the type check *execute*($\sigma[t]$) mean if $\sigma[t]$ is not closed. We can we wait until $\sigma[t]$ is closed or at least as long as possible? Otherwise the types will be used to generate instantiations of the variables. An alternative is to use a type checker and check the types before execution, but this restricts the set of allowed types.

A solution is to use a type checker and check the types before execution, but this restricts the set of allowed types. An advantage of using a type checker is that it is more efficient, since the cost of checking the types can be rather high. The untyped *Plus* program in example 7 computes the ground goal *Plus*(t_1, t_2, t_3) in O(t_1) time, whereas a typed one needs O(t_1^2) time.

THEOREM 9 (*execute* sound and complete). Let φ be a goal. $\Gamma \vdash \varphi$ iff *execute*(φ).

The theorem is proved by showing that the execution trace and the normal proof of a goal are isomorphic (for a proof see [Wal91]).

Schema-Based Transformations of Logic Programs

Norbert E. Fuchs
Markus P. J. Fromherz

Institut für Informatik
Universität Zürich
Switzerland
{fuchs, fromherz}@ifi.unizh.ch

Abstract

Transformation schemata are predefined abstract transformations of logic programs: input program schemata are transformed into output program schemata. Each transformation schema represents one transformation strategy, for example a particular sequence of applications of the unfold/fold rules, or the introduction of an accumulator data structure. The transformation of logic programs with the help of transformation schemata proceeds in three steps: *abstraction* of the programs to program schemata, *selection* of a transformation schema with these schemata as input and a suitable schema as output, and *specialization* of the output schema to the transformed program. Once the transformation schemata are available, user intervention is required only during the selection step. For standard transformation situations one can even envisage eliminating user interaction altogether by heuristics.

1 Introduction

Logic programming allows to write software specifications and the specified programs in the same language. But even when written in the same language, specifications and programs must not be confused. Specifications should describe the functionality of programs in a declarative, clear way, which usually means that they are not efficiently executable, while the programs themselves should be efficiently executable. Logic programming promises to bridge the apparent conflict by providing means to transform specifications into programs. For this reason transformations of logic programs into equivalent, but more efficient forms have a rather long tradition.

Often these transformations are based on unfold/fold rules which were introduced by Burstall and Darlington [2] in the context of functional programs. Tamaki and Sato [14] defined transformations of definite logic programs based on unfolding and folding. Their transformations generate equivalent programs in that the least Herbrand model and the computed answers are preserved. Gardner and Shepherdson [5] introduced slightly modified transformations for normal logic programs which preserve procedural semantics for SLDNF resolution and declarative semantics based on Clark's completion.

Though the unfold/fold rules preserve the semantics they cannot be used blindly. Their application requires user intervention and thus prevents transformations to be automated. Different strategies have been proposed to overcome practical problems of individual rules and to semi-automate transformations [8, 9, 11, 12]. However, these strategies do not lead easily to strategies for transformations consisting of several applications of the unfold/fold rules.

We suggest a radically different approach that is based on transformation schemata. Transformation schemata are predefined abstract transformations which transform schemata of logic programs into other schemata. Each transformation schema represents a transformation strategy, e.g. a particular sequence of applications of unfold/fold or other transformation rules. A set of transformation schemata constitutes an extensible transformation system. The transformation of individual programs is reduced to the search for an appropriate transformation schema. This approach allows considerable reduction and simplification of user interaction since users don't have to deal with the intricacies of the unfold/fold rules and can concentrate on the form of the transformed programs alone. Standard transformations promise to be completely automated by replacing user interaction by heuristics.

This paper has the following structure. In section 2 we define the three unfold/fold rules *definition, unfolding* and *folding* which we use in section 3 for an example transformation. Section 4 sketches practical problems with these unfold/fold rules and solutions suggested for some of the problems. In section 5 we introduce schemata for logic programs and briefly describe the set of schemata developed by Gegg-Harrison [6]. Section 6 defines transformation schemata as transformations of program schemata, and shows how programs can be transformed with the help of transformation schemata in the three steps *abstraction, selection,* and *specialization*. In section 7 we describe the implementation of an experimental transformation system based on transformation schemata. Section 8 contains examples of transformation schemata and of concrete program transformations. Finally, in section 9 we summarize the main results and indicate directions for further research.

2 Unfold/Fold Rules

Three of the unfold/fold transformation rules are especially important and are often used in combination: the definition of new predicates in terms of given predicates, unfolding new predicates with respect to the clauses of the given predicates, and folding of literals generated by unfolding. We will briefly define these three rules following Gallagher [4] and Gardner and Shepherdson [5]. Other transformation rules, e.g. goal replacement, more specific clauses, and using laws of the predicates, will not be discussed.

New Definition

Let P be a normal program and D a set of clauses. Define S as the new set of clauses p(...) <- Q_1, ... , p(...) <- Q_n where p is a predicate symbol not occurring in P, D, or Q_1, ... , Q_n. By letting P' = P $\cup$ S and D' = D $\cup$ S we transform P and D into P' and D'.

Unfolding

Let P be a normal program and C a clause in P of the form A <- Q_1, B, Q_2 where A and B are atoms and Q_1 and Q_2 conjunctions of literals. Let H_1 <- R_1, ... , H_n <- R_n be the clauses in P whose heads H_i unify with B with the mgu's θ_1, ... , θ_n. Unfolding C on B generates the clauses (A <- Q_1, R_1, Q_2)θ_1, ... , (A <- Q_1, R_n, Q_2)θ_n. Replacing C by these clauses transforms the program P into the program P'.

Folding

Let P be a normal program and D a set of clauses introduced by the new definition rule. Let C be a clause in P of the form A <- Qθ,R where Q and R are conjunctions of literals, and θ a substitution. Let C1 be a clause H <- Q in D which is not a variant of C. Folding C using C1 generates the clause C2 of the form A <- Hθ,R provided that unfolding C2 on Hθ with respect to D gives C, C1 is the only clause in D whose head unifies with Qθ, and θ maps variables which appear in Q, but not in H into distinct variables which do not occur in C2. Replacing C by C2 transforms P into P'.

3 An Example Transformation

As a basis for the subsequent discussion we present a standard example of the unfold/fold transformations. The predicate *average/2* calculates the average value of the elements of a list.

```
average([], 0).
average(List, Average) :-
        sum(List, Sum),
        length(List, Length),
        Average is Sum/Length.
```

Where the predicates *sum/2* and *length/2* are defined as

```
sum([], 0).
sum([First | Rest], Sum) :-
        sum(Rest, RestSum),
        Sum is RestSum + First.

length([], 0).
length([First | Rest], Length) :-
        length(Rest, RestLength),
        Length is RestLength + 1.
```

As defined, *average/2* is inefficient because it traverses the list twice to calculate its sum and its length though one traversal would suffice. To calculate sum and length in one traversal we define a new predicate *sumlength/3* as a composition of *sum/2* and *length/2*.

```
sumlength(List, Sum, Length) :-                    % A
        sum(List, Sum),
        length(List, Length).
```

Unfolding *sumlength/3* on *sum/2* yields the two clauses

```
sumlength([], 0, Length) :-                        % B1
        length([], Length).
sumlength(First | Rest], Sum, Length) :-           % B2
        sum(Rest, RestSum),
        Sum is RestSum + First,
        length(First | Rest], Length).
```

and unfolding these two clauses on *length/2* gives

```
sumlength([], 0, 0).                               % C1
sumlength([First | Rest], Sum, Length) :-          % C2
        sum(Rest, RestSum),
        Sum is RestSum + First,
        length(Rest, RestLength),
        Length is RestLength + 1.
```

Now we fold the conjunction *sum(Rest,RestSum),length(Rest,RestLength)* of clause C2 using the definition A of *sumlength/3*. We get

```
sumlength([First | Rest], Sum,Length) :-           % D2
        sumlength(Rest, RestSum, RestLength),
        Sum is RestSum + First,
        Length is RestLength + 1.
```

The predicate *sumlength/3* is now defined by the clauses C1 and D2, and a new version of *average/2* can be derived by a folding step as

```
average([], 0).
average(List, Average) :-
        sumlength(List, Sum, Length),
        Average is Sum/Length.
```

The new version of *average/2* runs about 30% faster than the old one; in other cases, transformations by the unfold/fold rules can lead to a much larger gain in efficiency.

4 Practical Problems with the Unfold/Fold Rules

The preceding transformation example looks straightforward, but in fact involves several careful decisions that amount to a transformation strategy.

Following a different strategy may have led us astray. Many practical problems prevent unfold/fold transformations from being performed routinely, or even automatically.

The definition of new predicates - also called *eureka* rule - is a creative act which requires our intuition and discretion. Introducing the predicate *sumlength/3* seems obvious, but how we got the idea in the first place remains unclear. Recently, attempts have been made to derive eureka definitions in a systematic way. Proietti and Pettorossi [12] introduced two methods to find eureka predicates. They applied these methods successfully to some classes of logic programs. In the realm of functional programs, Nielson and Nielson [9] showed that type information can be used to derive eureka definitions.

Unfolding is often possible in many different ways. In our example we unfolded *sumlength/3* on *sum/2* and the resulting clauses B1 and B2 on *length/2*.

Instead, we could have unfolded the clause B2 on *sum/2* to get

```
sumlength([First], Sum, Length) :-                    % E2
        Sum is First,
        length([First], Length).
sumlength([First, Second | Rest], Sum, Length) :-     % E3
        sum(Rest, RestSum),
        RestSum1 is RestSum + Second,
        Sum is RestSum1 + First,
        length([First, Second | Rest], Length).
```

The predicate *sumlength/3* is now defined by the clauses B1, E2, and E3.

Though the clauses E2 and E3 may be more efficient than B2, they are unnecessarily specific: E2 treats lists with one, and E3 lists with at least two elements. Further unfolding of B1, E2, and E3 yields additional clauses, most of which are quite useless since they deal with additional special cases. Unfolding increases the number of clauses and can even lead to a combinatorial explosion.

This means that human intervention is required to control unfolding, and that there is a great need for guidelines. For the case of specializing an interpreter by unfolding it with respect to an object program two strategies have been proposed. Pereira and Shieber [11] suggested to divide predicates into evaluable and residual ones. Lakhotia and Sterling [8] proposed to restrict the unfolding of the interpreter to its parsing component and to leave its execution component as residue. These strategies reduce and facilitate human intervention but do not eliminate it.

Folding also presents problems. The folding rule assumes that the literals to be folded are consecutive. In fact, in clause C2 the two literals *sum(Rest,RestSum)* and *length(Rest,RestLength)* are not consecutive. The independence of the computation rule of SLD resolution allows to rearrange the literals, but Prolog's left-to-right computation rule could lead to termination problems. If the literals to be folded are not consecutive it is also not clear where to put the literal resulting from the folding step. In clause D2 we carefully ordered the literals so that the predicate *sumlength/3* can be evaluated without generating an error message.

As we have seen, human assistance is required for all three transformation rules, thus preventing automatic transformations. One way to semi-automate transformations is to formulate human assistance as strategies for each transformation rule. In this paper we suggest a different approach based on transformation schemata. This approach allows to formulate strategies for complete sequences of transformation steps, thus reducing and simplifying user interaction. For standard transformation situations user interaction could be completely replaced by heuristics leading to automatic transformations.

5 Schemata for Logic Programs

Since the beginning of logic programming it has been recognized that many logic programs, e.g. list processing programs, are structured similarly, and can be understood as instances of program schemata.

Different sets of schemata have been proposed. O'Keefe [10] defined a set of schemata for recursive programs, while Deville and Burnay [3] suggested schemata as a basis for program construction derived from structural induction and generalization.

Schemata can also be used to abstract from programs which rely on the same programming technique, e.g. on accumulators or on difference lists. Brna et al. [1] defined a large number of these techniques. Robertson [13] showed how programming techniques can be used to teach the construction of logic programs. Lakhotia [7] demonstrated that programming techniques can be incorporated into initial programs with the help of partial evaluation.

By far the most comprehensive set of schemata was introduced by Gegg-Harrison [6] in the context of a tutoring system. Based on the notion of the most specific generalization, second-order schemata are produced. Applied to a large number of simple recursive list-processing Prolog programs, a hierarchy of Prolog schemata is created. At the top of this hierarchy are fourteen basic-level schemata which capture the majority of simple recursive list-processing Prolog programs.

To describe the schemata, Gegg-Harrison conceived a language which we will introduce by the example.of the basic-level schema A This schema classifies programs which recursively process all elements of a list from its front-end.

```
schema_A([], «&1»).
schema_A([Head|Tail], «&2») :-
        < pre_process(«&3», Head, «&4»), >
        schema_A(Tail, «&5»)
        <, post_process(«&6», Head, «&7») >.
```

Arguments and literals in angle brackets < ... > are optional, arguments and literals in double angle brackets « ... » are arbitrary, i.e. they can appear any number – including zero – of times. Schema variables are denoted by &n. We skip Gegg-Harrison's notation for permutations of arguments and literals.

Schema A describes many well-known programs, e.g. *append/3*, *length/2*, *merge/3*, and *naive_reverse/2*. It is interesting to note that two of O'Keefe's schemata for recursive list processing programs O'Keefe [10] – the *tower method* and the tail recursive *linear method* – are covered by schema A.

Schema B resembles schema A, but is doubly recursive. It is an abstraction of programs which rely on divide-and-conquer, e.g. *quicksort/2*, *mergesort/2*, and *flatten/2*.

The remaining twelve basic-level schemata describe other ways of processing the elements of a list, e.g. processing only a subset of the elements, or processing from the tail end. Details can be found in Gegg-Harrison [6].

6 Transformation Schemata

Let us assume that a program to be transformed can be described abstractly by a program schema, and the transformed program by another program schema. In this case, we may say that we transform an instance of one program schema into an instance of another one. This leads us to the idea to transform program schemata instead of programs, and to define *transformation schemata*. Transformation schemata are standardized transformations which transform input program schemata into output program schemata. Each transformation schema incorporates a fixed sequence of transformation steps, e.g. applications of unfold/fold rules. Transformation schemata incorporate our transformation decisions, i.e. the order and type of transformation steps, definitions of new predicates (eureka), selections of literals to be unfolded or folded, or any other information relevant to the transformation in question. In brief, each transformation schema represents one specific transformation strategy. Since the number of program schemata is limited we can – quasi at leisure – use all our intuition and our experience with individual program transformations to develop the transformation schemata.

Users of transformation schemata need not be concerned with individual transformation steps. Instead users can concentrate on the form of the input and output programs.

Transformation of a logic program means that a conjunction of literals

$Q_1, A_1, \ldots, A_n, Q_2$

is replaced by another conjunction of literals

Q_1, A, Q_2

Each A_i calls a predicate P_i while A calls a predicate P which is semantically equivalent to the predicates $P_1, \ldots, P_n$. Usually, we expect calculations using P to be more efficient than those using $P_1, \ldots, P_n$.

For conciseness we say that we transform the set of terms $\{P_1/A_1, \ldots, P_n/A_n\}$ into the term P/A. We derive P/A from $\{P_1/A_1, \ldots, P_n/A_n\}$ by the three steps *abstraction, selection,* and *specialization*.

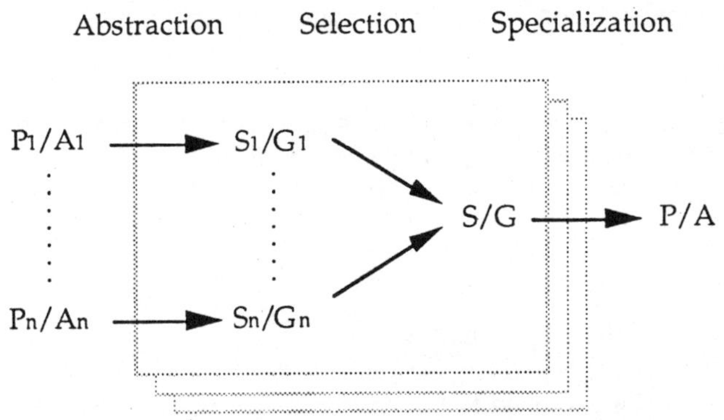

Abstraction
For each program P_i (i=1, ... , n) we identify a program schema S_i which describes P_i abstractly. This abstraction generates a set of substitutions θ_i for schema variables. The same abstraction leads from the literals A_i to the abstract literals G_i. In short, the abstraction step replaces each term P_i/A_i by its abstraction S_i/G_i, and we have $P_i/A_i = S_i\theta_i/G_i\theta_i$.

Selection
Transformation schemata transform the set of abstract terms $\{S_1/G_1, \ldots, S_n/G_n\}$ into an abstract term S/G, i.e. a transformation schema is defined as $\{S_1/G_1, \ldots, S_n/G_n, S/G\}$. In general there are several transformation schemata which have $\{S_1/G_1, \ldots, S_n/G_n\}$ as input. We select the transformation schema which generates a desired output program schema S together with an abstract literal G.

Specialization
We apply the substitution $\theta = \theta_1 \ldots \theta_n$ to S/G to get the transformed program $P=S\theta$ and the transformed literal $A=G\theta$.

Once the transformation schemata are available these three steps can be automated to a large degree. User intervention is only necessary in the selection step.

7 A Transformation System Based on Transformation Schemata

Following the preceding ideas we have implemented an experimental transformation system in Prolog.

We represent program schemata as lists, e.g.

```
[(Schema_A([], &1) :-
      true),
(Schema_A([H|T], &2) :-
      {process1},
      Schema_A(T, &4),
      {process2})]
```

Transformation schemata are similarly represented as facts *trafo/5*, e.g.

```
trafo(a1,
   [Schema_A1(L, &g1),                                          % G1
   Schema_A2(L, &g2)],                                          % G2
   [[(Schema_A1([], &11) :-                                     % S1
      true),
   (Schema_A1([H1|T1], &12) :-
      {process11},
      Schema_A1(T1, &14),
      {process12})],
   [(Schema_A2([], &21) :-                                      % S2
      true),
   (Schema_A2([H2|T2], &22) :-
      {process21},
      Schema_A2(T2, &24),
      {process22})]],
   [[Schema_A1, '_', Schema_A2, '_a1'](L, &g1, &g2)],           % G
   [([Schema_A1, '_', Schema_A2, '_a1']([], &11, &21) :-       % S
      true),
   ([Schema_A1, '_', Schema_A2, '_a1']([H1|T1], &12, &22) :-
      {process11},
      {process21},
      [Schema_A1, '_', Schema_A2, '_a1'](T1, &14, &24),
      {process12},
      {process22} )]).
```

The transformation schema a1 can be used to transform a conjunction of two literals abstractly represented by G_1 and G_2, and the two called programs represented by two copies S_1 and S_2 of program schema A into a literal represented by G and a program represented by S. This transformation schema is patterned after the transformation example of section 3. To derive S/G from S_1/G_1 and S_2/G_2 we have to perform the same transformation steps: one new definition, two unfolding steps, one folding step. This means that the transformation schema a1 incorporates a specific transformation strategy for programs described by program schema A.

The top predicate *transform(Literals,NewLiterals,NewClauses)* of the transformation system transforms the conjunction *Literals* of literals into the conjunction *NewLiterals* and the clauses of the predicates called by *Literals* into *NewClauses*. The predicate *transform/3* is defined by

```
transform(Literals, NewLiterals, NewClauses) :-
        trafo(Trafo, InLiterals, InSchemata, OutLiterals, OutSchema),
        abstract(Literals, InLiterals, InSchemata, Bindings),
        select(Trafo),
        specialize(Bindings, OutLiterals, OutSchema, NewLiterals, NewClauses).
```

The goal *trafo/5* chooses a suitable transformation schema *Trafo*. The goal *select/1* asks the user to accept or to reject this choice. Rejection causes backtracking if there is more than one suitable transformation schema. The goals *abstract/4* and *specialize/5* implement the transformation steps with the same names.

8 More Example Transformations

Additional examples will show the flexibility of the approach and the power of the experimental transformation system.

First we want to revisit the *sum-length* example of section 3. The transformation schema *a1* transforms the conjunction of literals *sum(Xs,S), length(Xs,L)* to the literal *sumlength(Xs,S,L)* and derives at the the same time the program *sum_length_a1/3*.

```
sum(Xs, S), length(Xs, L)                      % A1, A2

sum([], 0).                                    % P1
sum([E | Es], S) :-
        sum(Es, S1),
        S is S1+E.

length([], 0).                                 % P2
length([_ | Es], L) :-
        length(Es, L1),
        L is L1+1.

sum_length_a1([], 0, 0).                       % P
sum_length_a1([E | T], S, L) :-
        sum_length_a1(T, S1, L2),
        S is S1+E,
        L is L1+1.

sum_length_a1(Xs, S, L)                        % A
```

The same transformation schema *a1* can be used for the second example. Appending two lists by *append(L1,L2,L3)* and subsequently calculating the length of the first list by *length(L1,N)* involves two traversals of *L1*. We want to eliminate one traversal. The following transformation yields a program *append_length_a1(L1,L2,L3,N)* which appends *L1* and *L2* and calculates at the same time the length *N* of *L1*.

```
append(L1, L2, L3), length(L1, N)              % A1, A2

append([], L, L).                              % P1
append([X | L1], L2, [X | L3]) :-
        append(L1, L2, L3).

length([], 0).                                 % P2
length([_ | Es], N) :-
        length(Es, N1),
        N is N1+1.

append_length_a1([], L, L, 0).                 % P
append_length_a1([X | L1], L2, [X | L3], N) :-
        append_length_a1(L1, L2, L3, N1),
        N is N1+1.

append_length_a1(L1, L2, L3, N)                % A
```

The next example is based on the transformation schema *a2*

```
trafo(a2,
   [Schema_A1(X, Y, Z, &g1),                                                  % G1
   Schema_A2(Z, &g2)],                                                        % G2
   [[(Schema_A1([], L11, L11, &11) :-                                         % S1
      true),
   (Schema_A1([H1 | T11], L12, [H1 | T12], &12) :-
      {process11},
      Schema_A1(T11, L12, T12, &14),
      {process12})],
   [(Schema_A2([], &21) :-                                                    % S2
      true),
   (Schema_A2([H2 | T21], &22) :-
      {process21},
      Schema_A2(T21, &24),
      process22})]],
   [[Schema_A1, '_', Schema_A2, '_a2'](X, Y, Z, &g1, &g2)],                   % G
   [([Schema_A1, '_', Schema_A2, '_a2']([], [], [], &21) :-                   % S
      true),
   ([Schema_A1, '_', Schema_A2, '_a2']([], [H2 | T21], [H2 | T21], &11, &22) :-
      {process21},
      [Schema_A1, '_', Schema_A2, '_a2']([], T21, T21, &11, &24),
      {process22}),
   ([Schema_A1, '_', Schema_A2, '_a2']([H2 | T11], L, [H2 | T12], &12, &22) :-
      {process11},
      {process21},
      [Schema_A1, '_', Schema_A2, '_a2'](T11, L, T12, &14, &24),
      {process12},
      {process22})]).
```

We append two lists by *append(L1,L2,L3)* and calculate the length of the resulting list *L3* by *length(L3,N)*. Appending *L1* and *L2* means traversing *L1*, while calculating the length of *L3* means traversing *L3* of which *L1* is a prefix. As in the previous example, *L1* is traversed twice, but for the calculation of the length of *L3* the rest of *L3* must also be traversed. We want to eliminate the unnecessary second traversal of *L1*. With the help of the schema *a2* we get the program *append_length_a2(L1,L2,L3,N)* which appends *L1* and *L2* and calculates at the same time the length *N* of the resulting list *L3*.

```
append(L1, L2, L3), length(L3, N)                    % A1, A2

append([], L, L).                                    % P1
append([X|L1], L2, [X|L3]) :-
        append(L1, L2, L3).

length([], 0).                                       % P2
length([_|Es], N) :-
        length(Es, N1),
        N is N1+1.

append_length_a2([], [], [], 0).                     % P
append_length_a2([], [H|Es], [H|Es], N) :-
        append_length_a2([], Es, Es, N1),
        N is N1+1.
append_length_a2([X|L1], L2, [X|L3], N) :-
        append_length_a2(L1, L2, L3, N1),
        N is N1+1.

append_length_a2(L1, L2, L3, N)                      % A
```

Both transformation schemata *a1* and *a2* are based on unfold/fold rules. The following example shows that transformation schemata can also be derived using other transformation rules. Recursive predicates can be made tail-recursive or iterative by the introduction of an intermediate data structure called accumulator. The schema *t2* achieves this transformation.

```
trafo(t2,
    [Schema_T(L, R, &g1)],                           % G1
    [[(Schema_T([], I, &1) :-                        % S1
        true),
    (Schema_T([H|T], N, &2) :-
        {process1},
        Schema_T(T, N1, &4),
        Update(N1, HV, N, &5))]],
    [[Schema_T_t2](L, I, R, &g1)],                   % G
    [([Schema_T_t2]([], RN, RN, &1) :-               % S
        true),
    ([Schema_T_t2]([H|T], RN1, N, &2) :-
        {process1},
        Update(HV, RN1, N1, &5),
        [Schema_T_t2](T, N1, N, &4))]).
```

As a concrete example we transform the predicate *length/2* into its tail-recursive form *length_t2/3*. Note that the transformed literal *A* correctly initializes the accumulator to 0.

```
length(Xs, L)                                % A1

length([], 0).                               % P1
length([_|T], N) :-
      length(T, N1),
      N is N1+1.

length_t2([], N, N).                         % P
length_t2([_|T], N1, N) :-
      N2 is N1+1,
      length_t2(T, N2, N).

length_t2(Xs, 0, L)                          % A
```

Other transformation schemata have been implemented but will not be presented here because of the limited space.

9 Conclusions

There are several reasons why transformation schemata form a very powerful and flexible approach to program transformations.

Firstly, user interaction is enormously reduced and simplified. Instead of being confronted with the intricacies of the unfold/fold or other transformation rules, users can select a transformation by the very structure of the programs in question. If the transformation system offers a choice of possible transformation schemata, user interaction is reduced to yes/no decisions. For standard transformation situations one can even envisage eliminating user interaction altogether by heuristics.

Secondly, sets of transformation schemata can easily be extended and adapted by the addition of new schemata. The approach also allows to add transformation schemata for individual programs, especially for programs which do not fit into a given system of program schemata.

Thirdly, as demonstrated transformation schemata need not be derived from unfold/fold rules. Any set of semantics-preserving transformation rules can be used.

Fourthly, instead of deriving transformation schemata from transformation rules we could invent transformation schemata and post factum prove them correct. Waldau [15] proposes to validate transformation schemata by formal proofs based on intuitionistic logic.

These and other extensions of the basic approach will be used to develop a comprehensive and practical transformation system for logic programs.

Acknowledgements

We would like to thank the anonymous referees for their helpful and valuable comments on an earlier version of the paper. One of us (NEF) profited from intensive discussions during the LOPSTR '91 workshop at the University of Manchester.

This research has been partially supported by the Swiss National Science Foundation under contract 2000-5.449.

References

[1] P. Brna, A. Bundy, T. Dodd, M. Eisenstadt, C.K. Looi, H. Pain, B. Smith, M. van Someren, Prolog Programming Techniques, DAI Research Paper, 403, Department of Artificial Intelligence, University of Edinburgh, 1988

[2] R. Burstall, J. Darlington, Transformations for Developing Recursive Programs, JACM, Vol. 24, No. 1, 1977

[3] Y. Deville, J. Burnay, Generalization and Program Schemata. Proceedings of the North American Conference on Logic Programming 1989, E. L. Lusk, R. A. Overbeek (eds.), MIT Press, October 1989, pp. 409-425.

[4] J. Gallagher, Program Analysis and Transformation, Handout at Logic Programming Summer School LPSS '90, University of Zurich, August 1990

[5] P. A. Gardner, J. C. Shepherdson, Unfold/Fold Transformations of Logic Programs, Report PM-89-01, School of Mathematics, University of Bristol, 1989

[6] T. S. Gegg-Harrison, Basic Prolog Schemata, CS-1989-20, Department of Computer Science, Duke University, September 1989

[7] A. Lakhotia, Incorporating Programming Techniques into Prolog Programs. Proceedings of the North American Conference on Logic Programming 1989, E. L. Lusk, R. A. Overbeek (eds.), MIT Press, October 1989, pp. 426-440.

[8] A. Lakhotia, L. Sterling, How to Control Unfolding when Specializing Interpreters, in L. Sterling (ed.), The Practice of Prolog, MIT Press, 1990, pp. 171

[9] H. R. Nielson, F. Nielson, Eureka Definitions for Free – Disagreement Points for Fold/Unfold Transformations, Proceedings of ESOP '90, LNCS 432, 1990, pp. 291-305

[10] R. A. O'Keefe, The Craft of Prolog. MIT Press, 1990

[11] F. C. N. Pereira, S. M. Shieber, Prolog and Natural-Language Analysis, CSLI, Lectures Notes 10, 1987

[12] M. Proietti, A. Pettorossi, Synthesis of Eureka Predicates for Developing Logic Programs, Proceedings of ESOP '90, LNCS 432, 1990, pp. 306-325

[13] D. Robertson, A Simple Prolog Techniques Editor for Novice Users, Proceedings of ALPUK 91, 3rd Annual Conference on Logic Programming, Edinburgh, April 1991

[14] H. Tamaki, T. Sato, Unfold/Fold Transformation of Logic Programs, Proceedings of the Second International Conference on Logic Programming, Uppsala, 1984, S. - Å. Tärnlund (ed.), University of Uppsala, pp. 127 - 138

[15] M. Waldau, Formal Validation of Transformation Schemas Using First-Order Proofs, Proceedings of LOPSTR '91, University of Manchester, Springer Workshop in Computing Series (this volume), 1991

An Automatic Transformation Strategy for Avoiding Unnecessary Variables in Logic Programs*

Maurizio Proietti
IASI-CNR
Viale Manzoni 30
00185 Rome, Italy
E-mail: proietti@irmiasi.rm.cnr.it

Alberto Pettorossi
Electronics Department
University of Rome II
00173 Rome, Italy
E-mail: adp@irmiasi.rm.cnr.it

— Extended Abstract —

When writing programs one uses variables for storing input and output data. They can be considered as *necessary* variables, because they are needed for expressing the meaning of programs. Often one also uses variables which are *unnecessary*, in the sense that they are not required for describing the input-output relation. Unnecessary variables are used by the programmer because they often allow for a more transparent way of writing programs or an easier proof of their correctness.

It is the case that many strategies for program transformation which are given in the literature, are successful and improve program efficiency, precisely because they eliminate unnecessary variables, and thus, they avoid the construction of intermediate values and multiple traversals of data structures.

We propose some syntactically based techniques for avoiding unnecessary variables, which can be considered as a development of the tupling strategy and the composition strategy (also called loop-fusion, when used for merging consecutive loops).

For a presentation of those strategies in the case of functional programs the reader may refer to [BuD 77, Pet 77, Fea 86, Wad 88], while in the case of logic programs he may refer to [PeP 87, Deb 88].

We restrict our attention to definite logic programs and we consider two kinds of unnecessary variables, namely, the *existential* variables and the *multiple* variables. The existential variables of a clause C are the variables which occur in the body of C and not in its head, and the multiple variables of C are the variables which occur more than once in the body of C.

*This work has been partially supported by the "Progetto Finalizzato Sistemi Informatici e Calcolo Parallelo" of the CNR and MURST 40% (Italy). An expanded version of this paper was presented at PLILP 91, Passau, Germany, 26-28 Aug, 1991.

We present a strategy which drives the application of the unfold/fold rules [BuD 77, TaS 84], and automatically transforms initial program versions into new versions without multiple or existential variables. This strategy avoids the search for *eureka* definitions which is often required by other techniques described in the literature.

The basic part of our program transformation strategy consists in performing on any clause with unnecessary variables the following sequence of steps: an unfolding step, followed by some definition steps, followed by some folding steps.

Those steps eliminate all unnecessary variables from a given clause, at the expenses of possibly introducing definitions with unnecessary variables. However, we may repeat the unfolding-definitions-foldings steps w.r.t. the newly introduced definitions, in the hope that the process will terminate and all unnecessary variables will be eliminated.

It can be shown that the termination of the transformation process we have described above is undecidable. However, we have identified a suitable class of programs for which that process terminates, and thus, all unnecessary variables are eliminated. This class includes programs defined by induction on arbitrary data structures.

We also propose a variant of our strategy which *always* terminates, but, in general, this variant achieves a *partial* elimination of the unnecessary variables. This extension of the basic transformation strategy is obtained in two steps. We first introduce the notion of *relevant* predicates. The extended transformation strategy will eliminate the unnecessary variables from these relevant predicates only. We then introduce an additional transformation rule, called *Generalization + Equality Introduction*, and we show that, by making use of this rule, we can transform any program into an equivalent one for which the extended transformation strategy is applicable.

Finally, we show that the proposed transformation techniques can easily be enhanced by exploiting the functionality of some predicates in the initial program.

References

[BuD 77] R. M. Burstall and J. Darlington. *A Transformation System for Delevoping Recursive Programs.* JACM, Vol. 24, No. 1, January 1977, pp. 44-67.

[Deb 88] S. K. Debray. *Unfold/Fold Transformations and Loop Optimization of Logic Programs.* Proc. SIGPLAN 88, Conference on Programming Language Design and Implementation, Atlanta, Georgia, 1988.

[Fea 86] M. S. Feather. *A Survey and Classification of Some Program Transformation Techniques.* Proc. TC2 IFIP Working Conference on Program Specification and Transformation, Bad Tölz Germany, 1986.

[Pet 77] A. Pettorossi. *Transformation of Programs and Use of Tupling Strategy.* Proc. Informatica 77, Bled, Yugoslavia, 1977, pp. 3 103, 1-6.

[PeP 87] A. Pettorossi and M. Proietti. *Importing and Exporting Information in Program Development.* Proc. IFIP TC2 Workshop on Partial Evaluation and Mixed Computation, Gammel Avernaes, Denmark, North Holland 1987, pp. 405-425.

[TaS 84] H. Tamaki and T. Sato. *Unfold/Fold Transformation of Logic Programs* Proc. 2nd International Conference on Logic Programming, Uppsala, Sweden, 1984.

[Wad 88] P. L. Wadler. *Deforestation: Transforming Programs to Eliminate Trees.* Proc. ESOP 88, Nancy, France, 1988, Lecture Notes in Computer Science 300, pp. 344-358.

On Using Mode Input-output for Transforming Logic Programs

Francis Alexandre, Khaled Bsaies, Alain Quéré
CRIN-CNRS / INRIA-Lorraine
BP 239, Campus Scientifique
F-54506 Vandœuvre-lès-Nancy Cedex, FRANCE
e-mail: {alexandr, bsaies, quere}@loria.fr

Abstract

This paper discusses the transformation of logic programs by using mode input-output. We consider a system based on the Unfold/Fold transformations. First we introduce a notion of well-moded clause and well-moded definite program. We prove that under certain conditions the application of the Unfold/Fold transformations preserves the notion of well-modedness. We also define a transformation of a definite program into term rewriting system and we establish the correctness of this transformation.

1 Introduction

The general aim of our research is the derivation of program using transformations. This method is fruitful for producing correct and efficient programs [8], [4], [3], [13], [15].

This study can be inserted within the context of formal program development. Program is derived by application of rules, starting from a formal specification. The rules must guarantee the correctness of the derived programs. Two problems arise: the rules have a low level of abstraction and the application by hand is error prone; high-level rules (strategies) and machine support (development of a system) are essential. This approach generally consists in beginning with a simple and straightforward specification and in transforming it into a more efficient program. Within this context our initial specification is made in terms of Horn clauses, our objective is to get, by successive applications of the transformations, a correct and more efficient program.

In addition to the theoretical aspects, we are interested in the experimental approach. In this sense, we develop the Spes-system.

This paper is organized as follows. In section 2 we give some preliminary definitions and notations; Section 3 is devoted to the problems of the transformational approach. In section 4 we describe the mode input-output and we define a notion of well-moded program; in section 5 we establish some results relating to the preservation of the well-moded notion. In section 6 we define a transformation of definite program into term rewriting system and we establish the correctness of this transformation.

2 Preliminaries and notations

In the following we assume that the reader is familiar with the basic terminology of first order logic such as term, atom, formula, substitution, matching, most general unifier (m.g.u) and so on. A *constant* is a 0-ary function symbol. A *term* is a variable or a constant or of the form $f(t_1, ..., t_n)$ where f is an n-ary function symbol and $t_1, ..., t_n$ are terms. An *atom* is of the form $p(t_1, ..., t_n)$, where p is an n-ary predicate symbol and $t_1, ..., t_n$ are terms.

We assume knowledge of semantics of Prolog, minimum Herbrand model, SLD-refutations [10], [2]. We adopt the following notations:

- *p, q, r, identifiers (plus,...)* for the predicate symbols
- *f, g, h, s* for the function symbols
- $0, a, b, \ldots$ for the constants
- *t, u* for the terms
- *v, x, y, z* for variables
- A, B for the atoms and Γ, Δ, Λ, Φ for ordered conjunctions of atoms, for example, let Γ be $B_1, \ldots, B_n$ where "," stands for the logical connector "and". A definite clause (or Horn clause) has the following form: $A \leftarrow \Gamma$. A is called the clauses's ***head*** and Γ the clause's ***body***.

  A definite program is a sequence of definite clauses.
- c for the clauses and $\Box$ for the empty clause.
- $\mathcal{V}(t)$ (*resp.* $\mathcal{V}(A)$) is the set of the variables occurring in the term t (*resp.* atom A)
- An atom A is linear for x if x has at most one occurrence in A.

  An atom A is linear if A is linear for all variable.
- If V is a countable set of variables and F a finite set of function symbols, $T_F(V)$ is the set of the terms built with the symbols of F and the symbols of V.

  A substitution σ is a morphism of $T_F(V)$, such that $x\sigma = x$ except for a finite set of variables. The application of σ to the term t is denoted by $t\sigma$. We denote a substitution σ by a set $\{(x_1/t_1), ..., (x_n/t_n)\}$, where each x_i is a variable and each t_i is a term such that x_i does not occur in t_i. The ***domain*** and the ***image*** of the substitution σ are respectively the sets $Dom(\sigma) = \{x_1, ..., x_n\}$ and $Im(\sigma) = \{t_1, ..., t_n\}$.

  A p_substitution is a substitution σ such that

  1. σ is idempotent i.e.: $\mathcal{V}(Im(\sigma)) \cap \mathcal{V}(Dom(\sigma)) = \emptyset$.
  2. $\forall\ x, y \in Dom(\sigma)\ \ x \neq y \Rightarrow \mathcal{V}(x\sigma) \cap \mathcal{V}(y\sigma) = \emptyset$.
  3. $\forall\ x \in Dom(\sigma)\ x\sigma$ is linear.
- We assume also that the reader is familiar with the notions of rewriting [7] such as rewriting rules, term rewriting system and derivation. We denote a rewriting rule by $t_L \rightarrow t_R$ where t_L and t_R are terms.

3 Problems

In this section we point out some problems which arise in the area of the program transformation.

3.1 The correctness of the transformations

An essential point in the program transformation is that the transformations must preserve the semantics of the programs. For the definite programs Tamaki and Sato have shown that the transformation of unfolding, folding and new definition preserve the least Herbrand model of the programs [15]. In this paper we define a transformation of definite programs into term rewrite systems and we show the correctness of this transformation.

3.2 The strategies

The transformation rules generally have a low level of abstraction, so it is essential to define some strategies to guide the application of the basic transformations. The problem is to get some recursive definitions, more precisely the problem is to find a sequence of unfolding which permits the folding. If it is impossible to fold it is sometimes interesting to make a generalization. Pettorossi and Proietti have studied such strategies based on the synchronization descent rule (a rule which selects the atoms to be unfolded) [13],[12]. We have defined such strategies based on a static analysis using schema [1].

3.3 The improvement of the efficiency

A crucial point remains the problem of efficiency. The objective of the transformation is to improve the efficiency of the programs, but to our knowledge there are no results concerning this point; it is a very hard task which also relates to the complexity of the logic programs.

3.4 The problem of the eureka

Experience shows in many cases that the efficiency of the programs is improved by the application of a property (i.e. eureka). These properties are generally inductive theorems. The first problem is the invention of such properties which is a very hard task. The second problem is to prove such properties; it is a question of theorem proving.

4 Mode input-output

In this section we introduce the mode input-output which is a static program property. It can be derived or verified by static analysis. This property is useful for the elaboration of strategies. Modes analysis allows us to distinguish the arguments of the predicates; some arguments will be *output* while others will be *input*. It is well known that the evaluation of a query of a given *Prolog* program depends on the positions of atoms in the body of clauses. For this purpose, we are interested in the *mode*. By analyzing the *mode* of a program we can describe the *flow of data* among the body atoms of its clauses. Much research has been devoted to the *modes*; some of them are involved in the area of optimization of compilers [5], [6], [11] others in the area of program transformations[14]. In the following section, we give some definitions.

Definition 4.1 (Mode of predicate)
Let p be a predicate symbol of arity n, a mode m for p is a n_tuple $m = (m_1, \ldots, m_n)$ *over the set* { *in, out*}. *An* $i \in \{1, \ldots, n\}$ *such that* $m_i = in$ (*resp.* $m_i = out$) *is called an input (resp. output) position for p.*

Notation 4.1
Let $p(t_1, \ldots, t_n)$ be an atom and $m = (m_1, \ldots, m_n)$ a given mode of p.

$$\mathcal{V}_{in}(p(t_1, \ldots, t_n)) = \bigcup_{1 \leq i \leq n \text{ and } m_i = in} \mathcal{V}(t_i)$$

$$\mathcal{V}_{out}(p(t_1, \ldots, t_n)) = \bigcup_{1 \leq i \leq n \text{ and } m_i = out} \mathcal{V}(t_i)$$

In $p(t_1, \ldots, t_n)$ an occurrence x in t_i is one out-occurrence (resp. in-occurrence) if $m_i = out$ (resp. $m_i = in$).

A predicate p with a mode m is called *moded*.

Definition 4.2 (Mode of clause and program)
A clause (resp. program) is called moded if all its predicates (resp. clauses) are moded.

Notation 4.2
We assume that the predicates have some modes in the form (in,..., in, out,..., out), we separate the input from the output by a semicolon. For example, the notation in the clause

$$plus(s(x), y; s(z)) \leftarrow plus(x, y; z)$$

means that the predicate *plus* has the mode (in, in, out).

$q(; x)$ (resp. $q(x;)$), denotes that the predicate q has the mode (*out*) (resp. (*in*)).

Definition 4.3 (Dependency relation)
Let $c : A \leftarrow A_1, \ldots, A_n$ *a moded clause, the relation* $\mathcal{D}_c$ *defined in the set* $\{A_1, \ldots, A_n\}$ *by*

$$A_i \; \mathcal{D}_c \; A_j \;\; ifandonlyif \;\; \mathcal{V}_{out}(A_i) \cap \mathcal{V}_{in}(A_j) \neq \emptyset$$

is the dependency relation of c w.r.t. a given mode.

Such a relation makes it possible to arrange the atoms in the body of the clauses. If two atoms A and B of the body of c are such that $A \; \mathcal{D}_c \; B$, the atom A is evaluated before the atom B. Indeed B uses in *input* positions data produced in *output* position by A. This mechanism is well known in functional programming, it is the composition of functions. In addition, by giving to a function ground terms in *input* positions, this function must produce ground results, by the notion of well-moded programs and clauses we capture this notion.

Definition 4.4 (well-moded clause)
Let $c: A \leftarrow A_1, ..., A_n$ *a moded clause, c is called well-moded if the following conditions hold:*

1. $\forall x \in \mathcal{V}_{in}(A)$, *all occurrences of* x *in the body of* c *are in-occurrences.*

2. $\forall x \in (\mathcal{V}(c) \setminus \mathcal{V}_{in}(A))$ x *has once only out-occurrence in the body of* c.

3. $\forall i \in [1,n], \forall x \in \mathcal{V}_{in}(A_i) \setminus \mathcal{V}_{in}(A)$ $(\exists j \in [1, i-1],\ x \in \mathcal{V}_{out}(A_j))$.

Example 4.1
The clause: $mul(x, s(y); v) \leftarrow mul(x, y; z)\ plus(z, x; v)$ is well-moded.

Property 4.1
If the clause c is well-moded, then the relation $\mathcal{D}_c$ *is without circuit.*

Proof
The proof of this property is obvious. ∎

Definition 4.5 (well-moded program)
A given program is called well-moded iff all its clauses are well-moded.

5 Transformations

Unfold/fold transformations were introduced by Burstall and Darlington [4] in the context of the functional languages and formalized by Tamaki and Sato [15] for logic ones.

5.1 Basic transformations

Our basic transformations are:

Definition 5.1 (Unfolding)
Unfolding consists in applying SLD-resolution to a clause w.r.t. an atom of its body. Let:

(c_1): $A \leftarrow \Gamma,\ B,\ \Delta$ *and*
(c_2): $C \leftarrow \Phi$

be two clauses such that there exists σ, *an mgu of* B *and* C*; the result of Unfolding the atom* B *with the clause* (c_2) *is the following clause*

(c_3): $(A \leftarrow \Gamma, \Phi, \Delta)\sigma$.

Definition 5.2 (Folding)
Folding consists in replacing an instance of the body of a clause by the corresponding head instance of this clause: Let

(c_1): $A \leftarrow \Gamma,\ \Delta,\ \Phi$ *and*
(c_2): $B \leftarrow \Lambda$

be two clauses and σ *a substitution such that* $\Lambda\sigma = \Delta$, *the Folding of* (c_2) *in* (c_1) *is the clause*

(c_3): $A \leftarrow \Gamma,\ B\sigma,\ \Phi$.

Definition 5.3 (Introduction)
This consists in the introduction of a new predicate in terms of already existing ones. Indeed we introduce a new clause of the form:

$p(t_1, ..., t_k) \leftarrow A_1, ..., A_n$ *where p is a new predicate symbol and* $A_1, ..., A_n$, $t_1, ..., t_k$ *uses symbols already existing.*

Definition 5.4 (Property)
Let P be a program, a property of P is a first order formula of the form:

$\forall x_1, ..., \forall x_n (\exists y_1, ..., \exists y_m \Delta \Leftarrow \exists z_1, ..., \exists z_k \Lambda)$ *where:*

$\{x_1, ..., x_n\} = \mathcal{V}(\Delta) \cap \mathcal{V}(\Lambda)$

$\{y_1, ..., y_m\} = \mathcal{V}(\Delta) \setminus \mathcal{V}(\Lambda)$

$\{z_1, ..., z_k\} = \mathcal{V}(\Lambda) \setminus \mathcal{V}(\Delta)$

which is valid in the least Herbrand model of P. We denote this property by $(\Delta \Leftarrow \Lambda)$.

Definition 5.5 (Applying property)
Let: $(c) : \; A \leftarrow \Gamma, \Delta', \Phi$ *be a clause and*

$(\Delta \Leftarrow \Lambda)$ *a property such that there exists* σ *such that* $\Delta\sigma = \Delta'$, *the result of the application of the property* $(\Delta \Leftarrow \Lambda)$ *on (c) is the clause*

$(c') : \; A \leftarrow \Gamma, \Lambda\sigma, \Phi.$

Definition 5.6 (Goal inversion)
Let $(c) : \; A \leftarrow \Gamma, B_1, B_2, \Delta$ *be a well-moded clause such that* $\forall x \in \mathcal{V}_{in}(B_2)$ *implies* $x \notin \mathcal{V}_{out}(B_1)$, *the clause, obtained by the inversion of the atoms* B_1, B_2, *is*

$(c') : \; A \leftarrow \Gamma, B_2, B_1, \Delta.$

5.2 The transformations preserve the well-moded notion

Proposition 5.1 (Folding)
Let

$c_1 : \; A \leftarrow \Gamma, \Delta, \Lambda$

$c_2 : \; B \leftarrow \Delta'$

two clauses such that:

- c_1 *et* c_2 *are well-moded w.r.t. a given mode m*
- *there exists a p_substitution* σ *such that* $\Delta'\sigma = \Delta$
- σ *substitutes distinct variables for the internal variables of* c_2, *and those variables do not occur in* A, Γ, Λ.
- $\mathcal{V}_{in}(B) \subset \mathcal{V}(\Delta')$
- *B is out-linear, i.e. B is linear for all* $x \in \mathcal{V}_{out}(B)$

$c_3 : \; A \leftarrow \Gamma, (B\sigma), \Lambda,$ *is well-moded w.r.t. the mode m.*

Proof
The proof of this proposition is a consequence of the following lemmas. ▌

Lemma 5.1
Let c be a well-moded clause w.r.t. a given mode m and a p_substitution σ, then the clause cσ is well-moded w.r.t. the mode m.

Proof
Let x be in $\mathcal{V}(c\sigma)$.

- If $x \in \mathcal{V}(c)$, x is invariant by σ (condition1 of the definition of p_substitution) therefore the set of the occurrences of x in c is identical to the set of occurrences of x in $c\sigma$. Then $c\sigma$ is well-moded.
- If $x \notin \mathcal{V}(c)$. $\exists\ z \in \mathcal{V}(c)$ such that $x \in \mathcal{V}(z\sigma)$.
  The number of the occurrences of z in c is identical to the number of occurrences of x in $c\sigma$ (condition 2 and 3 of p_substitution) and the the mode of those occurrences is preserved by the application of σ. $c\sigma$ is then well-moded.

∎

Lemma 5.2
Let $c_1 : A \leftarrow \Gamma,\ \Delta,\ \Lambda$ *and* $c_2 : B \leftarrow \Delta$ *be two well-moded clauses w.r.t. a given mode m and verifying the following conditions:*

1. $(\mathcal{V}(\Delta) \setminus \mathcal{V}(B)) \cap \mathcal{V}(A, \Gamma, \Lambda) = \emptyset$
2. *B is out-linear*
3. $\mathcal{V}_{in}(B) \subset \mathcal{V}(\Delta)$

Then $c_3 : A \leftarrow \Gamma,\ B,\ \Lambda$ *is well-moded w.r.t. the mode m.*

Remarks 5.1
The lemma does not hold if one of its conditions fails:

1. for the condition (1), let us consider the following example:
   $c_1 : p(x;y) \leftarrow r(x;z),\ q(z;y),\ w(z;)$
   $c_2 : q'(x;y) \leftarrow r(x;z),\ q(z;y)$
   c_1 and c_2 are well-moded. Whenever
   $c_3 : p(x;y) \leftarrow q'(x;y),\ w(z;)$ is not well-moded..
2. for the condition (2), let us consider the following example:
   $c_1 : p(x;y) \leftarrow r(x;y),\ q(z;)$
   $c_2 : w(z;z) \leftarrow q(z;),$
   c_1 and c_2 are well-moded. Whenever
   $c_3 : p(x;y) \leftarrow r(x;y),\ w(z;z)$ is not well-moded.
3. and for the condition (3), let us consider the following example:
   $c_1 : p(x;y) \leftarrow q(x;z),\ w(z;y)$
   $c_2 : r(z,t;y) \leftarrow w(z;y)$
   c_1 and c_2 are well-moded. Whenever
   $c_3 : p(x;y) \leftarrow q(x;z),\ r(z,t;y)$ is not well-moded.

Proof [lemma 5.2]
Let $c_3 : A \leftarrow \Gamma,\ B,\ \Lambda$ be a well-moded clause:

1. Let $x \in \mathcal{V}_{in}(A)$

   - c_1 is well-moded then the occurrences of x in Γ and Λ are *in*.
   - If $x \in \mathcal{V}(B)$
     let us suppose that $x \in \mathcal{V}_{out}(B)$. By hypothesis c_2 is well-moded then x has one occurrence out in Δ. Contradiction with the fact that $x \in \mathcal{V}_{in}(A)$ and c_1 is well-moded. Then all the occurrences of x in B are in.

2. We remark that the condition 1 of c_2 well-moded can be rewriten in

$$(1) \qquad \mathcal{V}_{in}(B) \cap \mathcal{V}_{out}(\Delta) = \emptyset$$

   And from c_2 well-moded:

$$(2) \qquad \mathcal{V}_{out}(B) \subset \mathcal{V}_{out}(\Delta)$$

   Let $x \in \mathcal{V}(c_3) \setminus \mathcal{V}_{in}(A)$ and let us prove: x has once only out-occurrence in Γ, B, Λ

   - If $x \in \mathcal{V}(c_1)$ x has once only out-occurrence in Γ, Δ, Λ (c_1 is well-moded);
     - if this out-ocurrence is in Γ, Λ: $x \notin \mathcal{V}_{out}(\Delta)$ according to (2) $x \notin \mathcal{V}_{out}(B)$, therefore x has once only out-occurrence in Γ, Δ, Λ.
     - if this out-occurrence is in Δ: $x \in \mathcal{V}_{out}(\Delta)$ and according to (1) $C \notin \mathcal{V}_{in}(B)$; if $x \in \mathcal{V}_{out}(B)$ the result holds else $x \notin \mathcal{V}(B)$; according to the hypothesis (1) of the lemma $x \notin \mathcal{V}(A, \Gamma, \Lambda)$ therefore x does not occur in c_3, then we have a contradiction.
   - If $x \notin \mathcal{V}_{in}(c_1)$, $x \notin \mathcal{V}(A, \Gamma, \Delta, \Lambda)$ therefore $x \in \mathcal{V}(B)$ and $x \notin \mathcal{V}_{in}(B)$ (hypothesis 3). finally $x \in \mathcal{V}_{out}(B)$ and as B is out-linear, x has once only out-occurence in Γ, B, Λ

3. Let $\Gamma = A_1, ..., A_{k-1}$, $B = A_k$ *and* $\Lambda = A_{k+1}, ..., A_n$.

   and $c_3 : A \leftarrow A_1, ..., A_{k-1}, A_k, A_{k+1}, ..., A_n$.

   Let $x \in \mathcal{V}_{in}(A_i) \setminus \mathcal{V}(A)$ and let us prove:

$$(3) \qquad \exists j \ 1 \leq j < i \qquad x \in \mathcal{V}_{out}(A_j)$$

   - If $i \leq k-1$ the existence of j for (3) is assured since c_1 is well-moded.
   - If $i = k$ $x \in \mathcal{V}_{in}(B)$ therefore $x \in \mathcal{V}(\Delta)$ (hypothesis 3 of lemma), and, as c_2 is well-moded, all the occurrences of x in Δ are *in*, and as c_1 is well-moded, for each occurrence in of x in an atom H of Δ there exists one occurrence out of x in an atom previous H in the body of c_1. This atom is necessarily an atom of Γ (since all the occurrences of x in Δ are in).

- If $i > k \quad x \in \mathcal{V}_{in}(\Lambda)$.
  As c_1 is well-moded (condition 3) we have:
  $x \in \mathcal{V}_{out}(\Gamma, \Lambda)$ *or* $x \in \mathcal{V}_{out}(\Delta)$. If $x \in \mathcal{V}_{out}(\Gamma, \Lambda)$ the result holds, else, let us suppose that $x \in \mathcal{V}_{out}(\Delta)$. According to (1) we have $x \notin \mathcal{V}_{in}(B)$. If $x \in \mathcal{V}_{out}(B)$, the result holds ($B = A_k$ *and* $k < i$) else $x \notin \mathcal{V}(B)$; by the hypothesis 1 of the lemma $x \notin \mathcal{V}(A, \Gamma, \Lambda)$, in contradiction with $x \in \mathcal{V}_{in}(\Lambda)$.

▌

Proposition 5.2 (Unfolding)
Let $c_1 : A \leftarrow \Gamma, B, \Lambda$
$c_2 : B' \leftarrow \Delta$, *be two well-moded clauses w.r.t. a given mode m and there exists* $\theta = mgu(B, B')$ *such that* θ *is a p_substitution and* $(c_1) \cap \mathcal{V}(c_2) = \emptyset$
then $c_3 : (A \leftarrow \Gamma, \Delta, \Lambda)\theta$
is well-moded w.r.t. the mode m.

Proof
By renaming we can have $\mathcal{V}(c_1) \cap \mathcal{V}(c_2) = \emptyset$. The proof of this proposition is a consequence of the lemma 5.1 and lemma 5.3▌

Lemma 5.3
Let $c_1 : A \leftarrow \Gamma, B, \Lambda$
$c_2 : B \leftarrow \Delta$,
be two well-moded clauses w.r.t. a given mode m such that
$(\mathcal{V}(c_1) \cap \mathcal{V}(c_2)) \subset \mathcal{V}(B)$.
then the clause
$c_3 : A \leftarrow \Gamma, \Delta, \Lambda$, *is well-moded w.r.t. the mode m.*

Proof
Similar to the proof of the lemma 5.2▌

Proposition 5.3 (Introduction of new definition)
The transformation introduction of new definition preserves the notion of well-moded if the introduced clause is well-moded w.r.t. the mode of the current program.

Proof Obvious▌

Proposition 5.4 (Goal inversion)
The transformation goal inversion preserves the notion of well-moded program.

Proof Obvious▌

6 Transformation of definite program into term rewriting system

In this section we define a transformation of definite program into term rewriting system. It is interesting to transform a logic program into a functional program since reduction is generally more efficient that resolution.

The definite programs we transform belong to a particular class of well-moded program. Firstly we introduce the notion of unary and simple mode, secondly we define the transformation, thirdly we state two propositions which establish the correctness of the transformation.

6.1 Unary mode and simple mode

Definition 6.1 (Unary mode of a predicate)
A mode m_p of a predicate p with arity $n+1$, is unary if and only $m_p = (in, \ldots, in, out)$.

We denote an atom $p(\overline{t}; u)$ where $\overline{t} = (t_1, \ldots, t_n)$.

The notion of unary mode can be easily extended to the clauses and the programs.

Definition 6.2 (Simple mode of a program)
Let P be a moded program, the mode of P is simple if for all atoms $p(\overline{t}; u_1, \ldots, u_k)$ appearing in the body of a clause of P, the terms u_i are variables.

Example 6.1
Let (P) be the following moded-program:

$$(P)\left\{\begin{array}{ll} plus(0, x; x) & \leftarrow \\ plus(s(x), y; s(z)) & \leftarrow plus(x, y; z) \\ sum\_int(0; 0) & \leftarrow \\ sum\_int(s(x); y) & \leftarrow sum\_int\_iter(x, s(x); y) \\ sum\_int\_iter(0, v; v) & \leftarrow \\ sum\_int\_iter(s(x), y; z) & \leftarrow plus(s(x), y; v),\ sum\_int\_iter(x, v; z) \end{array}\right.$$

$sum\_int(x, y)$ holds if and only if $y = \sum_{i=1}^{i=x} i$

$sum\_int\_iter(x, y, z)$ holds if and only if $z = \sum_{i=1}^{i=x} i + y$.

The mode of P is

- an unary mode because each predicate has unique output place.
- a simple mode because the terms which occur in the output places in the bodies of the clauses are variables.

Definition 6.3 (Transformable program)
Let P be a program, and let m_P be a mode of P, P is transformable w.r.t. m_P if the following conditions hold

1. *P is well-moded w.r.t m_P*
2. *m_P is unary*
3. *m_P is simple.*

6.2 The transformation

In this section we assume we have some transformable programs and we give the definition of the transformation.

Let c be a clause of a transformable program P. The transformation of c consists in applying the following algorithm on c.

Let (R_1) and (R_2) be the following rules

$$\frac{A \leftarrow \Gamma,\ p(\overline{t}; y)}{(A \leftarrow \Gamma)\{(y/\widetilde{p}(\overline{t}))\}} \quad (R_1)$$

$$\frac{p(\overline{t}; u) \leftarrow}{\widetilde{p}(\overline{t}) \rightarrow u} \quad (R_2)$$

The algorithm of transformation consists in the two following steps:

1. Applying the rule (R_1) while we do not get a unit clause. At each application of (R_1) we select an atom $p(\overline{t}; x)$ which has no predecessor by the relation $\mathcal{D}_c$.

2. Applying once the rule (R_2).

Remark 6.1
The transformation of a clause is a term rewriting rule.
By transforming all the clauses of a definite program we get a term rewriting system.
At each predicate symbol p of the definite program corresponds a functional symbol $\widetilde{p}$ of the term rewriting system.

Example 6.2
Let P be the program of the example 6.1

$$(P)\begin{cases} plus(0, x; x) \leftarrow \\ plus(s(x), y; s(z)) \leftarrow plus(x, y; z) \\ sum\_int(0; 0) \leftarrow \\ sum\_int(s(x); y) \leftarrow sum\_int\_iter(x, s(x); y) \\ sum\_int\_iter(0, y; y) \leftarrow \\ sum\_int\_iter(s(x), y; z) \leftarrow plus(s(x), y; v),\quad sum\_int\_iter(x, v; z) \end{cases}$$

The transformation of the clause
$sum\_int\_iter(s(x), y; z) \leftarrow plus(s(x), y; v),\ sum\_int\_iter(x, v; z)$

$$\frac{sum\_int\_iter(s(x), y; z) \leftarrow plus(s(x), y; v),\ sum\_int\_iter(x, v; z)}{sum\_int\_iter(s(x), y; z) \leftarrow\ sum\_int\_iter(x, \widetilde{plus}(s(x), y); z)} \quad (R_1)$$

$$\frac{sum\_int\_iter(s(x), y; z) \leftarrow\ sum\_int\_iter(x, \widetilde{plus}(s(x), y); z)}{sum\_int\_iter(s(x), y; \widetilde{sum\_int\_iter}(x, \widetilde{plus}(s(x), y))) \leftarrow} \quad (R_1)$$

$$\frac{sum\_int\_iter(s(x), y; \widetilde{sum\_int\_iter}(x, \widetilde{plus}(s(x), y))) \leftarrow}{\widetilde{sum\_int\_iter}(s(x), y) \rightarrow \widetilde{sum\_int\_iter}(x, \widetilde{plus}(s(x), y))} \quad (R_2)$$

The transformation of the definite program P is the following term rewriting system (E); it is obtained by transforming all the clauses of the definite program P.

$$
(E)\left\{\begin{array}{l}
\widetilde{plus}(0,x) \rightarrow x \\
\widetilde{plus}(s(x),y) \rightarrow s(\widetilde{plus}(x,y)) \\
\widetilde{sum\_int}(0) \rightarrow 0 \\
\widetilde{sum\_int}(s(x)) \rightarrow \widetilde{sum\_int\_iter}(x,s(x)) \\
\widetilde{sum\_int\_iter}(0,y) \rightarrow y \\
\widetilde{sum\_int\_iter}(s(x),y) \rightarrow \widetilde{sum\_int\_iter}(x,\widetilde{plus}(s(x),y))
\end{array}\right.
$$

6.3 Correctness of the transformation

In this section we establish the correctness of the transformation.

Proposition 6.1
Let P be a transformable program and E the transformed term rewriting system of P. If we have the SLD-refutation in P

$$p(\bar{t};u) \overset{c_1,\theta_1}{\rightsquigarrow} \ldots \overset{c_m,\theta_m}{\rightsquigarrow} \square$$

where c_i are some clauses of P and θ_i some substitutions, then there exists a derivation in E of the following form

$$\widetilde{p}(\bar{t})\theta_1 \ldots \theta_m \rightarrow \ldots \rightarrow u\theta_1 \ldots \theta_m$$

Proof
The proof proceeds by induction on the length of the SLD-refutation [1].∎

Before establishing the converse of this proposition, we will present three counter-examples which show that the converse does not hold.

Example 6.3
Let P_1 be the following transformable program defined as follows :

$$
(P_1)\left\{\begin{array}{l}
p(x;y) \leftarrow q(x;z),\ r(x;y) \\
q(a;b) \leftarrow \\
r(b;a) \leftarrow
\end{array}\right.
$$

The transformation of P_1 produces the term rewriting system E_1

$$
(E_1)\left\{\begin{array}{l}
\widetilde{p}(x) \rightarrow \widetilde{r}(x) \\
\widetilde{q}(a) \rightarrow b \\
\widetilde{r}(b) \rightarrow a
\end{array}\right.
$$

In E_1 there is the derivation $\widetilde{p}(b) \rightarrow \widetilde{r}(b) \rightarrow a$

but in P_1 there is no SLD-refutation starting from $p(b,a)$, because it is impossible to eliminate the atoms in the form $q(b,\_)$ by resolution.

Let P_2 be the following definite program

$$
(P_2)\left\{\begin{array}{ll}
p(x;y) & \leftarrow q(x;z),\ r(z,z;y) \\
q(a;a) & \leftarrow \\
q(a;b) & \leftarrow \\
r(a,b;a) & \leftarrow
\end{array}\right.
$$

P_2 is transformable.
The transformation of P_2 gives the system E_2

$$(E_2)\left\{\begin{array}{ll}\widetilde{p}(x) & \rightarrow \widetilde{r}(\widetilde{q}(x),\widetilde{q}(x))\\ \widetilde{q}(a) & \rightarrow a\\ \widetilde{q}(a) & \rightarrow b\\ \widetilde{r}(a,b) & \rightarrow a\end{array}\right.$$

in E_2 we have the following derivation

$$\widetilde{p}(a) \rightarrow \widetilde{r}(\widetilde{q}(a),\widetilde{q}(a)) \rightarrow \widetilde{r}(a,\widetilde{q}(a)) \rightarrow \widetilde{r}(a,b) \rightarrow a$$

but in P_2 there is no SLD-refutation of the form

$$p(a,a) \rightsquigarrow \ldots \rightsquigarrow \square$$

We note here that the term $\widetilde{q}(a)$ has two normal forms a and b in E_2.
Let P_3 be the following definite program

$$(P_3)\left\{\begin{array}{ll} p(x,y;z) & \leftarrow q(x;u),\ r(x,y,u;z)\\ r(x,x,y;x) & \leftarrow\end{array}\right.$$

P_3 is transformable.
The transformation gives the term rewriting system E_3.

$$(E_3)\left\{\begin{array}{l}\widetilde{p}(x,y) \rightarrow \widetilde{r}(x,y,\widetilde{q}(x))\\ \widetilde{r}(x,x,y) \rightarrow x\end{array}\right.$$

Let a be a constant, in E_3 we have the following derivation

$$\widetilde{p}(a,a) \rightarrow \widetilde{r}(a,a,\widetilde{q}(a)) \rightarrow a$$

but in P_3 there is no SLD-refutation starting from $p(a,a,a)$

$$p(a,a,a) \rightsquigarrow \ldots \rightsquigarrow \square$$

The three previous examples show that we need some additional conditions to establish the converse of the proposition 6.1.

Proposition 6.2
Let P be a transformable *definite program with respect to a mode, let $Pred$ be the set of the predicate symbols of P and let $\widetilde{Pred} = \{\widetilde{p} \mid p \in Pred\}$. Let E be the term rewriting system resulting from the transformation of P.*

We assume the following hypothesis

- *For all the clause $c\ :\ A_0 \leftarrow A_1,\ldots,A_n$ of P, the dependency relation $\mathcal{D}_c$ defined on the set $A_0,A_1,\ldots,A_n$ is connex.*
- *E is canonical (i.e. E is has the property of Church-Rosser and E is nœtherian).*
- *All the rules $t_L \rightarrow t_R$ of E are such that $\mathcal{V}(t_L) = \mathcal{V}(t_R)$.*

then for every derivation of the form

$$\widetilde{p}(\overline{t}) \rightarrow \ldots \rightarrow u$$

and such that no symbol of $\widetilde{Pred}$ occurs in $\overline{t}$ and in u
there exists a SLD-refutation of the form

$$p(\overline{t},u) \rightsquigarrow \ldots \rightsquigarrow \square$$

Proof
The proof proceeds by induction on the length of the derivation [1]∎

7 Implementation

The work on Spes was started in 1987. Spes is implemented in CAML [9] and it runs on SUN3 and SUN4 workstations under the Unix Operating system.

Spes system makes it possible to define some specifications in terms of definite programs and to apply on them the basic transformations. Some tactics have been programmed. Some algorithms, which make it possible to infer automatically the types and the modes of the programs, have been implemented.

A graphical interface in Xwindows system is realized. It allows us to display the development tree, representing the history of the transformation process. A documentation about the implementation of the system is available on line and can be produced automatically. Ten thousand CAML lines code are developed.

We have also developed a high level language, which provides an interesting environment to define the transformations and to generate automatically the corresponding CAML functions.

8 Conclusion

In this article, we have defined the notion of well-moded program, and we have established some sufficient conditions for the preservation of this notion. These modes allow also the characterization of definite programs which can be transformed into term rewriting systems.

The notion of well-modedness must also permits the study of the termination of the transformed logic programs. Our further work is in this direction.

Acknowledgements

We would like to thank the referees for their helpful comments.

References

[1] F. Alexandre. Transformations de programmes logiques. Thèse de l'université de Nancy I, fevrier 1991.

[2] K.R. Apt and M.H Van Emden. Contribution to the theory of logic programming. *Journal of the Association for Computing Machinery*, 29(3):841–862, 1982.

[3] R.S. Bird. The promotion and accumulation strategies in transformational programming. *ACM TOPLAS*, 6(4):487–504, 1984.

[4] R.M Burstall and J.A Darlington. Transformation system for developing recursive programs. *Journal of the Association for Computing Machinery*, 24(1):44–67, 1977.

[5] S.K. Debray and D.S. Warren. Detection and optimization of functional computations in prolog. In E. Shapiro, editor, *Proceedings of the Third International Conference on Logic Programming, London*, volume 225 of *Lecture Notes in Computer Science*, pages 490–504. Springer-Verlag, 1986.

[6] S.K. Debray and D.S. Warren. Automatic mode inference for logic programs. *Journal of Logic Programming*, 5:207–229, 1988.

[7] N. Dershowitz and J. P. Jouannaud. *Rewriting systems.* Handbook of Computer Science. North Holland, 1989. To be published.

[8] M.S. Feather. A survey and classification of some program transformation techniques. In *Proc. TC2 IFIP Working Conference on Program Specification and Transformation, Bad-Tölz, F.R.G*, 1986.

[9] Projet Formel. *The CAML Reference Manual Version 2.6.* Inria, March 1989.

[10] J.W. Lloyd. *Foundations of Logic Programming.* Springer Verlag, 1988.

[11] C. S. Mellish. Some global optimizations for a prolog compiler. *Journal of Logic Programming*, 1:43–66, 1985.

[12] A. Pettorossi and M. Proietti. The automatic construction of logic programs. In *IFIP WG2.1 Meeting*, january 1989. Preliminary Version.

[13] A. Pettorossi and M. Proietti. Decidability results and characterization of strategies for the development of logic programs. In G. Levi and M. Martelli, editors, *6th International Conference on Logic Programming*, Lisbon (Portugal), 1989. MIT Press.

[14] U. S. Reddy. Transformation of logic programs into functional programs. In *International Symposium on Logic Programming, Atlantic City*, pages 187–196, 1984.

[15] H. Tamaki and T. Sato. Unfold/fold transformation of logic programs. In *Proceedings of the 2nd International Logic Programming Conference, Uppsala*, 1984.

Appendix: An example of a derivation with the Spes-system

In this appendix we present a session with the Spes-system.
Let SUM_INT be the following program :

$$(SUM\_INT)\left\{\begin{array}{lll}(1) & sum\_int(n,v) & \leftarrow list\_int(n,l),\ sum(l,v)\\ (2) & list\_int(0,nil) & \leftarrow\\ (3) & list\_int(s(n),cons(s(n),l)) & \leftarrow list\_int(n,l)\\ (4) & sum(nil,0) & \leftarrow\\ (5) & sum(cons(x,l),y) & \leftarrow sum(l,z),\ plus(z,x,y)\\ (6) & plus(0,x,x) & \leftarrow\\ (7) & plus(s(x),y,s(z)) & \leftarrow plus(x,y,z)\end{array}\right.$$

In this program 0 and s are the constructors of the integers, *nil* and *cons* are the constructors of the lists. The meaning of the predicates are the following :

sum_int(n, v) holds if and only if $v = \sum_{i=1}^{i=n} i$
list_int(n, l) holds if and only if l is the list of the n first integers.
sum(l, v) holds if and only if v is the sum of the integers of the list l.
plus(x, y, z) holds if z is the sum of x and y.
In the following session 0() is the constant 0 and nil() is the constant nil.

```
(* The initial program *)

1  sum_int(n,v)<-- list_int(n,l) sum(l,v)
2  list_int(0(),nil())<--
3  list_int(s(n),cons(s(n),l))<-- list_int(n,l)
4  sum(nil(),0())<--
5  sum(cons(x,l),y)<-- sum(l,z) plus(z,x,y)
6  plus(0(),x,x)<--
7  plus(s(x),y,s(z))<-- plus(x,y,z)
```

The first objective of the transformation is to eliminate the predicate *list_int* and to avoid the construction of the list l. To achieve this objective we seek a recursive definition of the predicate *sum_int* by applying the transformations of unfolding and folding.

We only write the new clauses which are generated at each step of the transformation process.

The unfolding transformation consists in applying the SLD-resolution. The second argument of the function "unfold" is the number of the selected clause, the first argument is the number of the selected atom in the body of this clause.

```
#unfold 1 1;;
8  sum_int(0(),v)<-- sum(nil(),v)
9  sum_int(s(n),v)<-- list_int(n,l) sum(cons(s(n),l),v)


#unfold 2 9;;
10  sum_int(s(n),v)<-- list_int(n,v1) sum(v1,z) plus(z,s(n),v)
```

The folding transformation consists in replacing an instance of the body of a clause by the corresponding instance of the head of this clause.

In the body of the clause (10) "list_int(n,v1) sum(v1,z)" is an instance of the body of the clause (1), then it is possible to fold (1) in (10)

```
#fold 1 10;;
11  sum_int(s(n),v1)<-- sum_int(n,z) plus(z,s(n),v1)
```

By unfolding the atom of the clause (8) we get the terminal case for the definition of the predicate sum_int.

```
#unfold 1 8;;
12  sum_int(0(),0())<--
```

The current program is the following

```
2  list_int(0(),nil())<--
3  list_int(s(n),cons(s(n),l))<-- list_int(n,l)
4  sum(nil(),0())<--
5  sum(cons(x,l),y)<-- sum(l,z) plus(z,x,y)
6  plus(0(),x,x)<--
7  plus(s(x),y,s(z))<-- plus(x,y,z)
11  sum_int(s(n),v1)<-- sum_int(n,z) plus(z,s(n),v1)
12  sum_int(0(),0())<--
```

In this program the predicate sum_int does not use the predicates list_int and sum, so we can eliminate the clauses 2,3,4 and 5.

```
#eliminate [2;3;4;5];;

6  plus(0(),x,x)<--
7  plus(s(x),y,s(z))<-- plus(x,y,z)
11  sum_int(s(v2),v1)<-- sum_int(v2,z) plus(z,s(v2),v1)
12  sum_int(0(),0())<--
```

We note that the definition of the predicate sum_int is not tail-recursive. The next objective is to define a new predicate in a tail-recursive form.

We define the new predicate sum_int_iter.

```
#add_new_clause << sum_int_iter(n,y,z) <-- sum_int(n,v) plus(v,y,z) >>;;
13  sum_int_iter(n,y,z)<-- sum_int(n,v) plus(v,y,z)
```

The objective is to get a recursive definition of sum_int_iter by application of unfolding and folding.

```
#unfold 1 13;;
14 sum_int_iter(s(v3),u,v1)<-- sum_int(v3,z) plus(z,s(v3),v2) plus(v2,u,v1)
15  sum_int_iter(0(),u,v1)<-- plus(0(),u,v1)
```

We apply the property number (2) which expresses the associativity of plus:

```
#display_list_of_properties();;
1  plus(x,y,z) <== plus(y,x,z)
2  plus(x,y,v) plus(v,z,w) <== plus(y,z,v1) plus(x,v1,w)
3  plus(y,z,v1) plus(x,v1,w) <== plus(x,y,v) plus(v,z,w)

#app_prop 2 14;;
16  sum_int_iter(s(v3),u,v1)<-- sum_int(v3,z) plus(s(v3),u,y) plus(z,y,v1)


#fold 13 16;;
17  sum_int_iter(s(z),v1,v2)<-- sum_int_iter(z,y,v2) plus(s(z),v1,y)
```

By unfolding the atom of the clause (15) we get the terminal case of the definition of sum_int_iter:

```
#unfold 1 15;;
18  sum_int_iter(0(),u,u)<--
```

By folding the clause (13) in the clause (11) we establish the link between the old predicate sum_int and the new sum_int_iter:

```
#fold 13 11;;
19  sum_int(s(v2),v1)<-- sum_int_iter(v2,s(v2),v1)
```

We get the following program:

```
6  plus(0(),x,x)<--
7  plus(s(x),y,s(z))<-- plus(x,y,z)
12  sum_int(0(),0())<--
17  sum_int_iter(s(z),v1,v2)<-- sum_int_iter(z,y,v2) plus(s(z),v1,y)
18  sum_int_iter(0(),u,u)<--
19  sum_int(s(v2),v1)<-- sum_int_iter(v2,s(v2),v1)
```

We compute the mode of the predicate sum_int_iter in (19). Then we order the atoms of the body of the clause (17) such that the clause (17) is well-moded.

```
#mode_clause  [("sum_int",[in;out])] 19;;
[[("sum_int",[in; out]);
  ("sum_int_iter",[in; in; out])]] :
 (string * mode list) list list

#echange 1 2 17;;
17  sum_int_iter(s(z),v1,v2)<-- plus(s(z),v1,y) sum_int_iter(z,y,v2)
```

The current program is the following:

```
6  plus(0(),x,x)<--
7  plus(s(x),y,s(z))<-- plus(x,y,z)
12  sum_int(0(),0())<--
19  sum_int(s(v2),v1)<-- sum_int_iter(v2,s(v2),v1)
18  sum_int_iter(0(),u,u)<--
17  sum_int_iter(s(z),v1,v2)<-- plus(s(z),v1,y) sum_int_iter(z,y,v2)
```

This program is well-moded, the next step of this session consists in transforming this program into a rewriting rules system. We get the following rewriting rules system :

```
plus3(0(),x) --> x
plus3(s(x),y)  --> s(plus3(x,y))
sum_int2(0())  --> 0()
sum_int2(s(v2))  --> sum_int_iter3(v2,s(v2))
sum_int_iter3(0(),u) --> u
sum_int_iter3(s(z),v1) --> sum_int_iter3(z,plus3(s(z),v1))
```

Abstract Interpretation and recursive behaviour of logic programs*

Christophe LECOUTRE
Philippe DEVIENNE
Patrick LEBEGUE

LIFL (Laboratoire d'Informatique Fondamentale de Lille),
USTL (Université des Sciences et Techniques de Lille-Flandres-Artois),
59655 Villeneuve d'Ascq cedex, FRANCE
{Lecoutre,Devienne,Lebegue}@lifl.lifl.fr

Abstract

We propose a general abstract interpretation based on the recursive behaviour study of Prolog programs. This abstract interpretation allows both the data-flow analysis of a program execution and the automatic derivation of some program properties.

First, we introduce a new notion: the limited-unfolding loop (abbreviated to lul). Roughly speaking, a tree t satisfies a lul m iff the leaf of the branch corresponding to the unfolding of the loop m is labelled with a constant. Instead of a term-groundedness analysis, our study can be seen as a "branch-groundedness" analysis. A finite set of luls can be regarded as a type which may be associated with a variable. Thus, a new algebra of atoms is built and substitution, unification (lub) and anti-unification (glb) operations are redefined in an easy way.

Then, a general abstract resolution (called abstract OLDT resolution) based on the work of H. Tamaki and T. Sato is presented. This abstract resolution always terminates and allows the collection of some information about the concrete resolution (i.e., the standard Prolog interpretation) of all program.

The three stages for our Prolog program abstract interpretation are: 1) computation of a finite set of "significant" luls by looking into the structure of a given Prolog program. 2) abstract resolution from a given call-pattern. 3) analysis of the abstract structure (result of the previous step) for establishing properties like, e.g., solution pattern(s), termination, boundedness, determinism, complexity, ...

1 Introduction

The recursive process of logic programming is a fundamental concept. A program can be viewed as a black box (figure 1), with some input and some output, and inside of which a possibly very complicated processing may be performed. The complexity of the

* This work is supported by the "GRECO de la programmation du CNRS"

program execution clearly depends on loops occurring during this execution. A good knowledge of the looping processes allows, from an input pattern, inferring behavioural properties like termination, complexity, parallelism, ... and an output pattern.

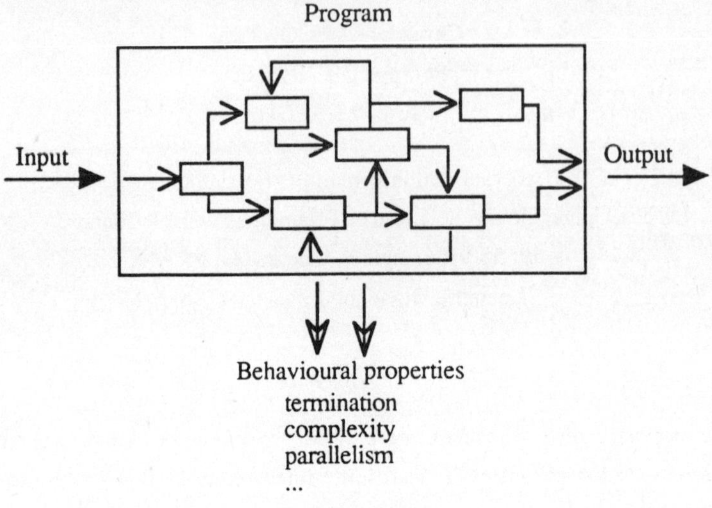

Figure 1

Several works have already been devoted to the recursivity in logic programming [Dev 88a, Dev 88b, DVB 90, Leb 88]. By way of abstract interpretation, we wish to study this concept.

The reader is expected to be familiar with some basic logic programming notions. Some proofs and some heuristic algorithms are omitted in this paper but are fully described in the following technical report [LDL 91].

2 Extension of the usual algebra

We introduce a variable typing in order to get abstractions of some sets of atoms. These abstractions will allow deriving some relevant properties. The usual algebra is extended via the introduced variable typing.

2.1 Some notations

V denotes a countable set of variables, V = {X,Y,...}. F denotes a finite set of function symbols, F = {a,b,...,f,g,...}. P denotes a finite set of predicate symbols, P = {p,q,...}. Note that variables are capital letters whereas function or predicate symbols are small letters.

Term(F,V) (resp. Term(F)) denotes the set of finite and infinite trees, called terms (resp. ground terms), built from F and V (resp. F). Atom(P,F,V) (resp. Atom(P,F)) denotes the set of finite and infinite trees, called atoms (resp. ground atoms), built from P, F and V (resp. P and F). Subs(F,V) (resp. Subs(F)) denotes the set of mappings, called substitutions (resp. ground substitutions), from V to Term(F,V) (resp. Term(F)). Let σ be a substitution, $Dom(\sigma) = \{X \in V \text{ such that } X \neq \sigma(X)\}$.

C represents the alphabet, each letter of which is a pair (f,i) denoted f_i such that f is a function symbol with a non-null arity and i is an integer designating the ith son of f. An elementary path m is a word built from C.

2.2 Variable typing

Let us consider the following program:

```
list([]) ←
list([X|L]) ← list(L).
← list(L')
```

Some tools as the weighted oriented graphs [Dev 88a, Dev 88b, Leb 88] can give some information about the recursive behaviour of Prolog programs. For instance in the weighted oriented graph attached to the second clause of the preceding program (figure 2), the positive loop indicates that at each recursive step an element of the list is removed.

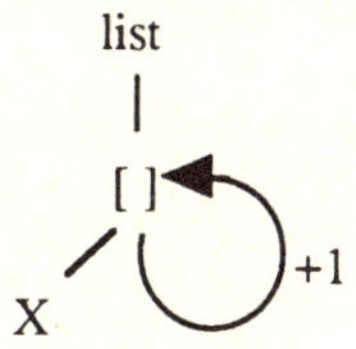

Figure 2

As the variable L' is free, it is clear that the program does not terminate. But we can ask ourselves which is the "minimal" constraint that can make the termination possible. We submit an answer: the variable L' can only be substituted by a term for which a function symbol different from [] appears (at a finite depth) on the rightmost branch (figure 3).

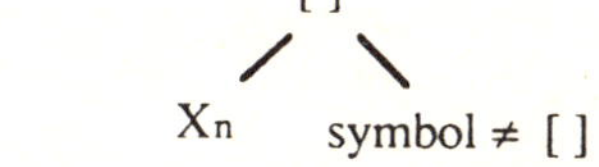

Figure 3

In fact, the basic information is the weighted oriented graph loop, that is the elementary path $[]_2$ composed of the node labelled with [] and the edge which connects this node to its second son. This loop (or this looping-path) is called a limited-unfolding loop (abbreviated to lul).

A certain parallelism can be made between the closure notion and the lul notion. The latter is a refinement of the former. Instead of speaking about term-groundedness, we can roughly speak about "branch-groundedness" (figure 4).

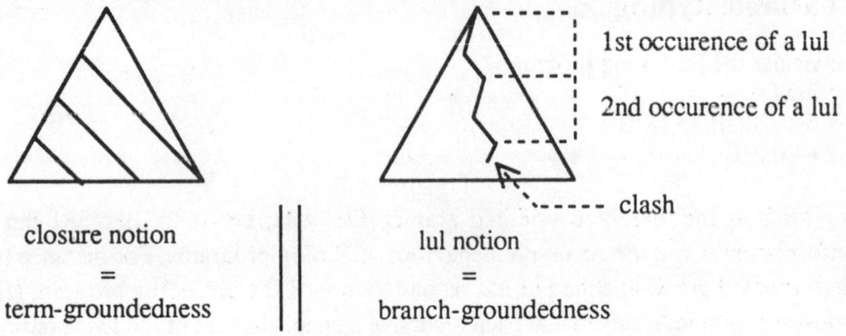

Figure 4

Each triangle represents an atom. Notice that the closure notion concerns the whole atom whereas the lul notion concerns only a precise branch of the atom.

Given a finite set L of luls, each subset of L corresponds to a type which may be associated with a variable.

<u>Notation</u>

L denotes a finite set of luls.

T denotes a finite set of types, $T = 2^L$.

Definition 1

Type is a mapping from V to T which maps a variable into its type.

Do understand the lul semantics: if a lul m belongs to the type of a variable X, this means that for any ground substitution of X, the loop m is unfolded in a finite way.

For example assume that $L = \{s_1,[]_2\}$ where s is a unary function symbol and [] a binary function symbol, $T = \{\emptyset,\{s_1\},\{[]_2\},\{s_1,[]_2\}\}$. Let us consider the atom P([A|X]) such that Type(X) = $\{[]_2\}$, this atom may generate: P([A]),P([A,B]),... P([a]),P([a,b]),... P([s(X)]),P([s(X),t(a,Y)]),... i.e., all atoms which respect the following restriction: the list of elements can never be infinite. Let us consider the atom P(X) such that Type(X) = $\{s_1\}$, this atom may generate: P(0),P(s(0)),... P(a),P(s(a)),... P(f(b)),P(s(t(Y)),... i.e., all atoms which respect the following restriction: the sequence of the function symbol s can never be infinite.

The introduced variable typing allows deriving some relevant program properties. For instance, if Type(L') = $\{[]_2\}$ we can deduce that for any concretization of L', i.e., any correct (see definition 2) substitution of the variable L' by an untyped term, the previous program terminates and the resolution complexity is bound to $|[]_2|_L$ where $|[]_2|_L$ denotes the length of the unfolding of the lul $[]_2$ attached to the variable L.

2.3 New algebra

Now, we can extend the usual algebra by considering the variable typing. Term(F,V,L) denotes the set of finite and infinite trees built from F, V and L. Atom(P,F,V,L) denotes the set of finite and infinite trees built from P, F, V and L. Subs(F,V,L) denotes the set of mappings from V×T to Term(F,V,L).

A variable X without type is equivalent to the variable X with an empty type (i.e., Type(X) = Ø). As it is always possible to associate a variable X with an empty type, by extension we have:

- Term(F) $\subseteq$ Term(F,V) $\subseteq$ Term(F,V,L)
- Atom(P,F) $\subseteq$ Atom(P,F,V) $\subseteq$ Atom(P,F,V,L)
- Subs(F) $\subseteq$ Subs(F,V) $\subseteq$ Subs(F,V,L)

A term (resp. an atom, a substitution) is represented as usually. However, information about type of the term variables is added. This information is represented by a set of pairs (variable,type of the variable) such that the variable belongs to the term and that the type of the variable is not an empty type.

We are only interested in some substitutions: the correct substitutions.

Definition 2

Let $\sigma \in$ Subst(F,V,L),

σ is correct iff $\forall X \in Dom(\sigma)$ and $\forall m \in Type(X)$, correct(m,σ(X))

where correct(m,t) represents a boolean operator defined as follows:

1 $correct(f_i.m, f(t_1,t_2,\ldots,t_n))$	$= correct(m.f_i,t_i)$
2 $correct(f_i.m, g(t_1,t_2,\ldots,t_n))$	= *true*
3 $correct(f_i.m, X')$	= *true if* $m' = f_i.m \in Type(X')$
	= *false otherwise*

Example

$\sigma = \{X/a, Y/g(a,Y')\}$ / $Type_\sigma = \{X/\{f_1\}, Y/\{g_2\}, Y'/\{g_2\}\}$ is correct.

$\beta = \{X/f(X'), Y/b\}$ / $Type_\beta = \{X/\{f_1\}, Y/\{g_2\}\}$ is not correct because $f_1 \notin Type(X')$.

From now on, we will only consider the correct substitutions. $\leq$ is a partial ordering on Atom(P,F,V,L). We keep the usual definition:

Definition 3

Let t and t' $\in$ Atom(P,F,V,L),

$t \leq t'$ iff $\exists \sigma \in$ Subst(F,V,L) such that $\sigma(t) = t'$

$t \cong t'$ iff $t \leq t'$ and $t \leq t'$

Henceforth, we consider Atom(P,F,V,L) modulo $\cong$ and enriched with a top element ^{T}, so this set is noted Atom(P,F,V,L)$^{T}/_{\cong}$.

The definitions related to the unification of two atoms are extended quite naturally to the new algebra, so we omit to recall them. On the other hand, we give the description of the extended unification algorithm (see appendix A) and an example.

Example

Let $t = app([],L,L) / Type_t = \{\emptyset\}$.

Let $t' = app(L1,L2,L3) / Type_{t'} = \{L1/\{[]_2\}, L2/\{[]_2\}\}$.

The application of the unification algorithm yields:

a) the most general unifier α

$$\alpha = \{L1/[], L/L3', L2/L3', L3/L3'\} / Type_\alpha = \{L1/\{[]_2\}, L2/\{[]_2\}, L3'/\{[]_2\}\}$$

b) the unified atom u

$$u = app([],L3',L3') / Type_u = \{L3'/\{[]_2\}\}$$

In a same way, the definitions related to the anti-unification of two atoms are extended quite naturally to the new algebra, so we omit to recall them. On the other hand, we give the description of the extended anti-unification algorithm (see appendix B) and an example.

Example

Let $L = \{[]_2\}$, it implies that $T = \{\emptyset,[]_2\}$.

Let $t = app([],L,L) / Type_t = \{\emptyset\}$.

Let $t' = app([X|L1],L2,[X|L3]) / Type_{t'} = \{L1/\{[]_2\}, L2/\{[]_2\}\}$.

The application of the anti-unification algorithm yields:

a) the most specific anti-unifier (β,β')

$$\beta = \{U/[], V/L, W/L\} / Type_\beta = \{U/\{[]_2\}\},$$

$$\beta' = \{U/[X|L1], V/L2, W/[X|L3]\} / Type_{\beta'} = \{U/\{[]_2\}, L1/\{[]_2\}, L2/\{[]_2\}\}$$

b) the anti-unified atom a

$$a = app(U,V,W) / Type_a = \{U/\{[]_2\}\}$$

Now that both operations of unification and anti-unification are defined, we can deduce that $(Atom(P,F,V,L)^T/_{\equiv},\leq)$ forms a complete lattice.

Theorem 4

$(Atom(P,F,V,L)^T/_{\equiv},\leq)$ is a complete lattice

Proof

Given a (possibly infinite) set S of atoms,

a) lub (least upper bound)

If there exists two atoms t and t' in S such that t and t' are not unifiable then ^{T} represents the lub of S, otherwise an atom u which is the unified atom of S represents the lub of S.

b) glb (greatest lower bound)

The anti-unified atom of S represents the glb of t and t'.

3 Abstract interpretation definition

Many studies [Bru 91, Cor 89, JS 87, MS 88, Mel 86] have been presented, all derive from the setting of P. Cousot and R. Cousot [CC 77]. An abstract interpretation is described by a 6-tuple $((2^{\mathbb{D}},\subseteq),(\mathbb{A},\leq),concr,abs,\mathbb{F},\mathbb{P})$:

- $\mathbb{D}$ is the concrete domain ($(2^{\mathbb{D}},\subseteq)$ denotes a partially ordered set)
- $\mathbb{A}$ is the abstract domain ($(\mathbb{A},\leq)$ denotes a partially ordered set)
- concr: $\mathbb{A} \rightarrow 2^{\mathbb{D}}$ is the monotonic concretization function
- abs: $2^{\mathbb{D}} \rightarrow \mathbb{A}$ is the monotonic abstraction function such that
  a) $\forall$ a $\in \mathbb{A}$, a = abs(concr(a))
  b) $\forall$ S $\in 2^{\mathbb{D}}$, S $\subseteq$ concr(abs(S))
- $\mathbb{F}$: $\mathbb{D} \rightarrow 2^{\mathbb{D}}$ is the concrete calculus
- $\mathbb{P}$: $\mathbb{A} \rightarrow 2^{\mathbb{A}}$ is the abstract calculus such that
  c) $\forall$ a $\in \mathbb{A}$, $\mathbb{F}$(concr(a)) $\subseteq$ concr($\mathbb{P}$(a))

The properties a) and b) mean the adjointness of the concretization and abstraction functions and the property c) means the safeness of the abstract calculus. Note that less restrictive conditions could have been imposed.

Now, we are going to define our abstract interpretation. First, we give the definition of the set of Herbrand atoms, denoted hatom, associated with an atom and with a set of atoms.

Definition 5

Let $t \in Atom(P,F,V,L)^T/_{\equiv}$, $hatom(t) = \{t' \in Atom(P,F)^T \,/\, t' \geq t\}$

Let $S \subseteq Atom(P,F,V,L)^T/_{\equiv}$, $hatom(S) = \cup \{hatom(t) \,/\, t \in S\}$

Then, we introduce a new partial ordering.

Definition 6

Let S and S' $\subseteq Atom(P,F,V,L)$,

$S \ll S' \Leftrightarrow hatom(S) \subseteq hatom(S')$

$S \approx S' \Leftrightarrow hatom(S) = hatom(S')$

We assume that F contains at least two elements, as a result: $Atom(P,F,V,L)^T/_{\equiv} = Atom(P,F,V,L)^T/_{\approx}$ and $(Atom(P,F,V,L)^T/_{\approx},\ll)$ forms a complete lattice inverted with respect to $(Atom(P,F,V,L)^T/_{\equiv},\leq)$. Thus for the new partial ordering ($\ll$), $\wedge$ denotes the meet operator and $\vee$ the join operator.

- $\mathbb{D}$, the concrete domain, refers to $Atom(P,F,V)^T/_{\equiv}$
- $\subseteq$, the partial ordering on $2^{\mathbb{D}}$, refers to $\ll$

- $\mathbb{A}$, the abstract domain, refers to $\text{Atom(P,F,V,L)}^{\text{T}}/_{\cong}$
- $\leq$, the partial ordering on $\mathbb{A}$, refers to «
- concr, the monotonic concretization function, is defined as follows:

Definition 7

Let $t \in A$, $concr(t) = hatom(t)$

Let $S \subseteq A$, $concr(S) = hatom(S)$

The concretization function is monotonic because for every atom t belonging to $\mathbb{A}$, t ≈ concr(t).

- abs, the monotonic abstraction function, is defined as follows:

Definition 8

Let $S \in 2^{D}$, $abs(S) = \wedge \{t \in S\}$

The properties a) and b) hold. Proofs are omitted.

Property 9

Let $t \in A$, $t \approx abs(concr(t))$

Let $S \in 2^{D}$, S « $concr(abs(S))$

- $\mathbb{F}$, the concrete calculus, refers to the concrete resolution (i.e., the standard Prolog interpretation). Let t ∈ $\mathbb{A}$, $\mathbb{F}$(t) denotes the set of success obtained by the standard Prolog interpretation.
- $\mathbb{P}$, the abstract calculus, refers to the abstract resolution (i.e., the abstract OLDT resolution). Let t ∈ $\mathbb{A}$, $\mathbb{P}$(t) denotes the set of success obtained by the abstract OLDT resolution. The abstract OLDT resolution is described in the following section.

The property c) (i.e., the safeness of the abstract calculus) holds.

Property 10

Let $t \in A$, $\mathbb{F}(concr(t))$ « $concr(\mathbb{P}(t))$

<u>Sketch of the proof</u>

$\mathbb{F}$(concr(t)) ≈ concr($\mathbb{F}$(t)) and $\mathbb{F}$(t) « $\mathbb{P}$(t).

We can summarize all these notions in a table (figure 5). On one side are presented operations related to the concrete domain, on the other side are presented operations related to the abstract domain. Notice that the concrete domain is equivalent to the abstract domain for which the set L of luls is empty.

The symbol '+' refers to an extension (i.e., the variable typing must be taken into account) whereas the symbol '-' refers to a restriction (i.e., the variable typing must be ignored).

Set of luls	Ø	L
Algebra	$Atom(P,F,V)^{T}/_{\cong}$	$Atom(P,F,V,L)^{T}/_{\cong}$
Order	$\leq$	$\leq_+$
Lub	$\vee$	$\vee_+$
Glb	$\wedge$	$\wedge_+$
Concrete calculus	$\mathbb{F}$	$\mathbb{F}_+$
Abstract calculus	$\mathbb{P}_-$	$\mathbb{P}$

Figure 5

4 Abstract OLDT resolution

A model of intelligent resolution was proposed by H. Tamaki and T. Sato [TS 86]: the OLDT resolution. The principle is to prevent the interpreter from achieving the evaluation of a goal previously considered.

Two kinds of nodes are manipulated in the OLD tree: the active (or solution) node which behaves in a usual way and the passive (or look up) node which looks up to the solutions of a more general active node. Two tables must be taken into account: the active table which associates each active node with a solution list and the passive table which associates each passive node with a position on a solution list.

Let us consider an example:

append([],L,L) ←
append([X|L1],L2,[X|L3]) ← append(L1,L2,L3)
← append($\underline{L1}$,$\underline{L2}$,L3)

An underlined variable means that the type composed of the single lul $[]_2$ is assigned to this one and thus that this variable is (in an approximative way) a finite-lengthed list.

The OLDT resolution is depicted by the figure 6 on which you can observe three kinds of nodes:

- an active node is represented by a rectangle
- a passive node is represented by an oval
- an empty node is represented by a small square

Let us comment on the resolution (figure 6):
The goal is an active node (it is the first node). A first refutation (or solution) is obtained by application of the first clause of the program. This solution is put in the solution list. A new node is then obtained by application of the second clause of the program. This node is registered passive because it is an instance of the active node. The first solution of the active node is then used to deriving a new refutation from the passive node. The pointer associated with the passive node is shifted and a new solution is added to the solution list. We can carry out this process infinitely, hence the OLDT resolution does not always terminate.

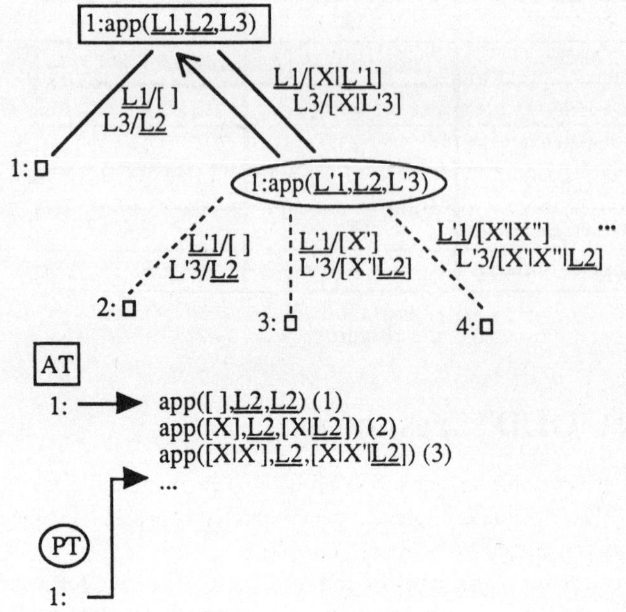

Figure 6

To get the termination of this resolution, we must make an approximation, just to go from an infinite OLDT resolution to an abstract finite OLDT resolution.

A first approach to this aim consists in limiting the complexity of atoms. So, the interpretation runs over a finite domain. We can mention the works of H. Tamaki and T. Sato [TS 86], T. Kanamori and T. Kawamura [KK 87], J. Gallagher, M. Codish and E. Shapiro [GCS 88]. We can take a look at this model of abstraction, called td-abstraction (td for term-depth), proposed by H. Tamaki and T. Sato. Given a parameter k, let us consider an atom A, if depth(A) > k then all branches of A are cut out from a depth equal to k and replaced by fresh variables. An illustration is given below (figure 7).

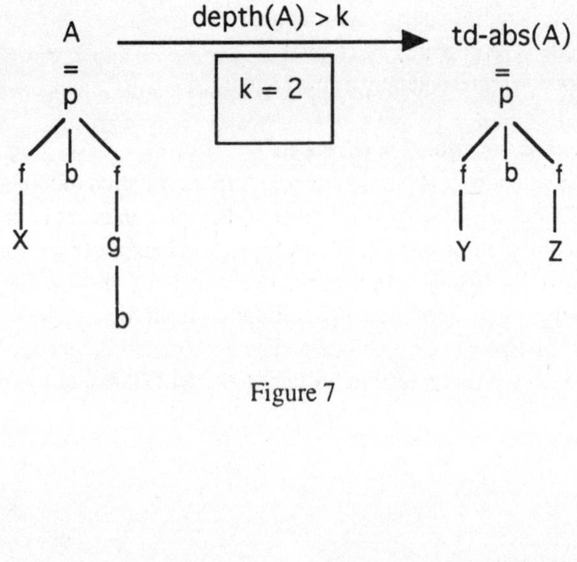

Figure 7

A slightly different approach consists in limiting the number of atoms which may be considered during an abstract calculus application. The considered atoms are not chosen beforehand, so the interpretation runs over a (possibly) infinite domain. This is our approach. Two abstraction models must be introduced in the OLDT resolution algorithm: the first model is associated with the entry list (i.e., the atom list of the active table) and the second model is associated with the solution lists. By limiting the number of atoms which may be taken into consideration in the entry list and in the solution lists, the termination can be proved.

Now, let us introduce a first model of abstraction, called ts-abstraction with anti-unification (ts for term-similarity). Given a parameter k and an atom list L, let us consider an atom A, we want to know if there exists an atom L_i (of L) such that L_i and A are quasi-similars (that is similars up to a depth equal to k), what we can formulate by the following question: Does there exists an atom L_i (of L) such that the depth of the anti-unified atom of A and L_i is greater than k ? If the answer is positive then an atom L_i is selected and the anti-unified atom of A and L_i is appended to L, otherwise the atom A is appended to L. An illustration is given below (figure 8).

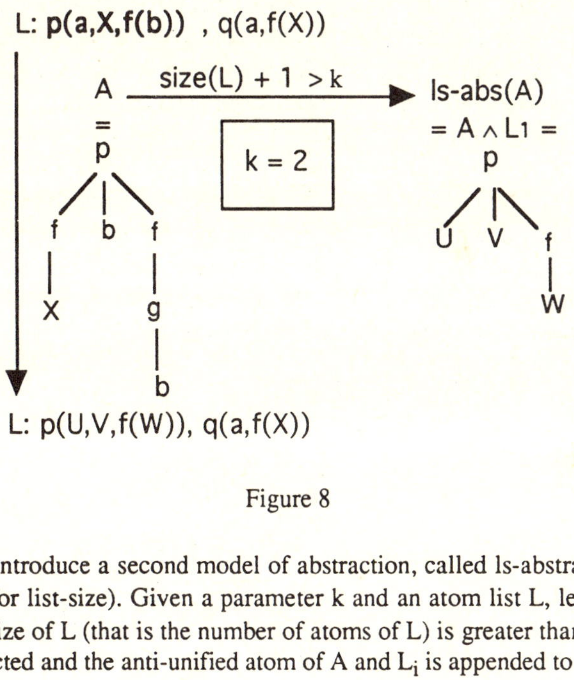

Figure 8

Now, let us introduce a second model of abstraction, called ls-abstraction with anti-unification (ls for list-size). Given a parameter k and an atom list L, let us consider an atom A, if the size of L (that is the number of atoms of L) is greater than k then an atom L_i (of L) is selected and the anti-unified atom of A and L_i is appended to L, otherwise the atom A is appended to L. An illustration is given below (figure 9).

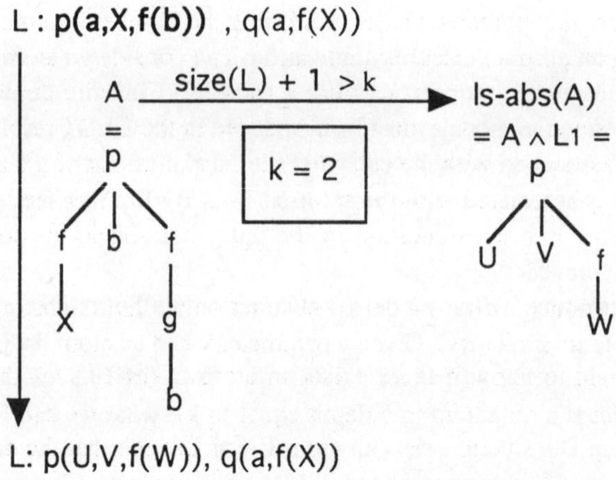

Figure 9

Now, let us consider an example of abstract OLDT resolution, let us take again the append program. The first model (namely the abstraction model associated with the entry list) is chosen as any abstraction model (because a single active node appears during resolution). The second model (namely the abstraction model associated with all solution lists) is chosen as the ls-abstraction (with k = 1).

Let us comment on the resolution (figure 10):
As before, a first solution (a) corresponding to the first refutation is put in the solution list. Then a second solution is taken into consideration, but as the size of the solution list is limited to one element, a new solution (b) which represents the anti-unified atom of the first and the second solution replaces the first solution (a). Lastly, a last solution is taken into consideration but as it is less general, nothing more is made.

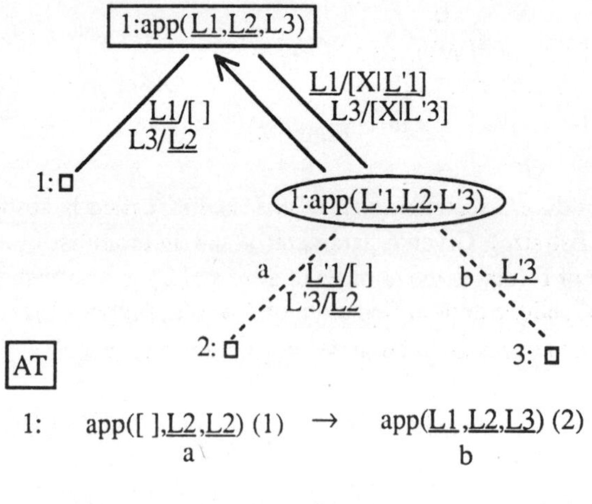

Figure 10

Remark

The result of an OLDT resolution is an OLDT structure, in a same way the result of an abstract OLDT resolution is an OLDT structure. Nevertheless, some information in an OLDT structure may be redundant or useless, consequently in order to get it more convenient we can transform the OLDT structure. We shall call the result of this transformation an abstract structure but we shall not describe this heuristic transformation.

5 Application of the abstract interpretation

The abstract interpretation of a pair (P,G) composed of a program P and a goal G consists of three stages:

5.1 Computation of L

Given a program P, the computation of L with respect to P is done. Let us call the atom $p(X_1, X_2, ..., X_n)$ where $X_1, X_2 ..., X_n$ denote distinct variables and n denotes the arity of p, the most general call associated with the predicate symbol p.

This stage consists in applying the abstract OLDT resolution over the concrete domain $\mathbb{D}$ to all most general calls associated with the program P. A loop analysis of the abstract structures allows computing the "significant" luls. Intuitively the "significant" luls correspond to either the increase or the decrease of some branches.

5.2 Abstract resolution

Given a goal G, the abstract OLDT resolution is applied.

5.3 Program analysis

This third stage allows inferring some program properties by way of an analysis of the abstract structure obtained at the previous stage.

Notation

For simplicity, a variable occurring in the leftmost atom of the label of a node n will be called a n-variable. Let l be a loop, the origin of which is a node n, in an abstract structure, decrease(l) denotes the set of all luls which belong to the type of the n-variables and which are unfolded at least once at each unfolding of the loop l.

Some properties are studied. From termination, properties are surveyed for any concretization of the goal.

5.3.1 Solution pattern(s)

The goal is an active node, then a solution list is associated with this node. To obtain a single solution pattern, we must carry out the anti-unification of all elements of the solution list.

5.3.2 Termination

The termination criterion is verified iff for each node n in the abstract structure, there exists a lul m which belongs to decrease(l) for every loop l, the origin of which is n, in the abstract structure.

5.3.3 Boundedness

The boundedness property means that there exists an equivalent non-recursive program. The boundedness criterion presents some analogy with the termination criterion. We do not describe this criterion.

5.3.4 Determinism

Given a variable X such that a lul m belongs to Type(X) and given two concrete terms t and t', the following definition indicates if it is possible to find an element c of the concretization of X (that is an element of $\mathbb{D}$) such that c may be substituted by t and t'. If the answer is negative then t and t' are incompatible with respect to m.

Definition 11

Let $m \in L$ *and let t and* $t' \in Term(F,V)$, *t and t' are incompatible w.r.t. m iff either* $t = f(t_1,t_2,\ldots,t_n)$, $t' = g(t'_1,t'_2,\ldots,t'_m)$ *and* $f \neq g$, *or* $t = f(t_1,t_2,\ldots,t_n)$, $t' = f(t'_1,t'_2,\ldots,t'_n)$, $m = f_i.m'$ *and* t_i *and* t'_i *are incompatible w.r.t.* $m'.f_i$.

The determinism criterion is verified iff for each node n in the abstract structure and for each pair of elementary derivations of n, a lul m belongs to the type of a n-variable X, X is substituted by a term t in the first derivation, X is substituted by a term t' in the second derivation and t and t' are incompatible with respect to m.

5.3.5 Complexity

The complexity of a program is expressed in terms of luls, thus a study of the overlapping loops of the abstract structure is necessary and allows under some hypotheses determining a complexity measure.

If we limit our study to the class of the ordered (ordered means that atoms in the body of rules appear from left to right with a decreasing ordering, where the order of an atom denotes the recursivity level of this one) deterministic quasi-rationnal programs, then the complexity criterion can be formulated as follows:

If there exists a loop l in the abstract structure such that decrease(l) is empty then no complexity measure can be given, otherwise the program complexity is equal to the complexity associated with the root node of the abstract structure.

- the complexity of a node n, denoted compl(n), is equal to

  max

  {

  decrease(l)*compl(n') / n and n' are respectively the first (the origin) and the second node of the loop l,

  max{compl(n') / n' is a son of n}

  }

- the complexity of an empty node is equal to 1.

If several luls appear in decrease(l) for a loop l, this represents a juxtaposition of different complexity measures. A lul m associated with a variable X is represented in regard to complexity by $|m|_X$, that is the length of the unfolding of the lul m attached to the variable X.

The description of the program analysis is succinct but is sufficient to give the reader an intuitive understanding.

6 Examples

The examples which are given now illustrate the possibilities and the limits of this abstract interpretation.

6.1 First example: append

The program is:

append([],L,L) ←
append([X|L1],L2,[X|L3]) ← append(L1,L2,L3)

6.1.1 Computation of L

The set of computed "significant" luls is: L = $\{[]_2\}$.

6.1.2 Abstract resolution

The goal is: ← append($\underline{L1}$,$\underline{L2}$,L3). The resolution has already been depicted (see the section 4).

6.1.3 Program analysis

Some properties can be derived:

- solution pattern: append($\underline{L1}$,$\underline{L2}$,$\underline{L3}$)
- termination: yes
- determinism: yes
- complexity: $|[]|_X$

Description of the analysis: The solution pattern indicates that the list L_3 is a finite-lengthed list. The termination is proved because when observing the structure we notice that the list L_1 is a finite-lengthed list and that at each recursive step an element of the list is removed. The determinism is proved because when still observing the structure we notice that for any concretization of the goal a single derivation instead of two is possible. The complexity is obviously equal to $|[]|_X$.

6.2 Second example: multiply

The program is:

add(0,X,X) ←
ass(s(X),Y,s(Z)) ← add(X,Y,Z)
mul(0,X,0) ←
mul(s(X),Y,Z) ← mul(X,Y,I), add(Y,I,Z)

6.2.1 Computation of L

The set of computed "significant" luls is: L = $\{s_1\}$.

6.2.2 Abstract resolution

The goal is: ← mul($\underline{X}$,$\underline{Y}$,Z).

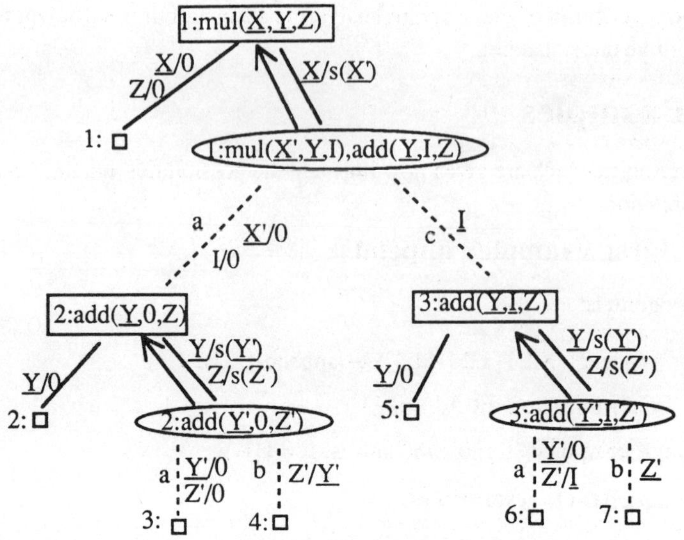

AT

1 : mul(0,Y,0) (1) → mul(X,Y,0) (2) → mul(X,Y,Z) (3)
a b c

2 : add(0,0,0) (2) → add(X,0,X) (3)
a b

3 : add(0,Y,Y) (5) → add(X,Y,Z) (6)
a b

Figure 11

An underlined variable means that the type composed of the single lul s_1 is assigned to this one and thus that this variable is (in an approximative way) an integer. The resolution is depicted by the preceding figure (note that the chosen abstraction models are the same as those of the previous resolution):

Let us comment on the resolution (figure 11):
The goal is an active node (it is the first node). A first solution is obtained by application of the third clause, this solution is put in the solution list of the first active node. Next a new node is obtained by application of the fourth clause. This node is registered passive because it is an instance of the first node. Then, the first solution is used to deriving a new active node. For this node, a first solution is obtained by application of the first clause, this solution is put in the solution list of the second active node. But it represents also a solution for the first active node, so a new solution (b) which represents the anti-unified atom of the first and the second solution replaces the first solution (a). And so on ...

6.2.3 Program analysis

Some properties can be derived:

- solution pattern: append(X,Y,Z)
- termination: yes
- determinism: yes

• complexity: $|s_1|_X * |s_1|_Y$

Description of the analysis: The solution pattern of the goal indicates that the third argument is an integer. The termination is proved because when observing the abstract structure we notice that for any loop the first argument is an integer and at each recursive step this integer is decremented. The determinism is proved because when still observing the abstract structure we notice that for any concretization of the goal a single derivation instead of two is possible. The complexity is equal to $|s_1|_X * |s_1|_Y$.

6.3 Third example: the quick-sort program

The program is:

```
quicksort([],[]) ←
quicksort([X|L],L') ← filter(X,L,L1,L2), quicksort(L1,L1'),
                      quicksort(L2,L2'), append(L1',[X|L2'],L')
filter(X,[],[],[]) ←
filter(X,[Y|L],[Y|L1],L2) ← X > Y, filter(X,L,L1,L2)
filter(X,[Y|L],L1,[Y|L2]) ← X ≤ Y, filter(X,L,L1,L2)
append([],L,L) ←
append([X|L1],L2,[X|L3]) ← append(L1,L2,L3)
```

6.3.1 Computation of L

The set of computed "significant" luls is: $L = \{[]_2\}$.

6.3.2 Abstract resolution

The goal is: ← quicksort($\underline{L}$,L'). We do not describe the resolution.

6.3.3 Program analysis

Only the solution pattern can be derived:

- solution pattern: quicksort($\underline{L}$,$\underline{L'}$)
- other properties: ?

Although the resolution terminates for any concretization of the goal, we cannot prove it. It results from the fact that our algebra is too limited. If we want more results, we must extend our model for instance to linear equations with luls.
We could express some relations like: $|[]_2|_L = |[]_2|_{L1} + |[]_2|_{L2}$

7 Conclusion

The improvements or extensions that we can perform can be made in the three domains (algebra, resolution, analysis) we have studied. But it is certainly the extension of the algebra which is the most interesting.

For instance, we can imagine an algebra for which each term represents a (rational, context-free, ...) language in terms of luls. Then, the unification comes down to the union of languages and anti-unification comes down to the intersection of languages. As we have already shown in the last example, extensions to systems of linear constraints can also be important to approach the operational semantics.

On the other hand, we can use the notion of limited-unfolding loop to carry out an implicit occur-check and thus to avoid performing it when it is unnecessary. To this aim, the unification algorithm must be modified (the explicit occur check must disappear), we must work with rational trees and the program must be typed (i.e., some variables of the program are typed) in order to performing an implicit occur check by means of unification. The lul notion (and more generally the type notion) can also be used by some synchronization processes such as the Wait in Mu-Prolog or the Freeze in Prolog 2 instead of the closure notion.

This study is developed within a software project called ORGANON grouping several universities (Bordeaux, INRIA ,Lille, Orleans).

Appendices

Appendix A

If two atoms t and t' are unifiable, then it is possible to construct the mgu (most general unifier) α and the unified atom u of t and t'.

A unification system S composed of a set of equations and a set of typing relations is associated with the unification problem of two atoms. Let l(S) denote the set of variables occurring at the left-hand side of an equation of S and let r(S) denote the set of variables occurring at the right-hand side of an equation of S. The unification algorithm consists of four stages:

Unify(t,t') =

1- Initialization

$S = \{t = t'\} \cup$ **$\{X : m / X \in Var(t) \cup Var(t')$ and $m \in Type(X)\}$**

2- Simplification = as far as possible, apply one of the following transformations :

2.1 $f(t_1,t_2,...,t_n) = f(t'_1,t'_2,...,t'_n) \Rightarrow$ replace by $t_1 = t'_1$, $t_2 = t'_2$, ..., $t_n = t'_n$

2.2 $f(t_1,t_2,...,t_n) = g(t_1,t_2,...,t_m) \Rightarrow$ stop with failure

2.3 $X = t$ $(X \notin Var(t)) \Rightarrow$ replace everywhere else X by t

2.4 $X = t$ $(X \in Var(t)) \Rightarrow$ stop with failure

2.5 $t = X \Rightarrow$ replace by $X = t$

2.6 $X = X \Rightarrow$ eliminate

2.7 $f(t_1,t_2,...,t_n) : f_i.m \Rightarrow$ replace by $t_i : m.f_i$

2.8 $X : Y$ and $X : m \Rightarrow$ replace $X : m$ by $Y : m$

2.8 $g(t_1,t_2,...,t_n) : f_i.m \Rightarrow$ eliminate

3- Normalisation = for every X belonging to r(S)

3.1 rename X X' (X' is a fresh variable)

3.2 add the equation $X = X'$

4- Computation of the mgu α and the unified atom u

4.1 $X \in l(S)$ and $X = t$ $\Rightarrow$ $\alpha(X) = t$

4.2 $X \in r(S)$ and $X : m_1, X : m_2, ..., X : m_n$ $\Rightarrow$ $Type(X) = \{m_1,m_2,...,m_n\}$

4.3 $u = \alpha(t) = \alpha(t')$

Let us put in some concise comments about the algorithm. First and second stage: with respect to the usual unification algorithm, the variable typing must be taken into account (note the bold rules). Third stage: for the variable typing to be unambiguous, a variable renaming is done.

Appendix B

Two atoms t and t' are always anti-unifiable, hence it is always possible to construct the msa (most specific anti-unifier) (ß,ß') and the anti-unified atom a of t and t'.
Anti-unify(t,t') = to resolve $t \wedge t'$
If it is possible apply the first rule, otherwise apply the second one:
1 $f(t_1,t_2,...,t_n) \wedge f(t'_1,t'_2,...,t'_n) = f(t_1 \wedge t'_1, t_2 \wedge t'_2,...,t_n \wedge t'_n)$
2 $t \wedge t' = \theta(t,t') = X$ and $ß(X) = t$ and $ß'(X) = t'$
where θ represents a bijection from $Atom(P,F,V,L)^T/_{\equiv} \times Atom(P,F,V,L)^T/_{\equiv}$ to $V \times T$
where X is a fresh variable / $\forall\ m \in T$, $m \in Type(X)$ iff correct(m,t) and correct(m,t')

References

[Bru 91] Bruynooghe M. A practical framework for the abstract interpretation of logic programs. Journal of Logic Programming, Feb 1991, pp 91-124.

[CC 77] Cousot P. and Cousot R. Abstract Interpretation: a unified lattice for static analysis of programs by construction of approximation of fixpoints. POPL 1977, Sigact Sigplan, 1977, pp 238-252.

[Cor 89] Corsini MM. Interprétation abstraite en programmation logique : théorie et applications. PhD thesis, Université de Bordeaux I, Jan 1989.

[Dev 88a] Devienne P. Weighted Graphs, a tool for expressing the behaviour of recursive rules in Logic Programming. FGCS conferences, Nov. 1988.

[Dev 88b] Devienne P. Weighted Graphs, a tool for studying the halting problem and time complexity in term rewriting systems and Logic Programming. ICOT technical report TR-437, 1988.

[DVB 90] De Schreye D., Verschaetse K. and Bruynooghe M. A practical technique for detecting non-terminating queries for a restricted class of Horn clauses using directed, weighted graphs. Report CW-109, Mar 1990.

[GCS 88] Gallagher J., Codish M. and Shapiro E. Specialisation of Prolog and FCP Programs using Abstract Interpretation. New Generation Computing, OHMSHA LTD and Springer-Verlag, 1988, pp 159-186.

[JS 87] Jones N. and Sondergaard H. A semantics-based framework for the abstract interpretation of Prolog. In Abstract interpretation of declarative languages, S. Abramsky and C. Hankin (Eds), Ellis Horwood, 1987.

[KK 87] Kanamori T. and Kawamura T. Analysing success patterns of logic programs by abstract hybrid interpretation. ICOT Technical Report, 1987.

[LDL 91] Lecoutre C., Devienne P. and Lebegue P. Abstract Interpretation and recursive behaviour of logic programs. LIFL Technical Report, Oct 1991.

[Leb 88] Lebègue P. Contribution à l'étude de la Programmation Logique par les Graphes Orientés Pondérés. PhD thesis, Université de LILLE I, Nov 1988.

[Mel 86] Mellish CS. Abstract Interpretation of Prolog programs. In Abstract interpretation of declarative languages, S. Abramsky and C. Hankin (Eds), Ellis Horwood, 1987.

[MS 88] Marriot K. and Sondergaard H. Bottom-up abstract interpretation of logic programs. Proceedings of the fifth ILCP, Seattle, August 1988, pp 733-748.

[TS 86] Tamaki H., Sato T. OLD resolution with Tabulation. Proceedings of the third ICLP, LNCS, 225, Springer-Verlag, 1986.

Speed-up Transformations of Logic Programs by Abstraction and Learning

Jutta Eusterbrock*

Intellektik – FB Informatik,

Alexanderstr. 10, D–6100 Darmstadt

email: jutta@intellektik.informatik.th-darmstadt.de

Abstract

This paper presents a formal framework for the automatic transformation of inefficient generate-and-test programs into equivalent programs by learning from the proofs of example queries. In the resulting program the search is guided by strategies based on abstracted proof traces obtained from the interpretation of example computations. Strategies are incrementally improved in an iterative process by a method for theory formation.

For the task of theory formation we developed a logic based method. It operates on a triple, consisting of a set of features augmented with taxonomic relations, a sequence of positive and negative facts and a set of hypotheses, which can also be the empty set. This triple is transformed into a set of hypotheses which implies all of the positive facts, but none of the negative facts and which is minimal in number of hypotheses. Hypotheses are constructed from facts by abstraction.

This method is embedded into a framework for program synthesis via constructive inductive proofs of input-output specifications. A prototypical implementation of the method was used in a mathematical application. The examples used in this paper are based on real problems that occurred during the generation of optimal mathematical algorithms.

1 Introduction

A logic program consists of a set of defining axioms and a query. Usually logic programs are interpreted by a uniform control strategy, eg., SLD-Resolution with depth-first search.

The depth-first execution of logic programs is inefficient in the following sense: if the direct proof of a query may be given in d steps, its derivation during the backtracking process requires an exponential number b^d of inferences depending on the branching rate b of the search tree.

However, for each situation occurring during the proof of a special query, there exists a sequence of defining axioms which reduces the amount of backtracking to a minimum if the program clauses are accessed accordingly. A proof strategy will be called optimal with respect to a logic program LP, if in each situation an appropriate subgoal is chosen, so that the proof complexity is minimized.

As a general method for controlling search the algorithm A^* [12] and its variants may be applied to this problem. The search process is guided by a heuristic, numerical cost function. Suttner and Ertel [19] demonstrated that a theorem prover

*This research was supported by the Deutsche Forschungsgemeinschaft under grant Bi:228/4-1.

can learn the parameters of a numerical cost function from example proofs. Using this learned function for the control in further proof processes, search complexities were remarkably reduced. However, from an analytical point of view, the coding of proof strategies by numerical cost functions is unsatisfying: numerical cost functions cannot provide insight into the structure of successful proof strategies. For instance, the retransformation of learned numerical functions into explanations of the form: *If a proof situation is characterized by the properties A, B, C, then substitute the axiom Ax by Ax'* is not directly possible.

In the area of machine learning, LEX [9] and LPRESS [16] investigated the improvement of problem-solving by learning from examples. Explanation-based learning (EBL) [10] is a method to derive an efficient logic program from a more general one — called the *domain theory* —, and a specific data base — called the *training example* . The resulting program, which is only applicable in cases similar to the training example, is more efficient, because it needs less inferences than the original domain theory. However, no attempt to change the control structures is made by the EBL approach. Harmelen and Bundy [6] showed that EBL is closely related to partial evaluation.

Most approaches to inductive inference employ the same procedure for constructing universally quantified formulas from ground formulas. This inductive inference is realized in two steps: first, certain constants occurring in the formula are replaced by variables. The latter are bound by universal quantifiers added in a second step. However, this technique fails to provide an explicit description of properties of the original formula. Therefore, it is inappropriate for our approach to speed-up transformations, because we need an explicit characterization of properties in order to generate rules that allow to control the search process during a proof. Thus, we employ an abstraction method instead of the common technique outlined above. Our notion of abstraction is closely related to natural concepts of abstraction which are discussed for example in [8] and can be used for proof discovery [3]. Abstraction is the computation of a set of properties which characterizes a given object, ie. assigns it to a certain class of objects. Properties are selected as relevant for the characterization, if they are shared by all members of the class. We formalize an appropriate abstraction method as part of our approach to speed-up transformations. It is based on abduction and induction.

Adopting some ideas from the contributions cited above, we propose a logical framework for the automatic transformation of inefficient logic programs into *equivalent* extended programs, ie. programs which describe the same set of answer substitutions. However, by reordering of subgoals, termination properties may be lost.

Using the extended logic programs for proving goals, the computation is speeded up. The transformation process is guided by the abstracted results of example computations.

Our transformation method is based on the following components

- a preliminary phase of metainterpretation of the original program on example queries;

- the abstraction of example proofs;
- the construction of a consistent and non-redundant set of formulas;
- the transformation of the original program into an equivalent one.

By metainterpretation information about the optimality of selection functions is gathered. This incomplete knowledge on the optimality of selection functions is transformed into general rules by abstraction.

Abstraction of a set of facts may cause inconsistencies. Shapiro has developed a general framework [14] for debugging incorrect Horn clause programs. Sets of formulas which are incomplete or incorrect with respect to an interpretation are modified such that the resulting set S of formulas subsumes, for a predicate $p(X)$, all ground instances $p(a)$ — called the positive formulas —, which are valid in the intended interpretation. On the other hand, none of the negative formulas — $p(a)$ is negative iff $\neg p(a)$ is positive — may be subsumed by S. Shapiro's method needs user support for the classification of ground formulas in positive and negative ones.

For debugging of a set of inconsistent hypotheses, we developed an incremental method. We distinguish hypotheses and proven formulas. The generalization and debugging process exploits a domain dependent, dynamically extensible, taxonomic theory. Using extended subsumption and antiunification algorithms [1, 5] the inference process is made efficient.

The paper is organized as follows: first, we present a "realistic" mathematical application problem, which serves to illustrate some aspects of our method. In section 3 an extension of Horn clause logic is introduced that provides the basis for our approach. In section 4 our method for theory formation is sketched. Some examples illustrate the construction and debugging of hypotheses based on positive and negative facts. In section 5 the components of the program transformation method are outlined. Especially we give the definition of a meta interpreter for controlling search processes. In section 6 empirical results are summarized. The paper concludes with a discussion of the transformation method.

2 A concrete Example

In this section, we present a "realistic" example problem arising from a mathematical application. The problem was solved by the transformation method introduced in this paper. It is not a mere illustrative toy problem, but a typical instance of the class of problems that have been solved by our method.

As a mathematical application we analyse the complexity of algorithms for the determination of the $I - th$ largest element of a totally ordered set, starting with an initially given partial ordering T, and using a given number B of comparisons. We examine constructive proofs of queries of the kind "$? - determine(I, T, B, Z)$", which are answered using the following program:

$$determine(I,T,B,Z) \Leftarrow B \geq 0, minimal\_solution(I,T,Z).$$

$$\begin{aligned} determine(I,T,B,Z) \Leftarrow\ & split\_elements(I,T,B,[N_1,N_2]),\\ & decompose([I,T,B],[N_1,N_2],[I_1,T_1,B'],[I_2,T_2,B']),\\ & determine(I',T_1,B',Z_1), determine(I',T_2,B',Z_2),\\ & compose\_solutions(Z_1,Z_2,Z). \end{aligned}$$

The program employs a tactic which is a variant of the principles "divide-and-conquer" and "global search" (cf. [18, 17]). The program is to be read as: to compute the I-th largest element Z of a partially ordered set represented by T, first select a split-element, then decompose the problem and compute the solutions Z_1, Z_2 of these subproblems, and finally compute the solution of the whole problem by composing the subsolutions.

In the following, we abbreviate part of the body of the above clause by defining

$$\begin{aligned} part\_body(I,T,B,Op,Z) \Leftrightarrow\ & decompose([I,T,B],Op,[I_1,T_1,B'],[I_2,T_2,B']),\\ & determine(I_1,T_1,B',Z_1), determine(I_2,T_2,B',Z_2)\\ & compose\_solutions(Z_1,Z_2,Z). \end{aligned}$$

The domain theory contains definitions of operations on the data type *partially ordered sets* . Partially ordered sets are implemented by special canonical terms called *graph terms* [4]. For example, the term $t = \lambda(a(d,e),b(d))$ represents the relation $\mathcal{R} = \{a > d, a > e, b > d\}$. From a given relation, a graph term is derived as follows: first, in the corresponding Hasse diagram all nodes with more than one parent node are copied according to the number of parents. The resulting forest structure is transformed into a graph term by introducing an artificial root λ. The figure below illustrates the forest obtained from $\mathcal{R}$.

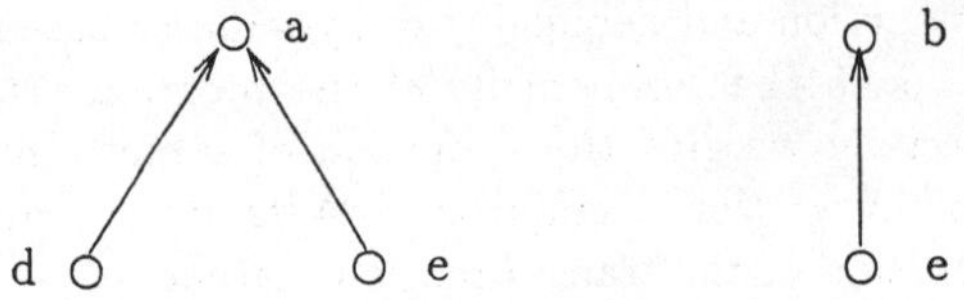

Some operations on the term algebra which simulate operations on partially ordered sets have been implemented. One of them is the operation $\uplus$, which simulates the adding of an edge. Eg., the result of $t \uplus (t_{|11}, t_{|2})$ represents the transitive closure of the set $\mathcal{R} \cup \{d > b\}$, if $T_{|N}$ denotes the subterm of T at occurence N, $N \in \mathcal{N}^*$.

Now the *decompose* and *compose_solutions* function can be defined:

$$\begin{aligned} & decompose([I,T,B],[N_1,N_2],[I_1,T_1,B'],[I_2,T_2,B']) \Leftarrow\\ & \quad T_1 = T \uplus (T_{|N_1}, T_{|N_2}), T_2 = T \uplus (T_{|N_2}, T_{|N_1}), B' = B - 1. \end{aligned}$$

$$\begin{aligned} & compose\_solutions(Z_1,Z_2,Z_1) \Leftarrow compare(Z_1,Z_2,<).\\ & compose\_solutions(Z_1,Z_2,Z_2) \Leftarrow compare(Z_1,Z_2,>). \end{aligned}$$

The complexity of a proof of a query of the form "? − $determine(I, T, B, Z)$" depends mainly on the sequence of values provided by the function *split_elements* during a backtracking process.

$split\_elements(\_, \_, \_, [last(2), last(1)]).$
$split\_elements(\_, \_, \_, [last(1), last(0)]).$
$split\_elements(T, \_, \_, [N_1, N_2]) \Leftarrow tree\_domain(T, N_1), tree\_domain(T, N_2).$

In this definition *tree_domain* represents a predicate enumerating all elements of the *tree domain* . The selector functions $last(0)$, $last(1)$, $last(2)$ are integrated into the definition, because it turned out that certain sets of examples can only be classified in a uniform way by use of these functions. The program enumerates the possible *split*-elements. This results in a combinatorial explosion of the proof complexity depending on the length of the graph term. In our implementation numerous filters are implemented, which allow us to avoid inadmissible or identical split-elements.

In the remainder of this paper, we will concentrate on the question how to transform logic programs that require enumerative searches into more efficient ones. We will develop a transformation method that, for instance, yields an equivalent version of the *split$_e$lements*-program which works without backtracking.

The intention of this article is to outline the transformation method, which is domain independent. It can be applied to further problems described in the specification language of section 3. Hence, we will furtheron neglect the details of our example application as far as possible. In the formulas the parts relevant for understanding the theory formation method are underlined.

3 The Specification Language

For the realization of our approach we need to augment definite Horn clauses with an explicit strategic component, thereby borrowing a concept of *concurrent logic programming* [15]. The first part of a clause's body consists of a conditional *guard* , built from type predicates.

Guarded clauses were introduced as a means to control the parallel execution of logic programs. However, in our specification language type predicates are applied to restrict the domain of variables. This strategic component allows to prefer or delay the proof of a given subgoal during the search process.

3.1 Types

First of all, we will introduce *types* . Types shall describe term properties, which are "easy" to verify. They are declared as unary predicates together with sets of defining axioms and subtype axioms. Subtype relations describe logical entailment. For reasons of efficiency they have to be declared explicitly. An expression of the form $p \sqsupset q$ will be used to abbreviate the formula $\forall X : p(X) \Leftarrow q(X)$. In the following, the symbols $\top, \bot$ denote *true* and *false*, respectively.

Example type systems. Given a signature Σ, types are predicates defined on the term algebra $\mathcal{T}_\Sigma$. Let $free\_of(s,T)$, $contains(s,T)$, $multiple\_occ(s,T)$ and $single\_occ(s,T)$ denote predicates, which are true, if a fixed subterm s doesn't occur in T, occurs in T, occurs several times or only once. $T_{|n}$ denotes the subterm S of T at occurrence n. $arity(T)$ denotes the arity of T. $|occ(S,T)|$ is the number of occurrences of S in T. $f(|T|)$ denotes an arithmetic function. $domt(S,T)$ is the subset of the tree domain of T, which contains the occurrences of the subterm S in T. $\subset$ denotes the subterm property.

As examples the type systems $\mathbf{Typ}_1, \mathbf{Typ}_2 \ldots \mathbf{Typ}_5$ are introduced by the defining relations $\mathbf{Def}_i$ and subtype declarations $\mathbf{Sub}_i$, $i = 1, 2, \ldots, 5$.

$$\begin{array}{ll} \mathbf{Def}_1 & \forall T: typ1_1(T) \Leftarrow contains(t,T). \\ & \forall T: typ1_2(T) \Leftarrow free\_of(t,T). \\ & \forall T: typ1_3(T) \Leftarrow multiple\_occ(t,T). \\ & \forall T: typ1_4(T) \Leftarrow single\_occ(t,T). \end{array}$$

$$\mathbf{Sub}_1 \quad \top \sqsupset typ1_1 \sqsupset typ1_3 \sqsupset \bot, typ1_1 \sqsupset typ1_4 \sqsupset \bot, \top \sqsupset typ1_2 \sqsupset \bot.$$

$$\begin{array}{ll} \mathbf{Def}_2 & \forall T: typ2_1(T) \Leftarrow arity(T_{|11}) - f(|T|) \geq 1. \\ & \forall T: typ2_2(T) \Leftarrow arity(T_{|11}) - f(|T|) \geq 2. \\ & \forall T: typ2_3(T) \Leftarrow arity(T_{|11}) - f(|T|) \geq 3. \\ & \forall T: typ2_4(T) \Leftarrow arity(T_{|11}) - f(|T|) < 1. \\ & \forall T: typ2_5(T) \Leftarrow arity(T_{|11}) - f(|T|) < 2. \end{array}$$

$$\begin{array}{ll} \mathbf{Def}_3 & \forall T: typ3_1(T) \Leftarrow |occ(T_{|11}, T)| \geq 2. \\ & \forall T: typ3_2(T) \Leftarrow |occ(T_{|11}, T)| \geq 3. \end{array}$$

$$\begin{array}{ll} \mathbf{Def}_4 & \forall T: typ4_1(T) \Leftarrow |\{S | S \subset T, |domt(S,T)| \geq 2\}| \geq 1. \\ & \forall T: typ4_2(T) \Leftarrow |\{S | S \subset T, |domt(S,T)| \geq 2\}| \geq 2. \\ & \forall T: typ4_3(T) \Leftarrow |\{S | S \subset T, |domt(S,T)| \geq 2\}| \geq 3. \end{array}$$

$$\begin{array}{ll} \mathbf{Def}_5 & \forall T: typ5_1(T) \Leftarrow arity(T_{|1}) - f(|T|) \geq 0. \\ & \forall T: typ5_2(T) \Leftarrow arity(T_{|1}) - f(|T|) \geq 1. \\ & \forall T: typ5_3(T) \Leftarrow arity(T_{|1}) - f(|T|) \geq 2. \end{array}$$

To achieve an efficient handling of type information, the class of admissible type systems will be restricted. Type systems are called admissible, if the relation $\sqsupset$ on the type symbols induces a forest structured lattice. The relation $\sqsupset$ on type symbols can be extended in a natural way to a relation $\sqsupset$ on sequences of type symbols. The computation of the most specific generalization and most general specialization of types and sequences of types with respect to the subtype relations are lattice operations $\sqcup, \sqcap$. We implemented these operations by special antiunification and subsumption algorithms (cf. [13, 5, 20, 7, 1]).

3.2 Formulas

Let p denote a distinguished predicate symbol, t a ground term. In our extended language we admit Horn clauses and, additionally, formulas of the form:

$$\neg p(t), typ_{p_1}(t), \ldots, typ_{p_r}(t) \mid q_1(t,\_), \ldots, q_p(t,\_)$$

$$\exists T : \neg p(T), typ_{p_1}(T), \ldots, typ_{p_r}(T) \mid q_1(T,\_), \ldots, q_p(T,\_)$$

$$\forall T : p(T) \Leftarrow typ_{p_1}(T), \ldots, typ_{p_r}(T) \mid q_1(T,\_), \ldots, q_p(T,\_)$$

$$\forall T : p(T) \stackrel{hyp}{\Leftarrow} typ_{p_1}(T), \ldots, typ_{p_r}(T) \mid q_1(T,\_), \ldots, q_p(T,\_)$$

where $typ_{p_1}, \ldots, typ_{p_r}$ are type predicates which check the arguments of p. Hence, the set $\{typ_{p_i}\}$ contains only predicates which don't modify their input variables. The subformulas p, $typ_{p_1}, \ldots, typ_{p_r}$ and $q_1(T,\_), \ldots, q_p(T,\_)$ are called the *head* , the *guard* and the *body* of the above formulas. The symbol ' | ' separates the guard from the body, as a logical connective it denotes the conjunction of guard and body. Contrary to common Prolog conventions, in this paper the notion of facts comprises ground clauses as well.

Formulas of the first and second type are called *negative formulas* , whereas Horn clauses and the implications of the third and fourth kind are *positive formulas* . The formulas of the fourth kind are called *hypotheses* .

Given a specification S, a formula of this kind represents an *admissible hypothesis* about a predicate p with respect to S, if the condition is *true*, p is only incompletely specified by positive and negative atoms with predicate symbol p, and the head of the formula does not contradict the specification.

Let h be a positive formula of the third or fourth kind with guard $prop'(T)$, head $p(T)$ and body $body(T)$ and let k be the formula $\exists T : \neg p(T), prop''(T)$. The pair h, k is *inconsistent* , if $prop' \sqsupset prop''$.

The computation of the most specific generalization, the test of logical entailment and the detection of inconsistencies with respect to a taxonomic theory are basic operations on a pair of formulas.

4 Theory Formation

In this section we will outline a method for theory formation. The method serves to transform a triple $< \mathbf{T}, \mathbf{H}, \mathbf{Ex}^+ \cup \mathbf{Ex}^- >$ into a set of hypotheses $\mathbf{H}^*$. In this context $\mathbf{T}$ denotes a set of type axioms; $\mathbf{H}$ a set of consistent hypotheses; $\mathbf{Ex}^+ \cup \mathbf{Ex}^-$ a set of positive and negative facts. The resulting set $\mathbf{H}^*$ represents all of the positive facts but no negative one (cf. [11]). Additionally $\mathbf{H}^*$ is a set with a minimal number of formulas with this property.

A thorough description of the method is beyond the scope of this paper, however, we will demonstrate the effects of the basic inference rules which constitute the core of the method with illustrative examples.

4.1 Abstraction by Abduction and Induction

The construction of hypotheses from facts is described by the following inference rule, called *abstraction* . t denotes a fixed term.

$$\frac{\begin{array}{r} p(t) \Leftarrow q_1(t,\_),\ldots,q_p(t,\_) \\ typ_1(t),\ldots,typ_r(t) \Leftarrow t \end{array}}{\forall T : p(T) \overset{hyp}{\Leftarrow} typ_1(T),\ldots,typ_i(T),\ldots,typ_r(T) \mid q_1(T,\_),\ldots,q_p(T,\_)}$$

This rule will be explained by an example. Let the term $t = \lambda(a(b(c),d),e(b(c)),f)$ represent a partially ordered set. Assume that the formula

$$\exists Z : split\_elements(3,t,4,[11,2]),$$

was proven.

Terms are abstracted with respect to the type system **Typ3**, which has been introduced in subsection 3.1. The minimal types which abstracts from the term t, the value 3 and the bound b are computed. This yields the most specialized formula which describes the above fact.

$$\exists Z : split\_elements(I,T,B,[11,2]) \overset{hyp}{\Leftarrow} |occ(T_{|11},T)| \geq 2, B \leq g(|T|), I \leq 3$$

4.2 Debugging

Constructing a rule from each positive and negative example may also cause inconsistencies. They are removed by *Weakening of inconsistent hypotheses* .

$$\frac{\begin{array}{r} \forall T : p(T) \overset{hyp}{\Leftarrow} typ_1(T),\ldots,typ_i(T),\ldots,typ_r(T) \mid q_1(T,\_),\ldots,q_p(T,\_) \\ \exists T : \neg p(T), typ_1'(T),\ldots,typ_i'(T),\ldots,typ_{r+1}'(T) \mid q_1(T,\_),\ldots,q_p(T,\_) \\ typ_1 \sqsupset typ_1',\ldots,typ_r \sqsupset typ_r' \\ typ_{r+1} \not\sqsupset typ_1',\ldots,typ_{r+1} \not\sqsupset typ_{r+1}' \end{array}}{\begin{array}{r} \forall T : p(T) \overset{hyp}{\Leftarrow} typ_1(T),\ldots,typ_r(T),typ_{r+1}(T) \mid q_1(T,\_),\ldots,q_p(T,\_) \\ \exists T : \neg p(T), typ_1'(T),\ldots,typ_i'(T),\ldots,typ_{r+1}'(T) \mid q_1(T,\_),\ldots,q_p(T,\_) \end{array}}$$

This rule will be explained by an example. The formulas

$$\exists Z : split\_elements(I,T,B,[11,2]) \overset{hyp}{\Leftarrow} |occ(T_{|11},T)| \geq 2, B \leq g(|T|), I \leq 3, \qquad (1)$$

$$\underline{\exists T}[\forall Z : \underline{\neg}(split\_elements(I,T,B,[11,2]), |occ(T_{|11},T)| \geq 2, B \leq g(|T|), I \leq 3. \qquad (2)$$

constructed with $t = \lambda(a(b(c),d),e(b(c)),f)$ (formula 1) and $t' = \lambda(a(b(c)),e(b(c)))$ (formula 2) are inconsistent. This inconsistency is removed by enriching the type system with the definitions $\mathbf{Def}_2 \cup \mathbf{Sub}_2$ (cf. subsection 3.1) and starting the abstraction process again with respect to the extended type system. This yields

$$\begin{array}{r} \exists Z : split\_elements(I,T,B,[11,2]) \\ \underline{\overset{hyp}{\Leftarrow} |occ(T_{|11},T)| \geq 2, arity(T_{|1}) - f(|T|) \geq 2,} B \leq g(|T|). \end{array} \tag{3}$$

$$\begin{array}{r} \underline{\exists T}[\forall Z : \underline{\neg}(split\_elements(I,T,B,[11,2]), \\ \underline{|occ(T_{|11},T)| \geq 2, arity(T_{|1}) - f(|T|) < 2,} B \leq g(|T|), I \leq 3]. \end{array} \tag{4}$$

4.3 Generalization

Constructing hypotheses from facts one-to-one may cause redundancy. For the compression of a set of constructed hypotheses we employ the following inference rules.

Elimination of redundant formulas

$$\begin{array}{r} \forall T : p(T) \overset{hyp}{\Leftarrow} typ_1(T), \ldots, typ_i(T), \ldots, typ_r(T) \mid q_1(T,\_), \ldots, q_p(T,\_) \\ \forall T : p(T) \overset{hyp}{\Leftarrow} typ'_1(T), \ldots, typ'_i(T), \ldots, typ'_r(T) \mid q_1(T,\_), \ldots, q_p(T,\_) \\ typ_1 \sqsupset typ'_1, \ldots, typ_r \sqsupset typ'_r \\ \hline \forall T : p(T) \overset{hyp}{\Leftarrow} typ_1(T), \ldots, typ_i(T), \ldots, typ_r(T) \mid q_1(T,\_), \ldots, q_p(T,\_) \end{array}$$

Generalization by omission of conditions

$$\begin{array}{c} \forall T : p(T) \overset{hyp}{\Leftarrow} typ_1(T), \ldots, typ_i(T), \ldots, typ_r(T) \mid q_1(T,\_), \ldots, q_p(T,\_) \\ \hline \forall T : p(T) \overset{hyp}{\Leftarrow} typ_1(T), \ldots, typ_i(T), \ldots, typ_{r-s}(T) \mid q_1(T,\_), \ldots, q_p(T,\_) \end{array} \tag{5}$$

Computation of the most specific generalization

$$\begin{array}{r} \forall T : p(T) \overset{hyp}{\Leftarrow} typ''_1(T), \ldots, typ''_i(T), \ldots, typ''_r(T) \mid q_1(T,\_), \ldots, q_p(T,\_) \\ \forall T : p(T) \overset{hyp}{\Leftarrow} typ'_1(T), \ldots, typ'_i(T), \ldots, typ'_r(T) \mid q_1(T,\_), \ldots, q_p(T,\_) \\ typ_1 = typ'_1 \sqcup typ''_1, \ldots, typ_r = typ'_r \sqcup typ''_r \\ \hline \forall T : p(T) \overset{hyp}{\Leftarrow} typ_1(T), \ldots, typ_i(T), \ldots, typ_r(T) \mid q_1(T,\_), \ldots, q_p(T,\_) \end{array}$$

Applying these inference rules from a set of hypotheses the most general hypotheses are computed, which are not rejected by a negative formula and which subsume the original set.

For example, the positive formula 3 is transformed applying the rule 5 into the formula

$$\exists Z : split\_elements(I,T,B,[11,2]) \underline{\overset{hyp}{\Leftarrow} arity(T_{|1}) - f(|T|) \geq 2}.$$

which is consistent with the negative formula 4.

5 Metainterpretation and Program Transformation

We now propose an incremental method for the transformation of declarative generate-and-test programs consisting of several iterations. Metainterpretation [21] will allow the system to keep track of the search process which led to the resulting proof. The information obtained this way will be evaluated yielding factual knowledge about the provability of subgoals and optimal selection functions for the problem to be solved. By abstraction, the obtained facts are transformed into more general hypothetical rules. Possibly incorrect hypotheses obtained this way are debugged, so that altogether an improved knowledge base is derived. Re-using the synthesized lemmata and exploiting the learned strategies, further queries can be proven.

5.1 Metainterpretation of Search Processes

A set of goals $\{q_1, \ldots, q_r\}$ is a *decomposition* of a goal p, iff

$$p \Leftarrow q_1 \wedge \ldots \wedge p \Leftarrow q_r.$$

A function, which maps decompositions into goals is called *selection* function. A selection function $\mathcal{O}$ is called *optimal* with respect to a decomposition $\{q_1, \ldots, q_r\}$ of the goal p, iff

$$\left\{ \begin{array}{l} \mathcal{O}(p) \text{ implies } p, \text{ if } p \text{ is provable,} \\ \mathcal{O} \text{ is arbitrarily defined, else.} \end{array} \right\}$$

Using an optimal selection function for controlling search processes avoids backtracking, if a goal is provable.

Questions which arise are, how to represent, to use and to acquire this control knowledge? In the remainder of this subsection we will concentrate on the first and the second problem, leaving the third for the next subsection.

In figure 1 a metainterpreter is introduced, which permits incomplete knowledge and hypotheses about the optimality of selection functions to be applied for the control of search processes. Hypotheses about the optimality of selection functions can change the order in which subgoals will be proven. This is due to the preference ordering that is imposed on the subgoals. The metainterpreter performs a deductive evaluation of the paths in the proof tree.

The metainterpreter allows

- the separation of declarative and control knowledge;
- flexible subgoal ordering;
- reasoning by analogy.

The proven statement, that $p(Args)$ is provable from the single subgoal $q(Args)$, if the arguments satisfy a certain condition, is represented by the formula $know\_select\_optimal(p(Args), [typ_1(Args), \ldots, typ_r(Args)], q(Args))$. In the formula above, the condition restricting the set of potential Args is conveyed by a list of type predicates. These are computed by *compute_type*. A similar construction can be used to represent hypotheses by the meta predicate *hyp_select_optimal*. Assertions about decompositions will be implemented by the formula $get\_dec(p(Args), [q_1(Args), \ldots, q_r(Args)])$. The predicate *add_lemma* serves to increment the database by inserting factual knowledge. Because an unrestricted addition of all knowledge that is generated during a proof search would result in an exponential growth of the data base, the procedure was modified. First, facts that can be considered as irrelevant with respect to a heuristic filter will be neglected. Lemmata concerning behavioural equivalences can then be used to derive propositions about equivalence classes from the given facts by deduction. These more comprehensive assertions can then be added to the related databases.

```
prove(Goal) ⇐
        get_dec(Goal, List_of_Subgoals),
        compute_type(Goal, Type),
        select_prove(Goal, Type, List_of_Subgoals).

select_prove(Goal, Type, _) ⇐
        know_select_optimal(Goal, Type, Subgoal),
        call(Subgoal).

select_prove(Goal, Type, List_of_Subgoals) ⇐
        hyp_select_optimal(Goal, Type, Subgoal),
        ((member(Subgoal, List_of_Subgoals),
                call(Subgoal));
        (add_lemma(know_neg_select_optimal(Goal, Type, Subgoal),
                delete(List_of_Subgoals, Subgoal, New_List_of_Subgoals),
        select_prove(Goal, Type, New_List_of_Subgoals)).

select_prove(Goal, Type, [Subgoal|_]) ⇐
        call(Subgoal),
        add_lemma(know_select_optimal(Goal, Type, Subgoal)).

select_prove(Goal, Type, [Subgoal|List_of_Subgoals]) ⇐
        add_lemma(know_neg_select_optimal(Goal, Type, Subgoal)),
        select_prove(Goal, Type, List_of_Subgoals).
```

Figure 1: Metainterpreter

5.2 Program Transformation

In this subsection we summarize a way to acquire, debug and to use strategic knowledge for proving by theory formation and program transformation, based on example computations.

Let the evaluation of the predicate q, whose computation causes exhaustive backtracking be necessary for the proof of a goal $p(Args)$. Then a logic program **LP** for p is transformed into an equivalent logic program **LP′** by the following steps. The search in **LP′** for goals $p(Args)$ is guided by strategic knowledge.

T1. Replace each occurrence $p(Args)$ of p in **LP** by $prove(p(Args))$;

T2. Replace the definitions of q by definitions of the predicate *get_dec*;

T3. Extend the logic program by the definitions of the metainterpreter *prove* (as given in figure 1);

Strategic knowledge is acquired and refined by the following steps, which can be performed sequentially but also as separated experiments.

L1. Define the type system;

L2. Access the strategic knowledge and hypotheses, which can be empty initially;

L3. Perform some example computations using **LP′**;

L4. Refine and build the theory on the basis of the constructed facts;

- L4.1 Debug the hypotheses;
- L4.2 Eliminate inconsistencies by the extension of the type system;
- L4.3 Compress the set of hypotheses by generalization;

L5. Verify the derived hypotheses by further example computations.

The definition of *determine* in the program introduced in Section 2 will be transformed thereby to

$$\begin{aligned}&prove(determine(I,T,B,Z)) \Leftarrow get\_dec(determine(I,T,B,Z), List\_of\_Subgoals),\\ &\quad compute\_type(determine(I,T,B), Type),\\ &\quad select\_prove(determine(I,T,B,Z), Type, List\_of\_Subgoals).\end{aligned}$$

In principle, each element in *List_of_Subgoals* represents a subgoal $\Leftarrow split\_elements(Args, Op), part\_body(Args, Op)$. However, in our application a more efficient implementation was chosen.

Thus, a Prolog program is transformed in two steps: first a specialized control strategy is explicitly defined. As a second part of the modification, more specialized rules are added. The declarative semantics of the program will not be changed, but the derived program should run more efficiently on examples similar to the training examples that have already been analysed.

5.3 Implementation Issues

The methods for theory formation and program transformation operate on sets of formulas. They can be implemented in Prolog by `assert` and `retract` or by using non-standard extensions as an interface to the Unix-System. This is unsatisfying, because, as some side effects may occur, even clearly structured abstract specifications cannot be implemented in a straightforward way. Instead, they have to be programmed by use of tricky idiosyncrasies of the given environment. Thus, the resulting programs scarcely reflect the logical structure of the original specification.

In our implementation this shortcoming was avoided by explicit definitions of predicates which operate on sets of formulas. A similar approach was proposed in [2]. The introduction of higher order predicates allows to establish relationships between theories, eg. the predicate $subsumption(OldTheory, Formula, NewTheory)$ allows to eliminate in a given set of formulas with the name $OldTheory$ all formula which are subsumed by $Formula$. $NewTheory$ is the resulting theory. Based on these fundamental set-theoretic operations the methods of theory formation and program transformation have been implemented.

Goals can be proven with respect to dynamically created and modified theories. For this reason theories can be accessed by context-switching [21].

6 Empirical Results

The transformation method proposed in this paper was implemented as a component in the program synthesis system ASK (**A**cquiring **S**ynthesis **K**nowledge) [4] in Prolog. ASK is a system which supports the incremental acquisition and the debugging of incomplete or incorrect knowledge for program synthesis tasks on the basis of example computations. Derived knowledge and hypotheses will be used for further syntheses. As of now, knowledge of the domain of topological sorting problems has been specified and implemented in the system, which forms the basis for the syntheses of algorithms. The method is used to automatically transform program parts, which cause costly searches.

In one of our experiments, we analysed the transformation of the declarative generate-and-test specification of the function *split_elements*, which is defined above (see section 2). We used a set of selected training examples.

The deductive evaluation of the search processes yielded a total of 1595 positive and negative facts concerning the optimality of applied decompositions. These facts were processed by the abstraction procedure with respect to a superset of the type system introduced in section 3.1. A subsequent application of the debugging-and-generalization algorithms resulted in a non-redundancy consistent set of formulas. The final output of the fully automated transformation process consisted of the following five hypotheses in figure 2.

- These hypotheses represent the complete factual knowledge about the optimality of the decompositions in a condensed form (compression factor $> 1/300$).

$$\begin{aligned}
split_elements(I,T,B,[11,2]) \overset{hyp}{\Leftarrow}\ & I \geq 3, B \geq g(|T|),\\
& |\{S|S \subset T, |domt(S,T)| > 1\}| = 0,\\
& arity(T_{|[1]}) \geq f(|T|)+1,\\
& |T|-1 \leq 6 * 2^{f(|T|)-1},\\
& 5 * 2^{f(|T|)-1} > |T|-1,
\end{aligned}$$

$$\begin{aligned}
split_elements(I,T,B,[last(2),last(1)]) \overset{hyp}{\Leftarrow}\ & I \geq 3, B \geq g(|T|),\\
& |\{S|S \subset T, |domt(S,T)| > 1\}| = 0,\\
& arity(T_{|[1]}) < f(|T|)+1,\\
& |T|-1 \leq 6 * 2^{f(|T|)-1},\\
& 5 * 2^{f(|T|)-1} > |T|-1.
\end{aligned}$$

$$\begin{aligned}
split_elements(I,T,B,[1,2]) \overset{hyp}{\Leftarrow}\ & I \geq 3, B \geq g(|T|),\\
& |domt(T_{|[1,1]},T)| = 1,\\
& |\{S|S \subset T, |domt(S,T)| > 1\}| = 1,\\
& arity(T_{|[1]}) \geq f(|T|)+1,\\
& |T|-1 \leq 6 * 2^{f(|T|)-1},\\
& 5 * 2^{f(|T|)-1} > |T|-1.
\end{aligned}$$

$$\begin{aligned}
split_elements(I,T,B,[last(2),last(1)]) \overset{hyp}{\Leftarrow}\ & I \geq 3, B \geq g(|T|),\\
& I \leq 2,\\
& |\{S|S \subset T, |domt(S,T)| > 1\}| = 0,\\
& |T|-1 \leq 10 * 2^{f(|T|)-1},\\
& 6 * 2^{f(|T|)-1} > |T|-1.
\end{aligned}$$

$$split\_elements(I,T,B,[last(1),last(0)]) \overset{hyp}{\Leftarrow} I \leq 2, B \geq g(|T|).$$

Figure 2: Synthesized Formulas

- The derived hypotheses can be employed to efficiently control the proof process of further example computations. Thus, they allow for a reasoning by analogy. A substantial reduction of search complexities can be achieved this way. In our application, several examples, which could not be processed due to limitations of computing time and memory, can now be solved in "reasonable" time.

- Additionally, we showed by structural induction that the definition of the *split_elements*-function given by the hypotheses yields complete and correct executable specifications of the following algorithms:

  Determination of the element at the

  - first, second and third

  rank in a totally ordered set, respectively. To obtain these algorithms, we have to replace the generic rules of the domain theory introduced in section 2 by the synthesized hypotheses. The resulting algorithms are optimal as far as the number of calls of the *compare*-function is concerned. Their complexity is given by a linear mapping.

The success of the transformation method relies heavily on a very careful choice of

- the examples used for learning, and
- the type predicates.

7 Discussion

Our method aims at the automatic transformation of inefficient declarative "generate-and-test" programs into equivalent programs that describe the same solution set, but differ from the initial one in a crucial point: With the modified sets of clauses the computation of a solution by a Prolog-Interpreter will be deterministic, ie. no backtracking will be needed. If a set of generated hypotheses can be proven to describe the solution span in a correct and complete way, then the intended enhanced programs are derived in the following way: Each of the original predicate definitions must be replaced by the corresponding synthesized formulas. In this special case, it is not necessary to use a metainterpreter in order to control the search process. However, machine learning usually does not provide a method that allows formal verification of constructed hypotheses.

Therefore, the transformation method will be embedded [4] into a deductive approach for program synthesis based on constructive inductive proofs for the input-output specification using program schemata. These tactics reduce the program synthesis task to the instantiation of predicate and function variables, which satisfy some preconditions. Although, in practice, for human beings the selection of appropriate parameters is often rather obvious, a more general and feasible technique for the automation of this process is missing. In this paper an approach is presented which supports the incremental acquisition of hypothetical knowledge.

Currently the discovery of suitable hypotheses from example computations for a non-trivial mathematical application is empirically analysed. The main problem using such an approach is the adequate abstraction from facts by features such that the constructed hypotheses are useful for the description of a class of problems. In order to define an appropriate type system, a user needs a fairly good understanding of the problem domain, however, no further knowledge about the problem solution is required.

Acknowledgements

I wish to thank the anonymous reviewers for their valuable comments, and U. Thiel for proof-reading the final paper.

References

[1] W. Buntine. Generalized subsumption and its application to induction and redundancy. *Artificial Intelligence*, 36:149–176, 1988.

[2] I. Cicekli. Design and implementation of an abstract metaprolog engine for metaprolog. In H. Abramson and M. Rogers, editors, *Meta-Programming in Logic Programming*, pages 417–434. MIT Press, 1989.

[3] S.L. Epstein and N.S. Sridharan. Knowledge representation for mathematical discovery: Three experiments in graph theory. *Journal of Applied Intelligence*, 1(1):7–32, 1991.

[4] J. Eusterbrock. *Wissensbasierte Verfahren zur Synthese mathematischer Beweise: Eine kombinatorische Anwendung.* PhD thesis, Institut für Informatik, Stuttgart, 1991.

[5] A.M. Frisch and D.C. Page. Generalization with taxonomic information. In *Proc. AAAI-90, Eigth Nat. Conf. on Artificial Intelligence*, volume 2, pages 755–761. AAAI Press/ The MIT Press, 1990.

[6] V. Harmelen and A. Bundy. Explanantion based generalization=partial evaluation. *Artificial Intelligence*, 36(3):401–412, 1989.

[7] J.L. Lassez and K. Marriot. Explicit representation of terms defined by counter examples. *Journal of Automated Reasoning*, 3:301–317, 1987.

[8] B. Meltzer. Proof, abstraction and semantics in mathematics and artificial intelligence. In A. Marzollo, editor, *Topics in Artificial Intelligence*, pages 2–9. Springer Verlag, Wien New York, 1979.

[9] T. M. Mitchell, P. E. Utgoff, B. Nudel, and R. Banerji. Learning problem solving heuristics through practice. In *Proc. of International Joint Conference on Artificial Intelligence*, pages 127–134, 1981.

[10] T.M. et al Mitchell. Explanation- based- generalization. *Machine Learning*, 1:47–80, 1985.

[11] K.S. Murray. Multiple convergence: An approach to disjunctive concept acquisition. In *Proc. Int. Joint Conf. on Artificial Intelligence*, pages 297–300, 1987.

[12] N. J. Nilsson. *Principles of Artificial Intelligence.* Tioga Publishing Company, Palo Alto, 1980.

[13] G. D. Plotkin. A note on inductive generalization. In B. Meltzer and D. Michie, editors, *Machine Intelligence 5*, 1970.

[14] E.Y. Shapiro. *Algorithmic Program Debugging.* ACM Distinguished Dissertations, The MIT Press, 1982.

[15] E.Y. Shapiro, editor. *Concurrent Prolog: Collected Papers.* MIT Press Series in Logic Programming, 1987.

[16] B. Silver. *Meta Level Inference.* North-Holland, Amsterdam,New York, Oxford, 1986.

[17] Douglas R. Smith. Structure and design of global search algorithms. Technical report, KES.U.87.12, 1987.

[18] D.R. Smith. Top-down synthesis of divide-and-conquer algorithms. *Artificial Intelligence*, 27:43–96, 1985.

[19] C.B. Suttner and W. Ertel. Automatic acquisition of search heuristics. In M. E. Stickel, editor, *Proc. 10th International Conference on Automated Deduction*, pages 470–484. Lecture Notes in Computer Science 449, Springer, 1990.

[20] Vere. Induction concept in the predicate calculus. In *Proc. IJCAI*, 1975.

[21] U. Yalcinalp and L. Sterling. An integrated interpreter for explaining prolog's successes and failures. In H. Abramson and M. Rogers, editors, *Meta-Programming in Logic Programming*, pages 205–216. MIT Press, 1989.

Pruning Operators for Partial Evaluation

P. M. Hill
Department of Computer Studies
University of Leeds
Leeds, UK.
Email: hill@dcs.leeds.ac.uk

Abstract

It is essential that any program transformation technique produces programs that, for given queries, can compute the same answers as the original programs. For logic programs, it has been shown that, under certain conditions, a partial evaluation of a program is computationally equivalent to the original program. Unfortunately, these results only apply to programs without control directives.

In this paper, we consider the difficulties of partially evaluating a logic program with a pruning operator such as the cut of Prolog and propose alternative pruning operators that overcome many of these problems.

1 Introduction

A specification language should be as close as possible to a language in which people can express their ideas. Logic can provide the basis for such a language. A programming language chosen for the implementation of a specification should be as close as possible to the specification language but such that the implementing program can run at speeds acceptable to the user. Prolog has been shown to run at speeds comparable with the speeds of other programming languages. It is therefore natural to implement a logical specification in a logic programming language such as Prolog. In this case, it is clearly desirable that the programmer should initially consider only the meaning of the predicates being defined and not their run-time efficiency. The programmer may then add control directives that can help the compiler produce executable code with improved efficiency as well as preventing the program falling into non-terminating loops. Such control directives may be in the form of declarations that modify the underlying computation rule, or as pruning operators that indicate parts of the search space that may be pruned.

With a naive implementation such a program may still be very inefficient so that the program may have to be transformed to an equivalent program which computes the same answers but with greatly increased efficiency. One well-known transformation technique, called 'unfolding', performs some of the computation at compile time. In addition, for a particular application, it may be possible to specialise a program so that the transformed program computes the required answers for only a restricted set of goals. Partial evaluation is a well-known program transformation that combines the unfolding and specialisation techniques. For a full account of partial evaluation in logic programming and additional references, see [6].

It is essential that any program transformation technique produces a program that, for a given form of queries, can compute the same answers as the original program. For logic programs, Lloyd and Shepherdson [6] show that, under certain conditions, a partial evaluation of a program is computationally equivalent to the original program. However, these results only apply to programs without control directives. In this paper, we consider the difficulties of partially evaluating a logic program with a pruning operator such as the cut of Prolog and propose alternative pruning operators that overcome many of these problems.

Hill, Lloyd, and Shepherdson [4] give a careful analysis of the deficiencies of the Prolog cut. Here, we are only interested in the problems created by the cut for partial evaluators. First, the presence of the cut in a program allows considerable uncertainty about what the underlying logical theory is. This is because programmers can exploit the sequential nature of the cut to leave "tests" out and when this is done the logic of the program cannot be obtained by simply removing all the cuts from the program. Since a program transformation technique can only be recommended if the semantics of a program is preserved, this uncertainty means that partial evaluation cannot easily be extended to programs with cuts. Secondly, the pruning defined by the cut can be changed by the unfolding. This is illustrated by the following Prolog program *Mlists*.

$$\begin{aligned} &member\_lists(X, Xs, Xss) :- list\_of\_lists(Xss), !,\\ &\qquad\qquad member(X, Xs), member(Xs, Xss). \end{aligned}$$

$$\begin{aligned} &member(W, [W|Ws]).\\ &member(W, [U|Ws] :- member(W, Ws). \end{aligned}$$

$$\begin{aligned} &list\_of\_lists([]).\\ &list\_of\_lists([[]|X]) :- list\_of\_lists(X).\\ &list\_of\_lists([[U|V]|X]) :- list\_of\_lists(X). \end{aligned}$$

The intended meaning of *member_lists* is that *member_lists*(X, Xs, Xss) is true whenever Xss is a list of lists, Xs is an element of Xss, and X is an element of Xs. A partial evaluation of *member_lists*(X, Xs, Xss) in *Mlists* (obtained by unfolding on the second call to *member*) is the following.

$$member\_lists(X, Xs, [Xs|Yss]) :- list\_of\_lists([Xs|Yss]), !, member(X, Xs).$$
$$member\_lists(X, Xs, [Ys|Yss]) :- list\_of\_lists([Ys|Yss]), !, member(X, Xs), member(Xs, Yss).$$

A partial evaluation $Mlists'$ of $Mlists$ is obtained from $Mlists$ by replacing the clause defining $member\_lists$ by the two partially evaluated clauses above. Then using Prolog's left to right computation rule and top down search strategy, the goal

$$?- member\_lists(2, ls, [[1], [2]])$$

succeeds with the $Mlists$ but fails with $Mlists'$.

When a cut is activated two types of pruning take place. First, all later clauses to the one containing the activated cut in the definition are pruned. This pruning is given by the *soft component* of the cut. Second, alternative ways of solving the subgoals before the cut are pruned away. This pruning corresponds to the *one solution component.*

Some Prolog languages have a one-solution pruning operator. For example, Nu-Prolog [8] has the *once* construct. Here, *once* *Goal* finds only the first solution (if any) to *Goal*. This pruning operator does not behave well under unfolding. Consider the following definition of *common* which uses the definition of *member* given above.

$$common(Xs, Ys) :- once(member(X, Xs), member(X, Ys)).$$

The intended meaning of *common* is that $common(Xs, Ys)$ is true whenever the lists Xs and Ys have a common element. A partial evaluation of $common(Xs, Ys)$ gives the following definition.

$$common([X|Xs], [X|Ys]).$$
$$common([X|Xs], [Y|Ys]) :- once(member(X, Ys)).$$
$$common([X|Xs], [Y|Ys]) :- once(member(Y, Xs)).$$
$$common([X|Xs], [Y|Ys]) :- once(member(U, Xs), member(U, Ys)).$$

Clearly, less pruning will be performed using the partially evaluated definition of *common* than with the original one.

Consider next the commit proposed in [4] and implemented in the logic programming language Gödel. The most general form of the Gödel *commit* is {...}_n, of which two special cases are denoted by | and {...}. The | is called a bar commit and is essentially the same as the commit (or symmetric cut) that has been proposed for Andorra Prolog [2]. The {...} is called a one-solution commit and obtains only a single answer to the goal in its scope. The bar and one-solution commits are adequate for most programming requirements. However, as for the commit of the concurrent languages, statements using the bar commit are not even syntactically closed under unfolding. Furthermore, the one-solution operator is equivalent to the *once* pruning operator described above so that the problems for partial evaluators are the same. Thus, for partial evaluators, the bar and the one-solution commits are replaced by the more general form of the Gödel commit.

Programs using only the general form of the Gödel commit are closed under unfolding. Furthermore, it is shown in [4] that any answer that could be obtained before partial evaluation can also be obtained after partial evaluation and, subject to conditions on the partial evaluation, the set of computed answers that can be obtained by the transformed program could also have been obtained by the original program. A detailed description of the Gödel commit will be presented in section 3.

Similarly to the cut, the general form of the Gödel commit has two components, a one-solution and a soft component. The one-solution is a special case of the general form of the Gödel commit and has the syntax described above. On the other hand, the soft component by itself cannot be expressed by means of a Gödel commit. This lack of expressiveness prevents a programmer declaring precisely the pruning required. In most cases where the bar commit is used, the goal before the bar (called the *guard*) is deterministic. In these cases a commit (called a *soft bar commit*) limited to the soft component can replace the bar commit. We will describe a general pruning operator (called a *soft commit*), for which the soft bar commit is a special case, that behaves significantly better under partial evaluation than the Gödel commit.

Finally, consider the pruning operators proposed for Andorra Prolog ([1], [2], [9]). Andorra Prolog supports a version of the cut that is strictly compatible with the usual Prolog cut. Of course this inherits all the problems outlined above. Furthermore, it has been shown that the cut is problematic in parallel languages since the procedural semantics of cut depend on the order of literals in a goal and the order of clauses in a program, thereby limiting the amount of exploitable parallelism. For this reason, Andorra Prolog extends the basic Prolog with a symmetric pruning operator called a commit. This commit is similar to the Gödel bar commit in that it allows non-determinism in any part of the clause (that is, both before as well as after the commit). The pruning that can be performed when the commit is activated is the same as for the Gödel bar commit. Kernel Andorra [1] also has a soft cut and soft commit. The soft commit pruning operator has similar behaviour to the soft bar commit proposed here.

In the next section, we give the basic concepts used in the rest of the paper. A full description of the Gödel commit is presented in section 3. In section 4, we describe the soft commit and illustrate its use by means of examples. In section 5, we show that the soft commit behaves well under partial evaluation. We conclude the paper by indicating directions for future research.

2 Basic Concepts

In this section, we give the basic concepts of partial evaluation. A knowledge of the basic theory of logic programming, as can be found in [5], is assumed.

Definition A *program clause* (resp., *definite program clause*) is a clause of the form

$A \leftarrow L_1, \ldots, L_n$

where A is an atom and $L_1, \ldots, L_n$ are literals (resp., atoms).

Definition A *normal program* (resp., *definite program*) is a finite set of program clauses (resp., definite program clauses).

Definition A *normal goal* (resp., *definite goal*) is a clause of the form

$\leftarrow L_1, \ldots, L_n$

where $L_1, \ldots, L_n$ are literals (resp., atoms).

The following definitions were introduced in [6].

Definition A *resultant* is a formula of the form

$Q_1 \leftarrow Q_2$

where Q_i is either absent or a conjunction of literals ($i = 1, 2$). Any variables in Q_1 or Q_2 are assumed to be universally quantified at the front of the resultant.

We will use more general definitions of SLDNF-derivation and SLDNF-tree than are given in [5]. In [5], an SLDNF-derivation is either infinite, successful or failed. Here we will also allow it to be *incomplete*, in the sense that at any point we are allowed to simply not select any literal and terminate the derivation. Similar remarks apply to the definition of SLDNF-tree employed here.

Definition Let P be a normal program, G a normal goal $\leftarrow Q$, and $G, G_1, \ldots, G_n$ an SLDNF-derivation of $P \cup \{G\}$, where the sequence of substitutions is $\theta_1, \ldots, \theta_n$ and G_n is $\leftarrow Q_n$. Let θ be the restriction of $\theta_1 \ldots \theta_n$ to the variables in G. Then we say the derivation has *length* n with *computed answer* θ and *resultant* $Q\theta \leftarrow Q_n$. (If n=0, the *resultant* is $Q \leftarrow Q$.)

Definition If A and B are atoms and there exists a substitution θ such that $A\theta = B$, then we say B is an *instance* of A. We say a set of atoms $\mathbf{A}$ is *independent* if no pair of atoms in $\mathbf{A}$ have a common instance.

Definition Let S be a set of first order formulas and $\mathbf{A}$ a finite set of atoms. We say S is $\mathbf{A}$-*closed* if each atom in S containing a predicate occurring in an atom in $\mathbf{A}$ is an instance of an atom in $\mathbf{A}$.

3 The Gödel commit

It is not the purpose of this paper to describe the language Gödel and the interested reader is referred to the Gödel report [3]. In this section, we describe the Gödel commit for normal programs. This is derived from the commit defined in [4] where a full description of it is given.

We first give the (top-level) syntax for normal clauses and goals containing commits. Since a Gödel commit only occurs in the body of a goal or a clause, we only need to give the top-level syntax for a body.

Body	$\longrightarrow$	[*CBody*] '|' [*CBody*] | *CBody*
CBody	$\longrightarrow$	'{' *CBody* '}' [_*Label*] | *CBody* '&' *CBody* | *Formula*

where the notation | indicates alternative forms, [...] indicates 0 or 1 occurrences of the included item, *Label* is a positive integer, and *Formula* is a conjunction of literals where & is used for conjunction and ~ for negation.

The bar and one-solution commits can be replaced by the general form of the Gödel commit. A body of the form V | W is replaced by {V}_n & W, for a suitable positive integer n. If V is empty, it is replaced by `True`. The label n must be the same for all bar commits in a definition[1] and different from any other commit labels in the definition. One-solution commits are given a label unique to the goal or definition in which they appear.

We now describe the procedural semantics of (the general form of) the Gödel commit, the details for which can be found in [4]. First we generalise the concept of an SLDNF-tree in such a way that each node in the tree can have commits appearing in it although all subsidiary SLDNF-trees, used at nodes in which a negative literal is selected, are on the underlying commit-free program which is obtained from the original program by removing all the commits. Using this generalised concept of an SLDNF-tree, we can define an l-child as follows.

Definition Let T be an SLDNF-tree, G_0 a non-leaf node in T, and G_1 a child of G_0. Then G_1 is an *l-child* of G_0 if **either**

1. G_0 contains a commit labelled l and the selected literal in G_0 is in the scope of this commit, **or**

2. G_1 is derived from G_0 using an input clause which contains a commit labelled l (after standardisation apart of the commit labels).

We say that G_1 is an l-child *of the first kind* (resp., *of the second kind*) if G_0 satisfies condition 1 (resp., 2) above.

The ideas of the previous definition are illustrated with program `P0`.

[1] It is not necessary to have a bar commit in a goal since the same pruning can be expressed by a one-solution commit.

```
MODULE        PO.

PROPOSITION   P,Q,R,S,T,U,V,W,Z,B.

P <- {Q}_1 & R.
P <- {S}_1 & T.
P <- U & {V}_2.
Q.
U <- W & Z.
R.
S <- B.
S.
T.
```

The following is an incomplete SLDNF-tree for program PO and goal <- P.

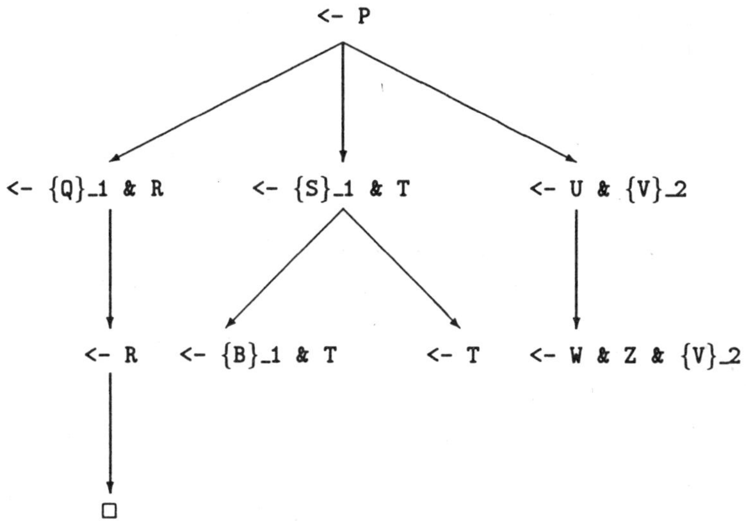

Then the nodes <- {Q}_1 & R, <- {S}_1 & T are 1-children and the node <- U & {V}_2 is a 2-child of <- P of the second kind. The nodes <- {B}_1 & T, <- T are 1-children of <- {S}_1 & T of the first kind. The node <- W & Z & {V}_2 is not a 2-child, as the selected literal is not in the scope of any commit.

We define the concept of a pruning step, which gives the procedural meaning of the Gödel commit.

Definition Let S be a subtree of an SLDNF-tree. We say that the tree S' is obtained from S by a *pruning step* in S at G_0 if the following conditions are satisfied.

1. S has a node G_0 with distinct l-children G_1 and G_2, and there is an l-free node G_2' in S which is either equal to or below G_2.

2. S' is obtained from S by removing the subtree of S rooted at G_1.

We say that G_1 is the *cut node* and the pair (G_2, G_2') is an *explanation* for the pruning step.

Consider the preceding SLDNF-tree. We can apply a pruning step to this tree to obtain the subtree S_1

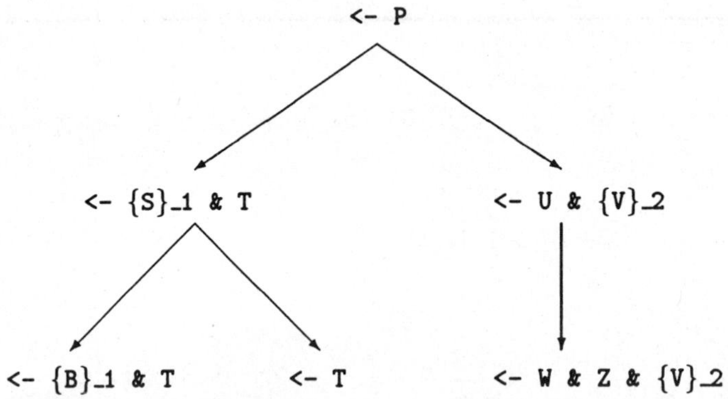

where the explanation for pruning the leftmost branch is (<- {S}_1 & T, <- T). We can apply another pruning step to S_1 to obtain the subtree S_2

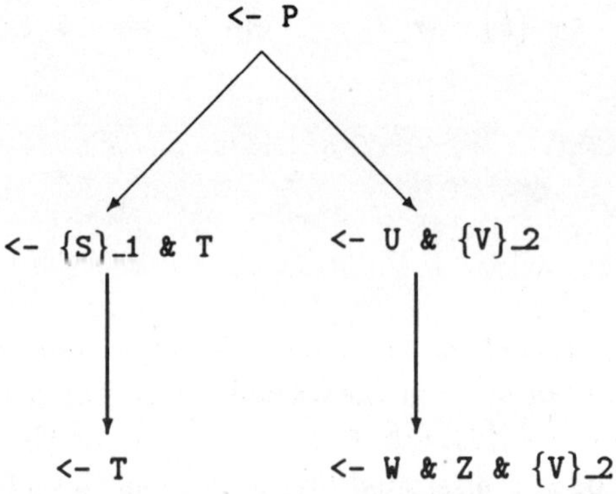

where the explanation for pruning the leftmost child of `<- {S}_1 & T` is the pair (`<- T`, `<- T`). No further pruning is possible.

Definition Let S be a subtree of an SLDNF-tree. A *pruning sequence* from S to S' of *length* n is a sequence $\{S_i\}_{i=0}^{n}$ of trees such that $S_0 = S$, $S_n = S'$, and S_i is obtained from S_{i-1} by a pruning step, for all $i \in \{1, \ldots, n\}$. We say that S' is a *pruned* subtree of S.

Soundness and completeness results have been proved for the partial evaluation of normal programs with Gödel commits (see [4, Theorems 3.1 and 3.2]). Before stating these results we need to define partial evaluation and related concepts for programs with Gödel commits.

Definition Let T be an SLDNF-tree. We say that T is *regular* if, for each node in T with more than one child in T, the selected literal is in the scope of all the commits at that node.

Definition Let P be a normal program, A an atom, and T a finite, non-trivial SLDNF-tree for $P \cup \{\leftarrow A\}$ such that, if the selected literal at a node $\leftarrow Q$ is an atom, then the commit labels in the matching clauses are standardised apart not only wrt the labels in $\leftarrow Q$ but also all goals in T which are not descendants of $\leftarrow Q$. Let S be a pruned subtree of T and $\{R_1, \ldots, R_r\}$ the set of all the resultants for S. Then the set $\{R_1, \ldots, R_r\}$ of program clauses is called a *partial evaluation of A in P*.

The partial evaluation is said to be *regular* if T is regular. The partial evaluation is said to be *free* if $S = T$.

Definition Let P be a normal program and $\mathbf{A}$ a finite set of atoms. A *partial evaluation of P wrt* $\mathbf{A}$ is a normal program obtained from P by replacing the set of clauses in P whose head contains one of the predicates appearing in $\mathbf{A}$ by the union of partial evaluations of the atoms in $\mathbf{A}$ in P.

The partial evaluation of P wrt $\mathbf{A}$ is said to be *regular* (resp., *free*) if the partial evaluation of each atom in $\mathbf{A}$ is regular (resp., free).

Theorem 3.1 *Let P be a normal program, G a normal goal, $\mathbf{A}$ a finite, independent set of atoms, and P' a free partial evaluation of P wrt $\mathbf{A}$ such that $P' \cup \{G\}$ is $\mathbf{A}$-closed. Then θ is a computed answer for $P \cup \{G\}$ iff θ is a computed answer for $P' \cup \{G\}$*

Note that, the completeness result proved in [4, Theorem 3.1] is slightly stronger but requires the additional concept of *persistence* (which we have not defined here).

Theorem 3.2 *Let P be a normal program, G a normal goal, $\mathbf{A}$ a finite, independent set of atoms, and P' a partial evaluation of P wrt $\mathbf{A}$ such that*

$P' \cup \{G\}$ is **A***-closed. If the partial evaluation is free and regular, and S' is a pruned subtree of an SLDNF-tree T' for $P' \cup \{G\}$, then there is a pruned subtree S of an SLDNF-tree T for $P \cup \{G\}$ which has the same set of computed answers as S'.*

Note that the second result requires the regularity condition. This severely restricts the choice of computation rule used for partial evaluation.

To illustrate this point, consider the Gödel program `Perm0` that can be used to find a permutation of a list of integers[2], where `True` is a built-in proposition that always succeeds. `Perm1` is a free partial evaluation of `Perm0` obtained by

```
MODULE         Perm0.

IMPORT         Lists.

PREDICATE      Permutation : List(Integer) * List(Integer).

Permutation([],[]) <-
               {True}_1.
Permutation([x|y],[u|v]) <-
               {True}_1 &
               Delete(u,[x|y],z) &
               Permutation(z,v).

PREDICATE      Delete : Integer * List(Integer) * List(Integer).

Delete(x,[x|y],y).
Delete(x,[y|z],[y|w]) <-
               x ~= y &
               Delete(x,z,w).
```

unfolding on the call to `Delete` in the second statement for `Permutation`. Now the goal

```
<- Permutation([1,2,3],x) & x = [2,1,3]
```

will succeed for program `Perm0` but could fail unexpectedly using `Perm1` by committing to the second statement. The problem was caused by unfolding on an atom outside the scope of the commit so that the regularity condition does

[2]In `Perm0` and `Perm1`, the module `Lists` defines the notation `[..|..]` for lists. The IMPORT declaration makes this module available for use in the current module.

```
MODULE          Perm1.

IMPORT          Lists.

PREDICATE       Permutation : List(Integer) * List(Integer).

Permutation([],[]) <-
                {True}_1.
Permutation([x|y],[x|v]) <-
                {True}_1 &
                Permutation(y,v).
Permutation([x|y],[u|v]) <-
                {True}_1 &
                u ~= x &
                Delete(u,y,w) &
                Permutation([x|w],v).

PREDICATE       Delete : Integer * List(Integer) * List(Integer).

Delete(x,[x|y],y).
Delete(x,[y|z],[y|w]) <-
                x ~= y &
                Delete(x,z,w).
```

not hold and hence the scope of the commit in **Perm1** includes the first call to **Delete**. Note that, as the commit in **Perm0** can only prune the alternative clause for **Permutation**, only the soft component is intended here.

4 The Soft Commit

We now describe a soft commit that only prunes branches at a single node of the SLDNF-tree. Although a simple syntax is adequate for most programming tasks it will suffer from the same problems as the bar commit in unfolding transformations. Thus we define a general form of the soft commit for which the soft bar commit is a special case. We use brackets $\{\cdots\}$ as before to indicate the scope of the soft commit. However, as shown in the programs **Perm0** and **Perm1**, labelling the bracket pair by a single integer does not give a sufficiently flexible control of the pruning operator.

Therefore, in order to distinguish the soft commit from the Gödel commit and have adequate control of the pruning, we extend the Gödel syntax for programs[3] so that a commit label can either be an integer or a pair of integers. If the label is a pair of integers, then we call the label a *soft commit label.* The intended meaning is that if the commit label is a positive integer, then the commit is a Gödel commit and its pruning is as described in section 3, and if the commit label is a pair of positive integers, then the commit is a soft commit and its pruning is described below. We use the notation λ to represent a label and refer to a *λ-commit* to mean a commit with label λ where λ is either an integer or a pair of integers. If a goal has no λ-commit it is said to be *λ-free.* The word *commit* is used to mean either a Gödel or a soft commit.

We generalise the concept of an SLDNF-tree for a normal program P and normal goal G with commits in such a way that the goal at a node in the tree can include (general forms of) both Gödel and soft commits. At each node, we need to standardise apart the labels in the definition used for the resolution steps at that node from the labels in the node. By *standardising apart,* we mean that if the selected literal at a node $\leftarrow Q$ is an atom, then the commit labels in the matching clauses are renamed such that:

1. each renamed Gödel commit label does not occur as a Gödel commit label or as the first integer of a soft commit label in $\leftarrow Q$;

2. the first integer in each renamed soft commit label does not occur as a Gödel commit label or as the first integer in a soft commit label in $\leftarrow Q$;

3. if l_1 and l_2 are Gödel commit labels renamed by l'_1 and l'_2, respectively, then $l'_1 = l'_2$ iff $l_1 = l_2$;

4. if (l_1, m_1) and (l_2, m_2) are soft commit labels renamed by (l'_1, m'_1) and (l'_2, m'_2), respectively, then $l'_1 = l'_2$ iff $l_1 = l_2$ and $m'_1 = m'_2$ iff $m_1 = m_2$;

5. if (l_1, m_1) and l_2 are commit labels renamed by (l'_1, m'_1) and l'_2, respectively, then $l'_1 \neq l'_2$.

As in section 3, to ensure soundness, the subsidiary SLDNF-trees (used at nodes in which negative literals are selected) are on the underlying commit-free program which is obtained from the original program by removing both forms of commits.

We extend the definition of an l-child to include the soft commit.

Definition Let T be an SLDNF-tree, G_0 a non-leaf node in T, and G_1 a child of G_0. Then G_1 is an *l-child of the third kind* of G_0 if

[3]It is not necessary to have soft commits in goals, since they can have no effect on the pruning.

3. G_1 is derived from G_0 using, as input clause, a program clause containing a commit with label (l, m), for some m (after standardisation apart of the commit labels).

We illustrate the idea behind this definition in program Q0

```
MODULE        Q0.

PROPOSITION   P,Q,R,S,T,U.

P <- {Q}_(1,2).
P <- {R}_(1,2).
P <- {S}_(1,3).
R <- T.
R <- U.
U.
```

The following tree T is an SLDNF-tree for Q0 with initial goal <- P

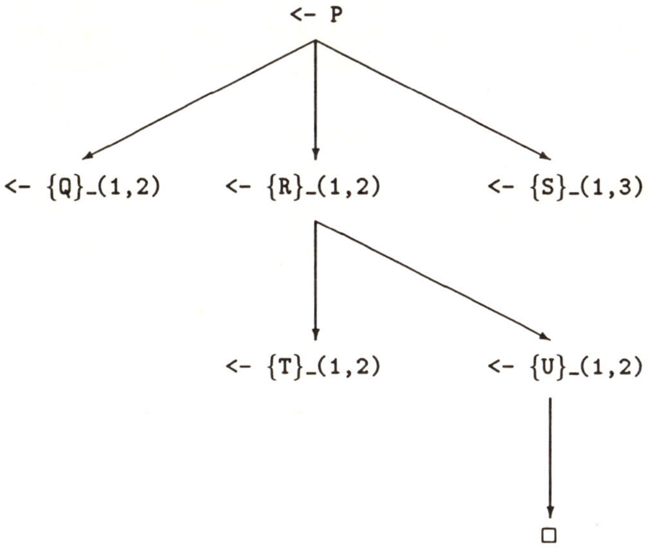

Then the nodes <- {R}_(1,2), <- {Q}_(1,2), and <- {S}_(1,3) are 1-children of <- P of the third kind but the nodes <- {T}_(1,2), and <- {U}_(1,2) are not 1-children of <- {R}_(1,2).

We now generalise the definition of pruning step (and hence that of a pruning sequence) to include the soft commit.

Definition Let S be a subtree of an SLDNF-tree. We say that the tree S' is obtained from S by a ***pruning step*** in S' at G_0 with label λ, cut node G_1, and explanation (G_2, G_2') if the following conditions are satisfied.

1. S has a node G_0 with distinct l-children G_1 and G_2 such that **either**

   (a) λ is an integer l and there is an l-free node G_2' in S which is either equal to or below G_2, **or**

   (b) λ is a pair of integers (l,m), G_2 has an (l,m)-commit, G_1 has an (l,m')-commit where $m \neq m'$, and there is an (l,m)-free node G_2' in S which is either equal to or below G_2.

2. S' is obtained from S by removing the subtree of S rooted at G_1.

For an illustration of this definition, consider again `Q0`. We can apply one pruning step to the tree T which prunes the subtree rooted at `<- {S}_(1,3)` using explanation (`<- {R}_(1,2)`, $\Box$). No other pruning is possible.

5 Partial Evaluation and the Soft Commit

We extend the results in [4] to include the soft commit. Clearly, the presence of soft commits does not affect the result of theorem 3.1. However, program `Q1` and its partial evaluation `Q1'` show that, without additional restrictions, theorem 3.2 is not true for programs with soft commits.

```
MODULE        Q1.

BASE K.
CONSTANT A,B,C : K.
PROPOSITION  S.
PREDICATE P,Q,R : K.

P(x) <- {Q(x)}_(1,2).
P(x) <- {R(x)}_(1,3).
Q(A) <- S.
Q(B) <- S.
R(C).
S.
```

```
MODULE        Q1'.

BASE K.
CONSTANT A,B,C : K.
PROPOSITION  S.
PREDICATE P,Q,R : K.
P(A) <- {S}_(1,2).
P(B) <- {S}_(1,2).
P(x) <- {R(x)}_(1,3).
Q(A) <- S.
Q(B) <- S.
R(C).
S.
```

There is an SLDNF-tree for Q1' with initial goal <- P(x)

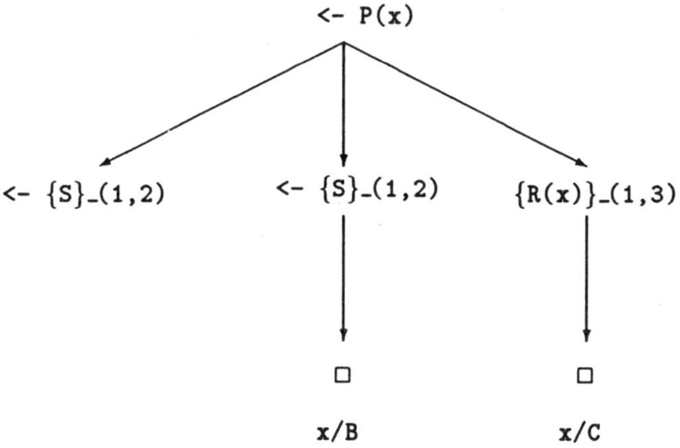

which can be pruned by first removing the left-most node <- {S}_(1,2), using the explanation (<- {R(x)}_(1,3),□), and then removing the subtree rooted at <- {R(x)}_(1,3) using the explanation (<- {S}_(1,2),□) to give just the computed answer {x/B}. However, there is no pruned subtree of an SLDNF-tree for Q1 with initial goal <- P(x) which has just this answer.

Thus, as shown in the above example, using the soft commit, pruning in some arbitrary order can achieve interesting although possibly unexpected results. In practice, the pruning will be performed in a systematic way and an implementation will have some pruning strategy. We define two such strategies.

Definition Let S be a subtree of an SLDNF-tree. We say that the tree S' is obtained from S by a *λ-pruning sequence* $\{S_i\}_{i=0}^n$ if $S = S_0$, $S' = S_n$, and there is a pruning step from S_{i-1} to S_i with label λ, for all $i \in \{1, \ldots, n\}$.

We say the λ-pruning sequence is *committed* if no pruning steps can be applied to S_n with label λ.

Definition Let S be a subtree of an SLDNF-tree. We say that the tree S' is obtained from S by a *label-based* pruning sequence $\{S_i\}_{i=0}^k$ if $S = S_0$, $S' = S_k$, and there is a committed λ_i-pruning sequence from S_{i-1} to S_i, for all $i \in \{1, \ldots, n\}$.

Note that, as a label-based pruning sequence is defined to be a sequence of pruning sequences, it can be easily flattened into a single pruning sequence.

Definition A *top down* pruning sequence is a pruning sequence $\{S_i\}_{i=0}^n$ such that, if S_i is obtained from S_{i-1} by a pruning step at G_i, for all $i \in \{1, \ldots, n\}$, then G_k is not above G_j, for all j and k such that $1 \leq j < k \leq n$.

This implies that, for all $i \in \{1, \ldots, n\}$, the subtree rooted at the cut node H_i for the pruning step from S_{i-1} to S_i is the same as the subtree rooted at H_i in S_0. The following result, proved in [4], shows that all pruning can be done top down.

Theorem 5.1 *(Top Down Pruning) Let S be a subtree of a SLDNF-tree. If S' is a pruned subtree of S, then there is a top down pruning sequence $\{S_i\}_{i=0}^n$ with $S_0 = S$ and $S_n = S'$.*

The regularity condition for partial evaluation trees, defined in section 3, applies only to the Gödel commit. It is not necessary to extend the condition to the soft commit. We do, however, require the following condition that applies to both commits.

Definition Let T be an SLDNF-tree. Then we say that T is *simple* if, whenever a commit label λ occurs in a node N in T, then λ occurs in every node below N.

If a partial evaluation P' of a normal program P wrt $\mathbf{A}$ uses simple SLDNF-trees for the partial evaluation, then we say the partial evaluation is *simple.*

Note that if a partial evaluation is simple, it must have been obtained using SLDNF-trees. Thus a simple partial evaluation is always free.

Theorem 5.2 *Let P be a normal program, G a normal goal,* **A** *a finite independent set of atoms, and P' a regular and simple partial evaluation of P wrt* **A** *such that $P' \cup \{G\}$ is* **A**-*closed. If S' is a pruned subtree of an SLDNF-tree T' for $P' \cup \{G\}$ obtained using a label-based pruning sequence, then there is a pruned subtree S of an SLDNF-tree T for $P \cup \{G\}$ (also obtained using a label-based pruning sequence) which has the same set of computed answers as S'.*

Proof Let G' be a node of T' from which is derived a child using one of the new program clauses as input clause. Then we call G' a *partially evaluated node of* T'. Since $P' \cup \{G\}$ is **A**-closed, the selected atom at G' will be an instance $A\phi$ of one of the atoms A in **A**. Since **A** is independent, A is uniquely defined and is the atom whose partial evaluation gave rise to this new clause. As the partial evaluation is free, the partial evaluation $\{R_1, \ldots, R_n\}$ of A will have been obtained using an SLDNF-tree T_0. Since we get a program procedurally equivalent to P' by replacing its clauses by variants, we may assume T_0 is chosen so that $R_1, \ldots, R_n$ are standardised apart so as to allow their use at the node G' in T'. Let $R_1, \ldots, R_n$ be indexed so that $R_1, \ldots, R_r$ are the only program clauses in $R_1, \ldots, R_n$ whose heads unify with $A\phi$ (where $r = 0$ is a possibility). Suppose G' has children $G'_1, \ldots, G'_r$ in T', where G'_i is obtained using input clause R_i and mgu ϕ_i, for each $i \in \{1, \ldots, r\}$.

As the partial evaluation is free, T_0 is an SLDNF-tree for $P \cup \{\leftarrow A\}$ and hence, by [4, lemma 3.3], there is a 'corresponding' SLDNF-tree $T_0(G')$ for $P \cup \{G'\}$. We construct a tree T from T' by replacing each partially evaluated node G' and the edges from G' leading to its children $G'_1, \ldots, G'_r$ by $T_0(G')$. By [4, lemma 3.3], each replacement is a perfect fit since, although the new tree $T_0(G')$ may have some additional failed branches, G' is the root node of $T_0(G')$, and the children of G' in T' are the same as the non-failed leaf nodes of $T_0(G')$. Also, by [4, lemma 3.3], the substitution in T' on the edge from G' to each child is the same as the substitution for the branch to the corresponding node in $T_0(G')$. Also, since the partial evaluation is free, by [6, theorem 4.3], the successful (resp., failed) negative calls in T' can be replaced by corresponding successful (resp., failed) negative calls in T. Thus the new tree T is an SLDNF-tree for $P \cup \{G\}$.

Given any subtree S of T, we define the *contraction* S^* of S to be the tree obtained from S by removing, for each partially evaluated node G', any failure branches in $T_0(G')$ contained in S and replacing each branch leading from G' to some leaf node G'_i of $T_0(G')$ in S by a single edge from G' to G'_i. Clearly, S^* is a subtree of T' and, if T^* is the contraction of T, $T^* = T'$.

The theorem is now a consequence of the lemma below by induction on the length of the label-based pruning sequence from T' to S'. ∎

Lemma 5.3 *Let P be a normal program, G a normal goal, $\mathbf{A}$ a finite independent set of atoms, and P' a regular and simple partial evaluation of P wrt $\mathbf{A}$ such that $P \cup \{G\}$ is $\mathbf{A}$-closed. If there is a pruned subtree S'_0 (resp., S_0) of an SLDNF-tree T' for $P' \cup \{G\}$ (resp., T for $P \cup \{G\}$) such that S^*_0 and S'_0 are the same, and a committed λ-pruning sequence from S'_0 to S', then there is an committed λ-pruning sequence from S_0 to a subtree S of T such that S^* and S' are the same.*

Proof By theorem 5.1, we can assume that there is a top down pruning sequence $\{S'_i\}_{i=0}^n$ from S'_0 to S'. We prove the result by induction on the length n of the pruning sequence. If the length is 0, then the result is obvious. Suppose $n > 0$ and the first pruning step from S'_0 to S'_1 is at a node G'. Let $\{S'_i\}_{i=0}^m$ $(m > 0)$ be the maximal initial subsequence such that, for each $i \in \{1, \ldots, m\}$, the pruning step from S'_{i-1} to S'_i is at the same node G'. Then, as the pruning sequence $\{S'_i\}_{i=0}^n$ is committed, there are no pruning steps with label λ that can be applied to S'_m at G'. We shall define a corresponding sequence $\{S_i\}_{i=0}^m$ from S_0 to S_m such that each step is either a pruning step using label λ or $S_i = S_{i-1}$ (a null step). If the null steps are removed, then the remaining sequence is a committed λ-pruning sequence. Let S^*_i be the contraction of S_i. Then we will show, by induction on i, that $S'_m \subseteq S^*_i$ and $S^*_i \subseteq S'_i$, for each $i \in \{0, \ldots, m\}$. Furthermore, we will show that if G' is not a partially evaluated node, then $S'_i = S^*_i$, for each $i \in \{0, \ldots, m\}$.

For the base case, as $S'_m \subseteq S'_0$ and $S'_0 = S^*_0$, the result follows. Suppose that $i > 0$. Let $G'_1, \ldots, G'_r$ be the children of G' indexed so that G'_i is the cut node of the pruning step from S'_{i-1} to S'_i, for each $i \in \{1, \ldots, m\}$.

Let (J, K) be the explanation of the last pruning step in $\{S'_i\}_{i=0}^m$. As J and K occur in S'_m, J and K must occur in S'_i, for all $i \in \{1, \ldots, m\}$. Thus all the pruning steps in $\{S'_i\}_{i=0}^m$ can use the same explanation (J, K).

We now define the pruning step from S_{i-1} to S_i and show that the contraction S^*_i of S_i has the required properties. If G'_i is not present in S_{i-1}, then we take $S_i = S_{i-1}$ and the result follows. Therefore, suppose G'_i is present in S_{i-1}. If G' is not a partially evaluated node, then the subtree rooted at G'_i in S_{i-1} can be pruned from S_{i-1}. We define the pruning step from S_{i-1} to S_i to have the cut node G'_i and explanation (J, K). By the inductive hypothesis, $S^*_{i-1} = S'_{i-1}$. Thus the contraction of the tree removed in this pruning step is the same as the tree removed in the pruning step from S'_{i-1} to S'_i. Therefore, $S^*_i = S'_i$ and as $S'_m \subseteq S'_i$, we have $S'_m \subseteq S^*_i$.

The crucial case is where G' is a partially evaluated node. Let H_i be the nearest common ancestor of J and G'_i in S_{i-1}, and L_i and M_i the children of H_i on the branches leading to G'_i and J, respectively.

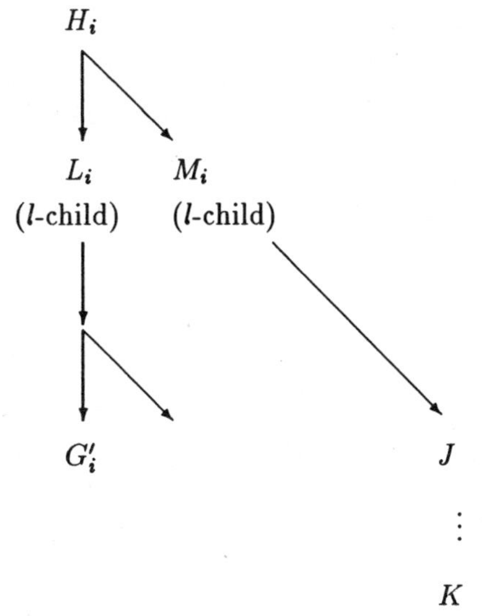

There are three cases.

1. *$\lambda = (l, m)$ is a soft commit label.*
   As the pruning step has label (l, m), the cut node G'_i must have a commit labelled (l, m_i) such that $m_i \neq m$. By standardising apart, the labels (l, m) and (l, m_i) must have been introduced at H_i so that L_i has the commit label (l, m_i) and M_i has a commit labelled (l, m). Thus we define the pruning step from S_{i-1} to S_i to be at H_i with cut node L_i and explanation (M_i, K).

   We must now show that this pruning step does not remove any G'_j that is in S'_m. Suppose G'_j is removed from S_{i-1} by this pruning step, for some $j \in \{1, \ldots, r\}$. Then G'_j must be below L_i in S_{i-1}. As the partial evaluation is simple, G'_j has a commit labelled (l, m_i). If G'_j occurs in S'_m, then (J, K) is an explanation for a pruning step at G' in S'_m with cut node G'_j, contradicting the fact that no pruning steps can be applied to S'_m at G' with label (l, m). Thus G'_j does not occur in S'_m, as required.

2. *$\lambda = l$ is a Gödel commit label and the selected literal at G' is within the scope of an l-commit.*
   As the partial evaluation is simple, every node in S_0 at or below G' and above J has an l-commit. As the partial evaluation is regular, every node in S_0 below G' and at or above J is an l-child of the first kind. Similarly, every node in S_0 below G' and at or above G'_i is an l-child of the first kind. Furthermore, as (J, K) is an explanation for a pruning step in S'_0, K is an l-free node. Thus the subtree rooted at L_i can be pruned with explanation (M_i, K). We define the pruning step from S_{i-1} to S_i to be

at H_i with cut node L_i and explanation (M_i, K).

Suppose G'_j is removed from S_{i-1} by this pruning step, for some $j \in \{1, \ldots, r\}$. Then G'_j must be below L_i in S_{i-1}. As the partial evaluation is simple and regular, G'_j is an l-child of the first kind in S'_0. If G'_j occurs in S'_m, then (J, K) is an explanation for a pruning step at G' in S'_m with cut node G'_j, contradicting the fact that no pruning steps can be applied to S'_m at G' with label l.

3. *$\lambda = l$ is a Gödel commit label and the selected literal at G' is not within the scope of a l-commit.*
Since, in S'_{i-1}, J must be an l-child of G' of the second kind and the introduced labels must be standardised apart from the labels in the current goal, G' will be l-free. There must be a node between G' and J and a (not necessarily distinct) node between G' and G'_i which include an l-commit but whose parents do not. By standardising apart, any labels of commits introduced below L_i and M_i would be distinct and hence the l-commit must be introduced either at L_i and M_i or at a node below G' and at or above H_i. If the l-commit is introduced at L_i and M_i, then they are l-children of H_i of the second kind. Otherwise, as the partial evaluation is simple, H_i contains an l-commit and, as the partial evaluation is regular, L_i and M_i are l-children of H_i of the first kind. In both cases, the subtree rooted at L_i may be pruned with explanation (M_i, K). Thus we define the pruning step from S_{i-1} to S_i to be at H_i with cut node L_i with explanation (M_i, K).

Suppose G'_j is removed from S_{i-1} by this pruning step, for some $j \in \{1, \ldots, r\}$. Then G'_j must be below L_i in S_{i-1}. As the partial evaluation is simple, G'_j has an l-commit. Since G' does not have an l-commit, G'_j is an l-child of G' of the second kind in S'_0. If G'_j occurs in S'_m, then (J, K) is an explanation for a pruning step at G' in S'_m with cut node G'_j, contradicting the fact that no pruning steps can be applied to S'_m at G' with label l.

As $S'_m \subseteq S^*_i$ and $S^*_i \subseteq S'_i$, for each $i \in \{0, \ldots, m\}$, we have $S^*_m = S'_m$. Therefore, by the inductive hypothesis, $S^*_n = S'_n$, as required. ∎

6 Conclusion

In the previous sections we have shown that the use of pruning operators affects the amount of unfolding that can be performed on a program. Here, we have studied the Gödel commit and defined a new pruning operator called the soft commit. These were chosen since, together, it is possible to express both a one solution operator and a soft pruning operator yet not unnecessarily restrict the unfolding of clauses. In practice, although the general forms of these pruning operators may appear fairly complicated, we have indicated that there are simplified forms of these that are adequate for the majority of programming tasks. In fact, only the soft bar commit and one-solution commit are required, since a Gödel bar commit can always be expressed as a combination of a soft bar commit and a one-solution commit. Furthermore, in most program statements with a bar commit, the guard is flat so that only a soft bar commit is needed.

The implementation of the commits is not discussed here and this is a topic for further research. However, it should be noted that Kernel Andorra Prolog [1] has a labelled form of its commit similar to the Gödel commit that is used in the definition of the computation model. We conjecture that implementing coroutining across the scope of a pruning operator is considerably simpler if it is a soft commit instead of a Gödel commit.

Ross [7, chapter 7], using CCS, has investigated the cut and the effect unfolding has on programs with cuts. He shows that unfolding atoms in a goal before the cut does not effect the operational semantics provided no cuts occur in the clauses used by the unfolding step. Note that this is even more restrictive than the regularity condition required for unfolding programs with the Gödel commit. However, we have not considered operational equivalence in this paper. It would be useful to apply his techniques to programs with the Gödel and soft commits and investigate their operational behaviour with respect to program transformations such as unfolding.

There are two forms of control available to a logic programmer. One is the pruning discussed in this paper, and the other is the computation rule. The computation rule is controlled by the ordering of the literals in the body of a clause as well as (in most logic programming languages) by means of mode declarations. There is a need for further research regarding the interplay between mode declarations and pruning operators and regarding the partial evaluation of programs with mode declarations.

Acknowledgements

We would like to thank Kerima Benkerimi who helped motivate the original idea for the soft commit and Tony Bowers for indicating that the problems of implementing the Gödel commit are not insuperable. Finally, we would like to thank John Lloyd for the many valuable discussions on pruning and control in logic programming.

References

[1] T. Franzen. Formal aspects of Kernel Andorra: I. Technical Report ISSN 0283–3638, Swedish Institute of Computer Science, 1990.

[2] S. Haridi and P. Brand. Andorra Prolog: An integration of Prolog and committed choice languages. In *Proceedings of the International Conference on Fifth Generation Computer Systems*, Tokyo, pages 745–754, 1988.

[3] P.M. Hill and J.W. Lloyd. The Gödel report (preliminary version). Technical Report CS-91-02, Department of Computer Science, University of Bristol, 1991.

[4] P.M. Hill, J.W. Lloyd, and J.C. Shepherdson. Properties of a pruning operator. *Journal of Logic and Computation*, 1(1):99–143, 1990.

[5] J.W. Lloyd. *Foundations of Logic Programming.* Springer-Verlag, second edition, 1987.

[6] J.W. Lloyd and J.C. Shepherdson. Partial evaluation in logic programming. Technical Report CS-87-09, Department of Computer Science, University of Bristol, 1987. Revised July 1989. To appear in The Journal of Logic Programming.

[7] B. J. Ross. *An Algebraic Semantics of Prolog Control.* PhD thesis, Edinburgh University, 1991.

[8] J. A. Thom and J. Zobel. Nu-prolog reference manual, version 1.3. Technical Report TR 86/10, Machine Intelligence Project, Department of Computer Science, University of Melbourne, 1988.

[9] D.H.D. Warren. The SRI model for or-parallel execution of Prolog – abstract design and implementation issues. In *Proceedings of the 1987 Symposium on Logic Programming*, San Francisco, pages 92–102. IEEE, 1987.

Specialisation of a Unification Algorithm *

D.A. de Waal
J. Gallagher
Department of Computer Science
University of Bristol
Bristol
United Kingdom

Abstract

Automatically specialising an algorithm for unification is a challenge to current techniques for partial evaluation. In this paper a study is made of several specialisations of unification that are typically needed. The limitations of existing partial evaluation techniques are examined and proposals for extensions are made. Partial evaluation is modified by adding condition goals which are used to evaluate or prune more of the computation tree than is possible with partial evaluation alone. It is shown that abstract substitutions can be introduced to allow information from infinite computation trees to be exploited. If infinite failures are removed from the computation tree the resulting specialised program does not preserve the procedural semantics given by SLDNF (which defines negation by finite failure). There is a short discussion on correctness results for such specialisations.

1 Introduction

Automatically specialising an algorithm for unification is of interest on two counts. Firstly it is a challenge to current specialisation techniques such as partial evaluation. A detailed study of this problem involves several key questions of partial evaluation including termination and the automatic control of unfolding. The study also suggests some areas where current techniques do not perform the required specialisation and should be extended. Secondly, specialising unification is a central part of the problem of compiling logic programs using the specialisation of an interpreter (that is, carrying out the first Futamura projection).

In the following, identifiers starting with lower case letters are variables, and those starting with upper case letters are constant, function or predicate symbols. The unification algorithm is formulated as a logic program U defining `Unify(x',y',s')` where `x'` and `y'` are representations of terms `x` and `y` respectively, and `s'` is a representation of `s`, a most general unifying substitution of `x` and `y`. We emphasise that we deal with *representations* of terms and substitutions. `Unify/3` is a meta predicate whose arguments are ground representations

*Work supported by ESPRIT II project PRINCE (5246)

of object language constructs [8]. Later we describe the representation scheme that we use. The program is included in appendix A. Contrast this formulation with the unification program given in [12], which manipulates ordinary Prolog structures including variables. That program may be more efficient but has to use non-logical features of Prolog, and hence does not have a declarative meaning. Specialising such programs is not impossible but correctness results are very difficult to obtain.

The aim of this study is to specialise the program U for various goals. The goals we consider are of the form:

- `<- Unify(t1,t2,s),C(t1,t2)`, where `t1` and `t2` are partially known terms to be unified and `C(t1,t2)` is some condition on the terms `t1` and `t2` where `C/2` is also defined by a logic program. Examples of such conditions are that `t1` or `t2` are ground, or that they share no variables. Such specialisations often require more sophisticated methods than partial evaluation. It is the purpose of this paper to develop such techniques. Rather than specialising the whole goal `<- Unify(t1,t2,s),C(t1,t2)`, we specialise the goal `<- Unify(t1,t2,s)` and use the condition `C(t1,t2)` to evaluate or prune more of the computation tree than is possible with partial evaluation of the goal `<- Unify(t1,t2,s)` alone. This is explained later in the paper.

We discuss first the specialisation of a number of typical examples. Then we discuss the algorithm for partial evaluation and examine the limitations of the algorithm for the given examples. An extension of current techniques of partial evaluation is proposed, in which the condition `C(t1,t2)` mentioned above is used to restrict the construction of the computation tree during partial evaluation. Information from infinite computations such as infinite failures and abstractions of infinite sets of solutions can also be useful during the specialisation. Abstract interpretation is used to obtain information on infinite computations, and it is incorporated into the partial evaluation algorithm.

2 Representation of Terms

A ground representation is used to represent terms to be unified and substitutions. Variables in the object language are represented as ground terms, `Var(1)`, `Var(2)`, `...`; atoms and terms in the object language are represented as ground terms `Struct(Predicate,Arguments)` and `Struct(Function, Arguments)` respectively, where `Predicate` and `Function` are constants representing predicate and function symbols and `Arguments` is a list of ground representations of the predicate and function arguments. Constants in the object language are regarded as 0-ary function symbols, and thus a constant is represented as a ground term `Struct(Constant,[])`. No distinction is made between atoms and terms in this unification algorithm. For example, the atom `'P(x,F(y))'` could be represented by a term `Struct(P',[Var(1),Struct(F',[Var(2)])])`.

3 Specialising for Particular Calls to Unify

The applications that are of interest occur during the execution of a logic program when unifying an atom and a copy of a clause head, which are standardised apart. This means that the general unification algorithm should not be needed in this case, since the occur check can be omitted in cases where a substitution pair is formed from a variable from one atom and a term from the other. Clearly, the variable does not occur in the term due to standardisation apart.

In all the examples of interest, the first argument of `Unify` is completely known, since it is the head of a logic program clause. As mentioned above, we also know that no variable in the clause head occurs in the call which is the second argument. We may also have partial information about the call in addition to knowing the first argument, such as mode, groundness or sharing information.

The following examples illustrate the kind of specialisation that need to be handled and the required results.

1. When unifying an atom `P(t1,t2)` in a goal with the head of a clause `P(x,y)`, we specialise a goal such as

```
<- Unify(Struct(P',[Var(1),Var(2)]),Struct(P',[t1,t2]),s),
   Noshare(Struct(P',[Var(1),Var(2)]),Struct(P',[t1,t2])).
```

   given a predicate `Noshare/2` that states that `t1` and `t2` do not share any variables. Specialisation is possible because of the known structure of the terms and because the variables in `Struct(P', [Var(1), Var(2)])` and `Struct(P',v)` are renamed apart. Specialising with respect to the above query gives the logic program clause

```
Unify(Struct(P',[Var(1),Var(2)]),Struct(P',[x0,x1]),
                                  [Var(1)/x0,Var(2)/x1]) <- .
```

2. If the head of the clause is `P(x,x)` we specialise with respect to the query

```
<- Unify(Struct(P',[Var(1),Var(1)]),Struct(P',[t1,t2]),s),
   Noshare(Struct(P',[Var(1),Var(1)]),Struct(P',[t1,t2])).
```

   giving as specialised program

```
Unify(Struct(P',[Var(1),Var(1)]),Struct(P',[t1,t2]),
                                  [Var(1)/t1 | s0]) <-
   Unify1(t1,t2,s0).
```

   where `Unify1` is a renamed call to the general unification procedure. (Note that the substitution returned by the unification procedure is not in idempotent form, so the partial result `[Var(1)/t1 | s0]` can be returned.)

3. Information about the modes of arguments in the call can also be exploited. Suppose the clause head `P(x,x)` is to be unified with a call `P(t,z)`, where `t` is a non-variable and `z` is a variable. The query to be specialised is of the form

```
<- Unify(Struct(P',[Var(1),Var(1)]),
                        Struct(P',[Struct(f,w),Var(2)]),s),
   Noshare(Struct(P',[Var(1),Var(1)]),
                          Struct(P',[Struct(f,w),Var(2)])).
```

   Specialisation gives the clause

```
Unify(Struct(P',[Var(1),Var(1)]),Struct(P',[Struct(f,w),
     Var(2)]),[Var(1)/Struct(f,w),Var(2)/Struct(f,w)] ) <-
   not(Occur(Var(2),w)).
```

   `P(x,x)` and `P(t,z)` are renamed apart and so the only time that the occur check may be violated is when `Var(2)` occurs inside `w`, the argument of the non-variable term `Struct(f,w)`. This is therefore the only check necessary.

4. If some argument of the call is known to be ground, the situation is more complex since groundness is a recursive property. Suppose the clause head `P(x,x)` is to be unified with a call `P(t,z)`, where `t` is ground and `z` is a variable. Then we specialise a goal of the form

```
<- Unify(Struct(P',[Var(1),Var(1)]),
                              Struct(P',[t,Var(2)]),s),
   Ground(t).
```

   given a predicate `Ground/1` that checks whether its argument represents a ground term. Because `t` is ground, `z` cannot appear in `t` and no occur check is necessary. `P(x,x)` and `P(t,z)` are renamed apart and specialisation therefore should give a clause

```
Unify(Struct(P',[Var(1),Var(1)]),Struct(P',[t,Var(2)]),
                              [Var(1)/t, Var(2)/t] ) <-
```

5. Sharing information within the call presents similar problems. Suppose the clause head `P(x,x)` is to be unified with a call `P(t1,t2)`, where `t1` and `t2` do not share any variables. Then we specialise a goal of the form

```
<- Unify(Struct(P',[Var(1),Var(1)]),Struct(P',[t1,t2]),s),
   Noshare(Struct(P',[Var(1),Var(1)]),Struct(P',[t1,t2])),
   Noshare(t1,t2).
```

   Specialisation gives a clause

```
Unify(Struct(P',[Var(1),Var(1)]),Struct(P',[t1,t2]),
                                  [Var(1)/t1 | s0] ) <-
   Unify1(t1,t2,s0).
```

where the partial substitution `s = [Var(1)/t1]` is computed, and the unification of `t1` and `t2` performed by `Unify1` can be simplified since `t1` and `t2` share no variables. (For example, if `t1 = Var(n)`, the substitution `[Var(n) / t2]` can be generated with no occur check.)

None of these results is straightforward using existing techniques of partial evaluation. We examine the reasons in more detail in section 5. To achieve the results shown we need to extend current partial evaluation techniques.

4 The Basic Specialisation Algorithm

The basic algorithm used for partial evaluation is based on the results in [10], the algorithm given in [1] and the unfold/fold transformation system in [11]. First we outline this algorithm and then show how it is modified to incorporate conditions to perform further specialisation. Secondly we show how to include abstract substitutions.

Let P be a normal program, and G a goal. The following algorithm, based on one in [1] computes a set of atoms from P and G.

```
begin
   A[0] := the set of atoms in G
   i := 0
   repeat
      P' := a partial evaluation
               of A[i] in P
      S := A[i] U
           { p(t) | B <- Q,p(t),Q' in P'
                    OR
                    B <- Q,not(p(t)),Q' in P'}
      A[i+1] := abstract(S)
      i := i+1
   until A[i] = A[i-1] (modulo variable renaming)
end
```

Definition 4.1 *abstract(S)*
The operation abstract(S) is any operation satisfying the following condition. Let S be a set of atoms; then A = abstract(S) implies A is a set of atoms with the same predicates as those in S, such that every atom in S is an instance of an atom in A.

The above algorithm is stated in a naive form that is quite inefficient, but a more efficient formulation was used in our study. If this algorithm terminates then every atom in P' and G is an instance of some atom in $A[i]$. However P' is not yet the required specialised program since $A[i]$ may not be *independent*, that is, two atoms in $A[i]$ may have common instances. As shown in [10], partial evaluation of a non-independent set of atoms is not correct. As in [1] we introduce renamings of atoms to handle the non-independence problem, but in a different way.

Definition 4.2 *renaming*
Let $p(t_1, \ldots, t_n)$ be an atom. Define a renaming of $p(t_1, \ldots, t_n)$ as an atom $p'(x_1, \ldots, x_m)$ where p' is a new predicate symbol and $\{x_1, \ldots, x_m\} = vars(p(t_1, \ldots, t_n))$. Let $A[i]$ be the set of atoms obtained when the above algorithm terminates. Define $\bar{A}$ to be a set of atoms obtained by renaming the atoms in $A[i]$ in such a way that each atom in $\bar{A}$ has a distinct predicate not occurring in P or G. Obviously $\bar{A}$ is independent.

Suppose $B \in A[i]$ and $\bar{B}$ is its renamed version in $\bar{A}$. For each atom define a clause $\bar{B} \leftarrow B$ and let $\bar{P}$ be the program obtained by adding these clauses to P.

The specialised program is then obtained by a process of unfolding and folding applied to $\bar{P}$, and is an instance of the transformations defined in [11] which preserve both answers and finite failures for stratified programs.

In the algorithm, there are two operations left unspecified. One is the process of computing P' as a partial evaluation of $A[i]$ in P. The other is the abstraction operation.

In the control of partial evaluation we make no explicit attempt to perform loop detection. In this aspect we differ from most other work on partial evaluation. (Nevertheless partial evaluation terminates). The control is based on looking for choice points, the rationale being that partial evaluation should perform as much determinate computation as possible, but that further computation may be counterproductive. Further details of the control strategy used may be found in [7].

The *abstract* operation is based on the idea of characteristic paths, presented in [5].

5 Limitations of the Basic Algorithm

The algorithm described in the previous section is limited in three main ways:

1. It uses only SLDNF computations to generate the resultants. This means that negative literals cannot be selected unless they are ground. However the occur check appears frequently in the computation: a typical resultant is:

   ```
   Unify(Var(1),t,[Var(1)/t]) <- not(Occur(Var(1),t))
   ```

   The call to `not(Occur(Var(1),t))` cannot be evaluated if `t` is not ground. However, if we have the information that `Var(1)` does not share with `t` (for instance if `t` represents a ground term) then this implies that `not(Occur(Var(1),t))` succeeds and should be eliminated.

2. The partial evaluation algorithm loses information in each iteration because when the set of atoms from the resultants is collected (to form the set `S` in the algorithm) the sharing information between atoms is lost. If the goal to be partial evaluated is of the form

```
G = <- Unify(x,y,s),C(x,y)
```

where `C(x,y)` is a condition, and both `Unify(x,y,s)` and `C(x,y)` have infinite computation trees, any partial evaluation of `G` must suspend at some stage and at that point the connection between the variables in the subgoals of `Unify(x,y,s)` and those of `C(x,y)` will be lost. As a result an over-general call to `Unify` may be generated.

3. Partial evaluation considers only a finite number of finite subtrees of the computation. But a goal such as

```
<- Occur(Var(1),t), Ground(t)
```

has an infinitely failed computation tree (though for each ground instance of `t` the computation fails finitely). More powerful evaluation techniques are needed to detect the infinite failure, and we propose abstract substitutions as a means to achieve this.

6 Partial Evaluation with Conditions

Given a goal `<- Unify(x,y,s), C(x,y)` we regard this as a goal `<- Unify(x,y,s)` with the condition `C(x,y)`, rather than a single goal. The condition `C(x,y)` is defined by a logic program, which we assume is included in the unification program. Intuitively, at each stage in the basic partial evaluation algorithm, the condition is used to evaluate or prune the resultants.

Definition 6.1 *condition pair*
Let A be an atom and $\{C_1, \ldots, C_k\}$ be a finite set of atoms, such that each C_j shares at least one variable with A. Then the pair $(A, \{C_1, \ldots, C_k\})$ is called a condition pair.

Let $(A, \mathbf{C})$ be a condition pair, and P a program defining the predicates in A and $\mathbf{C}$. Let $A\theta \leftarrow R$ be a resultant of A in P. We consider two operations on the resultant, using the condition $\mathbf{C}$.

T1 Let $\mathbf{C} = \{C_1, \ldots, C_k\}$. $\mathbf{C}\theta$ denotes the set $\{C_1\theta, \ldots, C_k\theta\}$. If the goal $\leftarrow R, \mathbf{C}\theta$ fails, then the resultant $A\theta \leftarrow R$ can be deleted from the partial evaluation of A in P, since the resultant is incompatible with the condition.

T2 Let $R = \neg L, Q$ where L is an atom and Q a conjunction of literals. Suppose the goal $\leftarrow L, Q, \mathbf{C}\theta$ fails, then the resultant $A\theta \leftarrow R$ can be replaced by $A\theta \leftarrow Q$ in the partial evaluation of A in P. A proof of the correctness of this transformation is short, and is a generalisation of the fact that if the atomic goal $\leftarrow L$ fails, then the goal $\leftarrow \neg L$ succeeds. This transformation was proposed in [3].

Definition 6.2 *conditioned resultants*
Let $(A, \mathbf{C})$ be a condition pair, and P a program. The set of conditioned resultants of $(A, \mathbf{C})$ in P is obtained by applying the above operations to the set of resultants of A in P, and is called a conditioned partial evaluation of $(A, \mathbf{C})$ in P. Given a set of condition pairs, its conditioned partial evaluation is the union of the conditioned partial evaluations of its elements.

Following the pattern of the basic partial evaluation algorithm, we wish to generate a set of condition pairs that is closed in some sense. Having generated a set of conditioned resultants from $(A, \mathbf{C})$, we need also to collect a set of condition pairs from the resultants. This is done as follows.

Let $A\theta \leftarrow R$ be a conditioned resultant of $(A, \mathbf{C})$ in P. Let B be an atom occurring in R. Consider the condition $C_1\theta, \ldots, C_k\theta$, and let $C_1\theta, \ldots, C_k\theta \leftarrow \mathbf{C}'$ be the resultant obtained by unfolding the condition so long as the unfolding is determinate; that is, each atom selected unifies with exactly one clause head in P. Then the condition pair associated with B is $(B, \mathbf{D})$, where $\mathbf{D}$ is the subset of literals in $\mathbf{C}$ sharing a variable with B. The requirement that $\mathbf{D}$ is the subset of literals in $\mathbf{C}$ sharing a variable with B is a safe approximation of the conditions imposed on B. The condition pairs obtained are used to generate further conditioned resultants, and the process is repeated until no new condition pairs (modulo renaming of variables) are obtained.

In order to ensure termination, we require again an abstraction operation. The notion of a condition subsuming another is defined as follows.

Definition 6.3 *subsumes*

Let $\mathbf{C}$ *and* $\mathbf{C}'$ *be conditions. Then* $\mathbf{C}'$ *subsumes* $\mathbf{C}$ *if* $\mathbf{C} = \mathbf{C}'\theta \cup \mathbf{D}$, *where* $\mathbf{D} \subseteq \mathbf{C}$.

Definition 6.4 *abstract'(S)*

Let S *be a set of condition pairs. A set abstract'*(S) *is any set such that if* $(A, \mathbf{C}) \in S$, *there exists a pair* $(A', \mathbf{C}') \in$ *abstract'*(S), *where* A *is an instance of* A' *and* $\mathbf{C}'$ *subsumes* $\mathbf{C}$.

We can now give the outline of an algorithm for partial evaluation with conditions. Let $A[0] = \{(B, \mathbf{C})\}$ contain an initial condition pair, and P be a program. B is the atom to be specialised, with the conditions $\mathbf{C}$.

```
begin
    A[0] := the set containing the initial condition pair
    i := 0
    repeat
        P' := a conditioned partial evaluation
                    of A[i] in P
        S := A[i] U
              { (p(t),D) | (B,C) in A[i],
                        B.theta <- Q,p(t),Q' in P'
                        OR
                        B.theta <- Q,not(p(t)),Q' in P',
                        (p(t),D) is the condition pair
                         obtained from B, C and theta}
        A[i+1] := abstract'(S)
        i := i+1
    until A[i] = A[i-1] (modulo variable renaming)
end
```

Example 1 *Consider the first case from Section 3.*

```
<- Unify(Struct(P',[Var(1),Var(2)]),Struct(P',[t1,t2]),s),
   Noshare(Struct(P',[Var(1),Var(2)]),Struct(P',[t1,t2])).
```

One of the resultants of the atom `Unify(Struct(P',[Var(1),Var(2)]), Struct(P',[t1,t2]),s)` is

```
Unify(Struct(P',[Var(1),Var(2)]),Struct(P',[t1,t2]),
                                    [Var(1)/t1 | s1]) <-
   not(Occurs(Var(1),t1)), Unify(Var(2),t2,s1).
```

The corresponding instance of the condition

```
Noshare(Struct(P',[Var(1),Var(2)]),Struct(P',[t1,t2]))
```

can be unfolded to the condition

```
Noshare(Var(1),t1),
Noshare(Var(1),t2),
Noshare(Var(2),t1),
Noshare(Var(2),t2).
```

The goal

```
<- Occurs(Var(1),t1), Noshare(Var(1),t1)
```

fails, and so by the transformation T2 given earlier the literal `not(Occurs(Var(1),t1))` can be omitted from the resultant.

An important point is that this goal fails infinitely; analysis is required to detect the absence of solutions. In the next section we present an algorithm incorporating abstract substitutions; the motivation for this is partly that operations on abstract substitutions provide sufficient conditions for detecting failure.

Note that the use of infinite failures implies that the finite failure set of the specialised program may be increased, so the correctness results for SLDNF of [10] do not apply. In a later section we discuss correctness results for the extended specialisation algorithm.

In the next section, abstract substitutions are used instead of conditions. The idea however is similar: the abstract substitutions are used to prune some of the computation tree during partial evaluation.

7 Extending Partial Evaluation with Abstract Interpretation

The main reason for introducing abstract interpretation into partial evaluation is to be able to use information from infinite computation trees. In partial evaluation as defined in section 4 only a finite part of the computation of a goal is evaluated.

Abstract interpretation provides a framework for computing approximations of a computation. For the purposes of this paper we introduce some of the concepts of abstract interpretation. Let us assume that some domain **Sub** of *abstract substitutions* is defined, with a partial order $\sqsubseteq$. Let $\sqcap$ be a greatest lower bound operator on **Sub**. Each element of **Sub** *describes* or represents a set of substitutions. There is a monotonic *abstraction* function α that maps a set of substitutions to an element of **Sub**. Given a program P and goal G, a procedure is defined for computing an abstract substitution Θ that describes all the computed answer substitutions for $P \cup \{G\}$. Θ is a *safe* approximation in the sense that if S is the set of computed answer substitutions for $P \cup \{G\}$, then $\alpha(S) \sqsubseteq \Theta$. That is, Θ describes an overestimation of the solutions. Let $\perp$ be the least element of **Sub**, representing the empty set of substitutions. Several frameworks for abstract interpretation of logic programs are described in the literature, such as [2].

The algorithm in section 4 is now modified to include abstract substitutions. The idea is to use the abstract substitutions as constraints on the generation of resultants. This is strongly related to the methods in [5] and [6].

The first stage of the algorithm generates a set of pairs of the form (A, Θ), where A is an atom and Θ is an abstract substitution.

The algorithm is modified from the basic algorithm. Let P be a program, A an atom and Θ (written `Theta` in the algorithm) an abstract substitution. The *greatest lower bound* operator on the set of abstract substitutions is written `glb`.

```
begin
   A[0] := {(A,Theta)}
   i := 0
   repeat
      P' := a partial evaluation
                of A[i] in P
      P" := {B.rho <- Q | (B,Phi) in A[i],
                B.rho <- Q in P',
                glb(alpha({rho}),Phi) \= bottom}
      S := A[i] U
           { (p(t),Beta) | (B,Phi) in A[i],
                B.rho <- Q,p(t),Q' in P"
                OR
                B.rho <- Q,not(p(t)),Q' in P",
                Beta = restrict(glb(alpha({rho}),Phi),p(t))}
      A[i+1] := abstract''(S)
      i := i+1
   until A[i] = A[i-1] (modulo variable renaming)
end
```

The line in the algorithm in which `P"` is computed is the stage at which the abstract substitution is used to prune some of the resultants from the partial evaluation. Say that a pair (B, Φ) exists in `A[i]`. B is partially evaluated in the standard way, giving a set of resultants in `P'` of the form $B\rho \leftarrow Q$. If $\alpha(\{\rho\}) \sqcap \Phi = \perp$ then the resultant is incompatible with the abstract substitution Φ and it is not included in `P"`.

The set of pairs `S` is formed by collecting all the atoms occurring in resultants in `P"`, and associating with each atom an abstract substitution. If $p(t)$ is an atom occurring in the resultant $B\rho \leftarrow Q$, then it is associated with the abstract substitution $(\alpha(\{\rho\}) \sqcap \Phi)|_{p(t)}$.

The operation *abstract''* is also an extension of the abstraction operator defined earlier.

Definition 7.1 *abstract''(S)*

Let S be a set of pairs of form (A, Θ) where A is an atom and Θ an abstract substitution. The operation abstract''(S) is any operation satisfying the following condition. $A = abstract''(S)$ implies A is a set of pairs such that for every pair (B, Φ) in A, the following conditions hold.

1. $\Phi = \Phi|_B$.

2. *There is a pair (A, Θ) in S where A is an instance of B, and $\Theta \sqsubseteq \Phi$.*

Example 2 *Suppose the unification algorithm is to be specialised for the case where two ground terms are being unified. A procedure defining ground terms is defined as follows:*

```
Ground(Struct(f,xs)) <-
      GroundArgs(xs).

GroundArgs([]).
GroundArgs([x|xs]) <-
     Ground(x),
     GroundArgs(xs).
```

The goal to be specialised is:

```
<- Unify(x,y,s,s1),Ground(x),Ground(y)
```

Here `Unify(x,y,s,s1)` is a predicate which is true if `s1` is the substitution obtained by unifying the terms obtained by applying the incoming substitution `s` to `x` and `y`. Note that a standard partial evaluation of this goal would not yield an interesting result, since the call `Unify(x,y,s,s1)` is completely general and would not result in any specialisation.

In this example we view the goals `Ground(x), Ground(y)` as constraints in the partial evaluation of `Unify(x,y,s,s1)`. The first step is to perform an abstract interpretation of the goal `Ground(x), Ground(y)`. As a suggestion, some abstract interpretation for type inference might be used. The type inference of [9] would give types essentially as follows:

$$Gr ::= Struct(\beta, List(Gr))$$

$$List(\alpha) ::= []; [\alpha | List(\alpha)]$$

The abstract solution for `Ground(x), Ground(y)` would then be $\{x/Gr, y/Gr\}$.

The algorithm is then applied to the pair $(Unify(x, y, s, s1), \{x/Gr, y/Gr\})$.

1. There are several resultants for $Unify(x, y, s, s1)$, but any in which x or y are bound to variables (that is terms **Var(n)**) are incompatible with the abstract substitution. After pruning away the incompatible resultants the only resultant generated is:

```
Unify(Struct(f,xs),Struct(f,ys),s,s1) <-
     UnifyArgs(xs,ys,s,s1).
```

2. The atom $UnifyArgs(xs, ys, s, s1)$ has as its associated abstract substitution
$\{xs/List(Gr), ys/List(Gr)\}$.

3. The procedure is then repeated for the pair $(UnifyArgs(xs, ys, s, s1),$ $\{xs/List(Gr), ys/List(Gr)\})$. The resultants of $UnifyArgs(xs, ys, s, s1)$ are:

```
UnifyArgs([],[],s,s).
UnifyArgs([x'|xs'],[y'|ys'],s,s2) <-
        Unify(x',y',s,s1),
        UnifyArgs(xs',ys',s1,s2).
```

Both of these are compatible with the abstract substitution. The abstract substitutions for the body atoms are then computed. The pairs obtained are as follows:

$$(Unify(x', y', s, s1), \{x'/Gr, y'/Gr\})$$
$$(UnifyArgs(xs', ys', s1, s2), \{xs'/List(Gr), ys'/List(Gr)\})$$

Both of these are variants of pairs occurring already, so the algorithm terminates.

The renaming in this case is trivial, so the program obtained is:

```
Unify(Struct(f,xs),Struct(f,ys),s,s1) <-
     UnifyArgs(xs,ys,s,s1).

UnifyArgs([],[],s,s).
UnifyArgs([x'|xs'],[y'|ys'],s,s2) <-
        Unify(x',y',s,s1),
        UnifyArgs(xs',ys',s1,s2).
```

This is a considerable simplification of the original unification algorithm, and implements an algorithm that just unifies two ground terms by checking whether they are identical.

8 Correctness Results with Infinite Failure Removal

As mentioned earlier, the correctness results in [10] no longer apply. The reason is that infinitely failed computations may be pruned, effectively turning them into finitely failed ones. Therefore the procedural semantics given by SLDNF is not preserved, as required in [10].

As an example, consider the following goal.

```
<- Occur(Var(1),y), Ground(y)
```

This has no solutions, but has an infinite computation tree. However for any given ground instance of **y**, the goal fails finitely.

The standard partial evaluation algorithm above does not specialise away such infinite failures. The algorithm incorporating abstract substitutions could do so. What are the problems and possibilities of removing infinite failures?

A limited but useful correctness property can be stated. If G is a goal and P' is a program obtained by eliminating infinite failures from $P \cup \{G\}$, and G' is an instance of G such that $P \cup \{G'\}$ has a finite computation tree, then $P' \cup \{G'\}$ also has a finite computation tree yielding the same answers (or finite failure) as $P \cup \{G'\}$.

9 Conclusions and Further Research

Specialisation of unification is an essential part of partial evaluation of a logic program interpreter, and presents a challenge to existing techniques for partial evaluation. The problems of specialising the unification algorithm were discussed. Extensions of existing methods for partial evaluation were needed to handle specialisations of unification goals involving conditions on the terms such as groundness. Two algorithms were outlined: the first incorporated conditions expressed as logic program goals, which were used to evaluate and prune resultants in the basic partial evaluation computation tree. Secondly, abstract substitutions were incorporated into a version of the basic partial evaluation algorithm.

The extended algorithms are more powerful than the standard algorithm in the sense that the standard algorithm is a special case of it. However, the extended algorithms are capable of removing infinite failures, and a correctness claim for such transformations was made. This stated that the behaviour of finite computations was preserved, but not of arbitrary computations. Further work to give more precise correctness results, with proofs, is to be done.

The incorporation of conditions and abstract substitutions into our existing partial evaluation algorithms in an efficient way is the most immediate topic for further work. The specialisation of unification is being used in the context of partial evaluation of an interpreter for logic programs using a ground representation of the object program. This work will also be relevant to partial evaluation of interpreters for other languages such as constraint logic languages.

References

[1] K. Benkerimi and J.W. Lloyd; A Procedure for Partial Evaluation of Logic Programs; Proceedings of the North American Conference on Logic Programming, November 1990, Austin, Texas; (eds. S. Debray and M. Hermenegildo); MIT Press 1990.

[2] M. Bruynooghe; A Practical Framework for the Abstract Interpretation of Logic Programs: to appear in *Journal of Logic Programming.*

[3] D. Chan and M. Wallace; A Treatment of Negation During Partial Evaluation; in *Meta-Programming in Logic Programming*; eds. H. Abramson and M.H. Rogers, MIT Press, 1989.

[4] J. Gallagher and M. Buynooghe; Some Low-Level Source Transformations for Logic Programs; Proceedings of Meta90 Workshop on Meta Programming in Logic, Leuven, Belgium, (April 1990).

[5] J. Gallagher and M. Bruynooghe; The Derivation of an Algorithm for Program Specialisation; 7th Int. Conf. on Logic Programming, Jerusalem, eds. D.H.D. Warren and P. Szeredi, MIT Press, June 1990.

[6] J. Gallagher, M. Codish, E. Shapiro; Specialisation of Prolog and FCP Programs Using Abstract Interpretation; *New Generation Computing*, 6 (1988) 159-186.

[7] J. Gallagher; SP: A System for Specialising Logic programs; Technical Report, University of Bristol.

[8] P.M. Hill and J.W. Lloyd; Analysis of Meta-Programs; in *Meta-Programming in Logic Programming*; eds. H. Abramson and M.H. Rogers, MIT Press, 1989.

[9] G. Janssens and M. Bruynooghe; Deriving Descriptions of Possible Valuam Variables by Means of Abstract Interpretation; Katholieke Univ. Leuven, CW-Report 108, 1990 (to appear in *Journal of Logic Programming*).

[10] J.W. Lloyd and J.C. Shepherdson; Partial Evaluation in Logic Programming; University of Bristol, Department of Computer Science, TR-87-09 (1987) (revised 1989); (to appear in *Journal of Logic Programming).*

[11] H. Seki; Unfold/Fold transformations of Stratified Programs; in Proc. of the 6th Int. Conf. on Logic Programming, Lisbon, 1989, eds. G. Levi and M. Martelli, MIT Press, 1989.

[12] L. Sterling and E. Shapiro; *The Art of Prolog*; MIT Press (1986)

A Ground Unification Algorithm

```
% Unification of ground terms with occurs check
% J. Gallagher & D.A. de Waal:  30/6/91
% unify(X,Y,S):  unifies X and Y giving substitution S (not
% idempotent in general).

unify(X,Y,S) :-
        unify(X,Y,[],S).

unify(var(N),T,S,S1) :-
        bound(var(N),S,B,V),
        unify(var(N),T,S,S1,B,V).
unify(struct(F,Args),var(N),S,S1) :-
        unify(var(N),struct(F,Args),S,S1).
unify(struct(F,Args1),struct(F,Args2),S,S2) :-
        unifyargs(Args1,Args2,S,S2).

unify(var(_),T,S,S1,B,true) :-
        unify(B,T,S,S1).
unify(var(N),T,S,S1,_,false) :-
        unify1(T,var(N),S,S1).

unifyargs([],[],S,S).
unifyargs([T|Ts],[R|Rs],S,S2) :-
        unify(T,R,S,S1),
        unifyargs(Ts,Rs,S1,S2).

unify1(struct(F,Args),var(N),S,[var(N)/struct(F,Args)|S]):-
        \+ occur_args(var(N),Args,S).
unify1(var(N),var(N),S,S).
unify1(var(M),var(N),S,S1) :-
        M \== N,
        bound(var(M),S,B,V),
        unify1(var(M),var(N),S,S1,B,V).

unify1(var(_),var(N),S,S1,B,true) :-
        unify1(B,var(N),S,S1).
unify1(var(M),var(N),S,[var(N)/var(M)|S],_,false).

bound(var(N),[var(N)/T|_],T,true) :-
        T \== var(N).
bound(var(N),[B/_|S],T,F) :-
        B \== var(N),
        bound(var(N),S,T,F).
bound(var(_),[],_,false).

dereference(var(N),[var(N)/T|_],T) :-
        T \== var(N).
```

```
dereference(var(N),[B/_|S],T) :-
        B \== var(N),
        dereference(var(N),S,T).

occur(var(N),var(M),S) :-
        dereference(var(M),S,T),
        occur(var(N),T,S).
occur(var(N),var(N),_).
occur(var(N),struct(_,Args),S) :-
        occur_args(var(N),Args,S).

occur_args(var(N),[A|_],S) :-
        occur(var(N),A,S).
occur_args(var(N),[_|As],S) :-
        occur_args(var(N),As,S).
```

Semantics–based Partial Evaluation of Prolog Programs

Brian J. Ross*
Department of Artificial Intelligence, University of Edinburgh
Edinburgh, Scotland

Abstract

A semantic characterisation of the partial evaluation of Prolog programs is presented. An algebraic semantics for Prolog which models Prolog's depth–first left–to–right control scheme is first outlined. This semantics is written in Milner's Calculus of Communicating Systems (CCS) [14]. This CCS semantics can be used to analyse how logic program control affects partial evaluation transformations of Prolog programs. Partial evaluation of a source program is accomplished by applying transforms onto a program's semantic representation. Correctness and completeness are preserved when such transformations respect the source program's semantic integrity. Because the semantic bisimilarities of Prolog control preserve behavioural equivalence, the semantic modelling of the basic control component of the partial evaluation process is possible. Conversely, the CCS semantics can determine whether particular partial evaluation transformations violate program completeness.

1 Introduction

Given a program and some particular instances of input data, partial evaluation involves the production of a new program specialised to that data. Prolog programs are well–suited to partial evaluation because Prolog partial evaluators are easily implemented as Prolog meta–interpreters. However, the formal justification of various phenomena which occur when partially evaluating logic programs have not been addressed in detail. Problems arise if a partial evaluator generates residual programs which behave differently than the original source program. This can happen when a partial evaluator uses a control scheme which differs from that used by the source program.

This paper suggests a semantic characterisation of the partial evaluation of Prolog programs. Using a formal semantics of Prolog programs, partial evaluation is modelled by equivalence–preserving transformations of the program's semantic representation. Because the semantics formally models Prolog's standard control scheme, the effects of this control on partial evaluation can be accounted for.

Section 2 gives a brief overview of a CCS semantics of sequential Prolog. Section 3 reviews the concept of partial evaluation. Then the semantics is

*Current address: Computer Science Department, University of Victoria, Victoria, British Columbia, Canada V8W 3P6 (email bjr@csr.uvic.ca).

applied towards partial evaluation transformations in section 4. Section 5 discusses the reasons why some partial evaluations do not preserve behavioral equivalence. A discussion and comparison to related work is in section 6.

A complete understanding of the semantics used in the paper requires an understanding of CCS. However, the main ideas can be understood without an intimate understanding of either the Prolog semantics or CCS. Appendix A reviews the basic concepts of CCS.

2 An algebraic semantics of Prolog control

A CCS semantics of Prolog's depth–first left–to–right control scheme is outlined here. See [17] for a thorough discussion, as well as for a treatment of the cut and negation by failure (also see [18]), and other control schemes such as breadth–first control.

The semantics is an AND/OR process model similar to ones in [3] [12]. Each AND and OR node in a program's AND/OR tree is modelled as a sequential CCS agent, rather than concurrent ones as in other process interpretations. Doing so introduces an *operational semantics* to the AND/OR tree: the AND and OR agents determine the manner in which the tree is explored.

The semantics is sound and complete with respect to a Prolog program's declarative and operational semantics. Soundness follows from the fact that the semantics models SLD resolution, and SLD resolution is sound relative to the declarative semantics of a logic program. The semantics is complete relative to standard Prolog control, as it models Prolog's search and computation rules, as well as negation by failure.

$$
\begin{aligned}
[f] &\equiv [\, succ'/succ,\ done'/done \,] \\
F &\equiv \{\, succ',\ done' \,\} \\
Done &\stackrel{\text{def}}{=} \overline{done}.\mathbf{0} \\
True &\stackrel{\text{def}}{=} \overline{succ(\epsilon)}\ .\ Done
\end{aligned}
$$

$$
P \,\mathbin{;}\, Q \stackrel{\text{def}}{=} (\, P[b/done] \mid b.Q \,) \setminus b
$$

$$
\begin{aligned}
P \rhd Q &\stackrel{\text{def}}{=} (P[f] \mid NextGoal_i) \setminus F \\
NextGoal_i &\stackrel{\text{def}}{=} succ(\theta)'.(Q\theta \,\mathbin{;}\, NextGoal_i) + done'.Done
\end{aligned}
$$

Figure 1: Control operators

The two events affecting control are success and termination, which are denoted by the actions $succ(\theta)$ and $done$ respectively. Executing a terminating program query results in the stream

$$
\overline{succ(\theta_1)}\ .\ \overline{succ(\theta_2)}\ .\ \cdots\ .\ \overline{succ(\theta_k)}\ .\ \cdots\ .\ \overline{done}\ .\ \mathbf{0} \qquad (k \geq 1)
$$

where the action $\overline{succ(\theta_i)}$ represents a successful derivation returning answer substitution θ_i, action $\overline{done}$ represents the end of the computation, "." separates stream elements, and the null agent **0** represents the end of all activity. The overlined *succ* actions represent output actions, and non–overlined ones used elsewhere are complementary input actions (see appendix). Finite failure is represented by termination with no success actions. Unless a logic program is non-terminating, $\overline{done}$ is eventually communicated. The computed answer substitution θ is a list of variable–term pairs representing variable bindings, for example, $\theta = \{ X \leftarrow a(Y),\ Y \leftarrow c \}$. Empty answer substitutions are denoted by ϵ. It is often convenient to represent $succ(\theta)$ by just *succ*, and assume that θ is implicit.

Because the semantics of control is primarily of interest here, the dataflow component is abstracted out of the semantics. A dataflow model corresponding to that of Prolog is assumed to be implicit throughout. Variables used in semantic expressions are logical variables, and computed answer subsitutions are constructed "appropriately". Unification is considered as a call to a unification algorithm. For example, the clause

$$P(X, b(Y)) \ :- \ a(X),\ ...$$

is equivalent to

$$P(A, B) \ :- \ (A, B) = (X, b(Y)),\ a(X),\ ...$$

where $=$ is a builtin unifier, and A and B are fresh variables. This clause is represented in CCS as

$$P_i(\tilde{X}) \stackrel{\text{def}}{=} (\tilde{X} = (X, b(Y))) \rhd a(X) \rhd \cdots$$

where $\tilde{X}$ is a tuple of variables, and $\tilde{t}_i$ is the tuple of terms factored out of the clause head. The definition of unification itself is:

$$\tilde{t}_1 = \tilde{t}_2 \stackrel{\text{def}}{=} \overline{succ(\theta)}.Done + Done$$

This $=$ agent returns either $\underline{succ(\theta)}.Done$ where θ is the most general unifier of $\tilde{t}_1$ and $\tilde{t}_2$ if it exists, or *Done* if $\tilde{t}_1$ and $\tilde{t}_2$ do not unify.

Two agent operators are used to represent Prolog control, a backtracking operator $\rhd$ for AND agents, and a sequencing operator $\fatsemi$ for OR agents (figure 1). Prolog's search rule uses the simple strategy of searching clauses according to their textual order in the program. This search strategy is modelled by the OR agent's use of $\fatsemi$. In $P \fatsemi Q$, the $\fatsemi$ operator sequences Q to execute after P terminates.

Prolog's computation rule resolves goals using their textual left–to–right order in a clause body or query. The $\rhd$ operator models the left–to–right backtracking behaviour of goals. In $P \rhd Q$, agent P is invoked. When a solution is computed from P, then Q is invoked, and any solutions from Q are generated. Upon Q's termination, checked through use of agent sequencing, the loop is re-executed to find the next solution of P. The $NextGoal_i$ loop is really an operator over Q, but for convenience is a separate agent uniquely named via the i index. Note that "$[f]$" relabels actions so that they are subscripted, while "$\backslash F$" restricts these relabelled actions to localise them within the operator. An example translation is in figure 2.

$$intersect(X,Y,M) : -\ member(M,X),\ member(M,Y).$$
$$member(A,[A|B]).$$
$$member(A,[H|T]) : -\ member(A,T).$$

$$\Updownarrow$$

$$\begin{array}{rcl} intersect(X,Y,M) & \stackrel{\text{def}}{=} & intersect_1(X,Y,M) \\ intersect_1(X,Y,M) & \stackrel{\text{def}}{=} & member(M,X) \rhd member(M,Y) \\ \\ member(X,Y) & \stackrel{\text{def}}{=} & member_1(X,Y) \fatsemi member_2(X,Y) \\ member_1(X,Y) & \stackrel{\text{def}}{=} & (X,Y) = (A,[A|B]) \\ member_2(X,Y) & \stackrel{\text{def}}{=} & (X,Y) = (A,[H|T]) \rhd member(A,T) \end{array}$$

Figure 2: Intersect program

The semantics of basic CCS as outlined in the appendix is applicable to the above semantics. However, the behaviour of the control operators is better described using the following high–level equivalences or *bisimilarities*, which represent various states of the sequencing and backtracking mechanisms:

$$\begin{array}{rrcl} \textbf{Seq}: & Done \fatsemi P & \approx & P \\ \textbf{Back}-\textbf{1}: & (\overline{succ(\theta)}.P) \rhd Q & \approx & P \rhd Q\theta \\ \textbf{Back}-\textbf{2}: & Done \rhd Q & \approx & Done \\ \textbf{Back}-\textbf{3}: & P \rhd \overline{succ(\theta)}.Q & \approx & \overline{succ(\theta)}.(P \rhd Q) \\ \textbf{Back}-\textbf{4}: & P \rhd Done & \approx & P \rhd Q \\ \textbf{Back}-\textbf{5}: & (\overline{succ(\theta)}.P) \rhd Q & \approx & Q\theta \fatsemi (P \rhd Q) \end{array}$$

The rule **Seq** sequences agents so that the previous agent first issues $\overline{done}$ before the next agent proceeds. The **Back** rules represent states of backtracking, and use a new backtracking operator:

$$P \rhd_i Q \stackrel{\text{def}}{=} (P[f] \mid (Q \fatsemi NextGoal_i)) \setminus F$$

The expression $A \rhd B$ represents the intermediate state of the backtracking mechanism in $A \rhd B$ when B is actively computing with last computed result from A. The "i" index denotes that $\rhd$ is an operator over $NextGoal_i$; because the context of $\rhd$ is always known, the index is omitted.

The following **Resol** bisimilarity represents one resolution step:

$$P_i(\tilde{t}) \approx \begin{cases} (i)\ Done & : \tilde{t} \text{ and } \tilde{t}_i \text{ do not unify} \\ (ii)\ \overline{succ(\theta)}.Done & : \theta = mgu(\tilde{t},\tilde{t}_i), \text{ and } P_i(\tilde{x}) \stackrel{\text{def}}{=} (\tilde{x} = \tilde{t}_i) \\ (iii)\ Q\theta & : \theta = mgu(\tilde{t},\tilde{t}_i), \text{ and } P_i(\tilde{x}) \stackrel{\text{def}}{=} (\tilde{x} = \tilde{t}_i) \rhd Q \end{cases}$$

Resol replaces a resolved goal with its resolvent, with the appropriate unifier applied to it.

3 Partial Evaluation

An active area of research is partial evaluation [19]. The concept was pioneered by [8], and was further expanded upon by [5]. Besides being a powerful program transformation technique, partial evaluation lends theoretical insight into program language theory, as well as compiler theory and development.

Partial evaluation or mixed computation is a programming language characterisation of the concept of *projection* in functional mathematics [15]. Given a program and part of its input, partial evaluation is the process that produces a residual program which, when executed with the remaining input of the original program, computes the same result that the original program would when given the complete input. For example, let L be a programming language, p be a program, and $< d_1, ..., d_n >$ be an n–tuple of data arguments such that each $d_i \in D$ for some domain D. Then the execution of p can be represented as

$$L(p)(< d_1, ..., d_n >) \rightarrow d$$

Here, L treats p and the d_i as data, and determines a semantic interpretation of p when executed with the d_i input. The partial evaluation process is represented by the following expression

$$L(mix)(p)(< x_1, ..., x_j, y_1, ..., y_k >) \quad = \quad L(r)(< y_1, ..., y_k >)$$

L is the target programming language, mix is the partial evaluation procedure, p is a program to be specialised for given input data $x_1, ..., x_j$, and $y_1, ..., y_k$ is the remaining input. The result of this procedure is the residual program r which, when executed on the y_i, produces the same result as the original program:

$$L(r)(< y_1, ..., y_k >) = L(p)(< x_1, ..., x_j, y_1, ..., y_k >)$$

Program r is specialised with respect to the x_i data, and may execute considerably more efficiently than the original program.

In logic programming, partial evaluation is the process of evaluating a goal at compile time with some of its arguments instantiated, and deriving a new residual logic program which produces the same output as the original program, except that it runs more efficiently. [13] present some soundness and completeness results of the partial evaluation of pure Prolog programs. They derive conditions which assure soundness and completeness, and also discuss the effects of unsafe negation as failure. Partial evaluation is sound and complete so long as some *closedness* conditions are observed, which assure that goals do not become too specialised so that viable solutions become uncomputable. They also discuss how the control strategy affects completeness. There are three stages which may use various control schemes:

(i) Source program control: the control used to execute the original program before partial evaluation

(ii) Partial evaluation control: the control employed by the partial evaluation procedure itself onto the original program

(iii) Residual control: the control used to execute the residual program

Ideally, if a fair computation strategy were to be employed, the particular control strategies of the partial evaluation algorithm would be of less concern. However, given unfair strategies such as Prolog's, the control used during partial evaluation is pertinent to the computational completeness of the residual program. For example, an original program may finitely fail when executed with a left–to–right computation rule, while its residual counterpart created with a partial evaluation algorithm which uses a right–to–left computation rule may loop. A consequence of this is the need for partial evaluation to produce a residual program R which preserves the observed behaviour of the pre–partial evaluated source program P, save for the added efficiency of the residual program. The possibility of using a different control strategy during the transformation procedure at stage (ii) means that this equivalence can be sacrificed. For example, an original program may finitely fail when executed with a left–to–right computation rule, while its residual counterpart created with a partial evaluation algorithm which uses a right–to–left computation rule may loop.

Because Prolog easily treats Prolog code as data, partial evaluators usually take the form of meta–interpreters written in Prolog [6] [22] [7]. There are different partial evaluation algorithms, which describe effective procedures for deriving efficient residual programs which retain computational completeness [7] [2]. One common characteristic of these algorithms is that some basic control component of SLDNF resolution is used by the partial evaluation algorithm (stage (ii) above), which is usually enhanced with analytical devices such as loop checking, closedness maintenance, and goal suspension. The simplest approach is to apply Prolog's standard depth–first–left–first control as a basic inference strategy. This is a sensible approach, given that programs to be partially evaluated are written with this control scheme in mind, and partially evaluating such programs using a different control scheme may result in undesirable behaviour. Algorithms are not contrained to use this control strategy, and may employ other control schemes, such as breadth–first or heuristic driven.

4 Semantically characterising partial evaluation

A fundamental tenet of programming languages and their formal semantics is that *computational mechanisms which are extensionally equivalent are substitutive with one another.* This concept permits more efficient programs to supercede less efficient ones. Likewise, language semantics reflect this by the notion of syntactic substitutivity of equivalent expressions, which is a prerequisite for a formal system to be equationally useful. The concept of substitutivity is taken a step further in [10] [11]. Hehner's *predicative programming* principle proposes that program code and its semantic meaning are substitutive within semantic expressions. This allows a program's concrete syntax and the formal semantic language to be intercomposed in semantic expressions. This is useful in applications such as program synthesis and verification, as it supports the step–wise refinement between program code and the semantics language within one formal context. It also assures that translations back and forth between the programming language and the semantic representation are sound.

The partial evaluation paradigm fundamentally depends upon the principle of program equivalence. When a logic program is partially evaluated, a residual program is desired which is behaviourally equivalent to the source program, except that it might be more efficient. Generally speaking, behavioural equivalence means that both the source and residual programs compute the same success and failure sets. A stricter criteria, however, requires that the original program and the residual program have identical output behaviour. This implies that the order of solutions is the same, as well as non-terminating and looping behaviour. As mentioned before, this strict characterisation of equivalence is required when unfair control strategies are being used; it could be relaxed if fair inference strategies are to be considered.

The substitutivity of equivalent agent expressions is fundamental to CCS theory. Using the concept of equivalence relations, if two agents are equivalent in CCS, then their corresponding expressions are substitutive within the calculus (under conditions based upon the theory of equivalence being used). CCS's observational equivalence relation can be used to describe the desired final result of partial evaluation. Let P be a Prolog program, and R be a residual program for P. Then the desired property which should hold between them is

$$P \approx R$$

Here, P and R are behaviourally equivalent with respect to their observed output, and therefore share the same nontermination and looping characteristics. Their internal state transitions (or computation trees) will differ, however, if R is a more efficient implementation.

Rudimentary partial evaluation is modelled in CCS by applying behaviourally equivalent transformations to the semantic expressions for programs. Because the behaviour of logic programs ultimately depends upon the control strategy used during execution, partial evaluation must consider the control scheme if behavioural equivalence is to be retained in the residual program. Given the semantics of a program for a particular control strategy, partial evaluation transformations must be applied which respect the integrity of this semantic meaning.

The following examples illustrate how basic partial evaluation can be performed directly on an object program's semantics. Given a program P and a query Q, bisimilarities for a given control strategy are applied to the semantic expression for P and Q to effect symbolic computation. Using Hehner's notion of predicative programming, the application of these bisimilarities to the program's semantic representation represent corresponding equivalence–preserving transformations of the source program. Criteria for freezing the expansion of terms in the semantic expression is applied at a meta–level. Eventually a CCS expression E results. This expression is normalised into a set of agent definitions and calls bisimilar to terms within E, which are in turn translated into equivalent Prolog code. This translation process may require unfolding and folding operations (which require creating new agent/predicate definitions); such activity has been studied elsewhere (eg. [21]) and is not discussed further here.

The first example is the program and CCS translation in figure 2 of section 2. The query $intersect(X,Y,M)$ is satisfied if the item in M is a member of both lists X and Y. First note how *member* generates multiple solutions through backtracking, for example,

$$member(M,[a,b]) \approx \overline{succ(\theta_1)}\,.\,\overline{succ(\theta_2)}\,.\,Done$$

where $\theta_1 = \{M \leftarrow a\}$ and $\theta_2 = \{M \leftarrow b\}$. Now consider the partial evaluation of the goal "?– $intersect([a,b],Y,M)$.", in which both Y and M are uninstantiated:

$$\begin{array}{ll}
intersect([a,b],Y,M) & \\
\approx \overline{member(M,[a,b])} \rhd member(M,Y) & : \mathbf{Con}\ intersect \\
\approx (\overline{succ(\theta_1)}.\overline{succ(\theta_2)}.Done) \rhd member(M,Y) & : subst\ member\ (above) \\
\approx member(a,Y) \,\S\, (\overline{succ(\theta_2)}.Done \rhd member(M,Y)) & : \mathbf{Back-5} \\
\approx member(a,Y) \,\S\, member(b,Y) \,\S & \\
\quad (Done \rhd member(M,Y)) & : \mathbf{Back-5} \\
\approx member(a,Y) \,\S\, member(b,Y) \,\S\, Done & : \mathbf{Back-2} \\
\approx member(a,Y) \,\S\, member(b,Y) & : P \,\S\, Done \approx P
\end{array}$$

Therefore $intersect([a,b],Y,M) \approx member(a,Y) \,\S\, member(b,Y)$. The call to $intersect([a,b],Y,M)$ is bisimilar to $intersect'([a,b],Y,M)$, where

$$\begin{array}{l}
intersect'(A,B,C) \stackrel{\text{def}}{=} intersect'_1(A,B,C) \,\S\, intersect'_2(A,B,C) \\
intersect_1(A,B,C) \stackrel{\text{def}}{=} (A,B,C) = ([a,b],Y,a) \rhd member(a,Y) \\
intersect_2(A,B,C) \stackrel{\text{def}}{=} (A,B,C) = ([a,b],Y,b) \rhd member(b,Y)
\end{array}$$

Using reverse translation via predicative programming, this represents the residual program

```
intersect'([a,b],Y,a) :- member(a,Y).
intersect'([a,b],Y,b) :- member(b,Y).
```

```
satisfiable(true).
satisfiable(X ∧ Y) :- satisfiable(X), satisfiable(Y).
satisfiable(X ∨ Y) :- satisfiable(X).
satisfiable(X ∨ Y) :- satisfiable(Y).
satisfiable(¬X) :- invalid(X).

invalid(false).
invalid(X ∨ Y) :- invalid(X), invalid(Y).
invalid(X ∧ Y) :- invalid(X).
invalid(X ∧ Y) :- invalid(Y).
invalid(¬X) :- satisfiable(Y).
```

Figure 3: Satisfiability program

$$
\begin{aligned}
satisfiable(E) &\stackrel{\text{def}}{=} satisfiable_1(E) \;\hat{;}\; satisfiable_2(E) \;\hat{;}\; satisfiable_3(E) \\
&\qquad \hat{;}\; satisfiable_4(E) \;\hat{;}\; satisfiable_5(E) \\
satisfiable_1(E) &\stackrel{\text{def}}{=} E = true \\
satisfiable_2(E) &\stackrel{\text{def}}{=} (E = X \wedge Y) \rhd satisfiable(X) \rhd satisfiable(Y) \\
satisfiable_3(E) &\stackrel{\text{def}}{=} (E = X \vee Y) \rhd satisfiable(X) \\
satisfiable_4(E) &\stackrel{\text{def}}{=} (E = X \vee Y) \rhd satisfiable(Y) \\
satisfiable_5(E) &\stackrel{\text{def}}{=} (E = \neg X) \rhd invalid(X) \\
\\
invalid(E) &\stackrel{\text{def}}{=} invalid_1(E) \;\hat{;}\; invalid_2(E) \;\hat{;}\; invalid_3(E) \\
&\qquad \hat{;}\; invalid_4(E) \;\hat{;}\; invalid_5(E) \\
invalid_1(E) &\stackrel{\text{def}}{=} E = false \\
invalid_2(E) &\stackrel{\text{def}}{=} (E = X \vee Y) \rhd invalid(X) \rhd invalid(Y) \\
invalid_3(E) &\stackrel{\text{def}}{=} (E = X \wedge Y) \rhd invalid(X) \\
invalid_3(E) &\stackrel{\text{def}}{=} (E = X \wedge Y) \rhd invalid(Y) \\
invalid_3(E) &\stackrel{\text{def}}{=} (E = \neg X) \rhd satisfiable(X)
\end{aligned}
$$

Figure 4: CCS translation

The second example is the program in figure 3 (from [20]) and its CCS translation in figure 4. This program determines whether a expression of propositional logic is satisfiable or invalid. It can be used to generate valid expressions (using a fair control scheme), or can verify the validity of expressions given to it. Consider the partial evaluation of the query

$$?- \ satisfiable(\neg(X \vee Y) \wedge \neg\neg(Y \vee Z)).$$

What is desired is a residual program specialised for expressions which unify with this expression schema. Logic variables will be treated as variables over expressions, and are intended to be instantiated at a later time. During partial evaluation, calls that have a single expression variable argument will be frozen. The partial evaluation and corresponding transformation step outline follow:

$$\begin{array}{ll}
satisfiable(\neg(X \vee Y) \wedge \neg\neg(Y \vee Z)) & \\
\approx satisfiable_1(E) \,\tilde{;}\, satisfiable_2(E) \,\tilde{;}\, satisfiable_3(E) \,\tilde{;} & :(1)\\
\quad satisfiable_4(E) \,\tilde{;}\, satisfiable_5(E) & \\
\approx satisfiable_2(\neg(X \vee Y) \wedge \neg\neg(Y \vee Z)) & :(2)\\
\approx satisfiable(\neg(X \vee Y)) \rhd satisfiable(\neg\neg(Y \vee Z)) & :(3)\\
\approx satisfiable_5(\neg(X \vee Y)) \rhd satisfiable_5(\neg\neg(Y \vee Z)) & :(4)\\
\approx invalid(X \vee Y) \rhd invalid(\neg(Y \vee Z)) & :(5)\\
\approx invalid_2(X \vee Y) \rhd invalid_5(\neg(Y \vee Z)) & :(6)\\
\approx invalid(X) \rhd invalid(Y) \rhd satisfiable(Y \vee Z) & :(7)\\
\approx invalid(X) \rhd invalid(Y) \rhd & :(8)\\
\quad (satisfiable_3(Y \vee Z) \,\tilde{;}\, satisfiable_4(Y \vee Z)) & \\
\approx invalid(X) \rhd invalid(Y) \rhd (satisfiable(Y) \,\tilde{;}\, satisfiable(Z)) & :(9)
\end{array}$$

Steps :

(1) **Con** *satisfiable*, $E = \neg(X \vee Y) \wedge \neg\neg(Y \vee Z)$
(2) $satisfiable_i \approx Done$ $(i \neq 2)$, *simplify*
(3) **Resol** $satisfiable_2$
(4) $satisfiable_i \approx Done$ $(i \neq 5)$ *for both*
(5) **Resol** *twice*
(6) $invalid_i(X \vee Y) \approx Done$ $(i \neq 2)$,
$invalid_i(\neg(Y \vee Z)) \approx Done$ $(i \neq 5)$
(7) **Resol** $invalid_{2,5}$
(8) $satisfiable_{1,2,5} \approx Done$
(9) **Resol** $satisfiable_{3,4}$

This residual expression is bisimilar to

$$\begin{aligned}
satisfiable'(E) &\stackrel{\text{def}}{=} satisfiable'_1(E)\\
satisfiable'_1(E) &\stackrel{\text{def}}{=} (E = \neg(X \vee Y) \wedge \neg\neg(Y \vee Z)) \rhd invalid(X)\\
&\qquad \rhd invalid(Y) \rhd new(Y, Z)\\
new(Y, Z) &\stackrel{\text{def}}{=} new_1(Y, Z) \,\tilde{;}\, new_2(Y, Z)\\
new_1(Y, Z) &\stackrel{\text{def}}{=} satisfiable(Y)\\
new_1(Y, Z) &\stackrel{\text{def}}{=} satisfiable(Z)
\end{aligned}$$

This represents the Prolog code:

$satisfiable'(\neg(X \vee Y) \wedge \neg\neg(Y \vee Z)) :- invalid(X),\ invalid(Y),\ new(Y, Z).$
$new(Y, Z) :- satisfiable(Y).$
$new(Y, Z) :- satisfiable(Z).$

This is supplemented with the original program from figure 3. This residual will efficiently determine the validity of propositional expressions matching this specific propositional formula .

Note that the above transformations are very straight–forward, and are well–suited to automation. The basic activity consists of the application of equivalence–preserving (bisimilar) transformations to a program's semantic representation. The only halting condition is a test which inspects the form of predicate arguments. Of course, this basic control can be further enhanced if desired.

5 Non–equivalence preserving transformations

The previous section used the semantics of a program as a basis for applying equivalence–preserving partial evaluation transformations. The semantics can also be used to show why particular types of transformations are invalid. In particular, some partial evaluation strategies produce residual programs which behave differently from the original program. This occurs when the control strategy used by the partial evaluation process differs from the control used to execute the original program. Semantically speaking, this happens when non–bisimilar transformations are applied to a program's semantic representation.

An example of a transformation which does not preserve program behaviour under Prolog's standard left–to–right computation rule is the partial evaluation of goals using a right–to–left computation rule. In the program,

$p(X) :- a(X), b(X).$
$a(1) :- a(1).$
$a(X).$
$b(3).$

Looping or livelock is represented in CCS by the agent $\perp$, which is defined as

$$\perp \stackrel{\text{def}}{=} \perp$$

Using a left–to–right computation rule, then $p(X) \approx \perp$. Partially evaluating $p(X)$ using a right–to–left computation rule results in the predicate "$p(3).$", which is not bisimilar to the original program's behaviour.

Incongruities result when non–bisimilar transformations are applied to a program. In the above example, the right–to–left computation rule (call it "$\lhd$") used during partial evaluation is not bisimilar to the left–to–right one used by standard Prolog. Consequently, the application of right–to–left bisimilarities to the program do not preserve behavioural equivalence with respect to the program's left–to–right semantic meaning. To illustrate this, note that $A \lhd B \approx B \rhd A$. It must therefore be shown that $A \rhd B \not\approx B \rhd A$. This inequality obviously holds due to the non–commutativity of $\rhd$ [17]. For example, let $A \approx \perp$ and $B \approx Done$. Then, because $\perp \rhd P \approx \perp$, then $A \rhd B \approx \perp \rhd B \approx \perp$. On the other hand, using **Back-2**, $B \rhd A \approx Done \rhd A \approx Done$. Thus the right–to–left partial evaluation of P will not preserve behavioural equivalence with Prolog's standard left–to–right computation rule.

Another example of an unsound transformation is when clause order is altered, which results because the clause sequencing operator $\mathbin{\hat{;}}$ is also non–commutative. Consider a predicate

$$P \stackrel{\text{def}}{=} P_1 \mathbin{\hat{;}} P_2$$

If P_1 and P_2 partially evaluate to P_1' and P_2' respectively, then the residual program

$$P' \stackrel{\mathrm{def}}{=} P_2' \,\hat{;}\, P_1'$$

is not bisimilar (ignoring degenerate cases).

6 Discussion

This paper presents a semantic characterisation of the partial evaluation of logic programs. Some perspectives afforded by this approach are:

- Given that the control strategy used to execute logic programs determines their computational behaviour, a formal consideration of control helps justify the correctness of program transformations. This applies to partial evaluation transformations as well. The CCS semantics of Prolog can ensure that partial evaluation transformations on a program preserve the computational equivalence between the original program and the residual program.

- Using the predicative programming principle, semantic expressions and program code are inter–translatable between one another. Even though a semantic expression may translate to many possible programs, predicative programming assures that the behaviour of such programs is equivalent and unambiguous.

- The control bisimilarities for standard Prolog control can model the basic control component of partial evaluation. Because CCS can model many types of control paradigms, including sequential and concurrent control, this semantic approach could be applied towards the partial evaluation of programs using other control strategies, including those which use a combination of different control schemes.

- The CCS semantics can be used to explain why some partial evaluations do not preserve behavioural equivalence. In particular, transformations which are not bisimilar to the control strategy under which the original program is executed will result in residual programs which behave differently from the original.

A quite strict notion of behavioural equivalence is used here, which specifies that programs and their residual counterparts produce identical observable output. This equivalence can be relaxed if fair control strategies are to be studied. However, strict equivalences such as this one are necessary when unfair computation strategies like that Prolog's are being considered.

The CCS semantics of Prolog is well–suited towards partial evaluation transformations of programs. Having a concise semantics of the control component permits a straight–forward partial evaluation of programs to be performed. Other semantics of Prolog, for example, denotational semantics [4] or proof–theoretic semantics [1], could also be applied to this same purpose, as long as the semantics model the control used by the inference mechanism. The practicality of using other semantics is dependent upon their conceptual complexity; to this ends, the usefulness of denotational semantics is suspect.

[13] discuss partial evaluation and its effect on the declarative and procedural semantics of pure logic programs. They illustrate how the computation and search rules affect completeness results of residual programs, and also discuss the effects of using unsafe negation as failure. The failure behaviour of programs and their residual counterparts is not necessarily preserved when different computation rules are used during partial evaluation. In addition, they show how clause order must be maintained in residual programs to preserve behavioural equivalence. Using the CCS semantics, these phenomena are shown to result when non–bisimilar transformations are performed on the program. In particular, backtracking and clause sequencing are non–commutative, and program transformations which do permute goal and clause order are unsound.

It should be stressed that the semantic approach proposed here models one aspect of the partial evaluation process – basic partial evaluation control. The bisimilarities for standard Prolog control were used to effect symbolic computation, which is a fundamental ingredient of partial evaluation transformations. However, the tactics used to apply these bisimilarities, such as when to freeze goals and create new predicates, were decided at a meta–level. Some of the partial evaluation algorithms suggested in the literature are considerably more sophisticated than the simple bisimilation transformations shown here. Including the program semantics within these other frameworks would permit a means of justifying the validity of more complex transformation strategies.

Prolog partial evaluators are typically implemented as meta–interpreters. One problem with meta–interpretive approaches is that the meta–interpreter's abstraction of programs as data objects obscures the semantics of the programming language being processed. The operational semantics of the target programming language is usually implicitly accounted for in the structure of the meta–interpreter, and relies on the operational semantics of the language in which the meta–interpreter itself is implemented. This can result in ad hoc, ill–founded program transformations and code generation. A consequence of this is the need to prove the correctness and completeness of these meta–interpretive program transformation systems, which can be a non–trivial task (eg. see [7]). On the other hand, semantically–sound transformations using a program's formal semantics affords a more verifiably sound transformation environment. This approach would offer a theoretically elegant explanation of partial evaluation, which meta–interpretive accounts do not afford. The semantic approach given here could be implemented via a term rewriting system, in which the bisimilarities and program semantics represent rewrite rules.

An important research topic is to study the circumstances under which alternate, non–bisimilar partial evaluation control strategies produce residual program with more desirable computational characteristics than the source program. Discovering these partial evaluation algorithms, and how to apply them, is an active area of research. Such systems will likely require sophisticated program analysis techniques.

An open research problem is to prove properties of the partial evaluation process such as termination. Some sort of meta–semantics of the partial evaluation algorithms would be useful in this regard. Work along this line has been done by [9]. He uses an inference system which uses inference rules defining the dynamic semantics of programming language interpreters, along with tactical inference rules which define partial evaluation strategies. The proof–theoretic semantics for Prolog in [1] could be used in such a system.

A similar approach to this one is taken in [16] towards partially evaluating imperative programs. An imperative program's relational semantics is represented by a logic program. This logic program is then treated as a pure Prolog program, and is partially evaluated using a Prolog meta-interpreter. Transformations of the logical semantics reflect correctness-preserving transformations of the imperative program. The residual logic program is translated back into imperative code using the predicative program principle.

Acknowledgements: Thanks to Alan Smaill for his helpful comments. Support through a University of Edinburgh Postgraduate Studentship and an ORS award is gratefully acknowledged.

References

[1] J.H. Andrews. *Logic Programming: Operational Semantics and Proof Theory.* PhD thesis, Department of Computer Science, University of Edinburgh, Edinburgh, Scotland, 1991.

[2] K. Benkerimi and J. Lloyd. A Partial Evaluation Procedure for Logic Programs. In *North American Conference on Logic Programming*, pages 343–358, 1990.

[3] J.S. Conery and D.F. Kibler. AND Parallelism and Nondeterminism in Logic Programs. *New Generation Computing*, 3(1):43–70, 1985.

[4] S.K. Debray and P. Mishra. Denotational and Operational Semantics for Prolog. *Journal of Logic Programming*, 5:61–91, 1988.

[5] A.P. Ershov. Mixed Computation: Potential Applications and Problems for Study. *Theoretical Computer Science 18*, 18:41–67, 1982.

[6] H. Fujita and K. Furukawa. A Self-Applicable Partial Evaluator and Its Use in Incremental Compilation. *New Generation Computing*, 6(2,3):91–118, 1988.

[7] D.A. Fuller and S. Abramsky. Mixed Computation of Prolog Programs. *New Generation Computing*, 6(2,3):119–141, 1988.

[8] Y. Futamura. Partial evaluation of computation process – an approach to a compiler-compiler. *Systems - Comput. - Controls*, 2(5):45–50, 1971.

[9] L. Hascoet. Partial Evaluation with Inference Rules. *New Generation Computing*, 6(2,3):187–209, 1988.

[10] E.C.R. Hehner. Predicative Programming Part I. *Communications of the ACM*, 27(2):134–143, February 1984.

[11] E.C.R. Hehner. Predicative Programming Part II. *Communications of the ACM*, 27(2), February 1984.

[12] G. Lindstrom and P. Panangaden. Stream-based execution of logic programs. In *Symposium on Logic Programming*, Atlantic City, 1984.

[13] J.W. Lloyd and J.C. Shepherdson. Partial Evaluation in Logic Programming. Technical Report CS-87-09, University of Bristol, December 1987.

[14] R. Milner. *Communication and Concurrency.* Prentice Hall, 1989.

[15] H. Rogers. *Theory of Recursive Functions and Effective Computability.* MIT Press, 1988.

[16] B.J. Ross. The Partial Evaluation of Imperative Programs Using Prolog. In *Meta-programming in Logic Programming.* MIT Press, 1989.

[17] B.J. Ross. *An Algebraic Semantics of Prolog Control.* PhD thesis, Department of Artificial Intelligence, University of Edinburgh, Edinburgh, Scotland, 1991. (forthcoming).

[18] B.J. Ross. Using Algebraic Semantics for Proving Prolog Termination and Transformation. In *Proc. UK ALP 91*, Edinburgh, Scotland, 1991. Springer–Verlag. (forthcoming).

[19] P. Sestoft and A.V. Zamulin. Annotated Bibliography on Partial Evaluation and Mixed Computation. *New Generation Computing*, 6(2,3):309–354, 1988.

[20] L. Sterling and E. Shapiro. *The Art of Prolog.* Prentice–Hall, 1986.

[21] H. Tamaki and T. Sato. A Transformation System for Logic Programs which Preserves Equivalence. Technical Report TR-018, ICOT, Tokyo, Japan, August 1983.

[22] R. Venken and B. Demoen. A Partial Evaluation System for Prolog: some Practical Considerations. *New Generation Computing*, 6(2,3):279–290, 1988.

A CCS definitions

An *agent* or *process* is a mechanism whose behavior is characterised by discrete actions. CCS is an algebra which allows the description and analysis of networks of communicating agents [14]. Agents are described using a set of *agent expressions*, $\mathcal{E}$. Letting E range over $\mathcal{E}$, then $\mathcal{E}$ are the formulae recursively constructed using the following equations:

$\alpha.E$	Prefix
$\sum_{i\in I} E_i$	Summation
$E_1 \mid E_2$	Composition
$E\backslash L$	Restriction
$E[f]$	Relabelling

Milner defines the semantics of these equational operators using the transitional rules of figure 5. These transitions are sequents in which the expression below the line can be inferred when the expressions above the line (if any) hold. The expression $E \xrightarrow{\alpha} E'$ represents the transition of agent E into agent E' through the action α. When multiple transitions occur, as in $E \xrightarrow{\alpha_1} \cdots \xrightarrow{\alpha_n}$, then $\alpha_1 \cdots \alpha_n$ an *action sequence* of E, and E' is a *derivative* of E. The meaning of the transitions in figure 5 are:

$$\textbf{Act}\quad \frac{}{\alpha.E \xrightarrow{\alpha} E} \qquad \textbf{Sum}_\mathbf{j}\quad \frac{E_j \xrightarrow{\alpha} E'_j}{\sum_{i\in I} E_i \xrightarrow{\alpha} E'_j}\ (j \in I)$$

$$\textbf{Com}_1\quad \frac{E \xrightarrow{\alpha} E'}{E|F \xrightarrow{\alpha} E'|F} \qquad \textbf{Com}_2\quad \frac{F \xrightarrow{\alpha} F'}{E|F \xrightarrow{\alpha} E|F'}$$

$$\textbf{Com}_3\quad \frac{E \xrightarrow{\ell} E' \qquad F \xrightarrow{\bar{\ell}} F'}{E|F \xrightarrow{\tau} E'|F'}$$

$$\textbf{Res}\quad \frac{E \xrightarrow{\alpha} E'}{E\backslash L \xrightarrow{\alpha} E'\backslash L}\ (\alpha, \overline{\alpha} \notin L) \qquad \textbf{Rel}\quad \frac{E \xrightarrow{\alpha} E'}{E[f] \xrightarrow{f(\alpha)} E'[f]}$$

$$\textbf{Con}\quad \frac{P \xrightarrow{\alpha} P'}{A \xrightarrow{\alpha} P'}\ (A \stackrel{\text{def}}{=} P)$$

Figure 5: Transitional semantics of basic CCS calculus

1. **Act**: This describes an agent transition in terms of its immediate actions α. The symbol "." is separates actions within a stream. $\mathcal{A}$ is a set of action *names*, and $\overline{\mathcal{A}}$ is the set of *co-names*. By convention, names are used for input actions, and co-names for output actions. The set of *labels* $\mathcal{L}$ is $\mathcal{L} = \mathcal{A} \cup \overline{\mathcal{A}}$. The set of *actions Act* is $Act = \mathcal{L} \cup \{\tau\}$, where τ is a distinguished silent action[1].

2. **Sum**$_j$: The expression $E_1 + E_2$ means that behaviors E_1 and E_2 are alternative choices of behavior.

3. **Com**$_i$: Agent composition represents how agents behave, both autonomously (**Com**$_1$, **Com**$_2$) and interactively (**Com**$_3$).

4. **Res**: Restriction removes the specified actions in set L from being observed externally.

5. **Rel**: A *relabelling function* $f : \mathcal{L} \rightarrow \mathcal{L}$ renames actions. A notation for finite relabelling functions is $[\ a_1/b_1, \ \cdots \ , a_k/b_k\ ]$ where each b_i is renamed by a_i.

6. **Con**: A *constant* is an agent whose meaning is defined by an agent expression. For every constant A, there exists an equation "$A \stackrel{\text{def}}{=} E$". The definition of an agent constant is semantically equivalent to the constant reference itself. The *null* or inactive agent is denoted **0**.

[1] "τ" is not used in this paper.

The most basic activity within a network of CCS agents is a *handshake*, which is a successful simultaneous communication between two agents. In order for a handshake to occur, two agents must simultaneously execute identical immediate actions, one of which is a co–action of the other. For example, in $(a.P + \overline{b}.Q) \mid (\overline{a}.R + c.S)$, a communication can occur between $a.P$ and $\overline{a}.R$, and results in a hidden "τ" action. A common form for CCS expressions is $(P_1 \mid \ldots \mid P_n) \setminus L$. The *expansion law* converts such an expression into one having a summation of terms with all immediate actions prefixed onto corresponding agent states. The (simplified) expansion law is as follows. Let $P = (P_1 \mid \ldots \mid P_n) \setminus L$ with $n \geq 1$. Then

$$\begin{aligned} P \quad = \quad & \sum\{\alpha.(P_1|\ldots|P_i'|\ldots|P_n)\backslash L \ : \ P_i \xrightarrow{\alpha} P_i', \alpha \notin L \cup \overline{L})\} \\ + \quad & \sum\{\tau.(P_1|\ldots|P_i'|\ldots|P_j'|\ldots|P_n)\backslash L \ : \ P_i \xrightarrow{\beta} P_i',\ P_j \xrightarrow{\overline{\beta}} P_j', i < j\} \end{aligned}$$

The first summation represents the agents which autonomously change state. The second summation represents the agents which change state interactively with one another (via hidden τ actions), which happens when a β and $\overline{\beta}$ handshake.

A significant part of CCS theory is devoted to various concepts of behavioral equality. A *bisimilarity* is an observed equivalence amongst agents. Observation equivalence is the most practical bisimulation to use. Let

$$A \stackrel{\hat{\alpha}}{\Rightarrow} A'$$

represent the transition of A into A' where the action sequence $\hat{\alpha}$ is one where all hidden "τ" actions are removed. Then $P \approx Q$ iff, for all $\alpha \in Act$,

(i) Whenever $P \xrightarrow{\alpha} P'$, then for some Q', $Q \stackrel{\hat{\alpha}}{\Rightarrow} Q'$, and $P' \approx Q'$.
(ii) Whenever $Q \xrightarrow{\alpha} Q'$, then for some P', $P \stackrel{\hat{\alpha}}{\Rightarrow} P'$, and $P' \approx Q'$.

This states that agents with identical external behavior can be considered equal, and that their equational descriptions are substitutive with each other within CCS expressions[2]. To prove bisimilarity of two expressions, it must be shown that the α–derivatives of the expressions generate the same behaviors, for all possible α.

[2]This does not hold in general with observational equivalence, but can be considered to be so in our constrained use of CCS.

Prolog Program Transformations and Meta-Interpreters

Anne Parrain, Philippe Devienne, Patrick Lebegue *
Laboratoire d'Informatique Fondamentale de Lille
Université de Lille I
59655 Villeneuve d'Ascq France
{parrain,devienne,lebegue}@lifl.lifl.fr

Abstract

Partial Evaluation in Prolog (generally associated to Folding/Unfolding techniques) is a code optimization technique, which transforms a readable and structured program in a more efficient program (that is to say better adapted to the interpreter or compiler). These programs are Prolog programs semantically equivalent with respect to the least Herbrand model. Our context is the operational equivalence of programs, and not the efficiency of program transformations.

We introduce first the notion of Strong Operational Equivalence (s.-o.e.), and then we propose to study strong operational equivalence preserving transformations. Strong operational equivalence means that the solution order is preserved and, when using inference as complexity unit, the runtime of any solution in the transformed program is linearly dependent on the runtime of the corresponding solution in the original program. This equivalence allows us to consider programs including non-logical features. We will restrict our study to Cut and Read/Write predicates and our framework is the standard resolution (depth first, leftmost atom).

Then, two meta-interpreters are studied. Using the Vanilla meta-interpreter and a new meta-interpreter (that we introduce and call quasi-iterative meta-interpreter), we show that any Prolog program P can be transformed to a meta-program (that is, an instance of these meta-interpreters) which is strongly operationally equivalent to the original one. The structure of the quasi-iterative meta-interpreter is the simpliest one known up to date, that is, composed of three unit clauses and one right linear recursive rule.

1 Introduction

The usual transformations (folding/unfolding techniques) preserve the semantics with respect to the least Herbrand model of the logic programs. These transformations cannot be applied directly to full Prolog programs, since they do not preserve the operational equivalence (with a standard interpreter) of programs. In this paper, we have tried to extend these transformations to take account of general Prolog programs. Our framework is the Prolog standard strategy (depth first and leftmost atom).

*partially supported by the G.D.R. Greco de la Programmation

We present the notion of strong operational equivalence, which is based on the relation ordering on solution nodes and on the linear dependency relation on the "size" of the standard SLD-tree. Some program transformations are studied and they are modified to preserve our equivalence. Then, we will validate two meta-interpreters by applying our transformations to them.

We have restricted our study to Cut and Read/Write predicates, for which we consider their usual behaviour. We have not considered other side-effect predicates (assert/retract, freeze, dif ...).

2 Notations and Definitions

2.1 Notations and Definitions

We call Prolog program an ordered set of Horn clauses, which can have side-effect predicates, and pure Prolog program an ordered set of Horn clauses without side-effect predicates. The relation ordering on clauses is necessary to preserve solution ordering. Derivation trees we consider are SLD-trees where we have replaced substitutions by systems of equations. Thus, any branch in a SLD-tree is labelled by systems of equations such that their union is solvable.

Definition 1 *The derivation tree for a program* Π *and a goal* G*, Tree(*Π*,*G*), is the SLD-tree s.t. :*

- *its nodes are labelled with atom conjunctions;*
- *its arrows are labelled with a number of rule and the system of equations* $\{root = head(rule)\}$

$$\begin{array}{c} A_1, \ldots, A_m \\ R_i \;\Big\downarrow\; \{A_1 = A\} \\ B_1, \ldots, B_n, A_2, \ldots, A_m \end{array} \qquad R_i:\;\; A :- B_1, \ldots, B_n$$

- *its solution-nodes are those labelled with the empty clause,* $\square$.

Definition 2 *The derivation tree in which we just consider paths and systems of equations associated is called the system tree.*

To measure the runtime of a program, we have chosen the number of unifications. Given a goal and a program, the complexity of a solution node is the number of unifications done before this node. (We consider usual definitions about relations ordering on nodes and paths.)

Definition 3 *Let* Π *be a Prolog program, and* G *be a goal for* Π*.*
The complexity for a solution-node Sol_Node is the function Φ*, defined by:*
$\Phi(Sol\_Node) = Card(\{N/N \text{ is a node in } Tree(\Pi,G) \text{ s.t. } N < Sol\_Node\})$

2.2 Strong Operational Equivalence

The basic idea is to preserve an equivalence in the sense of standard interpreters (unfair, depth first and leftmost atom). Two programs are equivalent, if they have the same solutions (in the sense of answer-substitutions), in the same order, with a runtime linear-dependence between them. That completes the logical and denotational semantics for standard interpreters by J.-P. Delahaye [Del88].

Definition 4 Strong Operational Equivalence
Let (Π_1,$Goal_1$) and (Π_2,$Goal_2$) be two program-goal couples, (Φ_1 and Φ_2 be their complexity function), they are strongly operationally equivalent if and only if :

1. *there exists a bijection Θ :*

   Θ : *Solution-Nodes*(Π_1,$Goal_1$) $\longrightarrow$ *Solution-Nodes*(Π_2,$Goal_2$)

   s.t. Θ is compatible with :

   (a) *the function Mgu : $Mgu_1 = Mgu_2 \circ \Theta$*

   (b) *the order relation on solution-nodes :*
   $\forall$ $nsol_1, nsol_2$ *solution-nodes,*
   $nsol_1 \leq nsol_2 \Leftrightarrow \Theta(nsol_1) \leq \Theta(nsol_2)$

   (c) *the complexity : $\forall$ nsol solution-node, there exist a_1, a_2, b_1 and b_2 rationals, with $a_1, a_2 > 0$,*
   $a_1 * \Phi_1(nsol) + b_1 \leq \Phi_2(\Theta(nsol)) \leq a_2 * \Phi_1(nsol) + b_2$

2. *there exists a bijection Θ' on infinite branches.*

Definition 5 Strong Operational Equivalence on a set of variables
Let S be a set of variables. The definition is the same as above, the only modified point is :
(a) *the function Mgu : $Mgu_1 \uparrow S = (Mgu_2 \circ \Theta) \uparrow S$*

Remarks :

- infinite derivations are not modified with respect to success derivations in the transformed program, because of the hypothesis 1-c). Intuitively, the SLD-tree built in this way, is an "elastic" tree with respect to the original tree. a_1 and a_2 are the modulus of elasticity, that is to say the factors of compression and stretching, of this "rubber-tree";

- two strongly operationally equivalent programs have the same success set SS and the same finite failure set FF. To preserve operational equivalence in the sense of standard interpreters (sets SSP and FFP of [Del88]), only the first infinite derivation needs to be preserved in the transformed program. Our equivalence, slightly stronger, preserves the SLD-tree in a more general manner.

3 Program Transformations and Strong Operational Equivalence

3.1 Unfolding transformation

3.1.1 Introduction

The definition of the unfold transformation proposed by H.Tamaki and T.Sato [TS84] is quite simple : it is a derivation step in a SLD-tree, with respect to any literal in a clause, for any computation rule.

example:

```
1.   a(X,Y) :- b(X), c(Y).
2.   b(0).
3.   b(1).
4.   c(0).
5.   c(1).
```

Order of solutions :
{(X=0,Y=0),(X=0,Y=1),
(X=1,Y=0),(X=1,Y=1)}

```
1.   a(X,0) :- b(X), c(0).
2.   a(X,1) :- b(X), c(1).
3.   b(0).
4.   b(1).
5.   c(0).
6.   c(1).
```

Order of solutions :
{(X=0,Y=0),(X=1,Y=0),
(X=0,Y=1),(X=1,Y=1)}

This transformation preserves neither the order of solutions, nor the complexity of a program. More hypotheses are needed :

- either the chosen literal must unify with only one head of rule (that is deterministic unfolding);
- either, let us call simple literal, any literal which unifies with only one fact, the unfolded literal must be the leftmost non-simple atom in the body part of the rule.

Second, to ensure the consistency with the side-effect predicates, the unfolding clause must have no Cut in its body. Changing the level of a Cut in a SLD-tree modifies entirely its behaviour : particularly, if the unfolding clause had a Cut in its body part, it would go up the Cut action in the SLD-tree, and then could prune branches with potential solutions.

Definition 6 Unfolding on leftmost literal
Let Π be a Prolog program, C be a clause in Π and B be a literal in the body of C.

C can be unfolded with respect to B if each atom before B in the body of C can be unified with at most one rule, this rule being a unit clause. Side-effect predicates on the left hand side of B are not allowed.

Let C_1, C_2, ..., C_k be clauses in Π,B_1,B_2, B_k be their heads, s.t.

- *each B_j can be unified with B by a mgu Θ_j;*
- *they have no Cut in their body.*

So, the clause C is replaced by clauses C'_1,C'_2, ..., C'_k (in this order). Each C'_j is obtained by inserting before B in C the equality $B = B_j$, then by replacing the atom B by the body of C_j in C.

C is called the unfolded clause, and C'_j unfolding clauses.

example :

The Vanilla-interpreter :

$\forall i \quad 1 \leq i \leq n$

```
1.i.    rule([a_i,b_i^1...b_i^ni]).

2.      solve([]).
3.      solve([A|B]) :-
  solve(A), solve(B).
4.      solve(A) :-
  rule([A|B]), solve(B).
```

Rule 4 is unfolded :

$\forall i \quad 1 \leq i \leq n$

```
1.i.    rule([a_i,b_i^1...b_i^ni]).

2.      solve([]).
3.      solve([A|B]) :-
  solve(A), solve(B).
```

$\forall i \quad 1 \leq i \leq n$

```
4.i.    solve(A) :- A = a_i,
  solve([b_i^1...b_i^ni]).
```

Proposition 1 *Strong Operational Equivalence is preserved by unfolding on leftmost literal.*

Remarks :

- No Cut is allowed on the left hand side of the unfolded literal :
- There cannot be Read/Write literals on the left hand side of the unfolded literal : as by unfolding one rule is replaced by k rules (if k is the number of rules which unifies with the unfolded literal), literals on the left hand of the unfolded literal are executed k times : it is a mistake when there are read/write literals.

Definition 7 Deterministic Unfolding
Let Π be a Prolog program, C be a clause in Π and B a literal in the body of C and s.t. B is not a side-effect predicate.

C can be unfolded w.r.t. B if B can be unified with only one head rule, called $D, D \neq C$, by the mgu Θ, and if this rule D does not have any Cut in its body.

C is then replaced by C' in Π. C' is obtained by replacing B in the body of C by the equality $\{B = D\}$ and by the body of D.

example :

The Vanilla-interpreter :

$\forall i \quad 1 \leq i \leq n$

```
1.i.    rule([a_i,b_i^1...b_i^ni]).
2.      solve([]).
3.      solve([A|B]) :-
        solve(A), solve(B).
```

$\forall i \quad 1 \leq i \leq n$

```
4.i.    solve(A) :- A = a_i,
        solve([b_i^1...b_i^ni]).
```

Rule 4.i is unfolded :

$\forall i \quad 1 \leq i \leq n$

```
1.i.    rule([a_i,b_i^1...b_i^ni]).
2.      solve([]).
3.      solve([A|B]) :-
        solve(A), solve(B).
```

The result is n new rules, some like :

```
4.i.    solve(A) :- A = a_i.
```

the others like :

```
4.i.        solve(A) :- A = a_i,
  solve(b_i^1),solve([b_i^2...b_i^ni]).
```

Proposition 2 *Strong Operational Equivalence is preserved by Deterministic Unfolding.*

3.2 Folding Transformation

3.2.1 Program Normalization

A necessary condition for the folding transformation is that variables appearing in the body part of the folding rule must appear in the head part of the rule. More precisely :

"As shown in [TS84], folding of a goal is correct if after unification of the goal and the body of the defining clause, all the internal variables remain uninstantiated, distinct from each other and from the variables surrounding the goal." [Sah91]

The technique we call normalization transforms a rule for verifying this condition. Adding a "holdall" argument to the head part of the rule is enough.

Definition 8 Normalized Program
Any program $(\Pi_1, Goal_1)$ *which all clauses verify* $Var(Head) \supseteq Var(Body)$, *is called a normalized program.*

Rule Normalization Algorithm

Let $(\Pi, Goal)$ be a program, R be the rule in Π we want to normalize and r the predicate defined by R.

If $Var(Body(R)) \subseteq Var(Head(R))$ then
  R is already normalized;
Else
  /* Now, wherever r appears in Π, an argument is added to it */
  1. for each literal, with predicate r, which appears in the body part of the rules
      the added argument is a fresh variable;
  /* Let us denote Π' the obtained program */
  2. for each rule defining r in Π'
      if the rule is a fact then
        the argument is [];
      else
        the argument added to the heads of the rules defining r is a term
        $[X_1, X_2, \ldots, X_n]$ s.t. $\{X_1, X_2, \ldots, X_n\} = Var(Body) - Var(Head)$;
End;

Proposition 3 *Normalizing a rule of a program* $(\Pi_1,\ Goal_1)$ *preserves the strong operational equivalence on variables of* $Goal_1$.

Proposition 4 *Any program* $(\Pi_1, Goal_1)$ *has a normalized program* $(\Pi_2, Goal_2)$ *strongly operationally equivalent to it.*

3.2.2 Folding Normalized Programs

Our definition is quite different from the definition of H.Tamaki and T.Sato. First, we introduce the normalization to improve the number of cases where folding can be applied. Second, we do not use the notions of P_{old} and P_{new}, which are essential for them. The folding clause is chosen in the current program. Third, the fold transformation can be applied only with respect to sequences of consecutive literals (without Cut). That is an essential condition to preserve Strong Operational Equivalence.

example :

original program	normalized program	folded normalized program
1. `a(X):-b,c(X),d(X).`	1. `a(X):-b,c(X),d(X).`	1. `a(X):-b,e(X,[X]).`
2. `e(X):-c(Y),d(X).`	2. `e(X,[Y]):-c(Y),d(X).`	2. `e(X,[Y]):-c(Y),d(X).`
3. `b.`	3. `b.`	3. `b.`
4. `c(0).`	4. `c(0).`	4. `c(0).`
5. `d(0).`	5. `d(0).`	5. `d(0).`
6. `d(1).`	6. `d(1).`	6. `d(1).`

Our fold transformation is the inverse of the deterministic unfold transformation, up to normalization.

Definition 9 Folding Normalized Programs
Let Π *be a Prolog program,* Θ *be a substitution,* C *be a clause in* Π *which has form*

$A : -A_1 \ldots A_{j-1}\Theta(\mathbf{A_j} \ldots \mathbf{A_{j+k}})A_{j+k+1} \ldots A_n$

and R *be another clause in* Π*, without any Cut in its body, which has form*

$G : -A_j \ldots A_{j+k}$

s.t. ΘG *unifies only with* $Head(R)$.

Then the clause R *is normalized and* G_N *is the normalized of* G*; then* C *is transformed in :*

$A : -A_1 \ldots A_{j-1}\Theta G_N A_{j+k+1} \ldots A_n$

Remark : R can be normalized only w.r.t. the variables which do not verify the condition mentioned in 3.2.1.

Proposition 5 *Strong Operational Equivalence is preserved by folding normalized programs.*

3.3 K-Factorization

3.3.1 Introduction

This program transformation is inspired by the program specification of [MNL88] and the algorithm of partial evaluation by H.Fujita ([Fuj87]).

A more specific version of a program [MNL88] is a program where at least one rule is more instantiated than in the original program. This transformation preserves the success set (SS), but can improve the finite failure set (FF) , because it does not preserve infinite derivations. The advantages of this technique are its equivalence in the sense of the success derivations and the fact that it prunes some failure derivations in the SLD-tree.

K.Marriott, L.Naish and J.-L.Lassez have defined a function $msg_P(G, L)$ (more/most specific goal) which, for a program P, a goal G and a depth L returns the most/more specific version of G. This function computes the least upper bound of the set of success answer-substitutions (which derivation depth is less than or equal to L) and partial answer-substitutions (which derivation depth is equal to L). It computes too the least upper bound of the set of uniquely success answer-substitutions (which derivation depth is equal to L).

Theorem 1 *([MNL88]): For any goal G, program P and derivation depth L, $msg_P(G, L)$ returns a tuple (Upr, Lwr) s.t. Upr is a more specific version of G for P which is infinite derivation preserving. Further, if $Upr \sim Lwr$ then Upr is the most specific version of G.*

We can give an informal definition:

Let p be a literal in a clause, E be the set of systems of equations of the branches of length less than or equal to k in the SLD-tree of root p, and S be the set of variables which are common for each system of equations in E.

If common-constraint(p) denotes the common constraint over the variables in S, then p and literals after p are instantiated w.r.t. this constraint.

In a more formal way, using the [MNL88] notations :

Let P be a Prolog program, and G a goal for P, $PD_P^k(G)$ denotes the set of partial answer-substitutions for the non-success(and non-failure) derivations w.r.t. the goal G, of length k; and $SD_P^k(G)$ denotes the set of answer-substitutions for the success derivations w.r.t. the goal G, of length k.

Definition 10 k-Factorization

Let P be a Prolog program, R be a clause in P, and B be a literal in the body of R.

R is replaced in P by the clause R', with R' obtained from R by executing this transformation :

- *if R is a clause like :*

  $A :- B_1 \ldots B_m G C_1 \ldots C_n \qquad (n \geq 0, m > 0)$

  then R' is the clause :

  $A :- B_1 \ldots B_m [G C_1 \ldots C_n] lub(SD_P^k(G) \cup PD_P^k(G)) \uparrow Var(G)$

- *if R is a clause like :*

  $A :- G C_1 \ldots C_n \qquad (n \geq 0)$

  then R' is the clause :

  $[A :- G C_1 \ldots C_n] lub(SD_P^k(G) \cup PD_P^k(G)) \uparrow Var(G)$

All clauses R_i in P, which have any literal with the same predicate as G in their body, are replaced by their k-factorized w.r.t. this literal. The program result, called P', is the k-factorized version of P w.r.t. the predicate of G.

example :

```
1.  p(X,Y):- a(X),e(X,Y).
2.  a(0):- b(X),c(X).
3.  a(1):- d(X).
4.  b(0).
5.  c(1).
6.  d(1).
```

when applying a 3-factorization w.r.t. a(X)
$lub(SD^3_P(\mathtt{a(X)}) \cup PD^3_P(\mathtt{a(X)})) \uparrow Var(\mathtt{a(X)})$
$= \{\mathtt{X} = 1\}$
the result is :

```
1.  p(1,Y):- a(1),e(1,Y).
2.  a(0):- b(X),c(X).
3.  a(1):- d(X).
4.  b(0).
5.  c(1).
6.  d(1).
```

Proposition 6 *Strong Operational Equivalence is preserved by k-factorization.*

3.4 Clause-Indexing

The clause-indexing method is in the Warren Abstract Machine the operation which selects the rule(s) to be executed, with respect to the type of the root of the current argument (free variable, constant, list, or an other function symbol). The transformation proposed by J.Gallagher and M.Bruynooghe([GB90]), which we call too clause-indexing, simplifies the literals by removing useless function symbols (or equality constraints). This transformation improves the clause-indexing method in the WAM by coming up to the root of the arguments the relevant information.

The clause-indexing is a term simplification. It allows to "clean up" the programs : by example, after a k-factorization, the constraints over terms set by the program, can be removed away from the literals.

Clause-indexing preserves strong operational equivalence. The transformed program complexity and original program complexity are equal, because that is the unification complexity which is simplified.

Definition 11 General Clause-Indexing on the Heads
Let Π be a Prolog program, p a predicate definite by n clauses in Π (we shall suppose that all literals in Π have one argument to simplify notations) :

$$p(t_1) : -B_1.$$
$$p(t_2) : -B_2.$$
$$\ldots$$
$$p(t_n) : -B_n.$$

The definition of p is replaced by the clause $p(T) : -q(X_1, X_2, \ldots, X_k).$, where

- *q is a new predicate symbol, never appearing before in Π,*
- *$T = t_1 \wedge t_2 \wedge \ldots \wedge t_n$,*
- *and arguments of q are distinct variables occurring in T.*

The definition of q is :

$$q(X_1.\Theta_1, X_2.\Theta_1, \ldots, X_k.\Theta_1) :- B_1.$$
$$q(X_1.\Theta_2, X_2.\Theta_2, \ldots, X_k.\Theta_2) :- B_2.$$
$$\ldots$$
$$q(X_1.\Theta_n, X_2.\Theta_n, \ldots, X_k.\Theta_n) :- B_n.$$

where Θ_i *is a substitution s.t.* $T.\Theta_i = t_i$

Then, whenever a literal $p(t)$ *appears in* Π, *it is replaced by*

$$\Theta.q(X_1, X_2, \ldots, X_k), E_{\Theta'},$$

where $p(t).\Theta' = p(T).\Theta$, *and* $E_{\Theta'}$ *is the system of equations associated to* Θ'.

example :

original program

```
1.  rev([X|Xs],Y-Z) :-
    rev(Xs,Y-[X|Z]).
2.  rev([],X-X).
:- rev(X,Y-[]).
```

indexed program

```
1.  rev(X,Y-Z) :- rev1(X,Y,Z).
2.  rev1([X|Xs],Y,Z) :-
    rev1(Xs,Y,[X|Z]).
3.  rev1([],X,X).
:- rev(X,Y-[]).
```

Proposition 7 *Strong Operational Equivalence is preserved by general clause-indexing on the heads.*

Definition 12 General Clause-Indexing on the Heads and on the Bodies
The definition is the same as upon, the only modified point is : $T = t_h \vee t_b$, *with*

- $t_h = t_1 \wedge t_2 \wedge \ldots \wedge t_n$;
- $t_b = t'_1 \wedge t'_2 \wedge \ldots \wedge t'_n$

where $p(t'_i)$ *is a literal appearing in* Π.

Proposition 8 *Strong Operational Equivalence is preserved by general clause-indexing on the heads and on the bodies.*

4 Strong Operational Equivalence and Meta-Interpretation

4.1 Introduction

Our framework is now pure Prolog, for which some simple meta-interpreters have been written. Many studies have been done about relations between different meta-interpreters. Thus, R.Kowalski's demo-interpreter can be transformed into the Vanilla-interpreter by partial evaluation ([Kow90]):

```
1. demo(t,true).
2. demo(t,G1) :- demo(t,G1 ↔ P1 ∧ Q),    G1 is an atom conjunction,
                                          and P1 is an atom in G1
                 demo(t,P2 ← R),          one rule is chosen
                 unify(P1,P2,Θ),
                 apply(Q ∧ R,Θ,G2),       the new goal G2 is built
                 demo(t,G2).
3. demo(t,not(P)) :- not (demo(t,P)).
```

The framework of this work was the relations between modal epistemic logic and two-valued logic. Our context is completely different (it is operational equivalence of programs), and we show :

- first, bindings between the Vanilla-interpreter and the program which it computes;
- second, bindings between an other meta-interpreter, with three facts and one right recursive rule, and the Vanilla-interpreter.

4.2 The Vanilla-Meta-interpreter

$\forall i \quad 1 \leq i \leq n$

```
1.i. rule([a_i, b_i^1,...b_i^ni]).
2.   solve([]).
3.   solve ([A|B]) :- solve(A), solve(B).
4.   solve (A) :- rule([A|B]),solve(B).
Goal :- solve([Goal_1,...,Goal_n])
```

By successive unfoldings (deterministic or with respect to the leftmost literal), the Prolog program (which is described by the clauses "`rule`") is obtained, with each literal included in the predicate solve.

Proposition 9 *The Vanilla-meta-interpreter preserves the strong operational equivalence of any pure Prolog program.*

Proof : Rule number 4 of the Vanilla-interpreter is unfolded with respect to the leftmost literal : the result is n rules with number 4.i. These clauses are then unfolded (by deterministic unfolding), until it cannot be applied, and then they are 1-factorized. The goal has now the form `:- solve(Goal_1), ..., solve(Goal_n)` and rules 1, 2 and 3 are useless : they can be removed. As we have only use strong operational equivalence preserving transformations, a new meta-program, which is equivalent to the original, is obtained :

$\forall i \quad 1 \leq i \leq n$

```
4.i.   solve (a_i) :- solve(b_i^1),...solve(b_i^(ni-1)),solve(b_i^ni).
Goal :- solve(Goal_1), ..., solve(Goal_n)
```

Thus, there is an equivalence (in the sense of s.o.e.) between a meta-program which has the form of the Vanilla-interpreter and the program that it computes.

4.3 The Quasi-Iterative Meta-Interpreter

Let us consider this Prolog meta-interpreter :

```
1. choice([Goal|L1]-L2, [[Goal|L3]-L1|List_of_Rules],L3-L2, Π).

2. choice(Goals, [Rule|List_of_Rules],Goals,List_of_Rules).

3. execute(L-L,[]).

4. execute(List_of_Goals_1,List_of_Rules_1) :-
     choice(List_of_Goals_1,List_of_Rules_1,
               List_of_Goals_2,List_of_Rules_2),
     execute(List_of_Goals_2,List_of_Rules_2).
```

Goal :- execute(Goals,Π)

Π is a list composed with n rules : $\Pi = [Rule_1, Rule_2, \ldots, Rule_n]$, with, for each $i, 1 \leq i \leq n$, $Rule_i$ is a difference list : $Rule_i = [a_i, b_i^1, \ldots, b_i^{mi}|L] - L$

example :

For the append example, the complete program is :

```
1. choice([Goal|L1]-L2,[[Goal|L3]-L1|List_of_rules],L3-L2,
        [[append([],Lapp1,Lapp1)|L]-L,
        [append([X|Lapp2],Lapp3,[X|Lapp4]),append(Lapp2,Lapp3,Lapp4)|LL]-LL]).

2. choice(List_of_Goals, [Rule|List_of_Rules], List_of_Goals, List_of_Rules).

3. execute(L-L,[]).

4. execute(List_of_Goals_1, List_of_Rules_1) :-
        choice(List_of_Goals_1,List_of_Rules_1,List_of_Goals_2,List_of_Rules_2),
        execute(List_of_Goals_2, List_of_Rules_2).
```

(In the Edinburgh syntax, the first letter of each variable is a capital letter.)

For the original goal append([1],[2,3],L), the corresponding goal in the quasi-iterative meta-interpreter will be :

```
Goal :- execute([append([1],[2,3],L1)]-[], [[append([],Lapp1,Lapp1)|L]-L,
        [append([X|Lapp2],Lapp3,[X|Lapp4]),append(Lapp2,Lapp3,Lapp4)|LL]-LL]).
```

This meta-interpreter needs the occur-check. However, it is enough to add the following body to the first rule, to avoid infinite terms (the occur-check is then no more needed):

```
choice([Goal|L1]-L2,[[Goal|L3]-L1|List_of_rules],L3-L2,Program) :-
     [Goal|L1] \== L2.
```

\== tests the literally equality in Quintus and in Sicstus.

This meta-program, with one recursive rule and three facts, is equivalent (in the sense of the strong operational equivalence) with the original program, because it can be transformed to the Vanilla-meta-interpreter using our transformations. So, there is an equivalence for the logic programming at the C.Böhm and G.Jacopini's theorem for the imperative programming : any program can be written with only one while.

Theorem 2 *Any logic program can be written with one recursive rule and three facts.*

5 Conclusion

We have studied the possibility to modify the classic code optimization techniques (folding, unfolding (H.Tamaki and T.Sato)), the specification of programs (K.Marriott, L.Naish and J.-L.Lassez) and the clause-indexing method (J.Gallagher and M.Bruynooghe) to take care of the strong operational equivalence of non-pure Prolog programs. With these techniques, we have shown that any pure Prolog program can be transformed to a quasi-iterative-meta-program, and that the C.Böhm and G.Jacopini's theorem has an equivalent form in logic programming.

We now try to define some folding/unfolding heuristics which will make a control of recursion and allow more non-logical features. The EUREKA-predicates (or definition rule) seem to be a good tool for a more efficient programs recursion. In an other side, we try to use the results of an abstract interpretation, and to apply these techniques to "typed" programs.

References

[BJ66] C.Böhm and G.Jacopini, *Flow diagrams, Türing machines and languages with only two formation rules*, Communications of ACM, vol.9, pages 366-371,1966.

[BuR89] M.Bugliesi and F.Russo, *Partial Evaluation in Prolog : some Improvements about Cut*, in Proceedings of the north-american conference on logic programming, pages 645-660, 1989.

[Del88] J.-P.Delahaye, *Sémantique logique et dénotationnelle des interpréteurs Prolog*, Informatique Théorique et Applications, Vol.22, n.1, 1988, pages 3-42.

[Den91] F.Denis and J.-P.Delahaye, *Unfolding, Procedural and Fixpoint Semantics of Logic Programs*, in Proceedings of STACS'91, Lecture Notes in Computer Science, vol.480, Springer-Verlag Ed., pages 511-522.

[Fuj87] H.Fujita,*An algorithm for partial evaluation with constraints*, ICOT Technical Memorandum, ICOT 1987.

[GB90] J.Gallagher and M.Bruynooghe, *Some low-level source transformations for logic programs*, in Proceedings of the second workshop on meta-programming in logic, April 1990, Leuven, Belgium, Bruynooghe editor, pages 229-244.

[KK88] T.Kawamura and T.Kanamori, *Preservation of stronger equivalence in unfold/fold logic transformation*, in Proceedings of the international conference on fifth generation computer systems, pages 413-421, ICOT 1988.

[Kow90] R.Kowalski, Imperial College, London, *Meta-matters*, in Second Workshop on Meta-programming in logic, April 1990, Louvain, Belgique.

[Lev89] M.Falaschi, G.Levi, C.Palamidessi and M.Martelli, *Declarative Modeling of the Operational Behaviour of Logic Languages*, in Theoretical Computer Science, vol.69, 1989, pages 289-318.

[Llo87] J.W.Lloyd, *Foundations of logic programming*, Springer-Verlag, 2nd ed., 1987.

[Mah87] M.J.Maher, *Equivalences of logic programs*, in Foundations of deductive databases and logic programming, J.Minker Ed., Morgan Kaufmann Publishers, pages 627-658, 1987.

[MNL88] K.Marriott, L.Naish and J.-L.Lassez, *Most specific logic programs*, in Proceedings of the Fifth International Conference and Symposium on Logic Programming,Washington, Seattle, August 1988, pages 909-923.

[PDL90] A.Parrain, P.Devienne and P.Lebegue, *Equivalence Opérationnelle et Evaluation Partielle*, Rapport Interne, LIFL, 1990.

[PP91] M.Proietti and A.Pettorossi, *Semantics Preserving Transformation Rules for Prolog*, ACM Symposium on Partial Evaluation and Semantics Based Program Manipulation, New-Haven, U.S.A., 17-19 June 1991.

[Sah91] D.Sahlin, *An Automatic Partial Evaluator for Full Prolog*, Ph.D.Thesis, Swedish Institute of Computer Science, Stockholm, March 1991.

[TS84] H.Tamaki and T.Sato, *Unfold/Fold transformation of logic programs*, in Proceedings of the second International Conference on Logic Programming, Uppsala, 1984, pages 127-138.

[VeB88] R.Venken and B.Demoen, *A Partial Evaluation System : some Practical Considerations*, in New Generation Computing, Vol.6, n.2,3, pages 279-290, 1988.

Global Search Algorithms and the Constraint Logic Programming Framework.

S. Schaeck [1]

University of Namur
rue Grandgagnage, 21
B-5000 Namur (Belgium)
Email: ssc@info.fundp.ac.be

Extended abstract

Global search is an improvement of the "generate & test" paradigm, which is particularly efficient for solving combinatorial problems. This paradigm was studied in the functional programming framework in [Smith88], and in the logic programming framework in [Schaeck91].

The constraint logic programming (CLP) framework is also a very interesting tool for designing programs solving combinatorial problems. A method for designing CLP programs, based on a general program schema, is studied in [Deville-Van Hentenryck90].

In our research, we first introduce a particular version of the schema for global search algorithms. The interest of this version is to explicitely separate the generation of candidate solutions and their feasibility test. We also show that this particular schema is indeed totally equivalent to the one presented in our earlier work (see [Schaeck91]).

We then show that each concept used in global search algorithms finds its counterpart in the schema used for constructing CLP programs or in the mechanisms of constraint logic programming languages. This convinces us that a CLP program can be considered as an instance of a global search algorithm, even if it does not have such an appearance.

We then propose a new schema for the design of CLP programs, which uses the full power of the global search paradigm. The main interest of this new schema is that the decomposition into subproblems is now justified by a semantical argument, and no more by a purely syntactical one.

[1]This work is sponsored by a research grant of the Belgian National Fund for Scientific Research.

References

[Deville-Van Hentenryck90] Yves Deville and Pascal Van Hentenryck, *Construction of CLP Programs*, research paper RP-90/6, Institut d'Informatique, FUNDP Namur, 1990.

[Schaeck91] Sébastien Schaeck, *Design of global search algorithms in the Logic Programming Framework*, technical report 27/91, Institut d'Informatique, FUNDP Namur, 1991.

[Smith88] Douglas R. Smith, *The Structure and Design of global search algorithms*, research report KES.U.87.12, Kestrel Institute, 1988.

AUTOMATED TRANSLATION OF OCCAM TO A CONCURRENT LOGIC LANGUAGE

Matthew Huntbach
Department of Computer Science
Queen Mary and Westfield College
London E1 4NS
email: mmh@dcs.qmw.ac.uk

Abstract

It is known that if we have an interpreter `I` written in a language L_I which interprets programs written in a language L_P, partially evaluating the interpreter with respect to some program `P` will give a program which behaves as `P` but is in language L_I rather than L_P. The combination of interpreter and partial evaluator may therefore be used to translate from L_P to L_I.

We discuss such a system in this paper, where L_P is a language close to Occam and L_I the concurrent logic language FGDC (Flat Guarded Definite Clauses - a development from Parlog).

We give an interpreter for an Occam-like language in FGDC and some examples of partial evaluation techniques used on the interpreter to translate Occam-like code to FGDC.

1. Translation through Partial Evaluation

Partially evaluating a program refers to executing it with only a subset of the input defined and at any point in the execution where the input is insufficiently defined to give a definite output leaving a residual program derived from the original program but specialised to cater only for examples which include the partial input.

Particular attention has been given to the use of partial evaluation in combination with interpreters [9]. If we have an interpreter `I` written in a language L_I which runs programs written in a language L_P, we can use it to run programs written in L_P on a system which does not know about L_P, but which can run L_I. The disadvantage of this is that there is a considerable overhead associated with interpretation. However, consider that `I` running a program `P` takes as input both `P` and `P`'s own input `i`. If we were to partially evaluate `I` with input `P` but leaving `i` undefined we would be left with a residual program in language L_I which takes input **i** and runs on the system which executes L_I, but gives the behaviour of the program **P** which was written in L_P. Thus the combination of interpreter and partial evaluator gives a system for translating from language L_P to language L_I.

Logic languages are well suited for this sort of program manipulation. As symbol-handling languages, interpreters may be written in them with ease. Their simple syntax, clean semantics, and declarative nature make them suited to program manipulation techniques such as partial evaluation.

Although Prolog is the most well-known logic language, a family of concurrent logic languages [13] has grown up which attempt to combine the concurrency of Dijkstra's CSP [5] with the declarative nature of Prolog. Such languages can support real parallel applications on distributed architectures. Since moving to distributed architectures necessitates the use of new languages it would be nice if programmers would take the opportunity to move to languages which are also declarative, thus avoiding the situation which has grown up with sequential programming of languages being used which are universally acknowledged to be clumsy and unfriendly but whose usage cannot be changed due both to human conservatism and the practical difficulty of changing a language once a software library has been established. Sadly, the mistakes that were made thirty years ago which led to the current commercial dominance of Cobol and Fortran are being made again. "Concurrent Fortran" in the shape of Occam appears to be the favoured language for use with distributed systems.

While all is not yet lost, there is already a need for translators from Occam and other imperative languages to concurrent declarative languages. In this paper we show how this may be done through the mechanism of partially evaluating an interpreter. The paper also serves to give a practical example of the power of this technique.

In this paper the concurrent logic language we use is FGDC (Flat Guarded Definite Clauses) [11]. This language is a version of Parlog86 [12], and is known in a commercial variant as Strand [1]. It has been argued that, with the addition of certain real time primitives, the language combines the power of Occam in expressing concurrent algorithms with the power of the logic programming paradigm for handling advanced symbolic applications [4]. This paper supports this argument by showing that Occam code can be automatically translated into FGDC.

2. An Interpreter for an Occam-style Language in FGDC

An interpreter for a simple block structured language can be written in which execution is achieved by explicitly passing the environment as a parameter. The call which executes a statement in the block-structured language takes as input the initial environment and returns as output the environment as updated by execution of the statement. This can form the basis of an interpreter in FGDC to Occam, since we can extend it by adding clauses to deal with the concurrency and indeterminism aspects of Occam.

An interpreter sufficient to implement a block structured language containing `if` statements, `while` loops (implemented by converting them to recursion) and assignments, though not procedure calls, is given in Appendix I.

In the interpreter the environment is a list of name/value pairs. To enable scoping rules to be implemented it may also contain the symbol `end`. When a block starts execution this symbol is put at the head of the environment list. When a block finishes execution, any name/value pairs which occur before the first `end` (i.e. variables declared within the block) are deleted. Expressions containing variables are evaluated with respect to their current environment; when a variable occurs its current value is looked up in the environment.

The interpreter contains code for variable declarations, which simply adds new variables initialised to zero to the environment; assignment statements which gives as output the input environment updated to change the value of the variable on the left hand side of the assignment as appropriate; `if` statements which calculates the value of a conditional expression and then gives as output the environment resulting from executing with the input environment the true or false branch of the conditional as appropriate; and `while` statements which evaluates a condition and returns the input environment unchanged if the conditional evaluates to false, otherwise the result of evaluating the statement within the loop followed by a recursive evaluation of the whole `while` statement. Sequencing is achieved by passing the input environment to the first statement in a block of statements, and using the output environment obtained as the input environment to any subsequent statements in the block.

The syntax of the source language is such that a program written in the language is also a valid FGDC tuple. Its BNF is:

```
<Program> ::= <Block>

<Block> ::= [ ]
```

```
<Block> ::= [ <Statement> { , <Statement> } ]

<Statement> ::= var(<Varlist>)

<Statement> ::= <Variable> := <Expression>

<Statement> ::= if(<Condition>,<Block>,<Block>)

<Statement> ::= while(<Condition>,<Block>)

<Variablelist> ::= [ <Variable> { , <Variable>} ]
```

where a `<Variable>` is a string starting with a **lower case** alphabetic character (i.e. it should be distinguished from an FGDC variable). An `<Expression>` follows the standard binding for arithmetic operators and may be composed of `<Variable>`s and integers.

For the language to be practical, it is necessary to add procedure calling mechanisms. Procedure names could be paired with code and parameter lists in the environment. A procedure call would extend the environment by linking the parameters with the arguments to the call. It would not be too difficult to add further extensions to allow call-by-name, and to ensure the scope rules gives static binding, but it is not necessary for the purpose of this paper to give further consideration to these issues.

A call doblock(InVars, Code, OutVars) where InVars gives the input in the form of a list of variables and their initial values will result in OutVars giving the output in the form of a list of variables and their final values.

For example, the call:

doblock([(acc,1),(n,6)], [while(n>1, [acc:=acc*n, n:=n-1])], OutVars)

will result in OutVars being bound to [(acc,720),(n,0)]. That is, the factorial of 6 has been calculated.

3. A Set of Rules for Partial Evaluation

In [10] we give a set of rule for partially evaluating concurrent logic programs. The rules were used to build an automated partial evaluator. They may be summarised as follows:

Let P be the initial program, and S be a set of pairs of goals, the set of previously encountered partial evaluations. To partially evaluate a goal g, if the pair (g',h') is in S, where g' is identical to g in all but variable names, return h where h is obtained from h' by replacing all variables which occur in g' by their equivalent in g.

Otherwise find all clauses in P to which *g* could commit. If there is only one such clause, and *g* is already sufficiently bound to enable the commitment to take place, replace *g* by the body of this clause with variables bound as they would be following the commitment, and partially evaluate the body as bound (in this case *g* is referred to as *immediately executable*). This may be considered a form of *unfolding* [2].

If there is more than one clause to which *g* could commit, given that *g* takes the form g(<Args>) and the clauses to which it may commit take the form:

g(<Args$_1$>) :– Body$_1$

...

g(<Args$_n$>) :– Body$_n$

construct a new set of clauses

h(<Args$'_1$>) :– Body$'_1$

...

h(<Args$'_n$>) :– Body$'_n$

where h is a new predicate name, Body$'_i$ is obtained from Body$_i$ by passing through any variable bindings made when g(<Args>) is unified with g(<Args$_i$>), and <Args$'_i$> are the values in <Args$_i$> with which the variables in <Args> must match for g(<Args>) to commit to the ith clause. Add the pair (g(<Args>), h(<Vars>)) to S where <Vars> are the variables occuring in <Args>, and partially evaluate each Body$'_i$. Replace *g* by h(<Vars>).

The first step in the partial evaluation of Body$'_i$ is to execute any primitive which is sufficiently bound to be executed and which does not bind a variable in <Args$'_i$>. This may cause further bindings to be made and give further scope for partial evaluation. The effect of adding (g(<Args>), h(<Vars>)) to S is to provide a halting condition so that, rather than continue indefinitely, partial evaluation halts and returns a recursive program when appropriate.

The partial evaluation described so far is essentially that described more formally by Furukawa et al [7]. To the UR-set of rules described in this reference, we add two extra rules which are applied after partially evaluating each h(<Args$'_i$>) :– Body$'_i$. The first rule *eliminates redundant variables*. If for any goal in the body f(<Vars$_f$>), <Vars$_f$> contains a variable X which does not otherwise occur in the body or in <Vars> in the head, this variable is redundant since it serves no practical purpose. The goal f(<Vars$_f$>) is replaced by f$'$(<Vars$_f$>$'$) where <Vars$_f$>$'$ is <Vars$_f$> with X removed and f$'$ is a new predicate name. A set of cases of redundant variable elimination, R, is kept and the tuple $(X, f(<Vars_f>), f')$ is added to R and a new set of clauses is constructed for f′ by taking those for f which do not require X to be bound for commitment, eliminating from the heads of these clauses that argument in the same position as X is in $<Vars_f>$ and applying redundant variable elimination recursively to the clauses for f′. During construction of this new set of clauses if an attempt is made to remove a redundant variable X from a goal p(Vars) and $(Y, p(Vars_r), p')$ is found in R where the position of Y in $Vars_r$ is equal to the position of X in Vars, p(Vars) is replaced by a call to p′(Vars′) where Vars′ is obtained from Vars by removing X. Again, this ensures that, rather than loop, partial evaluation terminates with a recursive program when appropriate.

The other rule for further transformation implements *goal fusion* [8]. This involves noting cases where a body contains two goals $p(<Args_p>)$ and $q(<Args_q>)$ where $<Args_p>$ and $<Args_q>$ share a common variable X which does not occur in the head of the clause and the clauses for q are such that $q(<Args_q>)$ cannot commit until X is bound. In this case the call $q(<Args_q>)$ is *dependent* on the call $p(<Args_p>)$. Both can be replaced by a single call $pq(<Args_{pq}>)$, where pq is a new predicate name and $<Args_{pq}>$ is the union of $<Args_p>$ and $<Args_q>$ less X. The dependency means that although the goals are expressed as runnable in parallel since it is not possible for them to simultaneously rewrite the fusion does not reduce the potential parallelism in the program. A set of cases of goal fusion, F, is maintained. The tuple $(X, p(<Args_p>), q(<Args_q>), pq(<Args_{pq}>))$ is added to F, and the clauses for $pq(<Args_{pq}>)$ are obtained by taking the clauses for $p(<Args_p>)$, replacing each $p(<Args_p>_i)$:- $Body_i$ by $pq(<Args_{pq}>_i)$:- $Body_i$, $q(<Args_q>_i)$ where $<Args_{pq}>_i$ and $<Args_q>_i$ are obtained from $<Args_{pq}>$ and $<Args_q>$ respectively by binding any variables which occur in $<Args_p>$ as they would need to be bound to match with $<Args_p>_i$. The goal $q(<Args_q>_i)$ may be further partially evaluated, and further goal fusion may be possible between the partially evaluated form of $q(<Args_q>_i)$ and a goal in $Body_i$. Once again, to avoid looping and produce recursive programs, before any new procedure is constructed by goal fusion a check is made on the set F to see whether an existing fusion identical in all but variable names has been made, and if so the fused goals are replaced by a call to the previously generated procedure. Recursion detection in goal fusion may be considered a form of *folding* [2].

In both redundancy removal and goal fusion, the transformations may result in primitives which bind variables becoming executable as the variables they bind no longer occur in the clause head. These primitives are then executed, binding variables in other goals which are then further partially evaluated.

When a set of clauses for a goal has been completely partially evaluated, they are added to the output program.

Some slight extensions to these rules are necessary to cope with the guards of FGDC. A consideration of the constraints which the guards impose can lead to further possibilities for partial evaluation [6].

FGDC partial evaluation may be considered an extended form of FGDC execution [11]. An FGDC computation consists of a set of goals, the clauses in the program being rewrite rules for these goals. Any goal which is immediately executable may be rewritten, there is no sense of ordering except as determined by data dependency. In actual execution a goal which is not immediately executable is suspended. In partial evaluation a specialised program for such a goal is constructed.

4. Partial Evaluation of the Block-Structured Language Interpreter

The interpreter for executing a block-structured language we described in section 2 is clearly not an efficient way of executing this language. Its importance is that if combined with a partial evaluator for FGDC it may be used to translate from the block-structured language to an efficient FGDC program. Thus if we partially evaluate the call

```
doblock([(acc,1),(n,N)], [while(n>1, [acc:=acc*n, n:=n-1])], OutVars)
```

we will obtain a FGDC program which will calculate the factorial of N and which will also be reasonably efficient.

The key to the improvement in efficiency is the fact that the predicates which manipulate environments, lookup and replace, do not depend on the actual value stored in the variable which is being looked up or replaced. Thus all calls to them can be executed during partial evaluation. The effect of partial evaluation is that the explicit environment is compiled away. In Appendix II we give a detailed working through the partial evaluation of the above factorial program which demonstrates this.

5. Implicit and Explicit Parallelism

The interpreter given in Appendix I for block-structured languages will detect any implicit parallelism and convert it to the implicit parallelism of FGDC. This implicit parallelism respects the data dependency of the sequencing of statements giving parallelism only where it has no effect on the result of the execution. Consider the execution of the assignments x:=*exp1*, y:=*exp2*, z:=*exp3* where *exp1*, *exp2* and *exp3* are arbitary expressions. The call dostatements(Env1, [x:=*exp1*, y:=*exp2*, z:=*exp3*], OutEnv) will evaluate to:

V1:= *evaluation of* *exp1* *in* Env1,
V2:= *evaluation of* *exp2* *in* Env2,
V3:= *evaluation of* *exp3* *in* Env3,
replace(x, V1, Env1, Env2),
replace(y, V2, Env2, Env3),
replace(z, V3, Env3, OutEnv)

Suppose the initial environment is [(x,1),(y,2),(z,3),(a,4),(b,5),(c,6)]. Then the call will evaluate to:

V1:= *evaluation of* *exp1* *in* Env1,
V2:= *evaluation of* *exp2* *in* Env2,
V3:= *evaluation of* *exp3* *in* Env3,
Env2:=[(x,V1),(y,2),(z,3),(a,4),(b,5),(c,6)],
Env3:=[(x,V1),(y,V2),(z,3),(a,4),(b,5),(c,6)],
OutEnv:=[(x,V1),(y,V2),(z,V3),(a,4),(b,5),(c,6)]

If *exp1*, *exp2* and *exp3* contain references to a, b and c only, they may be evaluated in parallel. If however, *exp2* contains references to x it will use V1 for x, and evaluation will be suspended until V1 is bound by evaluation of *exp1*. Similarly, evaluation of *exp3* will be halted if it contains references to x or y. In contrast a purely parallel execution of the assignments which does not respect data dependency could have indeterminate effect if *exp2* contains references to x or *exp3* contains references to x or y. The effect is as if the assignments were carried out in any order. If the assignments were [x:=y,y:=9,z:=2*x+y], the result would be that x is linked with either 2 or 9, and z any of 4, 6, 13 or 27.

In Occam this problem is solved by making variables shared between parallel computations read-only so that the situation of several processes simultaneously trying to assign a value to a single variable never arises. Another way of considering this is that computations executing in parallel take a copy of their environment but do not pass on any changes made to that environment. We distinguish between this explicit parallelism and the implicit parallelism mentioned previously. Explicit parallelism using the Occam solution to the problem of shared variables can be added to our language as follows. We add to the grammar:

```
<Statement> ::= par(<Blocklist>)

<Blocklist> ::= [ <Block> { , <Block> } ]
```

Additional code for the interpreter is given in Appendix III. The code for executing a `par` statement passes the input environment to each of its substatements and causes the substatements to be executed in parallel. The input environment is passed on unchanged as the output environment of the whole `par` statement, any changes made by any of the substatements being ignored.

6. Process Communication through Channels

The above introduction of parallelism avoids the problem of shared variables, but gives no way for parallel processes to communicate with each other. In Occam this is done through channels. An Occam channel can be imitated in FGDC by a shared unbound FGDC variable. In this imitation, to send a message on the channel the variable imitating the channel is bound to a pair consisting of the message and a new unbound variable. The next message on the channel can be sent by similarly treating this new variable, and so on for further messages. For a process to receive a message on a channel, the process is suspended until the channel variable has been bound to a pair consisting of the message and a new variable. The next message can be received by treating the new variable similarly, and similarly for further messages.

Thus Occam-type communication primitives can simply be added to the language of the interpreter with BNF:

```
<Statement> ::= <Variable> ? <Variable>

<Statement> ::= <Variable> ! <Expression>
```

The FGDC code to add these primitives to the interpreter is given in Appendix III. The code for `!` computes the value of the expression to be output, binds the channel variable and returns as output environment the input environment updated to link the channel name to the new unbound FGDC variable. The code for `?` makes a call to the predicate `waitin` whose third argument is the channel variable. This call cannot proceed until the channel variable is bound, when it does so it returns a new environment as output obtained by updating the Occam variable which received the input value and the FGDC value linked to the channel name to its new value to receive future communications.

The environments for parallel processes will share FGDC variables representing shared channels, thus the binding of a variable linked with a channel name in one process will cause the variable linked with the same name in the other processes to be changed, since it is the same variable. So, for example, suppose two processes share the environment [(chan,C),(x,3)]. If the first processes executes chan!4, it will bind C to [4|C1], and its environment will become [(chan,C1),(x,3)]. The second process will have the C in its environment bound, giving the environment [(chan,[4|C1]),(x,3)]. If the second process then executes chan?x its environment will become [(chan,C1),(x,4)]. Note how since x is an Occam variable, its new value is **not** shared between the processes.

7. Indeterminism

An essential part of Occam is the ability to express *indeterminism* or "don't care non-determinism", which derives from Dijkstra's guarded commands. In Occam this is expressed through the `alt` constructor. In FGDC this is expressed directly through the clause commitment mechanism. It is a limited form of OR-parallelism since attempts to satisfy each of the guards are made concurrently. However, when writing interpreters it is often necessary to simulate OR-parallelism by AND-parallelism in order to allow communication between the processes representing the various alternatives [3].

Occam's `alt` constructor enables a process to choose between a number of channels as possible sources of messages. It takes the form of a sequence of pairs of input commands and statements. When one of the input commands is executed, the statement linked with it is executed and the others abandoned. In our language we represent this by the BNF rule:

```
<Statement> ::= alt(<AltList>)

<AltList> ::= [ <GuardedCommand> { , <GuardedCommand} ]

<GuardedCommand> ::= <Variable> ? <Variable> : <Block>
```

Our implementation works as follows. Each guarded command is translated into three processes. The first waits for a message to arrive on a channel and if one arrives informs the second process by binding a flag variable. The second process creates a request for its guarded command to proceed and passes the request on in the case where the flag variable has been bound, or it passes on an alternative request from one of the following guarded commands in the case where one has been received; if both options are possible which is chosen is indeterminate, so the indeterminacy of Occam is mapped onto this indeterminacy in the interpreter. Requests include an *acceptance variable* which will be bound to yes or no depending on whether the request is accepted. The third process takes an acceptance variable and executes the statement associated with a guard if the request is accepted, halting without execution if it is not. A single process shared by all the guarded commands, the *request master* will receive just one of the requests and cause it to be accepted by binding its acceptance variable to yes; it kills off any processes which are still waiting for channel inputs by binding a termination variable (a single shared variable which when bound causes all the processes which share it to terminate). All other acceptance variables will be bound to no.

Full code for the implementation of `alt` is given in Appendix III. The three processes for each guarded command are given by the predicates alt_waitin, join_reqs and goahead respectively. The predicate selectalt sets them up. All goahead processes share the input and output environments but only the one whose request variable is bound to yes will update the input environment with the message and new channel value passed on from its alt_waitin process to give the output environment. The first two clauses for join_reqs represent the options mentioned above, the third clause represents the case where the process is killed off by the binding of the termination variable.

In Appendix IV as a simple example of partial evaluation techniques applied to our implementation of the `alt` construct, we consider in detail how we would deal with a process which has two input channels and one output channel, and waits for an input on either channel, outputting one constant value if the input is on one channel, another if it is on the other. Our factorial example showed a loop program converted to recursion by partial evaluation, this example shows a program involving a non-deterministic construct converted to a set of clauses. Conversion of a full-scale Occam program to FGDC would combine the techniques we have shown.

8. Conclusion

Occam is a language designed for programming multiprocessor systems. We have shown that the principal features of Occam may be represented in a concurrent logic language by demonstrating an interpreter in the concurrent logic language FGDC for an Occam-like language.

The declarative nature and simplicity of the concurrent logic languages make them open to program manipulation techniques such as partial evaluation. We gave a set of partial evaluation rules which in conjunction with the interpreter may be used to translate from Occam-like code to FGDC.

Our work demonstrates the power of the concurrent logic languages as general purpose languages for multiprocessor systems, as symbolic processing languages and as languages for use in program transformation systems.

References

[1]. Artificial Intelligence Ltd. *Strand88 User Manual.* 1988.

[2]. R.M.Burstall and J.Darlington. A Transformation System for Developing Recursive Programs. *Journal ACM 24,* pp.44-67 (1977).

[3]. M.Codish and E.Shapiro. Compiling OR-parallelism into AND-parallelism. *New Generation Computing 5,* 1 pp.45-61 (1987).

[4]. D.Cohen, M.M.Huntbach and G.A.Ringwood. Logical Occam, in P.Kacsuk and M.Wise (eds) *Distributed Prolog* (to be published) Wiley, 1991.

[5].E.W.Dijkstra. Guarded commands, nondeterminacy and formal derivation of programs. *Comm. ACM 18,* 8 pp.453-457 (1975).

[6]. H.Fujita, A.Okumura and K.Furukawa. Partial Evaluation of GHC Programs based on the UR-set with Constraints. In *Proc. Fifth Int. Conf. on Logic Programming,* pp.924-941. M.I.T. Press, 1988.

[7]. K.Furukawa, A.Okumura and M.Murukami. Unfolding Rules for GHC Programs. *New Generation Computing 6,* pp.143-157 (1988).

[8]. K.Furukawa and K.Ueda. GHC Process Fusion by Program Transformation. In *Proc. 2nd Annual Conf. of Japan Soc. of Software Science and Technology,* pp.89-92. 1985.

[9]. J.Gallagher. Transforming Logic Programs by Specialising Interpreters. In *European Conference on Artificial Intelligence (ECAI-86),* Brighton, UK, 1986.

[10]. M.M.Huntbach. Meta-Interpreters and Partial Evaluation in Parlog. *Formal Aspects of Computing 1,* pp.193-211 (1989).

[11]. G.A.Ringwood. *Pattern-Directed, Markovian, Linear Guarded, Definite Clause Resolution.* Tech.Rept. Dept. of Computing, Imperial College, 1987.

[12]. G.A.Ringwood. Parlog86 and the Dining Logicians. *Comm. ACM 31,* 1 pp.1-25 (1988).

[13]. E.Shapiro. The Family of Concurrent Logic Programming Languages. *ACM Comp. Surveys 21,* 3 pp.412-510 (1989).

Appendix I: An interpreter for a block-structured language

```
doblock(InEnv, Statements, OutEnv) :-
      dostatements([end|InEnv], Statements, OutEnv1),
      finish(OutEnv1, OutEnv).

finish([end | Env], OutEnv) :- OutEnv:=Env.
finish([(Name,Val) | Env], OutEnv) :- finish(Env, OutEnv).

dostatements(InEnv, [], OutEnv) :- OutEnv:=InEnv
dostatements(InEnv, [Stat | Statements], OutEnv) :-
      dostatement(InEnv, State, MidEnv),
      dostatements(MidEnv, Statements, OutEnv).

dostatement(InEnv, var(Vars), OutEnv) :-
      dodeclaration(InEnv, Vars, OutEnv).
dostatement(InEnv, Var:=Expr, OutEnv) :-
      doassignment(InEnv, Var, Expr, OutEnv).
dostatement(InEnv, while(Cond,Statements), OutEnv) :-
      dowhile(InEnv, Cond, Statements, OutEnv).
dostatement(InEnv, if(Cond,Stat1,Stat2), OutEnv) :-
      doif(InEnv, Cond, Stat1, Stat2, OutEnv).

doif(InEnv, Cond, Stat1, Stat2, OutEnv) :-
      evalinenv(InEnv, Cond, TruthVal),
      doif1(TruthVal, InEnv, Stat1, Stat2, OutEnv).

doif1(true, InEnv, Stat1, Stat2, OutEnv) :- doblock(InEnv, Stat1, OutEnv).
doif1(false, InEnv, Stat1, Stat2, OutEnv) :- doblock(InEnv, Stat2, OutEnv).

dowhile(InEnv, Cond, Statements, OutEnv) :-
      evalinenv(InEnv, Cond, TruthVal),
      dowhile1(TruthVal, InEnv, Cond, Statements, OutEnv).

dowhile1(false, InEnv, Cond, Statements, OutEnv) :- OutEnv:=InEnv.
dowhile1(true, InEnv, Cond, Statements, OutEnv) :-
      doblock(InEnv, Statements, MidEnv),
      dowhile(MidEnv, Cond, Statements, OutEnv).

dodeclaration(InEnv, [], OutEnv) :-
      OutEnv:=InEnv.
dodeclaration(InEnv, [Var | Vars], OutEnv) :-
      dodeclaration(InEnv, Vars, MidEnv),
      OutEnv:=[(Var,0) | MidEnv].
```

```
doassignment(InEnv, Var, Expr, OutEnv) :-
        evalinenv(InEnv, Expr, Val),
        replace(Var, Val, InEnv, OutEnv).

evalinenv(Env, N, V) :- integer(N) | V:=N.
evalinenv(Env, N, V) :- string(N) | lookup(N, Env, V).
evalinenv(Env, E1+E2, V) :-
        evalinenv(Env, E1, V1), evalinenv(Env, E2, V2), V is V1+V2.
evalinenev(Env, E1-E2, V) :-
        evalinenv(Env, E1, V1), evalinenv(Env, E2, V2), V is V1-V2.
evalinenev(Env, E1*E2, V) :-
        evalinenv(Env, E1, V1), evalinenv(Env, E2, V2), V is V1*V2.
evalinenev(Env, E1/E2, V) :-
        evalinenv(Env, E1, V1), evalinenv(Env, E2, V2), V is V1/V2.
evalinenev(Env, E1>E2, V) :-
        evalinenv(Env,E1,V1), evalinenv(Env,E2,V2), gt(V1,V2,V).
evalinenev(Env, E1<E2, V) :-
        evalinenv(Env,E1,V1), evalinenv(Env,E2,V2), lt(V1,V2,V).
evalinenev(Env, E1=E2, V) :-
        evalinenv(Env,E1,V1), evalinenv(Env,E2,V2), eq(V1,V2,V).
evalinenv(Env, not(E), V) :- evalinenv(Env, E, V1), negate(V1, V).

lt(V1, V2, V) :- V1<V2 | V:=true.
lt(V1, V2, V) :- V1>=V2 | V:=false.

gt(V1, V2, V) :- V1>V2 | V:=true.
gt(V1, V2, V) :- V1=<V2 | V:=false.

eq(V1, V2, V) :- V1==V2 | V:=true.
eq(V1, V2, V) :- V1=\=V2 | V:=false.

negate(true, V) :- V:=false.
negate(false, V) :- V:=true.

lookup(Var, [end | Env], Val) :- lookup(Var, Env, Val).
lookup(Var, [(Var1,Val1) | Env], Val) :- Var==Var1 | Val:=Val1.
lookup(Var, [(Var1,Val1) | Env], Val) :- Var=\=Var1 | lookup(Var, Env, Val).

replace(Var, Val, [end | Env1], Env) :-
        replace(Var, Val, Env1, Env2), Env:=[end | Env2].
replace(Var, Val, [(Var1,Val1) | Env1], Env) :- Var=\=Var1 |
        replace(Var, Val, Env1, Env2), Env:=[(Var1,Val1) | Env2].
replace(Var, Val, [(Var1,Val1) | Env1], Env) :- Var==Var1 | Env:=[(Var,Val) | Env1].
```

Appendix II: Example partial evaluation of a block-structured program

Here we give an example which shows how partial evaluation of the interpreter in Appendix I with input the block-structured code for computing a factorial using a while-loop is translated to FGDC clauses for computing a factorial. The partial evaluation is slightly simpler if we start with the environment [(acc,A),(n,N)] rather than [(acc,1),(n,N)], resulting in a program which leaves acc paired with the value A*(N!) in the environment.

```
doblock([(acc,A),(n,N)], [while(n>1, [acc:=acc*n,n:=n-1])], OutVars)
```

is immediately executable, rewriting to:

```
dostatements([end,(acc,A),(n,N)], [while(n>1, [acc:=acc*n, n:=n–1])], OutEnv),
finish(OutEnv, OutVars)
```

Here OutEnv is a new variable; new variable and predicate names would be generated by the partial evaluator. In our examples we will try where possible to invent meaningful names, though clearly this is a more difficult task when done automatically. The call to dostatements is immediately executable, causing the conjunction to be rewritten to:

```
dostatement([end,(acc,A),(n,N)], while(n>1, [acc:=acc*n, n:=n–1]), MidEnv),
dostatements(MidEnv, [], OutEnv),
finish(OutEnv, OutVars)
```

A few more rewrites of immediately executable goals will bring us to:

```
evalinenv([end,(acc,A),(n,N)], n, V1),
evalinenv([end,(acc,A),(n,N)], 1, V2),
gt(V1, V2, TruthVal),
dowhile1(TruthVal, [end,(acc,A),(n,N)], n>1, [acc:=acc*n, n:=n–1], MidEnv),
dostatements(MidEnv, [], OutEnv),
finish(OutEnv, OutVars)
```

Here we may note that evalinenv([end,(acc,A),(n,N)], n, V1) reduces to lookup(n, [end,(acc,A),(n,N)], n, V1) which will continue executing, eventually reducing to V1:=N. If we were actually executing a program using the interpreter rather than partially evaluating a call to the interpreter with respect to the program, N would be a value rather than an unbound integer. It may also be noted that evalinenv([end,(acc,A),(n,N)], 1, V2) reduces to V2:=1. Thus we have:

```
V1:=N, V2:=1, gt(V1, V2, TruthVal),
dowhile1(TruthVal, [end,(acc,A),(n,N)], n>1, [acc:=acc*n, n:=n–1], MidEnv),
dostatements(MidEnv, [], OutEnv),
finish(OutEnv, OutVars)
```

The assignments to V1 and V2 may be executed (the variables A and N, being in the top-level query, may be regarded as the head variables here) giving:

```
gt(N, 1, TruthVal),
dowhile1(TruthVal, [end,(acc,A),(n,N)], n>1, [acc:=acc*n,n:=n–1], MidEnv),
dostatements(MidEnv, [], OutEnv),
finish(OutEnv, OutVars)
```

The call gt(N, 1, TruthVal) gives a simple example of a call which can be specialised to particular arguments. We need to specialise the call to gt for the case when its second argument is 1. We will call this new procedure gt1 with clauses:

```
gt1(N, TruthVal) :- N>1 | TruthVal:=true.
gt1(N, TruthVal) :- N=<1 | TruthVal:=false.
```

We add the pair (gt(N,1,TruthVal), gt1(N, TruthVal)) to the set of previously encountered goals. This will ensure that if again we have a call gt(X,1,Y) we will rewrite it to gt1(X,Y) without generating another procedure.

We now need to generate a version of dowhile1 specialised with respect to the particular environment, condition and statements of the above call. This is a considerably more complex specialisation than the specialisation of gt. Let us call this specialised version doloop.

We add (dowhile1(TruthVal,[end,(acc,A),(n,N)],n>1,[acc:=acc*n,n:=n–1],MidEnv),
doloop(TruthVal,A,N,MidEnv))

to the set of previously encountered partial evaluations.

Our goals are now:

```
gt1(N, TruthVal),
doloop(TruthVal, A, N, MidEnv),
dostatements(MidEnv, [], OutEnv),
finish(OutEnv, OutVars)
```

The initial procedure for doloop is

```
doloop(false, A, N, OutEnv) :-
    OutEnv:=[end,(acc,A),(n,N)].
doloop(true, A, N, OutEnv) :-
    doblock([end,(acc,A),(n,N)], [acc:=acc*n,n:=n-1], Env1),
    dowhile(Env1, n>1, [acc:=acc*n,n:=n-1], OutEnv).
```

After several rewrites of immediately executable goals, the second clause becomes:

```
doloop(true, A, N, OutEnv) :-
    doassignment([end,end,(acc,A),(n,N)], acc, acc*n, Env2),
    dostatements(Env2, [n:=n-1], Env3),
    finish(Env3, Env1),
    dowhile(Env1, n>1, [acc:=acc*n,n:=n-1], OutEnv).
```

The call to doassignment will continue to rewrite, looking up the values of acc and n in its environment, but the arithmetic will not proceed as the values are unbound FGDC variables. This gives:

```
doloop(true, A, N, OutEnv) :-
    V is A*N,
    replace(acc, V, [end,end,(acc,A),(n,N)], Env2),
    dostatements(Env2, [n:=n-1], Env3),
    finish(Env3, Env1),
    dowhile(Env1, n>1, [acc:=acc*n,n:=n-1], OutEnv).
```

The rewrites of the call to replace show how the use of environments occurs only during the partial evaluation. There is no use of an environment in the multiplication in the resulting residual program:

```
doloop(true, A, N, OutEnv) :-
    V is A*N,
    Env2:=[end,end,(acc,V),(n,N)],
    dostatements(Env2, [n:=n-1], Env3),
    finish(Env3, Env1),
    dowhile(Env1, n>1, [acc:=acc*n, n:=n-1], OutEnv).
```

The variable Env2 is internal to the clause, so the assignment can be executed giving:

```
doloop(true, A, N, OutEnv) :-
    V is A*N,
    dostatements([end,end,(acc,V),(n,N)], [n:=n-1], Env3),
    finish(Env3, Env1),
    dowhile(Env1, n>1, [acc:=acc*n,n:=n-1], OutEnv).
```

The execution of n:=n-1 proceeds similarly to the execution of acc:=acc*n, leaving us with:

```
doloop(true, A, N, OutEnv) :-
    V is A*N, N1 is N-1,
    finish([end,end,(acc,V),(n,N1)], Env1),
    dowhile(Env1, n>1, [acc:=acc*n, n:=n-1], OutEnv).
```

The call to finish will just take off the first end from the environment, leaving us with:

```
doloop(true, A, N, OutEnv) :-
    V is A*N, N1 is N-1,
    dowhile([end,(acc,V),(n,N1)], n>1, [acc:=acc*n, n:=n-1], OutEnv).
```

If we continue by rewriting the call to dowhile and so on we will get:

```
doloop(true, A, N, OutEnv) :-
    V is A*N, N1 is N-1,
    gt(N1, 1, T),
    dowhile1(T, [end,(acc,V),(n,N1)], n>1 ,[acc:=acc*n,n:=n-1], OutEnv).
```

Here, the call to dowhile1 can be recognised as a version of the call we previously rewrote as doloop, and the call to gt as a version of the call rewritten as gt1. This gives us the following clauses for doloop:

```
doloop(false, A, N, OutEnv) :-
    OutEnv:=[end,(acc,A),(n,N)].
doloop(true, A, N, OutEnv) :-
    V is A*N, N1 is N-1,
    gt1(N1, 1, T),
    doloop(T, V, N1, OutEnv).
```

Our top level goals (with a slight rewriting that is possible) are:

```
gt1(N, TruthVal),
doloop(TruthVal, A, N, Env),
finish(Env, OutVars)
```

and we also have:

```
gt1(N, TruthVal) :- N>1 | TruthVal:=true.
gt1(N, TruthVal) :- N=<1 | TruthVal:=false.
```

We would also need the clauses for finish from the initial program.

Although this is adequate, and we have succeeeded in eliminating the explicit environment lookups, it is still not perfect. However, there is the possibility of goal fusion. Note that in the top level TruthVal communicates between gt1 and doloop. doloop cannot start executing until gt1 has bound TruthVal, therefore it is possible to fuse the two.

We define a new procedure doloopgt where doloopgt(A,N,Env1) is the fusion of gt1(N,T) and doloop(T,A,N,Env). We add (T, gt1(N,T), doloop(T,A,N,Env), doloopgt(A,N,Env)) to the set of previously encountered fusions. The clauses for doloopgt are:

```
doloopgt(A, N, Env) :- N>1 | T:=true, doloop(T, A, N, Env).
doloopgt(A, N, Env) :- N=<1 | T:=false, doloop(T, A, N, Env).
```

The assignments in the clause bodies may be executed:

```
doloopgt(A, N, Env) :- N>1 | doloop(true, A, N, Env).
doloopgt(A, N, Env) :- N=<1 | doloop(false, A, N, Env).
```

and the calls to doloop are now immediately executable, giving:

```
doloopgt(A, N, Env) :- N>1 | V is A*N, N1 is N-1, gt1(N1, T), doloop(T, V, N1, Env).
doloopgt(A, N, Env) :- N=<1 | Env:=[end,(acc,A),(n,N)].
```

In the first of these clauses it is possible to fuse gt1(N1, T) and doloop(T, V, N1, Env1), which will be recognised as a version of the previous fusion becoming: doloopgt(V,N1,Env1)

This gives us the program:

```
doloopgt(A,N,Env) :- N>1 | V is A*N, N1 is N-1, doloopgt(V, N1, Env).
doloopgt(A,N,Env) :- N=<1 | Env:=[end,(acc,A),(n,N)].
```

with top level goals:

```
doloopgt(A, N, Env),
finish(Env, OutVars)
```

Another fusion is possible at this point: doloopgt(A, N, Env) with finish(Env, OutVars) using the variable Env. This gives us a single top-level goal, let us call it factorial(A,N,OutVars). Its clauses are:

```
factorial(A, N, OutVars) :- N>1 |
    V is A*N, N1 is N-1,
    doloopgt(V, N1, Env),
    finish(Env, OutVars).
factorial(A, N, OutVars) :- N=<1 |
    Env:=[end,(acc,A),(n,N)],
    finish(Env, OutVars).
```

The calls of doloopgt(V, N1, Env) and finish(Env, OutVars) in the first clause can be fused, and noted as a version of the previous fusion, so they become factorial(V,N1,OutVars). In the second clause the assignment can be executed and the call to finish then becomes immediately executable. This gives us as the final program:

```
factorial(A, N, OutVars) :- N>1 |
    V is A*N, N1 is N-1,
    factorial(V, N1, OutVars).
factorial(A, N, OutVars) :- N=<1 |
    OutVars:=[(acc,A),(n,N)].
```

which is the program we would expect for factorial, with the environment occurring only in the final output.

Appendix III: Interpreter code for parallelism, process communication and indeterminism

```
dostatement(InEnv, par(Statements), OutEnv) :- dopar(InEnv, Statements, OutEnv).

dopar(InEnv, Blocks, OutEnv) :- OutEnv:=InEnv, par(Blocks).
par(InEnv, []).
par(InEnv, [Block | Blocks]) :-
    dostatements(InEnv, Block, OutEnv), par(InEnv, Blocks).


dostatement(InEnv, ChanName?Var, OutEnv) :-
    lookup(ChanName, InEnv, Channel),
    waitin(InEnv, ChanName, Channel, Var, OutEnv).

dostatement(InEnv, ChanName!Expr, OutEnv) :-
    evalinenv(InEnv, Expr, Message),
    lookup(ChanName, InEnv, Channel),
    Channel := [Message | Channel1],
    replace(ChanName, Channel1, InEnv, OutEnv).

waitin(InEnv, ChanName, [Message | Channel], Var, OutEnv) :-
    replace(Var, Message, InEnv, Env),
    replace(ChanName, Channel, Env, OutEnv).

dostatement(InEnv, alt(Alts), OutEnv) :-
    selectalt(K, InEnv, Alts, OutEnv, Req),
    req_master(Req, K).

selectalt(K, InEnv, [Channel?Var:Statements | Alts], OutEnv, Req) :-
    lookup(Channel, InEnv, ChanVar),
    alt_waitin(K, ChanVar, Message, NewChan, Done),
    join_reqs(K, Done, Go, AltReq, Req),
    goahead(Go, InEnv, Var, Message, Channel, NewChan, Statements, OutEnv),
    selectalt(K, InEnv, Alts, OutEnv, AltReq).
```

```
selectalt(K, InEnv, [], OutEnv, Req).

alt_waitin(K, [H|T], Message, NewChan, Done) :- Message:=H, NewChan:=T, Done:=done.
alt_waitin(kill, C, Message, NewChan, Done).

join_reqs(K, done, Go, AltReq, Req) :- Req:=req(Go).
join_reqs(K, Done, Go1, req(Go2), Req) :- Go1:=no, Req:=req(Go2).
join_reqs(kill, Done, Go, AltReq, Req) :- Go:=no.

goahead(yes, InEnv, Var, Message, Channel, NewChan, Statements, OutEnv) :-
      replace(Var, Message, InEnv, Env1),
      replace(Channel, NewChan, Env1, Env2),
      doblock(Env2, Statements, OutEnv).
goahead(no, InEnv, Var, Message, Channel, NewChan, Statements, OutEnv).

req_master(req(Go), K) :- Go:=yes, K:=kill.
```

Appendix IV: Example partial evaluation of code for indeterminism

Suppose the code we are interpreting is:

```
    alt([in1?x:[outc!8], in2?x:[outc!9]])
```

Then our initial call will be:

```
  dostatement([(in1,C1),(in2,C2),(outc,C3),(x,0)],
      alt([in1?x:outc!8,in2?x:outc!9]), OutEnv)
```

This will rewrite by immediately executable goals to:

```
  alt_waitin(K, C1, Val1, Chan1, Done1),
  alt_waitin(K, C2, Val2, Chan2, Done2),
  join_reqs(K, Done2, GoAhead2, Req2, Req1),
  goahead(GoAhead2,
      [(in1,C1),(in2,C2),(outc,C3),(x,0)], x, Val2, in2, Chan2, [outc!9], OutEnv)
  join_reqs(K, Done1, GoAhead1, Req1, Req),
  goahead(GoAhead1,
      [(in1,C1),(in2,C2),(outc,C3),(x,0)], x, Val1, in1, Chan1, [outc!8], OutEnv),
  req_master(Req, K).
```

The two calls to goahead are not immediately executable since they are dependent on the binding of their first argument which is not known at partial evaluation time. They will therefore rewrite to calls to two new procedures goahead1(GoAhead1,C1,C2,C3,Val1,Chan1,OutEnv) and goahead2(GoAhead2,C1,C2,C3,Val2,Chan2,OutEnv), with clauses:

```
  goahead1(yes, C1 ,C2 ,C3 ,Val1 ,Chan1 ,OutEnv) :-
      doblock([(in1,Chan1),(in2,C2),(outc,C3),(x,Val1)], [outc!8], OutEnv).
  goahead1(no, C1, C2, C3, Val1, Chan1, OutEnv).
  goahead2(yes, C1, C2, C3, Val2, Chan2, OutEnv) :-
      doblock([(in1,C1),(in2,Chan2),(outc,C3),(x,Val2)], [outc!9], OutEnv).
  goahead2(no, C1, C2, C3, Val2, Chan2, OutEnv).
```

Partially evaluating these clauses, and eliminating their redundant variables gives us the program:

```
alt_waitin(K, C1, Val1, Chan1, Done1),
alt_waitin(K, C2, Val2, Chan2, Done2),
join_reqs(K, Done2, GoAhead2, Req2, Req1),
goahead2(GoAhead2, C1, C3, Val2, Chan2, OutEnv),
join_reqs(K, Done1, GoAhead1, Req1, Req),
goahead1(GoAhead1, C2, C3, Val1, Chan1, OutEnv),
req_master(Req, K).
```

with new clauses:

```
goahead1(yes, C2, C3, Val1, Chan1, OutEnv) :-
    C3:=[8|C3T],
    OutEnv:=[(in1,Chan1),(in2,C2),(outc,C3T),(x,Val1)].
goahead1(no, C2, C3, Val1, Chan1, OutEnv).

goahead2(yes, C1, C3, Val2, Chan2, OutEnv) :-
    C3:=[9|C3T],
    OutEnv:=[(in1,C1),(in2,Chan2),(outc,C3T),(x,Val2)].
goahead2(no, C1, C3, Val2, Chan2, OutEnv).
```

We now proceed by goal fusion. Fusing the goals req_master(Req,K) and join_reqs(K,Done1,GoAhead1,Req1,Req) using the variable Req gives the goal join_req_master(K,Done1,GoAhead1,Req1) with clauses:

```
join_req_master(K, done, GoAhead1, Req1) :-
    Req:=req(GoAhead1),
    req_master(Req, K).
join_req_master(K, Done1, GoAhead1, req(Go2)) :-
    GoAhead1:=no,
    Req:=req(Go2),
    req_master(Req, K).
join_req_master(kill, Done1, GoAhead1, Req1) :-
    GoAhead1:=no.
```

Since Req does not occur in the head of these clauses, the assignments to Req within them may be executed and the calls to req_master(Req,K) become immediately executable giving:

```
join_req_master(K, done, GoAhead1, Req1) :- GoAhead1:=yes, K:=kill.
join_req_master(K, Done1, GoAhead1, req(Go2)) :- GoAhead1:=no, Go2:=yes, K:=kill.
join_req_master(kill, Done1, GoAhead1, Req1) :- GoAhead1:=no.
```

The next goal fusion fuses join_req_master(K,Done1,GoAhead1,Req1) with goahead1(GoAhead1,C2,C3,Val1,Chan1,OutEnv) on the variable GoAhead1, giving the new goal go_on1(K,Done1,Req1,C2,C3,Val1,Chan1,OutEnv). The assignments to GoAhead1 in the clause bodies for go_on1 are immediately executable. We can also eliminate the redundant variable Req in join_reqs(K,Done2,GoAhead2,Req2,Req1). This gives us:

```
alt_waitin(K, C1, Val1, Chan1, Done1),
alt_waitin(K, C2, Val2, Chan2, Done2),
join_reqs2(K, Done2, GoAhead2, Req1),
goahead2(GoAhead2, C1, C3, Val2, Chan2, OutVars),
go_on1(K, Done1, Req1, C2, C3, Val1, Chan1, OutVars).
```

with

```
join_reqs2(K, done, GoAhead2, Req1) :- Req1:=req(GoAhead2).
join_reqs2(kill, Done2, GoAhead2, Req1) :- GoAhead2:=no.
go_on1(K, done, Req1, C2, C3, Val1, Chan1, OutEnv) :-
    K:=kill,  C3:=[8|C3T],  OutEnv:=[(in1,Chan1),(in2,C2),(outc,C3T),(x,Val1)].
go_on1(K, Done1, req(Go2), C2, C3, Val1, Chan1, OutEnv) :- Go2:=yes, K:=kill.
go_on1(kill, Done1, Req1, C2, C3, Val1, Chan1, OutEnv).
```

join_reqs2(K,Done2,GoAhead2,Req1) and goahead2(GoAhead2,C1,C3,Val2,Chan2,OutEnv) may be fused on the variable GoAhead2 giving us:

```
alt_waitin(K, C1, Val1, Chan1, Done1),
alt_waitin(K, C2, Val2, Chan2, Done2),
go_on2(K, Done2, Req1, C1, C3, Val2, Chan2, OutEnv),
go_on1(K, Done1, Req1, C2, C3, Val1, Chan1, OutEnv).
```

with:

```
go_on1(K, done, Req1, C2, C3, Val1, Chan1, OutEnv) :-
    K:=kill,
    C3:=[8|C3T],
    OutEnv:=[(in1,Chan1),(in2,C2),(outc,C3T),(x,Val1)].
go_on1(K, Done1, req(Go2), C2, C3, Val1, Chan1, OutEnv) :-
    Go2:=yes,
    K:=kill.
go_on1(kill, Done1, Req1, C2, C3, Val1, Chan1, OutEnv).

go_on2(K, done, Req1, C1, C3, Val2, Chan2, OutEnv) :-
    Req1:=req(GoAhead2),
    goahead2(GoAhead2, C1, C3, Val2, Chan2, OutEnv).
go_on2(kill, Done2, Req1, C1, C3, Val2, Chan2, OutEnvs).
```

At this stage the clauses for goahead2 as given previously remain part of the residual program, as a call to goahead2 remains a subgoal of go_on2, the variable GoAhead2 not being sufficiently bound to make it immediately executable.

We can fuse the goal go_on1(K,Done1,Req1,C2,C3,Val1,Chan1,OutEnv) with alt_waitin(K,C1,Val1,Chan1,Done1), eliminating the variable Done1 to give:

```
waitin1(K, C1, C2, C3, Val1, Chan1, Req1, OutEnv),
alt_waitin(K, C2, Val2, Chan2, Done2),
go_on2(K, Done2, Req1, C1, C3, Val2, Chan2, OutEnv).
```

with:

```
waitin1(K, [H1|T1], C2, C3, Val1, Chan1, Req1, OutEnv) :-
    Val1:=H1, Chan1:=T1, K:=kill, C3:=[8|C3T],
    OutEnv:=[(in1,Chan1),(in2,C2),(outc,C3T),(x,Val1)].
waitin1(K, C1, C2, C3, Val1, Chan1, req(Go2), OutEnv) :- Go2:=yes, K:=kill.
waitin1(kill, C1, C2, C3, Val1, Chan1, Req1, OutEnv).
```

(note this fusion slightly extends the rule we gave earlier, in that here there are circumstances in which one goal will not commit until the other goal has, and circumstances in which it is the other way round; we cannot say that one goal is dependent on the other, but we can fuse the two because there are no circumstances in which they can commit in parallel).

A fusion of the goals alt_waitin(K,C2,Val2,Chan2,Done2) and go_on2(K,Done2,Req1,C1,C3,Val2,Chan2,OutEnv) eliminating Done2 gives:

```
waitin1(K, C1, C2, C3, Val1, Chan1, Req1, OutEnv),
waitin2(K, C1, C2, C3, Val2, Chan2, Req1, OutEnv).
```

with:

```
waitin2(K, C1, [H2|T2], C3, Val2, Chan2, Req1, OutEnv) :-
    Val2:=H2, Chan2:=T2, Done2:=done,
    go_on2(K, Done2, Req1, C1, C3, Val2, Chan2, OutEnv).
waitin2(kill, C1, C2, C3, Val2, Chan2, Req1, OutEnv) :-
    go_on2(kill, Done2, Req1, C1, C3, Val2, Chan2, OutEnv).
```

Eliminating the redundant variables Val1, Chan1, Val2 and Chan2, and executing the goals which are then immediately executable gives:

```
  waitin1(K, C1, C2, C3, Req1, OutEnv),
  waitin2(K, C1, C2, C3, Req1, OutEnv).
```

with:

```
  waitin1(K, [H1|T1], C2, C3, Req1, OutEnv) :-
      K:=kill,
      C3:=[8|C3T],
      OutEnv:=[(in1,T1),(in2,C2),(outc,C3T),(x,H1)].
  waitin1(K, C1, C2, C3, req(Go2), OutEnv) :-
      Go2:=yes,
      K:=kill.
  waitin1(kill, C1, C2, C3, Req1, OutEnv).
  waitin2(K, C1, [H2|T2], C3, Req1, OutEnv) :-
      Req1:=req(Go2),
      goahead2(Go2, C1, C3, H2, T2, OutEnv).
  waitin2(kill, C1, C2, C3, Req1, OutEnv).
```

A fusion of waitin1(K,C1,C2,C3,Req1,OutEnv) and waitin2(K,C1,C2,C3,Req1,OutEnv), eliminating at top level the variables K and Req1 gives:.

```
  waitin([H1|T1], C2, C3, OutEnv) :-
      K:=kill,
      C3:=[8|C3T],
      OutEnv:=[(in1,T1),(in2,C2),(outc,C3T),(x,H1)],
      waitin2(K, [H1|T1], C2, C3, Req1, OutEnv).
  waitin(C1, [H2|T2], C3, OutEnv) :-
      Req1:=req(Go2),
      goahead2(Go2,C1,C3,H2,T2,OutEnv),
      waitin1(K, C1, [H2|C2], C3, Req1, OutEnv).
```

which on rewriting the immediately executable goals becomes:

```
  waitin([H1|T1], C2, C3, OutEnv) :-
      C3:=[8|C3T],
      OutEnv:=[(in1,T1),(in2,C2),(outc,C3T),(x,H1)].
  waitin(C1, [H2|T2], C3, OutEnv) :-
      goahead2(Go2, C1, C3, H2, T2, OutEnv), Go2:=yes, K:=kill.
```

Further rewriting of the executable goals in the second clause gives:

```
  waitin([H1|T1], C2, C3, OutEnv) :-
      C3:=[8|C3T],
      OutEnv:=[(in1,T1),(in2,C2),(outc,C3T),(x,H1)].
  waitin(C1, [H2|T2], C3, OutEnv) :-
      C3:=[9|C3T],
      OutEnv:=[(in1,C1),(in2,T2),(outc,C3T),(x,H2)].
```

These are the clauses we would expect to use (except for the output in environment form) to give the desired effect of a process which waits for input on either of two channels, outputting a constant on a third channel which depends on which channel gave the input.

A Method for the Determinisation of Propositional Temporal Formulae

Philippe Noel*
Department of Computer Science
University of Manchester

Abstract

This paper is concerned with the generation of models for specifications expressed in a propositional temporal logic. These specifications represent dynamic and interacting systems and hence contain references to the environment in which the systems will execute.

In the current version of the executable temporal logic system, METATEM, a model may be generated directly from a given specification. However, in general, this model construction involves backtracking. We show how to transform an arbitrary specification, S, into another specification, S', from which a model can be generated without backtracking. S' is such that any of its models is a model of S, and it is satisfiable only if S is satisfiable.

1 Introduction

This paper is concerned with the implementation of specifications expressed in propositional temporal logic [10, 13, 14] with finite past time extension [9]. The specifications may involve *environment* variables, the behaviour of which is determined by the environment, as well as internal variables (sometimes called *component* variables), the behaviour of which is constrained by the specification. The work forms a part of the METATEM project [1, 2], the general aim of which is to provide facilities for executing temporal specifications.

A model for a specification is an infinite sequence of states (i.e. valuations for the formulae of the language) which satisfies the specification. To generate a model, one may use the original specification and, for every state, set the value of the internal variables in such a way that the specification is satisfied up to that state. When there is no consistent setting of the variables for which the specification is satisfied, backtracking has to be used in order to try alternative settings in previous states. However, this is not suitable for the interactive generation of a model, as required, for example, in the framework of concurrent communicating processes [5]. As in [11] we say that a specification is implementable only if it is possible to generate a model of it, in step with the input of values from the environment, without constraining the future behaviour of the environment. The generation of a model for an implementable specification may be achieved without backtracking to previous states. The purpose of the determinisation algorithm is to transform any implementable specification, S,

*This work was supported by SERC under project number GR/F/30123 (METATEM).

into another one, S', from which a model is easily constructed without backtracking. The transformation is such that S' has a model whenever S has a model, and all the models of S' are models of S.

A temporal formula with environment variables may be interpreted as the specification of a 'reactive program' which gives a valuation of the internal variables in each state, given the environment behaviour up to that state. Determinising the formula and providing an algorithm to generate a model for it is one way of synthesising such a program. In contrast to the automata-theoretic approach to synthesis [11], which is based on the determinisation of model-accepting automata, our approach is based on syntactic transformations.

The syntax and semantics of the temporal logic used are given in section 2. The determinisation algorithm itself is presented in sections 3 and 4 of the paper. Section 5 concerns the generation of models from a determinised specification. Finally, section 6 gives a brief overview of the automata theoretic-approach and attempts to relate it to our approach.

2 The logic

The specifications are expressed in propositional linear temporal logic with discrete time, finite past and infinite future. The adjective 'linear' refers to the fact that the interpretations of the logic are sets of states which are totally ordered. Since there is only a finite past extension, the ordering is well-founded. The qualification 'with discrete time' means that the set of states is countable. Thus the interpretations of the logic are actually infinite sequences of states. The syntax and semantics of the logic are formally given in the next two sections.

2.1 Syntax

In the following definition x represents a variable and f, f_1 and f_2 represent formulae of the language:

$$\begin{aligned} f \ := \quad & \mathit{True} \mid \mathit{False} \mid x \mid f_1 \wedge f_2 \mid f_1 \vee f_2 \mid \neg f_1 \\ & \mid \bigcirc f_1 \mid f_1 \,\mathcal{U}\, f_2 \\ & \mid \circledcirc f_1 \mid \bullet f_1 \mid f_1 \,\mathcal{S}\, f_2. \end{aligned}$$

The first line defines the syntax of the non-temporal part of the language. The second line introduces the future-time operators 'next' ($\bigcirc$) and 'until' ($\mathcal{U}$). The third line introduces the past-time operators 'strong last' ($\circledcirc$), 'weak last' ($\bullet$) and 'strong since' ($\mathcal{S}$). The semantics for these operators is given in the next section. The symbols defined below are also used:

Implication:	$f_1 \Rightarrow f_2$	$\equiv$	$\neg f_1 \vee f_2$
Bi-implication:	$f_1 \Leftrightarrow f_2$	$\equiv$	$f_1 \Rightarrow f_2 \wedge f_2 \Rightarrow f_1$
Sometime:	$\Diamond f_1$	$\equiv$	$\mathit{True}\,\mathcal{U}\, f_1$
Unless:	$f_1 \,\mathcal{W}\, f_2$	$\equiv$	$\neg(\neg f_2 \,\mathcal{U}\, (\neg f_1 \wedge \neg f_2))$
Always:	$\Box f_1$	$\equiv$	$f_1 \,\mathcal{W}\, \mathit{False}$
Sometime past:	$\blacklozenge f_1$	$\equiv$	$\mathit{True}\,\mathcal{S}\, f_1$
Weak since:	$f_1 \,\mathcal{Z}\, f_2$	$\equiv$	$\neg(\neg f_2 \,\mathcal{S}\, (\neg f_1 \wedge \neg f_2))$
Always past:	$\blacksquare f_1$	$\equiv$	$f_1 \,\mathcal{Z}\, \mathit{False}.$

2.2 Semantics

A *state* (or *world*) is a valuation of the formulae of the language over the set $\{true, false\}$ which satisfies the usual semantics of classical propositional logic; e.g. a state $\mathcal{M}$ satisfies $\mathcal{M}(True) = true$; $\mathcal{M}(f_1 \wedge f_2) = \mathcal{M}(f_1)$ *and* $\mathcal{M}(f_2)$.

For the logic considered in this paper, an *interpretation* (or *model*) is a family of states indexed by the natural numbers, $\{\mathcal{M}_i \mid i \in NAT\}$, such that:

$$
\begin{array}{lcl}
\mathcal{M}_i(\bigcirc f_1) & = & \mathcal{M}_{i+1}(f_1) \\
\mathcal{M}_i(f_1 \,\mathcal{U}\, f_2) & = & \exists j (j \geq 0) \mathcal{M}_{i+j}(f_2) \textit{ and } \forall n (0 \leq n < j) \mathcal{M}_{i+n}(f_1) \\
\mathcal{M}_{i>0}(\odot f_1) & = & \mathcal{M}_{i-1}(f_1) \\
\mathcal{M}_0(\odot f_1) & = & false \\
\mathcal{M}_{i>0}(\bullet f_1) & = & \mathcal{M}_{i-1}(f_1) \\
\mathcal{M}_0(\bullet f_1) & = & true \\
\mathcal{M}_{i>0}(f_1 \,\mathcal{S}\, f_2) & = & \exists j (0 \leq j \leq i) \mathcal{M}_{i-j}(f_2) \textit{ and } \forall n (0 \leq n < j) \mathcal{M}_{i-n}(f_1) \\
\mathcal{M}_0(f_1 \,\mathcal{S}\, f_2) & = & \mathcal{M}_0 f_2.
\end{array}
$$

Note that $f_1 \,\mathcal{S}\, f_2$ holds when f_2 holds. Some variants of this semantics, in which past formulae are evaluated using the states up to, but not including, the current state, are also found in the literature.

A formula f is valid iff it evaluates to *true* in every state of every interpretation. A formula f_1 logically implies a formula f_2 ($f_1 \models f_2$) iff, for every state of every interpretation, f_2 evaluates to *true* whenever f_1 evaluates to *true*. From these definitions, it is clear that $f_1 \models f_2$ iff $f1 \Rightarrow f2$ is valid.

An interpretation $\{\mathcal{M}_i \mid i \in NAT\}$ is said to satisfy a formula f in state j if $\mathcal{M}_j(f) = true$. In this paper, a *model* for a formula f is to be understood as an interpretation which satisfies f in the initial state or, equivalently, an interpretation which satisfies $\bullet False \wedge f$ (since $\bullet False$ may only be satisfied in the initial state). A formula is said to be satisfiable iff it has such a model.

3 Initial transformations

In this section, we describe transformations that are used to rewrite an arbitrary specification expressed in propositional temporal logic into an equivalent one in the form

$$I \wedge \Box \bigwedge_i (A_{1,i} \vee \bigcirc B_i) \wedge \Box \bigwedge_j (A_{2,j} \vee \Diamond \bigcirc L_j) \tag{1}$$

where I is a state (i.e. present-time) formula, the $A_{i,j}$ are disjuncts involving literals and/or formulae under the scope of a past-time operator, the B_i are non-empty disjuncts of literals, and the L_j are literals.

Without loss of generality, we will assume that the specifications, viewed as conjuncts of formulae, are written in the form $A \wedge \Box B$, where B is the conjunction of the formulae preceded by the operator $\Box$, and A is the conjunction of the other formulae. A will be called the 'initialisation' of the specification, B its 'body'. We will also assume that implications and equalities have been replaced by their definitions in terms of disjunctions and conjunctions.

In the current implementation, past-time operators are not eliminated. The general idea behind the transformation consists in replacing any subformula under the scope of a future-time operator, by a variable with the same temporal behaviour. Given that the fixed point definition of $a\mathcal{U}\,b$

$$\Box(a\mathcal{U}\,b \Leftrightarrow y) \Leftrightarrow \Box((y \Leftrightarrow (b \vee (a \wedge \bigcirc y))) \wedge (y \Rightarrow \Diamond b))$$

is valid, one could simply replace any expression of the form $a\mathcal{U}\,b$ by a variable y and add to the specification the right hand side of the main equivalence, in order to specify the behaviour of y. The formula to add, rewritten in conjunctive normal form, is:

$$\begin{array}{ll}\Box & ((\neg y \vee b \vee a) \wedge (\neg y \vee b \vee \bigcirc y) \wedge (\neg y \vee \Diamond b) \\ & \wedge(y \vee \bigcirc\neg b) \wedge (y \vee \bigcirc\neg a \vee \bigcirc\neg y)).\end{array}$$

The following equivalences could be used in the same way to replace the expressions of the form $a\mathcal{W}\,b$:

$$\Box(a\mathcal{W}\,b \Leftrightarrow y) \Leftrightarrow \Box((y \Leftrightarrow (b \vee (a \wedge \bigcirc y))) \wedge (\neg y \Rightarrow \Diamond\neg a)).$$

With such an approach, a future-time expression may be replaced by the same variable wherever it occurs in the original specification. However, some of the formulae defining the new variables are complex. The formulae need not be so complex if we rewrite the specification into a form in which the negation symbols apply only to variables. In the proposed implementation, first the next-time operators, and then the negation symbols, are moved to their innermost position. The subformulae under the scope of a future-time operator may then be replaced by variables using a set of transformations rules justified by derived inference rules of the logic. The innermost subformulae are the first to be transformed. The main transformation rules are discussed in section 3.1[1]. Section 3.2 indicates how the environment variables are processed during the transformations. Finally, the further transformations required to obtain the normal form specified in 1 are discussed in section 3.3.

3.1 Main rules

The set of inference rules underlying the transformations are in the form:

$$\frac{\begin{array}{l}F(y)\\ R(y)\end{array}}{F(exp)}$$

where exp is the expression to be replaced by the variable y, and F is a unary operator constructed on the set of literals of the language without using the negation symbol. In the case where F includes past-time operators, the inference rules are valid only under the implicit assumption $\bullet False$. The proof of the validity of the inference rules has been carried out using a temporal decision procedure based on semantic tableaux [7]. First, the implication $R(y) \Rightarrow \Box(y \Rightarrow exp)$ has been proved. Then the implications

$$\begin{array}{rcl}\Box(x_1 \Rightarrow exp_1) \wedge \Box(x_2 \Rightarrow exp_2) & \Rightarrow & \Box(G(x_1, x_2) \Rightarrow G(exp_1, exp_2)) \\ \Box(x \Rightarrow exp) & \Rightarrow & \Box(F(x) \Rightarrow F(exp))\end{array}$$

[1] A general framework for the transformation of temporal formulae within METATEM can be found in [6]

have been proved for the cases where G is a present or future-time binary operator (i.e. $\vee$, $\wedge$, $\mathcal{U}$, $\mathcal{W}$), and F is a future-time unary operator (i.e. $\bigcirc$, $\Box$, $\Diamond$). The following formulae are instances of the formulae above:

$$\begin{aligned} \Box(F_1(x) \Rightarrow F_1(exp)) \quad & \wedge \Box(F_2(x) \Rightarrow F_2(exp)) \\ & \Rightarrow \Box(G(F_1(x), F_2(x)) \Rightarrow G(F_1(exp), F_2(exp)) \\ \Box(F_1(x) \Rightarrow F_1(exp)) \quad & \Rightarrow \Box(F(F_1(x)) \Rightarrow F(F_1(exp))) \end{aligned}$$

where the F_i's are unary operators. Using structural induction, it may be deduced that if $(y \Rightarrow exp)$ holds, $(F(y) \Rightarrow F(exp))$ holds for any unary operator F constructed using the set of literals of the language and the standard present and future-time operators other than negation. In the case where F involves past-time operators, the same results holds only under the further assumption that $\bullet False$ holds, i.e. the formulae hold only in the first state. From the validity of the above implications it may be deduced that $R(y) \Rightarrow \Box(F(y) \Rightarrow F(exp))$ is valid under the assumption $\bullet False$ for any unary operator F constructed on the set of literals of the language without using the negation symbol. Thus $R(y) \Rightarrow (F(y) \Rightarrow F(exp))$ must be valid under the same assumptions, justifying the inference rule $F(y),\ R(y) \models F(exp)$.

Here are the transformations, expressed in the form of inference rules (the antecedents of the rule are the result of transforming the consequents):

1. $\mathcal{U}$ and $\mathcal{W}$.

   Until:

$$\frac{\begin{array}{l} F(y) \\ \Box(\neg y \vee \Diamond b) \\ \Box(\neg y \vee b \vee a) \\ \Box(\neg y \vee b \vee \bigcirc y) \end{array}}{F(a \mathcal{U} b)}$$

   Note the relation between this rules and the one presented earlier: only the disjuncts containing the negation of y are required.

   Unless:

$$\frac{\begin{array}{l} F(y) \\ \Box(\neg y \vee b \vee a) \\ \Box(\neg y \vee b \vee \bigcirc y) \end{array}}{F(a \mathcal{W} b)}$$

2. $\bigcirc$.

   The following rule is used to eliminate the operator $\bigcirc$ in the initialisation:

$$\frac{\begin{array}{l} F(y) \\ \Box(\neg y \vee \bigcirc a) \end{array}}{F(\bigcirc a)}$$

To eliminate from the body of the specification the next-time operators which do not apply to a literal, the following rule is used:

$$\frac{\begin{array}{l} F(\bigcirc y) \\ \Box(\neg y \vee a) \end{array}}{F(\bigcirc a)}$$

3. $\Diamond$.

The following rule is used to eliminate the operator $\Diamond$ in the initialisation:

$$\frac{\begin{array}{l} F(y) \\ \Box(\neg y \vee \Diamond a) \end{array}}{F(\Diamond a)}$$

The following rule, in conjunction with the equivalence $\Diamond a \Leftrightarrow a \vee \Diamond \bigcirc a$, is used to ensure that the operators $\Diamond$ in the body of the specification always apply to next-state literals:

$$\frac{\begin{array}{l} F(\Diamond \bigcirc y) \\ \Box(\neg y \vee a) \end{array}}{F(\Diamond \bigcirc a)} .$$

A remark concerning the use of the equivalence $\Diamond a \Leftrightarrow a \vee \Diamond \bigcirc a$ is in order. Some unwanted delay may result from the transformation since the fairness algorithm, which ensures that every outstanding eventuality is satisfied, will attempt to satisfy $\bigcirc a$ as soon as $\neg a$ holds, rather than satisfy a as soon as possible.

It has already been argued that, under the assumption $\bullet False$, the above inference rules are valid for any operator F constructed on the set of literals without using negation. Their inverse are valid without assumption for appropriate instantiations of the extra variables: in the rule concerning $\mathcal{U}$, for instance, this is true if y is instantiated by $a \mathcal{U} b$. The fact that, for each rule, the formulae resulting from the transformation imply the original formula under the assumption $\bullet False$, ensures that any model of the new specification is a model of the original one (assuming that the language of the original specification includes the new variables). The fact that the original formulae are equivalent to the transformed formulae for some instantiation of the new variables, ensures that, for any model M of the original specification, there is a model of the new specification which differs from M only by the valuation of the new variables. From this may be deduced, in particular, that the new specification is satisfiable whenever the original one is satisfiable.

3.2 Dealing with the environment

As mentioned in the introduction, the variables of the language are partitioned into a set of environment variables and a set of internal variables. Recall that a specification is said to be implementable if it is possible to generate a model of it without constraining the future behaviour of the environment. More precisely, a specification S is implementable iff it is possible to generate a model of S in such a way that, for every partially generated model $s_0, s_1, \ldots, s_n$ and environment input for state s_{n+1}, there is a way of completing s_{n+1} which ensures that, for all possible future environment behaviours, the sequence of states $s_0, s_1, \ldots, s_n, s_{n+1}$ is the prefix of a model of S. We also assume that we have no knowledge concerning the environment. Accordingly, if the future-time component of a disjunct is a disjunction of environment literals which is not valid, it may be eliminated from the disjunct (the past/present component of the disjunct must always be satisfiable in order to avoid constraining the environment in the next state). The environment literals may not, in general, be eliminated if the future-time component includes internal variables. Consider for instance a specification with a body consisting of the formulae $\bigcirc a \vee \bigcirc e$ and $\bigcirc \neg a \vee \bigcirc \neg e$, where e is an environment variable and a is an internal variable. The specification is implementable since a model for it may be generated, in step with the environment input, without constraining the future behaviour of the environment. If the subformulae involving e were eliminated, the resulting specification would be unsatisfiable, leading to the incorrect conclusion that the original specification is not implementable.

It is also the case that a specification is not implementable if it imposes some constraints on the first set of values from the environment. This happens when the conjunctive normal form of the initialisation contains a non valid disjunct consisting only of environment literals.

3.3 Normalisation

After a repeated use of the rules described in 3.1, the body of the specification may be rewritten as a conjunction of formulae of the form:

$$r \vee \bigcirc d_1 \vee \Diamond \bigcirc d_2$$

where r is a past/present disjunct, and d_1 and d_2 are disjuncts of literals (possibly empty). It remains to replace such formulae by formulae of the form

$$p \vee \bigcirc d \qquad \textit{and} \qquad q \vee \Diamond \bigcirc l$$

where p and q are past/present disjuncts, l is a literal, and d is a disjunct of literals. This last transformation may involve the definition of a new variable to stand for $\bigcirc d_1$ when d_2 is not empty and one to stand for d_2 when d_2 is not a literal.

A particularly important case is the one where d_1 and d_2 are both empty disjuncts. In this case, the past/present disjunct r is 'lifted' to the next state: r is added to the initialisation and is replaced by $\bigcirc r$ in the body of the specification; $\bigcirc r$ is further transformed into the required format by using recursively the equivalences:

$$
\begin{array}{lcl}
\bigcirc(a \vee b) & \Leftrightarrow & \bigcirc a \vee \bigcirc b \\
\bigcirc(a \wedge b) & \Leftrightarrow & \bigcirc a \wedge \bigcirc b \\
\bigcirc a \,\mathcal{S}\, b & \Leftrightarrow & (\bigcirc b \vee (\bigcirc a \wedge a \,\mathcal{S}\, b)) \\
\bigcirc a \,\mathcal{Z}\, b & \Leftrightarrow & (\bigcirc b \vee (\bigcirc a \wedge a \,\mathcal{Z}\, b)) \\
\bigcirc \odot a & \Leftrightarrow & a \\
\bigcirc \bullet a & \Leftrightarrow & a.
\end{array}
$$

During lifting, the next-time components consisting only of environment literals are replaced by *False*. The process of lifting a formula terminates, since the number of subformulae involved is obviously finite and the size of the subformulae decreases at every step of the recursion. However, the resulting formula may still contain past/present disjuncts; thus lifting itself must be used recursively. The set of past/present disjuncts generated during such a recursive process has a tree structure. It can be shown that, within a finite distance from the root, every branch of the tree has a node which, either has no successor, or has a unique successor identical to itself. In the latter case, there is a past present formula f and a conjunction of disjuncts with a next-time component, g, such that the equivalence $\bigcirc f \Leftrightarrow f \wedge g$ holds. Given that the formula

$$\bullet \mathit{False} \Rightarrow \square(\bigcirc x \Leftrightarrow x \wedge y) \Rightarrow (\square x \Leftrightarrow x \wedge \square y)$$

is valid, it is clear that a formula f satisfying the above condition may be replaced by g in the body of the specification if f is added to the initialisation.

Finally, the initialisation of the specification may be simplified. Since we are only interested in interpretations making formulae true in the first state, the initialisation may be transformed into a state formula using the semantic equivalences holding in the first state:

$$\begin{array}{rcl} a\,\mathcal{S}\,b & \leadsto & b \\ a\,\mathcal{Z}\,b & \leadsto & a \vee b \\ \odot a & \leadsto & \mathit{false} \\ \bullet a & \leadsto & \mathit{true} \end{array}$$

where the symbol $\leadsto$ represents the transformation.

4 Determinisation

In this section, we describe the transformations that are used to rewrite a specification in the form 1 (see beginning of section 3), into one in the form

$$I \wedge \square \bigwedge_i (A_i \vee \bigcirc B_i) \tag{2}$$

where I is a state formula, the A_i are disjuncts involving literals and/or formulae under the scope of a past-time operator and the B_i are non-empty disjuncts of literals. The transformation is such that, if 1 is implementable, then 2 is implementable and any model of 2 is a model of 1. The resulting specification has also the following property: if M is the prefix of a model of the specification and $\{A_i \mid i \in I\}$ is the set of A_i which evaluate to *false* in the last state of M, then every valuation s for which $\bigwedge_{i \in I} B_i$ is *true* is such that the sequence Ms is also the prefix of a model. This property guarantees that backtracking to previous states will not be necessary.

The first part of the determinisation concerns the disjuncts without eventuality operators. The transformation consists of making explicit enough information to ensure that a model for this part of the specification may be generated without backtracking. A resolution rule is used for this purpose. The second part of the determinisation consists in replacing the disjuncts of the body containing an eventuality symbol by a set of formulae which specifies when the eventuality literals (i.e. the literals under the scope of the symbol $\Diamond$) are to be set.

Section 4.1 presents the resolution rule and discusses its use. Section 4.2 gives first an overview, and then a more formal presentation, of the method to determinise the eventualities. Two simple examples of determinisation are given in appendix A.

4.1 Resolution

Resolution generates a resolvent from two parent formulae in disjunctive form, using the rule:

$$\frac{\begin{array}{l} p \vee \bigcirc a \\ q \vee \bigcirc \neg a \end{array}}{p \vee q}$$

where p and q may contain the operator $\bigcirc$. The resolution rule applies only to the cases which involve the unification of literals in the future-time component of the disjunctions. This is an instance of the classical resolution rule since the symbol $\neg$ may be moved in front of the symbol $\bigcirc$. If the resolvent is a past/present formula, it is lifted in the way specified in section 3.3. If the resolvent is the empty disjunct (the formula $False$), the specification is not implementable.

The rule is applied recursively to the body of the specification, and the resulting resolvents are added to the specification. The following argument shows that subsumption checking may be used to ensure termination. Let us call a basic subformula any subformula which is not prefixed by a disjunction, conjunction or negation. A formula involves only a finite number of basic subformulae. When lifting a formula to the next state the only new basic subformulae which may be added are terms of the form $\bigcirc l$ where l is a literal. Thus the disjuncts in the resolvents, as well as the disjuncts of the original specification, are constructed from a finite set of subformulae. The set of disjuncts of this kind, such that no disjunct subsumes another one is clearly finite.

Resolution is used to make explicit the conditions that any state must satisfy in order that a model, constructed up to and including that state, may be completed. For instance, if $p \vee \bigcirc a$ and $q \vee \bigcirc \neg a$, where p and q are past/present disjuncts, belong to the body of the specification, then the resolvent $p \vee q$ expresses explicitly a past/present condition that every state must satisfy in order that there exists a consistent next state. In particular, if $p \vee q$ simplifies to the formula $False$, the specification is not implementable. There is another reason for performing resolution on the specification: the formulae which constrain the satisfaction of any eventualities are of the form $l_1 \vee \bigcirc \neg l_0 \vee \bigcirc e_1$, where l_0 is a literal under an eventuality symbol, l_1 is a past/present disjunct, and e_1 is a state formula involving only environment literals; such constraints are made explicit through the use of resolution.

When all the relevant resolvents from the body of a specification have been obtained, classical resolution is applied to the initialisation. The specification is not implementable if the process produces either the resolvent $False$, or a non valid resolvent consisting only of environment literals.

4.2 Determinisation of the eventualities

4.2.1 Overview

In the proposed determinisation method, a past/present formula is chosen to represent the allocation of a priority to an eventuality literal. This is simply a flag to indicate which eventuality is to be satisfied next. The priority is allocated to each unsatisfied eventuality literal in turn, and it remains allocated to the same literal until the eventuality is satisfied. Determinisation is achieved by expressing explicitly the conditions under which the eventualities are satisfiable and by adding a set of formulae (the 'determinising formulae'), consistent with the specification, which schedule the setting of the eventuality literals. Now, setting an eventuality literal l_0 in a particular state is possible only if the specification does not enforce $\neg l_0$ in that state. Disjuncts of the form $l_{1,j} \vee \bigcirc\neg l_0 \vee \bigcirc e_{1,j}$, where $e_{1,j}$ is a state formula involving only environment literals, express a constraint on the setting of l_0. One must take account of the formulae with an environment component because it is always possible that the environment makes $e_{1,j}$ *false*, and thus that $l_{1,j} \vee \bigcirc\neg l_0$ holds. Resolution ensures that any derivable disjunct, the next-time component of which involves a single internal literal, is expressed explicitly. Let us call l_1 the formula $\bigwedge_j l_{1,j}$. To be able to set l_0 in a given state, whatever the behaviour of the environment, l_1 must hold in the previous state. However, l_1 may itself be constrained by formulae of the form $l_{2,j} \vee \bigcirc\neg l_1 \vee \bigcirc e_{2,j}$. In the most general case, the satisfaction of l_0 is constrained by a sequence of sets of constraints. If the sequence is circular, i.e. if l_n implies l_m $(m \leq n)$, a formula is added to the specification to express the fact that one of the sets of constraints in the sequence must eventually be disabled, that is l_i must eventually hold for some i. Whether the sequence is finite or circular, the determinising formulae are added to ensure that once l_i holds, the disabling of constraints 'ripples through' until l_0 may be set.

The second example of appendix A provides an illustration of the case where finite sequences of constraints are involved. The body of the specification rewrites to:

$$
\begin{array}{ll}
 & f_A \vee \bigcirc\neg eaten_A \\
\wedge & f_B \vee \bigcirc\neg eaten_B \\
\wedge & \bigcirc\neg f_A \vee \bigcirc\neg f_B \\
\wedge & eaten_A \vee \Diamond\bigcirc eaten_A \\
\wedge & eaten_B \vee \Diamond\bigcirc eaten_B .
\end{array}
$$

The setting of the literal $eaten_A$ $(= l_0)$ is constrained by the formula $f_A \vee \bigcirc\neg eaten_A$. However, there is no formula constraining the setting of f_A $(= l_1)$. A similar sequence consisting of a single constraint affects the setting of $eaten_B$.

The proposed determinisation enforces the setting of only one outstanding literal at a time. In the worst cases, it is not possible to do better. However, should there be a requirement that as many outstanding literals as possible be set within the constraints imposed by the specification, then a more sophisticated method would be called for.

The allocation of the priority flag is discussed in section 4.2.2. The determinisation itself is discussed in section 4.2.3 for the particular case where the environment variables may be eliminated from the constraints. The general case is considered in section 4.2.4.

4.2.2 Allocation of priority

Given the formula $p \vee \Diamond \bigcirc l$, let us call $outs(l)$ the expression $\neg l \, \mathcal{S} \neg p$ (i.e. $outs(l)$ asserts that the literal l is outstanding at the beginning of the next state), and $priority(l)$ the formula specifying that the priority is allocated to l. $priority(l)$ must satisfy the following constraints:

- $\neg priority(l) \vee \neg priority(m)$ must hold at every state for every eventuality literal m such that $m \neq l$, i.e. the priority may only be allocated to one literal at a time;
- if $priority(l)$ holds then it must hold until $\bigcirc l$ holds;
- if $outs(l)$ holds in a state, $priority(l)$ must hold in the same sate or sometime afterwards, as long as l is still outstanding.

Within the limits imposed by these constraints, any priority scheme may be chosen. The currently implemented priority scheme ensures that one of the oldest outstanding eventualities is satisfied as soon as possible. Given a set of eventuality literals, $\{l^j \mid j < n\}$, the allocation of the priority to the outstanding literal l^i is given by the formula:

$$\begin{array}{ll} & \bigwedge_{j<i} \neg(unsatisfied(l^j)\, \mathcal{S} \neg unsatisfied(l^i)) \\ \wedge & \bigwedge_{i<j<n} (unsatisfied(l^i)\, \mathcal{S} \neg unsatisfied(l^j)) \end{array}$$

where $unsatisfied(l)$ stands for $\odot outs(l) \wedge \neg l$

The first example of appendix A may be used as an illustration. This is a simple example of resource allocation. The body of the specification includes the disjuncts

$$\begin{array}{l} \neg e_1 \vee \Diamond \bigcirc a_1 \\ \neg e_2 \vee \Diamond \bigcirc a_2 \end{array}$$

where e_1 and e_2 are environment variables. For this specification, we have the following definitions:

$$\begin{array}{rl} outs(a_1) & \equiv \neg a_1 \, \mathcal{S} \, e_1 \\ outs(a_2) & \equiv \neg a_2 \, \mathcal{S} \, e_2 \\ priority(a_1) & \equiv ((\odot(\neg a_1 \, \mathcal{S} \, e_1) \wedge \neg a_1) \, \mathcal{S} \, (\neg(\odot(\neg a_2 \, \mathcal{S} \, e_2)) \vee a_2)) \\ priority(a_2) & \equiv \neg priority(a_1). \end{array}$$

4.2.3 Determinisation without environment components

The Sequences of Constraints.

Generally, given an eventuality formula $p \vee \Diamond \bigcirc l_0$, the formulae which constrain the eventuality are the formulae of the body which may be written in the form:

$$l_{i,j} \vee \bigcirc \neg l_{i-1} \vee \bigcirc e_{i,j}$$

where l_k stands for $\bigwedge_j l_{k,j}$, and $e_{i,j}$ is a state formula involving only environment literals. In order to identify the formulae which constrain l_{i-1} (for $i > 1$), a new variable v_{i-1} is used to define l_{i-1}, and the formulae $l_{i,j} \vee \bigcirc\neg v_{i-1} \vee \bigcirc e_{i,j}$ are derived after resolving the definition $v_{i-1} \Leftrightarrow l_{i-1}$ with the body of the specification (note that the specification itself is left unchanged: resolution is used simply to identify the constraints on the eventualities). In this section we only consider the case where no next-time environment literal appearing in a constraint also appears in its negated form in another constraint. It is worth considering this particular case separately because it leads to a more efficient algorithm than the general case. For the specification to be implementable, the eventualities must be satisfiable under the strongest constraints that the environment may produce, that is, in this case, under the constraints which result from setting all the next-time environment components to *false*. Thus, after merging the formulae with identical future-time components, the constraints may be represented by a sequence of formulae in the simple form:

$$l_i \vee \bigcirc\neg l_{i-1}.$$

The identification of the constraints may be stopped when either:

1. no formula constraining l_n may be found, and thus the sequence is finite;
2. some formulae of the form $l_{n+1,j} \vee \bigcirc\neg l_n \vee \bigcirc e_{n+1,j}$ is found and l_{n+1} implies l_m for some $m \leq n$ (this includes the case where l_{n+1} is the empty disjunct, i.e. the formula *False*); when this condition holds, the sequence is circular.

Using an argument similar to the one of section4.1, it can be shown that that the above process always terminates, and therefore the generated sequence of l_i's is finite.

Determinising Formulae and Satisfiability Condition.

Determinisation is achieved by replacing each disjunct of the form $p \vee \Diamond\bigcirc l_0$ in the body of the specification by a set of determinising formulae and, in some cases, a formula expressing explicitly the condition under which the eventuality is satisfiable. If the sequence of constraints is empty, the determinising formula for l_0 is simply $\neg outs(l_0) \vee \neg priority(l_0) \vee \bigcirc l_0$. If the sequence is not empty, the determinising formulae consist of the following formulae, rewritten in conjunctive normal form (recall that the l_i stand for past/present formulae):

$$\neg outs(l_0) \vee \neg priority(l_0) \vee (\bigvee_{1 \leq j < i} l_j) \vee \neg l_i \vee \bigcirc l_{i-1} \qquad (0 < i \leq n).$$

It is clear that the past/present component of only one of these formulae may evaluate to false at any one time, and that, when this occurs, the right-hand side may be set to *true*. Thus, the determinising formulae may be added to the body of the specification without introducing an inconsistency. Furthermore, since the satisfaction of these formulae in a state may be achieved without affecting the previous states, they may be added without requiring resolution to be performed.

The determinising formulae ensure that, once one of the l_i's holds, l_0 eventually holds. It only remains to ensure that, whenever $outs(l_0) \wedge priority(l_0)$ holds, one of the l_i's eventually holds afterwards. When the sequence of constraints is finite, it is easy to see that, whenever $outs(l_0) \wedge priority(l_0)$ holds in a state, l_n may be set in the next state without imposing constraints on the previous states. Thus the formula

$$\neg outs(l_0) \vee \neg priority(l_0) \vee \bigvee_{i \leq n} \bigcirc l_i$$

may be simply added to the body of the specification without requiring resolution to be performed.

When the sequence of constraints is circular however, the formula

$$\neg outs(l_0) \vee \bigvee_{i \leq n} \bigcirc l_i$$

must be true in every state of every model, the generation of which does not constrain the future behaviour of the environment. This can be argued as follows. $\neg l_{n+1}$ is implied by $\neg l_m$ for some $m \leq n$. Thus, if $\bigwedge_{i \leq n} \neg l_i$ holds, then $\bigwedge_{i \leq n+1} \neg l_i$ holds. But then $\bigwedge_{i \leq n} \bigcirc \neg l_i$ holds for some environment behaviour. Thus whenever the condition $\bigwedge_{i \leq n} \neg l_i$ holds in a state, $\neg l_0$ holds in that state and forever afterwards for some environment behaviour. The formula $\square(\neg outs(l_0) \vee \bigvee_{i \leq n} \bigcirc l_i)$ expresses explicitly a condition for the satisfiability of the eventuality. The satisfaction of this formula in any given state puts some restrictions on the choice of the previous states. Such restrictions are made explicit by adding the formula to the disjuncts without eventuality symbols in the body of the specification, and performing resolution. As a result, the constraints may have to be identified anew. Therefore the identification of the sequences of l_i's for all the eventuality literals must be performed recursively. A function to perform such an identification is described in section 4.3.

4.2.4 The general case

Generally, the set of constraints may include pairs of next-time environment literals which are the negation of each other. There is not a constant valuation of these literals which constitutes a 'worst case'. Their values in a state determine which constraints are disabled in that state. We may still, however, eliminate the other next-time environment literals.

Following the method of section 4.2.3, one could identify, for each eventuality literal, the conditions under which the eventuality may not be satisfied and add to the specification some derivable formulae stating that such conditions should not occur when the eventuality is outstanding. However, the general case is complicated by the fact that such an identification has to be considered for all possible environment behaviours, and that the resulting satisfiability conditions do not provide a scheduling for the satisfaction of the eventuality. A different method is suggested below, in which the formulae which ensure the satisfaction of the outstanding eventualities are simply consistent with the specification.

The constraints directly affecting the eventuality literal l_0 have the form $l_{1,j} \vee \bigcirc\neg l_0 \vee \bigcirc e_{1,j}$, where $e_{0,j}$ is a state formula involving only environment literals. As before, let us call l_i the expression $\bigwedge_j l_{i,j}$, where the $l_{i,j}$ are formulae such that

$$l_{i,j} \vee \bigcirc(\bigvee_{k<i} \neg l_k) \vee \bigcirc e_{i,j}$$

is derivable and $l_{i,j} \neq l_{k,l}$ for all l and all $k < i$. The end of the sequence of sets of constraints is reached if either no formula constraining l_n may be found, or the formulae of the form $l_{n+1,j} \vee \bigcirc\neg l_n \vee \bigcirc e_{n+1,j}$ are such that $l_{n+1,j}$ implies $l_{m,k}$ for some k and some $m \leq n$.

The formula $\bigvee_{i\leq n} l_i$ must eventually hold in order that l_0 may eventually hold. When the sequence of l_i's is finite and $outs(l_0) \wedge priority(l_0)$ holds, l_n, and therefore $\bigvee_{i\leq n} l_i$, may be set in the next state without imposing constraints on the previous states. Thus, as in the particular case of section 4.2.3, the formula $\neg outs(l_0) \vee \neg priority(l_0) \vee \bigvee_{i\leq n} \bigcirc l_i$ may be simply added to the body of the specification without requiring resolution to be performed.

When the sequence is circular a formula must be found, consistent with the specification, which specifies the scheduling of $\bigvee_{i\leq n} l_i$. One possible formula is specified as follows. Let L be a disjunct of expressions $l_{i,j}$ containing at least one $l_{i,j}$ for every value of i and let $\neg L'$ be the disjunct of expressions $\neg l_{i,j}$ such that $l_{i,j}$ does not occur in L. It can be easily verified that, if the specification is implementable, and if it admits some models for which $\neg L \wedge L'$ holds in some state s, then one of these models must be such such that l_0 holds after s and before $\neg L$ holds again. Therefore, if the specification is implementable, every conjunct $\neg L \wedge L'$, defined in the way specified above, must be such that the formula $\Box(\neg(outs(l_0)\,\mathcal{S}\,(\neg L \wedge L')) \vee \bigcirc L)$ is consistent with it. Thus, for a single eventuality literal, the formula $\neg(outs(l_0)\,\mathcal{S}\,(\neg L \wedge L')) \vee \bigcirc L$ may be added to the body of the specification without introducing an inconsistency. When there are more than one eventuality literal, the weaker formulae

$$\neg priority(l_0) \vee \neg(outs(l_0)\,\mathcal{S}\,(\neg L \wedge L')) \vee \bigcirc L$$

must be used instead in order to ensure that L is enforced in the next state only when $outs(l_0) \wedge priority(l_0)$ holds, and thus that the setting of L for an eventuality literal is not prohibited by the setting of L for another one. Adding these formulae to the body of the specification and performing resolution may, of course, alter the constraints. The identification of the l_i's has to be performed recursively, using, for instance, the function defined in section 4.3.

The resulting specification includes a schedule for the satisfaction of the disjunct $\bigvee_{i\leq n} l_i$. This may be seen by noting that, since the number of possible disjuncts L is finite, the above formulae ensure that, within a finite number of states after $priority(l_0)$ has been set, either l_0 is set or all the possible instantiations of L are true, at which point $\bigvee_{i\leq n} l_i$ must hold.

Efficiency may be improved by adding a specific scheduling of $\bigvee_{i\leq n} l_i$ whenever possible. For instance, given the constraints

$$l_{1,0} \vee \bigcirc\neg l_0 \vee \bigcirc e_{1,0}$$
$$l_{2,0} \vee \bigcirc\neg l_1 \vee \bigcirc e_{2,0}$$
$$l_{2,1} \vee \bigcirc\neg l_1 \vee \bigcirc\neg e_{1,0}$$
$$l_{1,0} \vee \bigcirc\neg l_2,$$

adding the formula

$$\neg outs(l_0) \vee \neg priority(l_0) \vee l_{1,0} \vee l_{2,1} \vee \neg l_{2,0} \vee \bigcirc(l_1 \vee l_0)$$

ensures that $l_1 \vee l_0$ holds just after $\neg l_{1,0} \wedge \neg l_{2,1} \wedge l_{2,0}$ ($= \neg L \wedge L'$) holds. Without it the scheduling would simply ensure that $l_{1,0} \vee l_{2,1}$ ($= L$) holds until l_0 is set.

The scheduling of l_0, once $\bigvee_{i \leq n} l_i$ is set may be performed by adding determinising formulae, as specified in section 4.2.3.

4.3 A function which identifies the sequences of constraints

The function 'id_lis', defined below, returns the sequence of l_i's together with the updated specification. The argument 'spec' denotes the specification, 'events' denotes the list of eventuality literals and 'lis' the corresponding list of sequences of l_i's. 'new_constraints' denotes the same sequences, together with values specifying whether the sequence is finite or circular, and whether the next-time environment literals have been eliminated or not. The function 'get_new_spec' adds to the specification a set of formulae which expresses explicitly the condition that, for every sequence of l_i's which is circular, $\bigvee_{i \leq n} \bigcirc l_i$ eventually holds whenever l_0 is outstanding. Here is the definition of the function:

```
function   id_lis (spec, events, lis)   =
           new_constraints   =   get_new_constraints events
               (* get the sequences of li's together with their kind *)
           new_lis   =   get_lis new_constraints
               (* extract from it the sequences of li's *)
           if equivalent (new_lis, lis)
               (* if the new sequences are equivalent to the old ones *)
               then (spec,lis)
                    (* then return the specification and the sequences *)
               else id_lis ((get_new_spec spec new_constraints)
                                events
                                new_lis)
                    (* otherwise update the specification
                                  and repeat the process *)
end
```

The facts that the sequence of l_i's is finite, that the number of basic subformulae is also finite, and that each formula l_i is a conjunction which is simply expanded from one step of the recursion to the next ensure that, within a finite number of recursion steps, the identified l_i's are semantically equivalent to to the corresponding l_i's in the next step, and thus that the algorithm terminates.

5 Generating models

There are several ways of generating a model from the specification. The method which is currently implemented is dynamic, in the sense that the future-time components of the disjuncts in the final form of the specification may themselves be disjuncts, and the selection of the next state literal occurs at run time. A state is defined by a set of assignments of truth values to the subformulae of the specification which are either variables or expressions under the scope of a past-time operator. Past expressions are evaluated in every state using the equivalences described in section 3.3 (e.g. $\bigcirc a\,\mathcal{S}\,b \Leftrightarrow (\bigcirc b \vee (\bigcirc a \wedge a\,\mathcal{S}\,b))$).

Once the first set of environment variables is received, the first state is fully defined by choosing a consistent conjunct from the initialisation of the specification and by making use of the default strategy. Given any state, the body of the specification partially defines the next state. If the past/present component of a disjunct evaluates to *false* in the current state, its future-time component is selected. This process results in a set of disjuncts of literals. Once the current set of environment variables is received, a consistent set of literals is selected from the set of disjuncts, selecting an environment variables whenever possible (i.e. whenever one agrees with the actual input). The default strategy is used to evaluate the variables not appearing in the resulting list of literals. The new state is constructed from the old one and the new variable setting.

6 Related work

As mentioned in the introduction, [11] uses automata-theoretic techniques to achieve the synthesis of a specification in propositional temporal logic (without past time extension) with environment variables. The general idea consists in constructing a non-deterministic Büchi automaton which accepts the models of the specification, and then transforming it into an automaton which accepts trees representing sets of models for all possible settings of the environment variables. The final automaton is a deterministic transducer, i.e. it accepts a single tree. Given a specification ϕ, the synthesis consists in four stages:

1. Construction of a non-deterministic sequential Büchi automaton A accepting the sequential models of ϕ. This is a standard construction, which may be found in [3] for instance.

2. Determinisation of the Büchi automaton using a subset construction [3, 12]. In this context, the word 'determinisation' refers simply to the fact that the transition function of the automaton is deterministic. The resulting automaton B, accepts the same sequences as A, i.e. the models of ϕ. However, what is required is an automaton which accepts sets of models of ϕ, containing one model for each possible setting of the environment variables. Let x be the set of environment variables and y the set of internal variables. If δ is the transition function of the determinised automaton, the state following state s_i after input $< x, y >$ is given by $\delta(s_i, < x, y >)$. The automaton B may be seen as a tree automaton B' if the transition function δ is replaced by the multifunction δ' with projection along input x given by $\delta'(s_i, y) \Downarrow x = \delta(s_i, < x, y >)$. B' may only accept trees of values of y defined for every nodes of a full x-tree. In any accepting run of B', a finite path in the full x-tree specifies the current value of y .

3. Construction of a finite tree automaton C which accepts a tree iff B' accepts an infinite tree. [8]

4. Determinisation (where 'determinisation' has the same meaning as in the rest of the paper). The automaton C is transformed into a deterministic transducer.

It is difficult to compare the automata-theoretic approach to synthesis with our approach. However, at a general level, one can see that the first approach reasons directly about the semantics of the specification, while the second approach reasons about its syntax. In both approaches, the result may be interpreted as a function which specifies a current state, given the past states of a model and the current values of the environment variables. I am not aware that any implementation of the suggested algorithm for automata transformation has been attempted yet.

Note finally that transformation rules of the kind presented in section 3 are used in [4] as part of a temporal resolution method based on the graph-theoretic representation of temporal formulae.

7 Conclusion

A method has been given to transform any implementable propositional temporal specification into a 'deterministic specification, i.e. one from which a model of the original specification may be generated without backtracking. The set of models of the transformed specification is a subset of the set of models of the original one, entirely specified by the strategy used to allocate the priority to outstanding literals (if the priority is allocated only after time t, then all the models of the original specification will be available up to time t). The transformed specification may be used to generate deterministically a single model, characterised by the method used to choose the literals which hold in the next state and by the chosen default strategy.

An implementation in ML of the determinisation is in the process of being tested. Here are some of the remaining problems:

- There may be some delays in the setting of eventuality literals. For instance, the transformation of subformulae of the form $p \vee \Diamond a$ ensures only that a is set in the state following the one where $\neg p$ holds. There may also be unwanted delays for subformulae of the form $p \vee \Diamond \bigcirc a$, when the satisfaction of a is constrained.

- The transformations are sometimes very slow: although various versions of the resource allocation problem and the dining philosopher problem (simple examples of which are given in appendix A) take less than 1 min to determinise on a sun 4, the specification

  $$\Diamond \neg z \wedge \Box((\neg a \vee \Box \neg b) \wedge (z \vee \Diamond a) \wedge (z \vee \Diamond b))$$

  takes about 5 mins.

There is much scope to improve the efficiency of both the transformation and the generation of models. More work is also required at the theoretical level to ensure that the eventualities are satisfied in an optimal way (i.e. that as many eventualities as possible are satisfied, as early as possible). The possibility of determinising first-order temporal specifications is being investigated.

Acknowledgements: I would like to thank Michael Fisher, who has repeatedly provided me with useful comments and information concerning this work.

Appendices

A Simple Examples

Two very simple examples are used in this section to illustrate the determinisation algorithm. In both cases, the transformation does not introduce new variables.

A.1 Resource allocation

Original specification:

$$\begin{array}{ll}\Box & ((\neg a_1 \vee \neg a_2)\\ & \wedge(\Diamond \bigcirc a_1 \vee \neg e_1)\\ & \wedge(\Diamond \bigcirc a_2 \vee \neg e_2))\end{array}$$

This formula specifies that resource a_1 must eventually be allocated when the environment variable e_1 is set, and resource a_2 must eventually be allocated when e_2 is set, with the constraint that a_1 and a_2 may not be allocated in the same state.

Specification after the initial transformations:

$$\begin{array}{ll} & (\neg a_1 \vee \neg a_2)\\ \wedge\Box & ((\bigcirc\neg a_1 \vee \bigcirc\neg a_2)\\ & \wedge(\Diamond \bigcirc a_1 \vee \neg e_1)\\ & \wedge(\Diamond \bigcirc a_2 \vee \neg e_2))\end{array}$$

Determinised specification:

$$\begin{array}{ll} & (\neg a_1 \wedge a_2)\\ \wedge\Box & ((\bigcirc a_1 \vee \neg(\neg a_1 \mathcal{S}\, e_1)\\ & \qquad \vee\neg((\bullet(\neg a_1 \mathcal{S}\, e_1) \wedge \neg a_1)\, \mathcal{S}\, (\neg(\bullet(\neg a_2 \mathcal{S}\, e_2)) \vee a_2)))\\ & \wedge(\bigcirc a_2 \vee \neg(\neg a_2 \mathcal{S}\, e_2)\\ & \qquad \vee(\bullet(\neg a_1 \mathcal{S}\, e_1) \wedge \neg a_1)\, \mathcal{S}\, (\neg(\bullet(\neg a_2 \mathcal{S}\, e_2)) \vee a_2))\\ & \wedge(\bigcirc\neg a_1 \vee \bigcirc\neg a_2))\end{array}$$

The outstanding formulae and the priority formulae are identified as follows:

$outs(a_1)$ is $\neg a_1 \mathcal{S}\, e_1$; $outs(a_2)$ is $\neg a_2 \mathcal{S}\, e_2$.

$priority(a_1)$ is $((\bullet(\neg a_1 \mathcal{S}\, e_1) \wedge \neg a_1)\, \mathcal{S}\, (\neg(\bullet(\neg a_2 \mathcal{S}\, e_2)) \vee a_2))$;

$priority(a_2)$ is $\neg priority(a_1)$.

Sample run:

states				
1	e_1	e_2	$\neg a_1$	$\neg a_2$
2	e_1	e_2	a_1	$\neg a_2$
3	$\neg e_1$	e_2	$\neg a_1$	a_2
4	$\neg e_1$	$\neg e_2$	a_1	$\neg a_2$
5	$\neg e_1$	$\neg e_2$	$\neg a_1$	a_2
6	e_1	$\neg e_2$	$\neg a_1$	$\neg a_2$
7	e_1	e_2	a_1	$\neg a_2$
8	$\neg e_1$	$\neg e_2$	a_1	$\neg a_2$
9	$\neg e_1$	$\neg e_2$	$\neg a_1$	a_2
	end run			

Once the environment has provided an evaluation for e_1 and e_2, the current state is completed. The response to the environment request occurs in the next state or later, according to the constraint imposed by the specification.

A.2 Simple dining philosopher problem

Original specification:

$$\begin{array}{ll} \Box & ((\bigcirc(\neg eaten_A) \vee f_A) \\ & \wedge(\bigcirc(\neg eaten_B) \vee f_B) \\ & \wedge(\neg f_A \vee \neg f_B) \\ & \wedge\Diamond eaten_A \\ & \wedge\Diamond eaten_B) \end{array}$$

This formula specifies that, at every state, both philosopher A and philosopher B must eventually have eaten ($eaten_X$ means that philosopher X has eaten in the previous state). There is only one fork, which is either in A's possession (f_A) or in B's possession (f_B). The philosophers can eat only if they have the fork.

Specification after the initial transformations:

$$\begin{array}{ll} & ((\neg f_A \vee \neg f_B)) \\ \wedge\Box & ((\bigcirc\neg eaten_A \vee f_A) \\ & \wedge(\bigcirc\neg eaten_B \vee f_B) \\ & \wedge(\bigcirc\neg f_A \vee \bigcirc\neg f_B) \\ & \wedge(\Diamond\bigcirc eaten_A \vee eaten_A) \\ & \wedge(\Diamond\bigcirc eaten_B \vee eaten_B)) \end{array}$$

Determinised specification:

$$
\begin{array}{ll}
 & (\neg f_A) \\
\wedge\Box & ((\bigcirc eaten_A \vee eaten_A \vee \neg f_A \\
 & \quad \vee\neg((\circledbullet\neg eaten_A \wedge \neg eaten_A)\,\mathcal{S}\,(\neg(\circledbullet\neg eaten_B) \vee eaten_B))) \\
 & \wedge(\bigcirc eaten_B \vee eaten_B \vee \neg f_B \\
 & \quad \vee(\circledbullet\neg eaten_A \wedge \neg eaten_A)\,\mathcal{S}\,(\neg(\circledbullet\neg eaten_B) \vee eaten_B)) \\
 & \wedge(\bigcirc f_A \vee eaten_A \vee f_A \\
 & \quad \vee\neg((\circledbullet\neg eaten_A \wedge \neg eaten_A)\,\mathcal{S}\,(\neg(\circledbullet\neg eaten_B) \vee eaten_B))) \\
 & \wedge(\bigcirc f_B \vee eaten_B \vee f_B \\
 & \quad \vee(\circledbullet\neg eaten_A \wedge \neg eaten_A)\,\mathcal{S}\,(\neg(\circledbullet\neg eaten_B) \vee eaten_B)) \\
 & \wedge(\bigcirc\neg eaten_A \vee f_A) \\
 & \wedge(\bigcirc\neg eaten_B \vee f_B) \\
 & \wedge(\bigcirc\neg f_A \vee \bigcirc\neg f_B))
\end{array}
$$

Note that the setting of f_A and f_B, as well as the setting of $eaten_A$ and $eaten_B$, are explicitly scheduled. The outstanding formulae and the priority formulae are identified as follows: $outs(eaten_A)$ is $\neg eaten_A$; $outs(eaten_B)$ is $\neg eaten_B$. $priority(eaten_A)$ is $((\circledbullet\neg eaten_A \wedge \neg eaten_A)\,\mathcal{S}\,(\neg(\circledbullet\neg eaten_B) \vee eaten_B))$; $priority(eaten_B)$ is $\neg priority(eaten_A)$.

Sample run:

states					
1	*true*	$\neg eaten_A$	$\neg eaten_B$	$\neg f_A$	$\neg f_B$
2	*true*	$\neg eaten_A$	$\neg eaten_B$	f_A	$\neg f_B$
3	*true*	$eaten_A$	$\neg eaten_B$	$\neg f_A$	$\neg f_B$
4	*true*	$\neg eaten_A$	$\neg eaten_B$	$\neg f_A$	f_B
5	*true*	$\neg eaten_A$	$eaten_B$	$\neg f_A$	$\neg f_B$
6	*true*	$\neg eaten_A$	$\neg eaten_B$	f_A	$\neg f_B$
7	*true*	$eaten_A$	$\neg eaten_B$	$\neg f_A$	$\neg f_B$
8	*true*	$\neg eaten_A$	$\neg eaten_B$	$\neg f_A$	f_B
9	*true*	$\neg eaten_A$	$eaten_B$	$\neg f_A$	$\neg f_B$
	end run				

The symbol *true* indicates that there is no environment variable. Note that there is a better implementation, in which $\neg f_A \wedge \neg f_B$ never occurs. The failure to get the best implementation results from specifying the fact that one of the l_i's must occur (see section 4.2.3) by the formula

$$\neg outs(l) \vee \neg priority(l) \vee \bigcirc l_0 \vee \bigcirc l_1$$

thus forcing l_1 to hold only in the next state when $\neg l_0$ holds in the current state, while in this particular case, it is possible to satisfy:

$$\neg outs(l) \vee \neg priority(l) \vee l_1.$$

References

[1] H. Barringer, M. Fisher, D. Gabbay, G. Gough, and R. Owens. METATEM: A Framework for Programming in Temporal Logic. In *REX Workshop on Stepwise Refinement of Distributed Systems: Models, Formalisms, Correctness (LNCS Volume 430)*, pages 94–129, Mook, Netherlands, June 1989. Springer Verlag.

[2] H. Barringer, M. Fisher, D. Gabbay, and A. Hunter. Meta-Reasoning in Executable Temporal Logic. In James Allen, Richard Fikes, and Erik Sandewall, editors, *Proceedings of the International Conference on Principles of Knowledge Representation and Reasoning*, Cambridge, Massachusetts, April 1991. Morgan Kaufmann.

[3] E.A. Emerson and A.P. Sistla. Deciding full Branching Time Logic. *Information and Control*, 61:175–201, 1984.

[4] M. Fisher. A Resolution Method for Temporal Logic. In *Proceedings of the International Joint Conference on Artificial Intelligence*, Sydney, Australia, August 1991. Morgan Kaufman.

[5] M. Fisher and H. Barringer. Concurrent METATEM Processes — A Language for Distributed AI. In *Proceedings of the European Simulation Multiconference*, Copenhagen, Denmark, June 1991.

[6] M. Fisher and P. Noel. Transformation and Synthesis in METATEM – Part I: Propositional METATEM. METATEM project report, May 1991.

[7] G.D. Gough. Decision Procedures for Temporal Logic. Master's thesis, Department of Computer Science, University of Manchester, 1984.

[8] A. Hossley and C. Rackoff. The Emptiness Problem for Automata on Infinite Trees. In *13th IEEE Symposium on Switching and Automata Theory*, pages 121–124, 1972.

[9] O. Lichtendtein, A. Pnueli, and L.Zuck. The Glory of the Past. In *Proc. Workshop on Logic of Programs*, pages 196–218. Springer-Verlag, 1985. LNCS 193.

[10] A. Pnueli. The Temporal Logic of Programs. In *Proceedings of the Eighteenth Symposium on the Foundations of Computer Science*, Providence, November 1977.

[11] A. Pnueli and R. Rosner. On the Synthesis of a Reactive Module. In *16th ACM POPL*, pages 179–190, January 1989.

[12] A.Prasad Sistla, Moshe Y. Vardi, and Pierre Wolper. The Complementation Problem for Buchi Automata with Application to Temporal Logic. *Theoretical Computer Science*, 49:217–237, 1987.

[13] P. Wolper. The Tableau Method for Temporal Logic: An overview. *Logique et Analyse*, 110–111:119–136, June-Sept 1985.

[14] P. Wolper. On the Relation of Programs and Computations to Models of Temporal Logic. In *Temporal Logic in Specification*, pages 75–123. Springer-Verlag, 1987. LNCS 398.

Program Transformations Directed by the Evaluation of non Functional Properties

Yamine Aït Ameur
O.N.E.R.A-C.E.R.T-D.E.R.I
2,Avenue Edouard Belin BP 4025 31400 TOULOUSE FRANCE
Email : yamine@tls-cs.cert.fr

Extended Abstract

1 Introduction

Program transformation aims at producing efficient programs from lucid specifications or preliminary versions. Two classes of program transformations can be distinguished [Fea87]. The first class deals with automatic transformations. They are achieved mechanically and no external intervention is needed. Examples are compilation, transformations following a partial evaluation, ...

The second one is the class of semi-automatic transformations. External interventions are necessary to transform programs. The programmer gives some informations (properties, eurekas,...) to guide the transformations supported by a transformation system. Our work is concerned with the second class. It focuses on the semi-automatic transformation of equational programs.

A transformational program development is defined as a set of transformation steps. Each step is the application of a transformation rule $rule_i$ to one or several intermediate objects obj_i, giving another intermediate object obj_{i+1}. The initial object is the problem specification (or a first version of the program to be transformed) and the last object is the resulting transformed program. The rules to be applied belong to a transformation system. The Fold/Unfold transformation system of Burstall and Darlington [BD77] has been chosen to illustrate our approach.

2 Program transformations based on functional properties

Most of the program transformations are based on functional properties. These properties are explicitly stated as algebraic equations (commutativity, associativity,...) in the theory where the transformations are conducted. They can be qualified syntactic

or structural.
Transformation rules use these properties in applicability conditions and check them syntactically (unification, pattern matching, ...) or by static semantic control (type checking,...).

Transformation rules produce a new version of a program equivalent to a previous one. Moreover, a transformation rule is not used alone. It is combined with other rules to build tactics. The aim of applying a tactic is to produce a program more efficient than the initial one. The practice of program transformation has led to the development of several tactics which can be used when applicability conditions are met. The problem is then, *how to detect in a given state what are the applicability conditions which are satisfied so as to select the corresponding transformation tactic?*

Huet and Lang in [HL78] have proposed some transformation templates. They are based on program schemes expressed in a second order language. The templates are formally proved when a set of axioms are given. These axioms represent essentially functional properties. The applicability conditions consist in the matching of the template.

3 Program transformations based on operational properties

The main part of our work aims at introducing the applications of transformation tactics based not only on functional properties as stated above but also on operational properties of the objects to be transformed.

Such operational properties are not structural and must be computed and evaluated. Examples are space and time complexity, or properties related to parallelism. So, the rules cannot check them syntactically as it is done for functional ones. An additional tool is required to compute and verify this kind of properties.

We particularly focus on this last point. Indeed, a particular property in relation with time analysis [Weg75] of a program to be transformed is studied. If the property does not hold for this program at a given transformation stage, a transformation tactic is applied to produce a new equivalent object satisfying it. To apply this tactic, two questions must be given an answer.

First, *does the property hold for* obj_i *at a given stage?* A formal tool to evaluate the properties is required. For this purpose, an extension of abstract interpretation [CC77][Myc81][BHA86] is defined on the objects produced by transformational developments. The property calculus will be safe if the abstract interpretation is correct.

Second, *how to make sure that the applied tactic preserves the standard semantics of* obj_i*?* This is the problem of tactic validation. Two answers are possible. The first one is to give global validation of the tactic. This approach implies to apply mathematical proof methods on the objects and tactics. It is not supported by generic tools and so it is hardly usable.
The second one is to prove the validity of the tactic on some templates and use

it where applicability conditions are met. It is a generalization of the templates introduced by Huet and Lang [HL78] which adds non functional properties verifications to the syntactic applicability conditions (pattern matching,...) and to the functional properties.

4 Conclusion and further work

The approach we presented aims at taking into account operational properties during program transformations. This approach is based on a totally formal expression of the properties and the transformation tactics. This formal expression makes it possible to prove the correction of the property calculus (by a safe abstract interpretation) and the validity of transformation tactics as stated above. As tactics are associated to properties, we can envisage to drive the transformations by these properties and try to achieve them automatically.

The transformations and tactics previously defined have been supported by and developed with the *DEVA* development language.[CCJ+91]

Although our approach is quite general, we have taken into account only one property related to time complexity. Our future work, aims at considering not only one property but many properties. It seems more difficult since we do not know whether the achieved transformations for a given property do or do not preserve the other ones.

Bibliography

[BD77] R.M. Burstall and J. Darlington. A transformation system for developping recursive programs. *JACM*, 24(1):44–67, 1977.

[BHA86] G.L. Burn, C.L. Hankin, and S. Abramsky. Strictness Analysis of Higher Order Functions. *Science of Computer Programming*, 7:249–278, 1986.

[CC77] P. Cousot and R. Cousot. Abstract Interpretation: A unified Lattice Model for Static Analysis of Programs by Construction of Approximation of Fixpoint. *4th POPL*, pages 238–252, 1977.

[CCJ+91] J. Cazin, P. Cros, R. Jacquart, M. Lemoine, and P. Michel. *Construction and Reuse of Formal Program Developments.* In Springer Verlag, editor, *TAPSOFT 91.* LNCS, 4 91.

[Fea87] M. S. Feather. *A Survey and Classification of Some Program Transformation Approaches and Techniques.* In North Holland, editor, *IFIP*, 87.

[HL78] G. Huet and B. Lang. *Proving and Applying Transformations Expressed with Second-Order Patterns . Acta Informatica*, 11(1):31–55, 1978.

[Myc81] A. Mycroft. *Abstract Interpretation and Optimising Transformations for Applicative Programs.* PhD thesis, University of Edimburgh, 1981.

[Weg75] B. Wegbreit. Mechanical Program Analysis. *communications of the ACM*, 18:528–539, 1975.

Using a Prolog Prototype for Designing an Object Oriented Scheme

Christine Solnon
Michel Rueher

I3S - CNRS, Université de Nice - Sophia Antipolis
06560 Valbonne, FRANCE

Abstract

The purpose of this paper is to define a reverse engineering technique for recovering structural design information through the analysis of a Prolog prototype. Prolog is widely used for making prototypes due to its high level of abstraction, and object oriented programming has emerged as a successful paradigm for software development. However, object oriented modelling is difficult to achieve. Thus, we propose to extract an object oriented scheme from the Prolog prototype. We show that the identification of the inclusion polymorphism expressed by Prolog clauses allows us to define an inheritance hierarchy.

In the first section, we define a polymorphic denotational type system for Prolog, and we show that a Prolog program expresses relationships between types which allow us to capture inclusion polymorphism. In the second section, we present an algorithm that infers relationships between types expressed in a Prolog program. These relationships are used to define an object oriented scheme, where the inheritance hierarchy only depends on the semantic relations specified by the clauses of the program. Finally, we compare our approach with some related works, and we show the advantage of our system for well capturing inheritance relations.

1 Introduction

1.1 Motivations

Prototyping is widely used to refine and validate specifications prior to constructing a production version [Bal89]. A prototype quickly provides feedback about the behaviour and the structure of the application product and then constitutes a reference for the production version development [Rue91]. Prolog is widely used for prototyping due to its high level of abstraction [Gal87, LeR89]. Its main qualities are:

- a particular ability for a fast development thanks to its facilities for writing, modifying and stepwise refining of programs,
- an exceptional capacity to experiment different solutions (multiple entry points, tests which may be driven both by input and by output data, the combining of both concrete and symbolic execution which enables us to get a solution for a particular case as well as for a class of problems).

Object oriented programming has emerged as a very successful paradigm for software development, due to its ability for structuring knowledge [Mey88, Cox89]. The success of object oriented languages mainly comes from their facilities in reusing well structured components. When designing an application with an object oriented language, the programmer has to identify the different objects and operations, and to classify them by means of classes and class inheritance. However, this modelisation, which is a central key of object oriented design, is difficult to achieve, especially when the specifications of all components of the application product are not yet completely defined.

In order to provide an effective support for identifying the objects, classes of objects and relationships between them, we propose to reuse the Prolog prototype when designing the production version. The goal is to enable us to achieve a very convenient exploration of a problem (thanks to Prolog's facilities) while keeping up the structural information gathered during the prototyping step. Thus, we propose to extract an object oriented scheme from the Prolog prototype validated by the user. The purpose of our approach is to define a reverse engineering technique for recovering structural design information through the analysis of the Prolog prototype.

1.2 The object oriented paradigm

Many definitions of object oriented programming have been proposed (e.g. [Bra83, DaT88, Cox89]). In this paper, we assume that an object oriented language provides linguistic support for defining objects, classes of objects and inheritance relations defined as follows [Weg90]:

- **Objects** are collections of methods that share a state. The **methods** determine the messages to which the object can respond, while the shared state is hidden from the outside world and is only accessible to the object's methods.

- **Classes** specify an interface of a collection of objects with a uniform behaviour (i.e. objects which are accessible through the same methods).

- **Inheritance** allows us to reuse the properties of one or more classes in the definition of a new class. Inherited classes are called **superclasses**, while inheriting classes are called **subclasses**. Inheritance expresses classification, specialization or evolution relations.

In object oriented programming, inheritance is an essential means to express inclusion polymorphism. Thus, identifying inclusion polymorphism will be a major problem when extracting an object oriented scheme from a Prolog prototype. In order to avoid any confusion about inclusion polymorphism, we recall below Cardelli and Wegner classification of polymorphism.

1.3 Classification of polymorphism

Polymorphism denotes the fact that a feature can have more than one type. The classification of polymorphism defined by Cardelli and Wegner [CaW85] is displayed in Figure 1.

$$\textit{polymorphism} \begin{cases} \textit{universal} \begin{cases} \textit{parametric} \\ \textit{inclusion} \end{cases} \\ \\ \textit{adhoc} \begin{cases} \textit{overloading} \\ \textit{coercion} \end{cases} \end{cases}$$

Figure 1: Varieties of polymorphism.

Two major kinds of polymorphism are distinguished: **universal polymorphism** which allows a feature to have an infinite number of related types (all the types having a given common structure), and **ad-hoc polymorphism** which allows a feature to have a finite set of different and potentially unrelated types.

There are two kinds of universal polymorphism:

- **Parametric polymorphism**, where a type parameter determines the type of the argument for each application of a feature. For example, if we define a parametric type ∀*T,List[T]* and a parametric method ∀*T,f(x:List[T])* then *x1:List[Int]* and *x2:List[Char]* are instances of the type *List* while *f(x1)* and *f(x2)* are well-typed calls to *f*. Parametric polymorphism is also referred to as **genericity**.

- **Inclusion polymorphism**, where a feature can be viewed as belonging to many different types that need not be disjoint (i.e. there may be subtyping or inclusion of types). As subtyping relations are expressed in object oriented programs via inheritance, inclusion polymorphism is also called **inheritance polymorphism** [Weg87]. For example, if a type *RealList* inherits a type *List*, and a type *IntList* inherits the type *RealList*, then both *RealList* and *IntList* are subtypes of *List*. A method *f(x:List)* will accept every argument of type *List*, *RealList* or *IntList*.

There are also two different kinds of ad-hoc polymorphism:

- **Overloading**, where the same name is used to denote different semantic features. Overloading is just a convenient syntactic abbreviation. For example, the operator + may be overloaded to define addition on integers and conjunction on booleans.

- **Coercion**, which allows the user to omit semantically necessary type conversions. The required type conversions are determined by the system and inserted in the program to be executed. For example, the operator + may be only defined for the addition of reals, but when integer arguments are used, they are coerced into being real numbers.

In the next chapter, we define a denotational and polymorphic type system for Prolog and we show that Prolog clauses express relationships between types which capture polymorphism.

2 A type system for Prolog

As we have mentionned, inheritance is closely related to inclusion polymorphism. To capture the inheritance relations expressed in a Prolog program, we propose to capture inclusion polymorphism. Prolog is an untyped language: the two available standard structures are the term and the atom (i.e. a predicate symbol and its arguments), whose instances all belong to the Herbrand universe and the Herbrand base. However, these can be decomposed into subsets of objects that have a uniform behaviour and that actually denote types.

2.1 Notation

The notation $p(\ldots, T_i, \ldots)$ expresses the fact that the term T is at position i in the atom p. We denote by Tp the type of a predicate p and by $Tp(i)$ the type of the argument at position i in the predicate p:

PredType ::= 'T' PredName
ArgType ::= 'T' PredName '(' Position ')'

The position of an argument can be composed in order to take into account compound terms (i.e. functional terms whose arity is different from zero):

Position ::= Integer | Integer '.' FunctorName '(' Position ')'

If X is a term, and $T = p(T1, \ldots, Tn)$ is an atom or a compound term, then the position of X in T is computed by using the following rules:

$Position(X,T) = i$ if $X = Ti$ and $i \in 1..n$,
$Position(X,T) = i.f(Position(X,Ti))$ if X appears in a compound term $Ti = f(U1, \ldots, Um)$ and $i \in 1..n$.

For example, in the atom $p(a,g(b,c,X),e)$, the argument X is at position $2.g(3)$, the type of X is $Tp(2.g(3))$, and the type of $p(a,g(b,c,X),e)$ is Tp.

2.2 A denotational type system

We associate potentially different types with each predicate and with each argument position in a predicate. Types are defined as follows:

- The type Tp of a predicate p corresponds to the set of the **logical consequences** of p (i.e. the denotation of p),
- The type $Tp(i)$ of the term at position i in a predicate p corresponds to the **successful instantiations** of this term, i.e. the set $\{T \,/\, p(\ldots, T_i, \ldots) \in Tp\}$.

An example of denotational types is given in Figure 2. One can notice that our proposed definition of types is more restrictive than the one usually proposed for type checking in Prolog (e.g. [Mis84]). For example, in the program *P0* of Figure 2, most of the type systems for Prolog would have considered $p(c)$ as well typed for Tp, although $p(c)$ is not a logical consequence of the program. Such a syntax oriented definition of type is appropriate for type checking, but it is less well suited for infering semantic relationships — such as inheritance — between types.

Program *P0*:	Types associated with *P0*: ($T : S$ means that the type T is described by the set S)	
s(a).	*Ts* : {*s(a)*}	*Tr(2)* : {*a,b*}
r(f(b,1),a).	*Ts(1)* : {*a*}	*Tp* : {*p(a), p(b)*}
r(f(c,2),b).	*Tr* : {*r(f(b,1),a), r(f(c,2),b)*}	*Tp(1)* : {*a,b*}
p(X) :- s(X).	*Tr(1)* : {*f(b,1), f(c,2)*}	*Tt* : {*t(X,X)*}
p(X) :- r(f(X,1),Y).	*Tr(1.f(1))* : {*b,c*}	*Tt(1)* : {*X*}
t(X,X).	*Tr(1.f(2))* : {*1,2*}	*Tt(2)* : {*X*}

Figure 2: An example of denotational types.

2.3 A polymorphic type system

According to the proposed semantics of a type, Prolog is polymorphic. In order to illustrate this polymorphism, let us examine the different types of the feature *a* in the program *P0* of Figure 2:

- Parametric polymorphism is illustrated by the types *Tt(1)* and *Tt(2)* which are described by the set {*X*}. The variable *X* can be viewed as a type variable which is universally quantified. Thus, each value of the Herbrand universe — for example *a* — can be both of types *Tt(1)* and *Tt(2)*.

- Inclusion polymorphism is illustrated by *Ts(1)* and *Tp(1)*. The clause "*p(X) :- s(X)*" expresses the fact that "*for all X, if X is of type Ts(1) then X is also of type Tp(1)*". Hence, each value of the Herbrand universe which is of type *Ts(1)* — for example *a* — is also of type *Tp(1)*. Actually, *Ts(1)* is a subtype or a specialization of *Tp(1)*.

- Overloading is illustrated by the types *Ts(1)* and *Tr(2)*: the value *a* occurs in both atoms *s(a)* and *r(f(b,1),a)* so that *a* can be of type *Ts(1)* and *Tr(2)*. This can be interpreted as "*Ts(1) is a subtype of Tr(2)*". However, this subtyping relationship does not result from a universal rule as in the previous case, but from a syntactical duplication. In fact, the constant *a* can have been overloaded so that it does not have the same meaning (interpretation) in the two clauses.

Hence, parametric polymorphism, inclusion polymorphism and overloading in Prolog allow a value of the Herbrand universe to have several types:

- In parametric polymorphism, a variable allows a type to have an infinite number of subtypes.

- In inclusion polymorphism, a type *T1* is a subtype of another type *T2* because there is a clause that specifies that each object of type *T1* is also of type *T2*. This expresses the fact that *T1* is a specialization (a subtype) of *T2*.

- Overloading allows us to use the same symbol of function or constant for different terms although there is no semantic relationship between the corresponding types.

In the following section, we make explicit the different kinds of relationships between types expressed by Prolog clauses. These relationships will allow us to capture inclusion polymorphism, and then, to design an inheritance hierarchy corresponding to a Prolog prototype.

2.4 Relationships between types in Prolog

2.4.1 The type of a predicate is related to the cartesian product of the types of its arguments

Let the predicate *r* be:

r(f(b,1),a).
r(f(c,2),b).

The types *Tr*, *Tr(1)* and *Tr(2)* are described by the sets:

Tr : {*r(f(b,1),a), r(f(c,2),b)*}
Tr(1) : {*f(b,1), f(c,2)*}
Tr(2) : {*a,b*}

Thus, *Tr* is related to the types of its arguments: the first argument of an atom of type *Tr* is of type *Tr(1)* and the second argument of an atom of type *Tr* is of type *Tr(2)*. We denote this relationship by:

$$Tr = r(Tr(1) \times Tr(2))$$

where $r(Tr(1) \times Tr(2))$ denotes the set of the successful instantiations of *r*, which is a subset of $\{r(X1,X2) / X1 \in Tr(1) \text{ and } X2 \in Tr(2)\}$.

More generally, the type of a predicate *p* of arity *n* — where $n \geq 1$ — is related to the cartesian product of the types of its arguments:

$$Tp = p(Tp(1) \times \ldots \times Tp(n))$$

Predicates without argument are not considered for generating an object oriented scheme.

2.4.2 The type of an argument in a predicate is related to the union of the types of this argument in the different clauses defining the predicate

Let the predicate *p* be:

p(X) :- s(X).
p(X) :- q(X).

The logical formula defining *p* is: $p(X) \Leftarrow s(X) \vee q(X)$. Thus, *Tp(1)* is related to the disjunction of *Ts(1)* and *Tq(1)*. We denote this relationship by:

$$Tp(1) = Ts(1) \cup Tq(1)$$

More generally, let the predicate r be:

$r(\ldots,T1_i,\ldots)$:- $body\_1$.

...

$r(\ldots,Tn_i,\ldots)$:- $body\_n$.

The type $Tr(i)$ is related to the disjunction of n type expressions: $E1, \ldots, En$, so that Ej describes the type of Tj_i in the jth clause that defines r. We denote this relationship by:

$$Tr(i) = E1 \cup E2 \ldots \cup En$$

The type expression Ej depends on the nature of the term Tj_i, which can be a compound term, a head and body variable (i.e. a variable that both occurs in the head and in the body of a clause), a head only variable (i.e. a variable that only occurs in the head of a clause) or a constant. In the following subsections, we study the type expressions associated with these different kinds of terms.

2.4.3 Type expression associated with a compound term

Let be the clause:

r(f(b,1),a).

The type of the compound term *f(b,1)* is related to the types of its two arguments *b* and *1*, i.e. $Tr(1.f(1))$ and $Tr(1.f(2))$. Thus, the type expression associated with *f(b,1)* is:

$$f(Tr(1.f(1)) \times Tr(1.f(2)))$$

More generally, the type expression of a compound term $f(T1,\ldots,Tm)$ at position i in a clause of functor p is defined as follows:

$$f(Tp(i.f(1)) \times \ldots \times Tp(i.f(m)))$$

2.4.4 Type expression associated with a head and body variable

Let be the clause:

p(X) :- q(X), r(X).

The logical formula defining this clause is: $p(X) \Leftarrow q(X) \wedge r(X)$. Thus, the type expression associated with X is the conjunction of $Tq(1)$ and $Tr(1)$. This is denoted by:

$$Tq(1) \cap Tr(1)$$

This has to be refined in order to take into account the other terms that occur in the body of a clause:

- **Shared variables** (i.e. variables that occur more than once in the body of a clause) restrict the resolution set of a variable. Let be the clause:

  p(X) :- q(X,Y), r(X), s(Y).

The resolution set S of X is:

$$S = \{X / X \in Tq(1) \text{ and } X \in Tr(1) \text{ and } q(X,Y) \in Tq \text{ and } s(Y) \in Ts\}.$$

S is a subset of the conjunction of $Tq(1)$ and $Tr(1)$:

$$S \subseteq \{X / X \in Tq(1) \text{ and } X \in Tr(1)\}$$

Thus, the type expression associated with X is a new type Ti defined by the relationship:

$$Ti \leq Tq(1) \cap Tr(1)$$

- **Ground terms** that occur in the body of a clause restrict in the same way the resolution set of a variable. Let be the clause:

  p(X) :- q(X,a), r(X).

  The resolution set S of X is:

  $$S = \{X / X \in Tq(1) \text{ and } q(X,a) \in Tq \text{ and } X \in Tr(1)\}.$$

  S is a subset of the conjunction of $Tq(1)$ and $Tr(1)$:

  $$S \subseteq \{X / X \in Tq(1) \text{ and } X \in Tr(1)\}$$

  Thus, the type expression associated with X is a new type Ti defined by the relationship:

  $$Ti \leq Tq(1) \cap Tr(1)$$

In the following, we shall say that a variable X in the body of a clause is restricted if there is a constant or a shared variable other than X in the body of the clause.

More generally, let be the clause:

p(...,X,...) :- body

where X is a variable which occurs in *body* at position i^1 in an atom of name p^1, ..., and at position i^n in an atom of name p^n. If X is restricted, then the type expression associated with X is a new type Ti defined by the relationship:

$$Ti \leq Tp^1(i^1) \cap Tp^2(i^2) \cap \ldots \cap Tp^n(i^n)$$

otherwise the type expression is:

$$Tp^1(i^1) \cap Tp^2(i^2) \cap \ldots \cap Tp^n(i^n).$$

2.4.5 Type expression associated with a head only variable

Let be the clause: "*p(...,X,...) :- body*" where X is a variable which does not occur in *body*. This clause is generic and the type expression associated with X is a type variable:

- If X only occurs once in the head of the clause (or if X is the anonymous variable "_"), then the type expression associated with X is the universal type μ.
- If X occurs more than once in the head of the clause, then the type expression associated with X is X itself.

2.4.6 Type expression associated with a constant

Let be the clause: *"p(...,c,...) :- body"* where c is a constant. The type expression associated with c is the set $\{c\}$.

3 Inference of an object oriented scheme

In the previous section, we have defined a polymorphic and denotational type system for Prolog, and we have made explicit relationships between types expressed by Prolog clauses. In this section, we show how these relationships enable us to define an object oriented scheme corresponding to a Prolog prototype. The emphasis is on defining an inheritance hierarchy based upon the relationships between types. Thus, the object oriented hierarchy does not depend on the data of the program (that may be incomplete or overloaded) but on the semantic relations specified by the clauses.

First, we present an algorithm for defining the types of a Prolog program by means of their relationships with other types. We then show how these relationships between types can be used for defining an object oriented scheme.

3.1 A relationship inference system

From a Prolog program, we can infer three kinds of relationships that respectively describe the type of a predicate, the type of an argument and the subtype of a conjunction of types:

Relationship ::= PredRelation | ArgRelation | SubtypeRelation

The type of a predicate is described by the cartesian product of its arguments (if it has at least one argument):

PredRelation ::= PredType '=' PredName '(' ArgType ('×' ArgType) ')'*

where *PredName* denotes the name of a predicate, *PredType* denotes the type of a predicate and *ArgType* the type of an argument (cf. section *2.1*). The type of an argument in a predicate is described by the union of its type expressions in the different clauses that define the predicate:

*ArgRelation ::= ArgType '=' TypeExp ('∪' TypeExp)**

where *TypeExp* describes the type of an argument T in a clause, and depends on the nature of T:

TypeExp ::=	
'{' Constant '}'	% T is a constant,
| *FunctorName '(' ArgType ('×' ArgType)* ')'*	% T is a compound term,
| *Variable* | *'μ'*	% T is a head only variable,
| *ArgType ('∩' ArgType)**	% T is a non restricted head and body variable,
| *'T' Integer*	% T is a restricted head and body variable.

In this last case, *"'T' Integer"* is the name of a new type which is the subtype of a conjunction of types. Thus, it is defined by the relationship:

*SubtypeRelation ::= 'T' Integer '≤' ArgType ('∩' ArgType)**

An algorithm which infers the relationships between types for a Prolog program is given in annex A, and is illustrated by means of two classical examples in annex B. This algorithm is directly derived from the above definition of relationships, and is self explanatory.

When applying the algorithm, we assume that the Prolog program has been transformed so that each body of clause is a conjunction of atoms, different predicates with the same name but with a different arity have been renamed, and variables have been renamed so that there is no name conflict between different clauses. In a first step, we only consider clauses without negative or extra logical subgoals.

3.2 The object oriented scheme

The relationships between types described above are used for designing an object oriented scheme in the following way:

- A class of objects is associated with each different type. The set of the objects of a class associated with a type T is defined by using the following rules:

$$
\begin{aligned}
&Obj(T) = Obj(T1) \times \ldots \times Obj(Tn)\\
&\qquad \text{if } T \text{ is defined by the relation } T = p(T1 \times \ldots \times Tn)\\
&Obj(T) = ObjExp(E1) \cup \ldots \cup ObjExp(En)\\
&\qquad \text{if } T \text{ is defined by the relation } T = E1 \cup \ldots \cup En\\
&Obj(T) \subseteq Obj(T1) \cap \ldots \cap Obj(Tn)\\
&\qquad \text{if } T \text{ is defined by the relation } T \leq T1 \cap \ldots \cap Tn\\
&ObjExp(T1 \cap \ldots \cap Tn) = Obj(T1) \cap \ldots \cap Obj(Tn)\\
&ObjExp(f(T1 \times \ldots \times Tn)) = f(Obj(T1) \times \ldots \times Obj(Tn))\\
&ObjExp(X) = \{X\}\\
&ObjExp(\mu) = \{\mu\}\\
&ObjExp(\{c\}) = \{c\}
\end{aligned}
$$

- Subtyping relations are defined as follows: a type $T1$ is a subtype of another type $T2$ if all features of type $T1$ are also of type $T2$. This is denoted by $T1 \leq T2$. We compare types by using the two rules:

$$
\begin{aligned}
&T1 \cup \ldots \cup TN \leq U1 \cup \ldots \cup UM\\
&\qquad \text{if } \forall i \in 1..N,\ \exists j \in 1..M \text{ so that } Ti \leq Uj\\
&T1 \cap \ldots \cap TN \leq U1 \cap \ldots \cap UM\\
&\qquad \text{if } \forall i \in 1..M,\ \exists j \in 1..N \text{ so that } Tj \leq Ui
\end{aligned}
$$

- Inheritance relations between classes are defined according to the order relationships between types. The class associated with a type $T1$ inherits of the class associated with another type $T2$ if $T1 \leq T2$. Actually, subtyping relations denote inclusion polymorphism and correspond in the object oriented scheme to inheritance relations.

- Composition relations between classes are defined as follows: the class associated with a type T is composed of the classes associated with the types $T1$, $T2$, ..., Tn if there is a relationship $T = f(T1 \times T2 \times \ldots \times Tn)$ and $n \geq 2$.

The object oriented scheme corresponding to one of the examples of annex B is displayed in annex C.

4 Discussion

4.1 Further works

The algorithm that infers relationships between types has been implemented in Prolog, but we still have to produce a program that will use these relationships for modelling an object oriented scheme.

In some cases, all type information is not present in the Prolog program. Thus, the inferred object oriented scheme has to be interactively refined by the user, and a graphical editor would be useful. We plan to construct such an editor in order to support the design of an object oriented scheme that can be directly implemented in the Eiffel language.

The relationship inference sytem described in this paper has to be improved in order to better deal with the generic clauses. Hence, describing a type by means of its relationship with a parametric type can be meaningless. Let be the program:

eq(X,X).
p(A) :- f(B), eq(A,B).

The algorithm will infer the following relationships for this program:

$$Teq = eq(\ Teq(1) \times Teq(2)\ )$$
$$Teq(1) = X$$
$$Teq(2) = X$$
$$Tp = p(\ Tp(1)\ )$$
$$Tp(1) \leq Teq(1)$$

As $Teq(1)$ is related to the type variable X, the relationship $Tp(1) \leq Teq(1)$ is not enough accurate. In fact, when a parametric type T occurs in the right hand side of a relationhip, the type variables that are used in the relationship describing T should be instantiated when possible. In our example, one notices that the variable B expresses a local closure between $Tf(1)$ and $Teq(2)$. Thus, the variable X should be instantiated to $Tf(1)$, and the relationship that describes $Tp(1)$ becomes $Tp(1) \leq Teq(1)[X \leftarrow Tf(1)]$. We are currently investigating a generalization and automation of this reasoning.

We are also looking for a possible extension and improvement of the rules used for defining inheritance relations between types. At present, we can only compare non parametric nor recursive clauses and this is insufficient for treating real applications.

4.2 Related work

The integration of object oriented features into logic languages has been widely studied (e.g. [KTM87, MeN87, ANS89, AnP90, HoM90]). Besides the technical difficulties that arise when one tries to perform an effective preservation of both logic and object oriented qualities, a language integrating these two powerful paradigms also appears to be difficult to use [RuM90, Rue91]. Moreover, such a language would be likely to be less convenient for rapid prototyping than Prolog. Thus, instead of integrating the object oriented and logic paradigms into a new single language, we prefer to provide facilities for designing an object oriented program from a Prolog prototype.

The relationships inference system described in this paper is closely related to different work concerned with types and logic programming. Two main approaches of types in logic programming can be persued: a declarative one and an inferential one. We are going to illustrate them on the program of Figure 3.

```
man(a).          father(Father,Child) :- parent(Father,Child), man(Father).
man(b).          gd_father(GdF,GdC) :- father(GdF,C), parent(C,GdC).
woman(c).        person(P1) :- man(P1).
parent(b,a).     person(P2) :- woman(P2).
parent(a,c).     person(d).
parent(a,d).
```

Figure 3: Program example.

4.2.1 A declarative approach

Mycroft and O'Keefe have defined a type system for a large subset of Prolog, where the programmer has to declare the types of the functors and predicates [MyO84]. The program is then type-checked, with type reconstructions where necessary. The scheme of types allowed is given by the grammar:

$$Type ::= Tvar \mid Tcons(Type^{*})$$

so that *Tcons* denotes type constructors and *Tvar* type variables. The programmer declares the types of all the functors and predicates by using the following grammar:

$$Declaration ::= type\ Tcons(Tvar^{*}) \Rightarrow Functor(Type^{*}) \mid pred\ Predicate(Type^{*})$$

Different type declarations can correspond to the same program, depending on the programmer's intents. For example, Figure 4 gives a type declaration for the program example of Figure 3.

```
type Tperson => a, b, c, d     pred parent(Tperson,Tperson)
pred man(Tperson)              pred father(Tperson,Tperson)
pred woman(Tperson)            pred gd_father(Tperson,Tperson)
pred person(Tperson)
```

Figure 4: A type declaration for the program example of Figure 3.

4.2.2 An inferential approach

Mishra has proposed a type inference system that deals successfully with a restricted class of Prolog predicates (non polymorphic predicates), and that does not require any type definitions to be made by the user, nor does it require the types of predicates to be declared [Mis84]. Zobel and Azzoune also defined similar type inference systems, extended to generic predicates [Zob87, Azz89]. In all these works, types are viewed as subsets of the Herbrand Universe and approximate the domain of the values that a variable can take. Figure 5 describes the types corresponding to the program example of Figure 3 inferred by a type inference system à la Mishra.

man(T1)	with *T1* = $\{a,b\}$
woman(T2)	with *T2* = $\{c\}$
person(T3)	with *T3* = $\{a,b,c,d\}$
parent(T4,T5)	with *T4* = $\{a,b\}$ and *T5* = $\{a,c,d\}$
father(T6,T7)	with *T6* = $\{a,b\}$ and *T7* = $\{a,c,d\}$
gdfather(T8,T9)	with *T8* = $\{a,b\}$ and *T9* = $\{a,c,d\}$

Figure 5: Types inferred by a type inference system à la Mishra

Then, if we consider that U is a supertype of T if $U \supseteq T$, we obtain the hierarchy displayed by Figure 6.

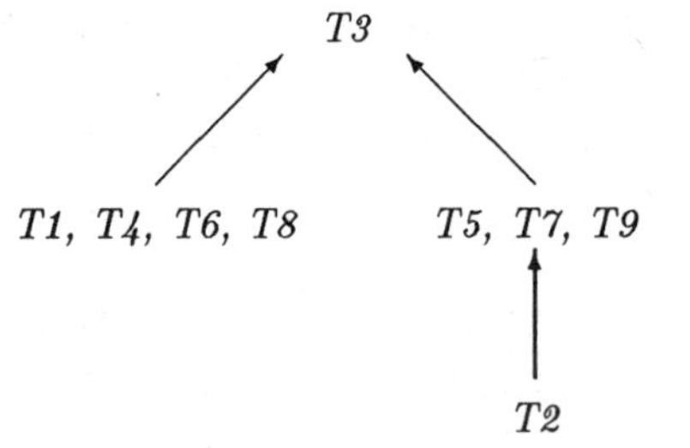

where $A \longrightarrow B$ means that A is a subtype of B

Figure 6: Inheritance hierarchy corresponding to the types of Figure 5.

4.2.3 Specificity of our approach

The motivations of our type system are different from the one of Mishra, Mycroft and O'Keefe. The goal of Microft and O'Keefe type system is to detect errors at compile time while Mishra's aim is to improve the program efficiency. The semantics of their type system would not be appropriate for inferring an object oriented scheme from a Prolog prototype:

- In a context of prototyping, explicit type declarations — like the one proposed by Mycroft and O'Keefe — are heavy and imply a loss of flexibility:

the declarations of Figure 4 are nearly as long as the typed program. Indeed, empirical evidence tends to show that such typed Prolog are not relevant for rapid prototyping [Rue91].

- The type inference system proposed by Mishra is not appropriate for specifying an object oriented structure because it does not capture relationships between types. Types are defined by sets of values, and thus, subtyping relationships between types are dependant on test cases. Moreover, overloading of constant symbols can lead to inconsistent subtyping relationships.

The relationship inference system described in this paper allows us to define a type by means of its relationships with other types expressed by Prolog clauses. These relationships do not depend on test sets but are inherent to the definition of the clauses. Thus, our type system properly captures inclusion polymorphism, and is well appropriate for designing an object oriented scheme. Of course, the emphasis on relationships between types is particularly relevant in our context, where the Prolog program is a prototype that has been validated by the customer and that constitutes a reference for the final program development. Actually, we are not interested in detection of errors, debugging or optimization but in specifying the structure of a program.

References

[AnP90] JM. Andreoli, R. Pareschi: *Linear objects: logical processes with built-in inheritance*, Proc. of the 7th ICLP 1990, pp 495-510

[ANS89] H. Ait-Kaci, R. Nasr, J. Seo: *Implementing a Knowledge Based Library Information System with Typed Horn Logic*, Information Processing and Management, Vol.25, No.4, 1989, 35p

[Azz89] H. Azzoune: *Types in Prolog. A type inference system and its applications* (in french), Thèse de Doctorat, Institut National Polytechnique de Grenoble, 1989, 177p

[Bal89] R. Balzer: *Draft Report on Requirements for a Common Prototyping System*, SIGPLAN Notices, Vol.24, No.3, 1989, pp 93-114

[Bra83] R.J. Brachman: *What IS-A is and isn't : an analysis of taxonomics links in semantics networks*, IEEE computer, 1983, pp 30-36

[CaW85] L. Cardelli, P. Wegner: *On understanding Types, Data Abstraction, and Polymorphism*, ACM Computing Surveys, Vol.17, No.14, 1985, pp 471-522

[Cox89] B. Cox: *Object oriented technology and the software industrial revolution... Necessary but sufficient*, Proc. of OOPSLA'89, Special issue of ACM SIGPLAN Notices, Vol.24, No.10, 1989, pp 510-522

[DaT88] S. Danforth, C. Tomlinson: *Type Theories and Object Oriented Programming*, ACM Computing surveys, Vol.20, No.1, 1988, pp 29-72

[Gal87] H. Gallaire: *Boosting Logic Programming*, Proc. of the 4th ICLP, MIT Press, 1987, pp 962-988

[HoM90] J.S. Hodas, D. Miller: *Representing objects in a logic programming language with scoping constructs*, Proc. of the 7th ICLP, 1990, pp 511-526

[KTM87] K. Kahn, E.D. Tribble, M.S. Miller et al.: *Vulcan: Logical Concurrent Objects*, in "Research directions in Object Oriented Programming", MIT Press, 1987, pp 75-112

[LeR89] B. Legeard, M. Rueher: *An approach for prototyping in Prolog* (in french), TSI Dunod, Vol.8, No.5, 1989, pp 423-438

[MeN87] P. Mello, A. Natali: *Objects as communicating Prolog units*, Proc. of the ECOOP'87, pp 233-243

[Mey88] B. Meyer: *Object Oriented Software Construction*, Prentice Hall, 1988, 534p

[Mis84] P. Mishra: *Towards a theory of types in Prolog*, Proc. of the IEEE Int. Symp. of LP, 1984, pp 289-298

[MyO84] A. Mycroft, R.A. O'Keefe: *A polymorphic type system for Prolog*, Artificial Intelligence (23), 1984, pp 295-307

[Rue91] M. Rueher: *Contribution à l'étude du prototypage exploratoire: vers une programmation multistyle*, Mémoire d'habilitation, Université de Nice Sophia Antipolis, 1991, 135p

[RuM90] M. Rueher, C. Michel: *Using objects evolution for software processes representation*, Proc. Software track HICSS23, IEEE Computer Society Press, 1990, pp 121-130

[Weg87] P. Wegner: *The Object Oriented Classification Paradigm*, in Research directions in object oriented programming, MIT Press, 1987, pp 481-560

[Weg90] P. Wegner: *Concepts and paradigms of Object Oriented Programming*, OOPS Messenger, Vol.1, No.1, 1990, ACM Press, pp 7-87

[Zob87] J. Zobel: *Derivation of polymorphic types for Prolog programs*, Proc. of the 4th ICLP, 1987, pp 817-838

A Algorithm

infer_type_relationships

S : a set of Relations $\leftarrow \emptyset$
For each predicate p of arity n, defined by the clauses *cl1*, ..., *clm*
  $S \leftarrow S + \{Tp = p(Tp(1) \times \ldots \times Tp(n))\}$
  For i in $1..n$: $S \leftarrow S + \{Tp(i) = type(i,cl1) \cup \ldots \cup type(i,clm)\}$
treat_recursive_relations
return S

type(*j*: a position, *p(X1,...,Xn) :- body*: a Prolog clause)
case the argument at position j in *p(X1,...,Xn)* is
- a constant c : return $\{c\}$
- a compound term *f(B1,...,Br)* :
  for k in $1..r$:
    Let the predicate p be defined by the clauses *cl1*, ..., *clm*,
    $S \leftarrow S + \{Tp(j.f(k)) = type(j.f(k),cl1) \cup \ldots \cup type(j.f(k),clm)\}$
  return $f(Tp(j.f(1)) \times \ldots \times Tp(j.f(r)))$
- a variable X :
  if X does not occurs in *body*
  then if X only occurs once in *p(X1,...,Xn)* or X = '_'
    then return 'μ' else return X
  else let X occurs k times in *body* :
    at the position *l1* in an atom *p1*,
    ...,
    at the position *lk* in an atom *pk*,
    if X is restricted in *body*,
    then $S \leftarrow S + \{T\_i \leq Tp1(l1) \cap \ldots \cap Tpk(lk)\}$
      return *T_i*
    else return $Tp1(l1) \cap \ldots \cap Tpk(lk)$

treat_recursive_relations

Each relation of S "$T = T \cup T1 \cup \ldots \cup Tn$" becomes "$T = T1 \cup \ldots \cup Tn$"
Each relation of S "$T = T$" becomes "$T = \mu$"
For all relations *R1*, ..., *Rn* of S so that :
  R1 is "$T1 = f1(T2) \cup T11 \cup \ldots$"
  R2 is "$T2 = f2(T3) \cup T21 \cup \ldots$"
  ...
  Rn is "$Tn = fn(T1) \cup Tn1 \cup \ldots$",
R1 becomes "$T1 = f1(f2(\,..(fn(T1) \cup Tn1 \cup ..)\,..) \cup T21 \cup ..) \cup T11 \cup ..$"
R2 becomes "$T2 = f2(f3(\,..(f1(T2) \cup T11 \cup ..)\,..) \cup T31 \cup ..) \cup T21 \cup ..$"
...
Rn becomes "$Tn = fn(f1(\,..(fm(Tn) \cup Tm1 \cup ..)\,..) \cup T11 \cup ..) \cup Tn1 \cup ..$"
  (where m is the abbreviation for $n\text{-}1$)

B Examples

B.1 Example 1: the member predicate

member(X1,cons(X1,_)).
member(X2,cons(_,L)) :- member(X2,L).

Before treating recursivity, the algorithm infers :
$Tmember = member(\ Tmember(1) \times Tmember(2)\ )$
$Tmember(1) = X1 \cup Tmember(1)$
$Tmember(2) = cons(\ Tmember(2.cons(1)) \times Tmember(2.cons(2))\ )$
$Tmember(2.cons(1)) = X1 \cup \mu$
$Tmember(2.cons(2)) = \mu \cup Tmember(2)$

The recursive relations become :
$Tmember(1) = X1$
$Tmember(2) = cons(\ Tmember(2.cons(1)) \times (\mu \cup Tmember(2))\ )$
$Tmember(2.cons(2)) = \mu \cup cons(Tmember(2.cons(1)) \times Tmember(2.cons(2)))$

These two last relations correspond to the infinite sets :
$Tmember(2) = \{cons(T,\mu), cons(T,cons(T,\mu)), cons(T,cons(T,cons(T,\mu))), \ldots\}$
$Tmember(2.cons(2)) = \{\mu, cons(T,\mu), cons(T,cons(T,\mu)), \ldots\}$
(where T is the abbreviation for $Tmember(2.cons(1))$).

B.2 Example 2: family relationships

man(a).
man(b).
woman(c).
parent(b,a).
parent(a,c).
parent(a,d).

father(Father,Child) :- parent(Father,Child), man(Father).
gd_father(GdF,GdC) :- father(GdF,C), parent(C,GdC).
person(P1) :- man(P1).
person(P2) :- woman(P2).
person(d).

Relations between types inferred by the algorithm are :
$Tman = man(\ Tman(1)\ )$ $\quad Tman(1) = \{a\} \cup \{b\}$
$Twoman = woman(\ Twoman(1)\ )$ $\quad Twoman(1) = \{c\}$
$Tperson = person(\ Tperson(1)\ )$ $\quad Tperson(1) = Tman(1) \cup Twoman(1) \cup \{d\}$
$Tparent = parent(\ Tparent(1) \times Tparent(2)\ )$
$Tparent(1) = \{b\} \cup \{a\}$
$Tparent(2) = \{a\} \cup \{c\} \cup \{d\}$
$Tfather = father(\ Tfather(1) \times Tfather(2)\ )$
$Tfather(1) = Tparent(1) \cap Tman(1)$
$Tfather(2) = T1$ % *Father* is a shared variable that restricts the resolution set of *Child*
$T1 \leq Tparent(2)$
$Tgd\_father = gd\_father(\ Tgd\_father(1) \times Tgd\_father(2)\ )$
$Tgd\_father(1) = T2$ % *C* is a shared variable that restricts the resolution set of *GdF*
$T2 \leq Tfather(1)$
$Tgd\_father(2) = T3$ % *C* is a shared variable that restricts the resolution set of *GdC*
$T3 \leq Tparent(2)$

C Object oriented scheme corresponding to the "family" example

C.1 Composition relationships

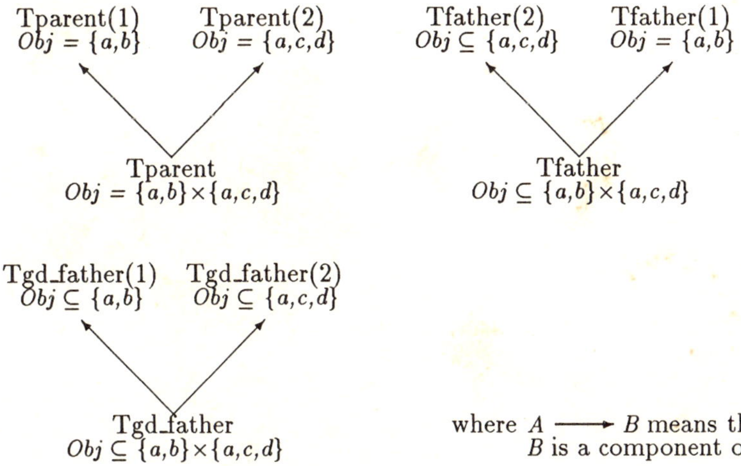

where $A \longrightarrow B$ means that B is a component of A

C.2 Inheritance hierarchy

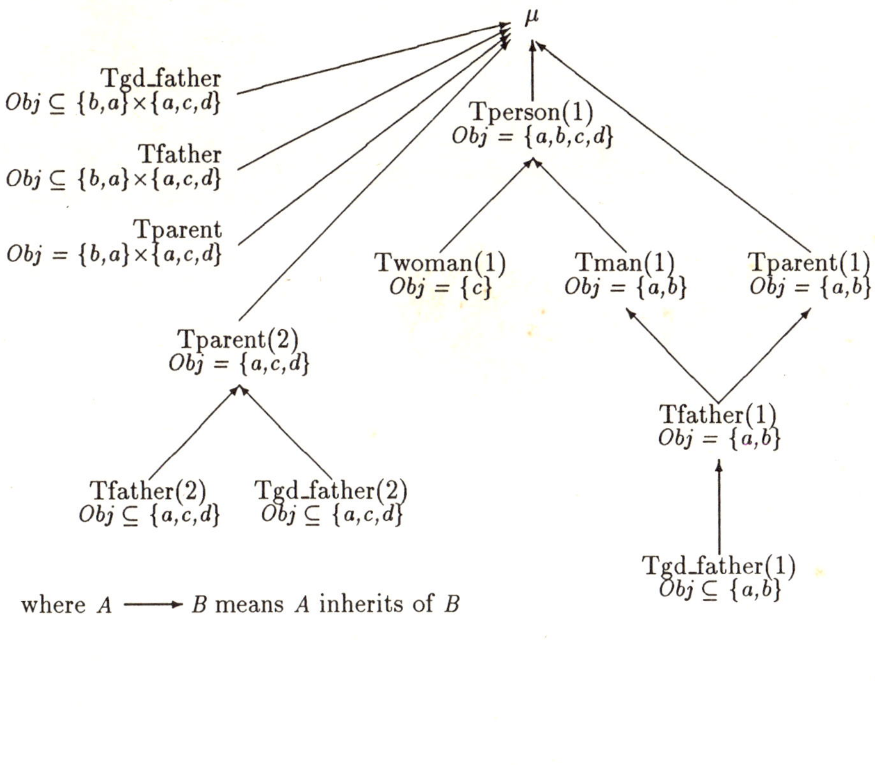

where $A \longrightarrow B$ means A inherits of B

Non-Determinism and Lazy Evaluation in Logic Programming

Sergio Antoy*

Department of Computer Science
Portland State University
Portland, OR 97207-0751
antoy@cs.pdx.edu

Abstract

We propose a transformation of term rewriting systems in logic programs. The systems we consider may be non-confluent and/or non-terminating. The programs we generate compute lazily. Our approach is based on a generalization of the concept of definitional trees. We propose an algorithm for code generation and discuss code optimization. We present a benchmark comparing the efficiency of various approaches to program design. We address the adequacy of Prolog to interpret the generated programs. We characterize a situation in which non-determinism and lazy evaluation do not mix well. We show the application of our ideas to two simple, but non-trivial problems.

1 Introduction

The transformation of term rewriting systems in logic programs has received considerable attention. Early work, summarized in [14], was directed toward prototyping algebraic specifications through their direct implementation and/or through the use of Prolog-supported automatic theorem provers. More recent efforts [5, 6] aim at the integration of functional and/or equational programs into logic programs. An extensive analysis and comparison of several transformation methods appears in [3]. These methods, all based on rewriting [11], follow two broad strategies in selecting redexes. The *innermost* strategy contracts a redex which has no proper sub-redexes and roughly corresponds to eager evaluation, the parameter passing mechanism called *by-value* in many programming languages. The *outermost* strategy contracts a redex which has no proper super-redexes and roughly corresponds to lazy evaluation or *call-by-need.*

[7] regards the latter as a fundamental attribute of modern functional programming languages, since it makes efficient use of computational resources and supports a programming style which includes infinite structures. For the same reasons this strategy is appealing in logic programming too. More interestingly, lazy evaluation plays a specific role in the composition or reuse of a class of logic programs. Motivating and illustrative examples will be provided later.

*This material is based upon work supported by the National Science Foundation Grant No. CCR-8908565.

The problem of knowing exactly which redexes must be reduced for computing a normal form is unsolvable [9] and many outermost methods, such as those reported in [3], tend to perform also unnecessary reductions. [12] first proposed an approach which, with some well-understood exceptions, reduces only needed redexes. This approach is not based on rewrite rules and requires a non-trivial semantic analysis of the logic program to ensure the correctness of the transformation and the laziness of the computations. [2] suggests a transformation scheme ¿from rewrite rules to logic programs which fully implements a lazy reduction strategy and is based on a syntactic property of a rewrite system expressed through the concept of *definitional tree*. This approach is limited to confluent term rewriting systems [8] and does not allow non-determinism. In this note we lift this limitation by generalizing the concept of definitional tree and extending the associated transformation scheme, and we analyze the effects of non-determinism on the computations of the generated programs.

2 Preliminaries and Notations

We consider a term rewriting system $\mathcal{R}$ with a many-sorted signature partitioned into a set $\mathcal{C}$ of *constructors* and a set $\mathcal{D}$ of *(defined) operations*. We assume an arbitrary, but fixed ordering, called *standard*, among the constructors of each sort. The rules of $\mathcal{R}$ are characterized below.

$\mathcal{X}$ denotes a set of sorted variables. Variables are denoted by upper case letters or, when anonymous, by the symbol "_". $T(\Sigma)$ is the set of terms built over the signature Σ. Any term referred to in this note type checks. The leading symbol or principal functor of a term t is called *root* of t. The elements of $T(\mathcal{C})$, $T(\mathcal{C} \cup \mathcal{X})$, and $T(\mathcal{C} \cup \mathcal{D})$ are respectively called *values*, *constructor terms*, and *ground terms*. A term t of the form $f(x_1, \ldots, x_n)$, where f is an operation and the arguments are constructor terms is called *f-rooted constructor term*. The rules in $\mathcal{R}$ are characterized by having an operation-rooted constructor term as lhs, i.e. $\mathcal{R}$ follows the constructor discipline.

An *occurrence* is a path identifying a subterm in a term. An occurrence of a term t is either the empty string, which is denoted by Λ and identifies t itself, or is $o{\cdot}i$, for some occurrence o and positive integer i, and identifies the i-th argument of the subterm of t identified by o. For terms t and t', occurrence o, and variable X, t/o denotes the subterm of t identified by (at) o; $t[o \leftarrow t']$ denotes the term obtained by replacing the subterm t/o by t'; and $\{t'/X\}t$ denotes the term obtained by substituting every occurrence of X in t by t'.

3 Transformation

A generalized definitional tree of an operation f in a term rewriting system $\mathcal{R}$ is a structure containing the set of rules defining f in $\mathcal{R}$, i.e. those having f as root of the lhs. This structure is the basis of a transformation scheme ¿from rewrite rules to Horn clauses described below. A less general form of this concept is described in [2].

Definition 1 A *generalized partial definitional tree* (abbreviated *gpdt*) is a 4-tuple $\langle l, s, o, d\rangle$, where:

l is the left side of a rewrite rule,

s is a set of right sides for l,

o is either Λ or the occurrence of a variable in l,

d is a list of *gpdt*'s depending on o as follows: if $o = \Lambda$, then d is the empty list; otherwise if u is the sort of l/o and $c_1, \ldots, c_k$ are the constructors of u, in standard ordering, then $d = d_1, \ldots, d_k$ and for all i, $1 \leq i \leq k$, the first component of d_i is $l[o \leftarrow c_i(X_1, \ldots, X_{a_i})]$, where a_i is the arity of c_i and $X_1, \ldots, X_{a_i}$ are new variables.

Definition 2 A *generalized definitional tree* is a pair $\langle f, d \rangle$ where f is a k-ary operation and d is a *gpdt* such that the first component of d is $f(X_1, \ldots, X_k)$, where $X_1, \ldots, X_k$ are distinct variables.

If $\langle f, d \rangle$ is a generalized definitional tree, with some abuse of terminology, we call d a generalized definitional tree of f. A *gpdt* of the form $\langle l, s, \Lambda, [] \rangle$ is more conveniently denoted by $\langle l, s \rangle$.

The following rewrite rules non-deterministically compute a permutation of a list. Lists are denoted in the usual Prolog notation. The operation *insert* makes a non-deterministic choice. On input an element e and a list l, *insert* either returns a list with e as head and l as tail, or if l evaluates to some non-empty list $[h|t]$, *insert* returns a list with h as head and $insert(e, t)$ as tail.

$$\begin{aligned} permute([]) &\to [] \\ permute([H|T]) &\to insert(H, permute(T)) \\ insert(E, L) &\to [E|L] \\ insert(E, [H|T]) &\to [H|insert(E, T)] \end{aligned} \tag{1}$$

The sets of rules defining each operation are organized in the following generalized definitional tree, where $\{\}$ denotes the empty set.

$$\begin{aligned} &\langle permute(\_), \{\}, 1, [\langle permute([]), \{[]\}\rangle, \\ &\qquad\qquad \langle permute([H|T]), \{insert(H, permute(T))\}\rangle]\rangle \\ &\langle insert(E, L), \{[E|L]\}, 2, [\langle insert(E, []), \{\}\rangle, \\ &\qquad\qquad \langle insert(E, [H|T]), \{[H|insert(E, T)]\}\rangle]\rangle \end{aligned} \tag{2}$$

A generalized definitional tree is pictorially represented by a tree-like structure easier to read than the corresponding 4-tuple representation. The trees of display (2) are pictorially represented in figure 1. The transformation of a term rewriting system $\mathcal{R}$ in a logic program $\mathcal{H}_\mathcal{R}$ is based on the algorithm shown, in Ada-like syntax, in figure 2. The procedure *Translate* takes a *gpdt* d as input and outputs a set of Horn clauses "generated by" d. These clauses contain only one binary predicate denoted by the infix symbol $\Rightarrow$. The logic program $\mathcal{H}_\mathcal{R}$ is the union of the clauses generated by applying the procedure *Translate* to the generalized definitional trees of all the operations in $\mathcal{R}$, plus a few additional clauses described later.

The procedure *Translate* applied to the generalized definitional trees of *permute* and *insert* generates the following clauses shown in Edinburgh Prolog

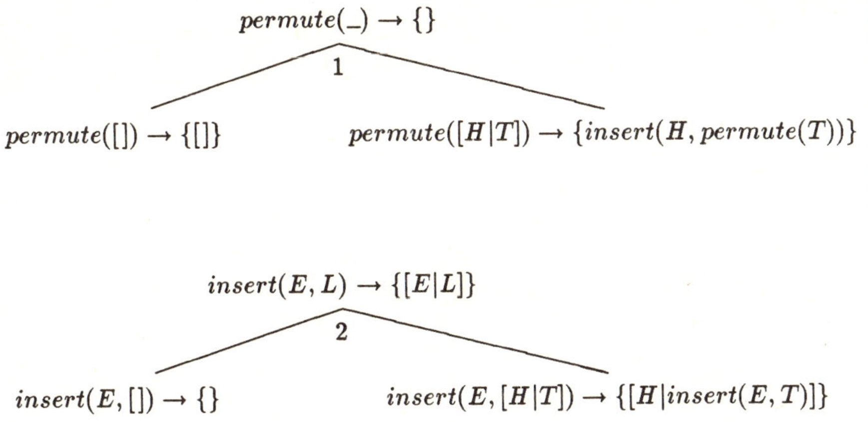

Figure 1: Pictorial representations of the definitional trees of the operations *insert* and *permute* defined in display (1) and represented by 4-tuples in display (2). Each node represents a possibly empty set of rewrite rules sharing a common left side. The occurrence below a branch node identifies the variable of the left side instantiated in the node's children.

syntax [4].

```
permute([]) ==> [] .
permute([A|B]) ==> C :- insert(A,permute(B)) ==> C .
permute(A) ==> B :- A ==> C , permute(C) ==> B .
insert(A,B) ==> [A|B] .
insert(A,[B|C]) ==> [B|insert(A,C)] .
insert(A,B) ==> C :- B ==> D , insert(A,D) ==> C .
```
(3)

4 Evaluation

The relation $\Rightarrow$ satisfies a *simplification* property which is crucial to our treatment. First observe that for any ground terms t and t', if $t \Rightarrow t'$, then $t \overset{*}{\rightarrow} t'$. Following [12], we refer to this condition as *soundness* and further elaborate on it in the next section. We discuss the simplification property now, since it justifies why we need to augment $\mathcal{H}_{\mathcal{R}}$ with a few clauses not generated by the procedure *Translate*.

Soundness. The relation $\Rightarrow$ on ground terms is contained in the relation $\overset{*}{\rightarrow}$.

Simplification Property. For any ground terms t and t', if $t \Rightarrow t'$, then t is operation-rooted and t' is constructor-rooted.

The proof of both claims is by structural induction on a proof tree [16] of a goal $t \Rightarrow t'$, for any two ground terms t and t'. A constructor-rooted term is also called *root stable* [13] or *head normal form*, since its outermost portion is

```
Procedure Translate(d : gpdt) is
  -- The output is a set of Horn clauses
  -- Assume d = ⟨l, s, o, d'⟩
  -- Let X, Y, Z, X_1, ..., X_k ... be new variables
begin
  for each term r in s loop
    case r is
      when r is constructor-rooted:
        output l ⇒ r;
      when r is operation-rooted:
        output l ⇒ X :- r ⇒ X;
      when r is a variable:
        for each constructor c of the sort of r loop
          output {c(X_1, ..., X_k)/r}(l ⇒ r);
        end loop;
        output l ⇒ X :- r ⇒ X;
    end case;
  end loop;
  for each gpdt d'' in d' loop
    Translate(d'');
  end loop;
  output l[o ← Z] ⇒ X :- Z ⇒ Y, l[o ← Y] ⇒ X;
end Translate;
```

Figure 2: Algorithm for the transformation of a generalized definitional tree in a set of clauses.

in normal form. Thus, $\Rightarrow$ "reduces" a term enough to determine the root of its normal form and formalizes a notion of *useful simplification* introduced in [12]. In our framework this notion is more general, since it is independent of any type, rather than being limited to lists, and it is uniformly lazy, rather than being strict in the first argument of *cons*.

Through a sequence of useful simplifications we attempt to compute the normal form of a ground term t. For this task we need a "driver" which repeatedly applies $\Rightarrow$ to some subexpression of t which needs to be simplified. This driver is implemented by another binary relation denoted by the infix symbol $\twoheadrightarrow$ and defined below. Intuitively, the driver "skips over" the constructors of a term and applies $\Rightarrow$ to any operation-rooted subterm.

Definition 3 For all ground terms t and t', $t \twoheadrightarrow t'$ if and only if one of the following conditions holds:

1. $t' = c(t'_1, \ldots, t'_k)$, if $t = c(t_1, \ldots, t_k)$ for some constructor c and terms $t_1, \ldots, t_k$, for some $k \geq 0$, and for all i, $1 \leq i \leq k$, $t_i \twoheadrightarrow t'_i$,
2. $t \Rightarrow t''$ and $t'' \twoheadrightarrow t'$, for some term t''.

The logic implementation of the relation $\twoheadrightarrow$ requires one clause to satisfy condition 2 and, for each constructor in $\mathcal{R}$, one clause to satisfy condition 1. The driver for the clauses of display (3) follow.

```
[] ->> [] .
[A|B] ->> [C|D] :- A ->> C , B ->> D .          (4)
A ->> B :- A ==> C , C ->> B .
```

We show in an example how to use the clauses of displays (3) and (4). A permutation of a list l is computed by satisfying the goal $permute(l) \twoheadrightarrow T$. If $l = [x_1, \ldots, x_k]$ and each x_i has a normal form, then the satisfaction of the goal instantiates T to some permutation of $[\bar{x}_1, \ldots, \bar{x}_i]$, where for all i, $1 \leq i \leq k$, $\bar{x}_i$ is a normal form of x_i. Through backtracking we generate each permutation exactly once.

5 Correctness

Informally, the transformation performed by the procedure *Translate* is correct when any result computed in $\mathcal{H}_{\mathcal{R}}$ is computed in $\mathcal{R}$ and vice versa. We refer to the first condition as *soundness* and to the second one as *completeness*. We need to refine the latter, since our transformation desirably constrains some non-determinism of $\mathcal{R}$ to improve efficiency. In the following we propose our notions of soundness and completeness, justify their appropriateness for our transformation, and briefly sketch why they hold in the hypotheses we are considering.

Soundness. The relation $\twoheadrightarrow$ on ground terms is contained in the relation $\overset{*}{\rightarrow}$.

Thus, both relations $\Rightarrow$ and $\twoheadrightarrow$ are sound in the most straightforward sense. The proof of the soundness of $\twoheadrightarrow$ is by structural induction on a proof tree of a goal $t \twoheadrightarrow t'$, for any two ground terms t and t', and it is based on the soundness of $\Rightarrow$.

Completeness. The relation $\overset{*}{\rightarrow}$ on $T(\Sigma) \times T(C)$ is contained in $\twoheadrightarrow$.

In other words, for any ground term t and value v, if $t \overset{*}{\rightarrow} v$, then $t \twoheadrightarrow v$. The containment of both relations $\Rightarrow$ and $\twoheadrightarrow$ in $\overset{*}{\rightarrow}$ is strict. In general $t \overset{*}{\rightarrow} t'$, for some ground terms t and t', does not imply $t \Rightarrow t'$ or $t \twoheadrightarrow t'$. Informally speaking, $\Rightarrow$ is a specialization of $\overset{*}{\rightarrow}$ concerned with the simplification of a term and $t \Rightarrow t'$ holds only if t' is obtained by an "outermost" simplification of t'. Similarly, $\twoheadrightarrow$ is the specialization of $\overset{*}{\rightarrow}$ concerned with the "result" of a computation represented by t. For example, for every term t, $t \overset{*}{\rightarrow} t$, but $t \not\Rightarrow t$ and $t \twoheadrightarrow t$ only if t is a value. Note that the constructor discipline implies that any value is a normal form, but not vice versa. Normal forms which are not values are undesirable in constructor systems and the relation $\twoheadrightarrow$ properly captures this fact.

To prove the completeness of $\twoheadrightarrow$ we rely on the fact that the notion of descendant of a redex [9] is meaningful in the class of systems under consideration. Intuitively, suppose we have a reduction sequence $t \overset{*}{\rightarrow} t'$ and a subterm s of t. The descendants of s in t' are computed as follows. Underline the root of s and perform the reduction sequence $t \overset{*}{\rightarrow} t'$. The descendants of s in t' are the subterms of t' which have an underlined root [11]. Furthermore, we rely on a non-deterministic variation of the *Parallel Moves Lemma* [9]. Suppose that a term t has two distinct redex occurrences, o and p, reducible by the rewrite rules $l_o \rightarrow r_o$ and $l_p \rightarrow r_p$ respectively, and let t_o and t_p be the corresponding reducts. Then, both t_o and t_p are reducible to some term t'. To reduce t_o to t' we reduce each descendant of p in t_o by the rule $l_p \rightarrow r_p$. The symmetric situation holds for t_p. Let us consider "equivalent" these reductions of t to t'

The completeness of $\twoheadrightarrow$ is proved as follows. Let α be a reduction sequence of t to v. In the class of reductions equivalent to α there is an element $\bar{\alpha}$ which reduces t to v with the "least amount" of work[1]. Each reduction step of $\bar{\alpha}$ is associated to a reduction step in α involving the "same" redex (possibly having multiple instances) and the same rewrite rule, but loosely speaking, $\bar{\alpha}$ contracts shallow redexes first. The proof of completeness is by induction on the length of the least costly reduction sequence of t to v.

6 Non-Determinism

In this section we address pragmatic issues related to non-determinism and the ability to compute with programs generated by our transformation. Prolog's depth-first search strategy is, with two exceptions discussed shortly, incomplete to implement $\twoheadrightarrow$. The reason is that Prolog's computation rule is inherently sequential, while the class of rewrite systems we consider is not.

Prolog is complete for a restricted class of rewrite systems, namely those whose operations admit a *definitional tree* [2]. A definitional tree is a generalized definitional tree in which the second component of the 4-tuple, i.e. the set of rhs', is empty in a branch node and is a singleton in a leaf node. For example, the tree of the operation *permute* in figure 1 satisfies this condition. A system in this class is sequential [9] and a computation in such a system has at most one result. A logic program generated by the procedure *Translate* ¿from a system in this class reduces only needed redexes [2]. This implies that if a term t has a normal form in $\mathcal{R}$ (more intuitively, a computation has a result), then a Prolog interpreter satisfies the goal $t \twoheadrightarrow T$ by instantiating T to the normal form of t. Furthermore, this computation is optimal in the sense that no redex is unnecessarily reduced.

The other situation in which Prolog adequately implements $\twoheadrightarrow$ is when $\mathcal{R}$ is terminating. This is trivial, since any computation in $\mathcal{H}_\mathcal{R}$ is terminating too. If we desire to compute all the normal forms of a term, then the programs generated by the procedure *Translate* can be optimized by the cut. Let $d = \langle l, s, o, d' \rangle$ be the input of the procedure. Any two clauses generated by distinct subtrees of d are mutually exclusive. In fact, if $l_1 \Rightarrow r_1$ and $l_2 \Rightarrow r_2$ are the heads of two such clauses, then the roots of the subterms of l_1 and l_2 at o are distinct non-variable symbols. Thus any term t which unifies with l_1 does not unify with l_2, and vice versa. Similarly, any clause c_1 generated by the recursive invocation of *Translate* at line 20 is mutually exclusive with the clause c_2 generated at line 22. In fact, if $l_1 \Rightarrow r_1$ and $l_2 \Rightarrow r_2$ are the heads of c_1 and c_2 respectively, then the roots of the subterms of l_1 and l_2 at o are

[1] The number of reduction steps of $\bar{\alpha}$ is not necessary the minimum in its class. Our intuitive description relies on the convention that shallow redexes are less expensive to reduce than deep ones.

respectively a constructor and a variable. If the first subgoal of c_2 succeeds, then, by the simplification property of $\Rightarrow$, such a variable is instantiated to an operation-rooted term. Thus, any goal succeeding via c_1 cannot succeed via c_2 and vice versa. Accordingly, the code of display (3) is optimized as follows.

```
permute([]) ==> [] :- ! .
permute([A|B]) ==> C :- ! , insert(A,permute(B)) ==> C .
permute(A) ==> B :- A ==> C , permute(C) ==> B .
insert(A,B) ==> [A|B] .                                        (5)
insert(A,[B|C]) ==> [B|insert(A,C)] :- ! .
insert(A,B) ==> [C|insert(A,D)] :- B ==> [C|D] .
```

Similarly, it is easy to see, using the simplification property of $\Rightarrow$, that the clauses implementing the relation $\twoheadrightarrow$ are mutually exclusive as well. Accordingly, the code of display (4) is optimized as follows.

```
[] ->> [] :- ! .
[A|B] ->> [C|D] :- ! , A ->> C , B ->> D .                     (6)
A ->> B :- A ==> C , C ->> B .
```

Combining non-determinism with lazy evaluation has one non-obvious interaction. Consider the following system, where the constructors of the natural numbers are denoted 0 and *succ*. The symbol "1" is a shorthand for *succ*(0).

$$\begin{aligned} \mathit{flip} &\rightarrow 0 \\ \mathit{flip} &\rightarrow 1 \\ 0 + Y &\rightarrow Y \\ \mathit{succ}(X) + Y &\rightarrow \mathit{succ}(X+Y) \\ \mathit{double}(Z) &\rightarrow Z + Z \end{aligned} \tag{7}$$

The operation *flip* non-deterministically returns either 0 or 1. The operation *double* doubles its argument using addition. The lazy evaluation of the term *double*(*flip*) goes through *flip*+*flip* and eventually yields some value in $\{0, 1, 2\}$, which might not be the intended behavior. The situation stems from the non-linearity of the rhs of the rule defining *double*. Using only eager evaluation the value of *double* cannot be 1 for any argument.

Our final consideration concerns the coexistence, within the same program, of code generated by the procedure *Translate* with handwritten code. This is a standard technique in many transformational approaches, often it is a necessity for using built-in predicates or types, e.g. numbers [12, 18]. In our situation, this technique offers the possibility of integrating lazy with eager evaluation. Our transformation is inherently simple and the programs generated by the procedure *Translate* are easy to read and hence to modify. The program presented in the appendix shows this possibility. In the benchmark of the next section, all the programs resulting from a transformation, i.e. (3), (4), and (5), share mechanically generated code with handwritten one.

7 Benchmark

We use the well-known N queens problem to informally measure the time efficiency of the logic programs generated by our transformation. We compare the performance of 5 programs to solve the problem.

(1) Naive

The "naive" generate-and-test program described in [16, Program 14.2]. The predicate *range* is eliminated for compatibility with the other programs involved in the experiment. The predicate *queens* is called with $[1, 2, \ldots N]$ as first argument, computes a permutation of it, and checks whether it is *safe*.

(2) Accumulator

An improved version of program (1), described in [16, Program 14.3], which pushes the tester inside the generator. This program does not compute the permutations of $[1, 2, \ldots N]$, rather it checks the safety of a (possibly incomplete) configuration as soon as a queen is placed on the board. Thus, it implements an *ad hoc* form of lazy evaluation.

(3) Narain

The program presented in [12, page 263]. Lazy evaluation is limited to tails of lists. All other computations are eager, for example the predicate *noattack* is defined as

```
noattack(Q1,Q2,N) :- Q1>Q2, Diff is Q1-Q2, Diff \== N.
noattack(Q1,Q2,N) :- Q1<Q2, Diff is Q2-Q1, Diff \== N.     (8)
```

(4) Actual

The program generated by the procedure *Translate* on input the rewrite rules of display (1) and the following ones.

$$\begin{aligned}
queens(L) &\to safe(permute(L)) \\
safe([]) &\to [] \\
safe([Q|L]) &\to [Q|safe(nodiagonal(Q, L, 1))] \\
nodiagonal(_, [], _) &\to [] \\
nodiagonal(Q, [H|L], N) &\to [noattack(Q, H, N)|nodiagonal(Q, L, N+1)]
\end{aligned} \tag{9}$$

Although Narain's method is not based on rewriting, the above set of rules is *de facto* derived from [12]. For compatibility with Narain's program, we adopt the same evaluation strategy. In particular, we use the same *noattack* predicate and we replace the second clause of the driver, display (6), with the following one

```
[A|B] ->> [A|C] :- ! , B ->> C .     (10)
```

since each operation yielding a list yields a list whose first element is a normal form when the operation's arguments satisfy the same property.

(5) vEM

The program generated by the *vEM* transformation [18] applied to the same rules used to generate program (4). This transformation implements a non-deterministic innermost reduction strategy. For compatibility with the other programs of the benchmark, this program too uses the same *noattack* predicate.

The following table shows the time that each program takes to compute all the solutions to the N queens problem, for N ranging from 4 to 8. The environment is a Sequent S27 under Dynix running C-Prolog version 1.4. The tabular entries show, in seconds, the sum of user plus system times.

N	4	5	6	7	8
Accumulator	0.3	0.6	2.0	8.2	36.3
Actual	0.6	1.3	3.7	15.5	69.3
Narain	0.5	1.4	4.2	17.3	75.2
vEM	0.3	1.1	6.5	51.9	512.2
Naive	0.4	1.4	8.3	64.0	595.7

(11)

This limited experiment shows that the procedure *Translate* generates logic programs whose efficiency is competitive with those generated by other transformation schemes. This program is representative of a class of problems involving search known as *generate-and-test*, a common technique in algorithm design. Logic programming provides, with backtracking, an ideal environment for the application of this technique. Unfortunately, as the *Naive* program shows, this approach can be prohibitively inefficient. The *Accumulator* program shows an impressive improvement in performance, but has a downside: "the test is completely intertwined with the generator" [16]. Thus, reuse of code becomes impossible and programs become more difficult to write and understand. By contrast, our approach promotes transparent reuse of code with a slight penalty in efficiency, less than a factor 2, with respect to a carefully handcrafted solution.

8 Scope

Our transformation requires rewrite systems that both follow the constructor discipline and admit generalized definitional trees for each operation. In this section we try to assess how limiting these conditions are.

Constructor systems are the underlying model of several functional programming languages. Often using constructor systems is a convenience rather than a limitation. Systems not based on constructors are used, for example, for symbolic simplification and aspects of theorem proving. Our method is not directly applicable to such systems. However, [17] shows that any system can be transformed in an equivalent one satisfying the constructor discipline. We have not investigated the interactions of Thatte's transformation with our second requirement: the existence of generalized definitional trees.

The existence of a generalized definitional tree for each operation is a more stringent condition. Still, it does not appear particularly limiting. Definitional trees are obtained as a by-product of a design strategy for rewrite rules presented in [1]. This strategy, discussed only for deterministic and completely defined operations, extends naturally to more general situations. This work also shows that for certain large classes of functions, for example the binary functions on natural numbers, deterministic and complete definitions imply the existence of definitional trees.

However, there exist simple, plausible definitions of operations that do not admit generalized definitional trees. In some of these situations we might find alternate sets of rules that define the same operations and admit generalized definitional trees. For example, consider the following rewrite rules defining logic disjunction of boolean values with a technique referred to as "parallel or". The name stems from the fact that if either argument of *or* yields *true*, then the result of the computation becomes known. This set of rules has no generalized definitional tree.

$$\begin{aligned} or(true, \_) &\rightarrow true \\ or(\_, true) &\rightarrow true \\ or(false, false) &\rightarrow false \end{aligned} \tag{12}$$

A definition of boolean conjunction for which there exists a definitional tree is trivial and can be obtained with the help of the strategy defined in [1]. Two such definitions, or_1 and or_2, appears below. Contrary to *or*, the operation or_i needs to evaluate its i-th argument no matter what the value of the other argument is, thus it may fail to terminate for some inputs on which *or* yields a result. A new operation *or* somewhat equivalent to the old one, is defined below through or_1 and or_2.

$$\begin{aligned} or(X,Y) &\rightarrow or_1(X,Y) \\ or(X,Y) &\rightarrow or_2(X,Y) \\ or_1(false,Y) &\rightarrow Y \\ or_1(true,\_) &\rightarrow true \\ or_2(X,false) &\rightarrow X \\ or_2(\_,true) &\rightarrow true \end{aligned} \tag{13}$$

The sets of rules (12) and (13) are equivalent in the following sense. In both systems, for any ground terms t_1 and t_2, the sets of values computed from $or(t_1, t_2)$ are the same and the computation involves a non-deterministic choice. The difference is that in (13) the choice of which argument of *or* should be evaluated first is made by chosing a rule. Neither argument of *or* is *needed* in a technical sense [9], though in practice we may not be able to compute a normal form without evaluating, at least partially, both [10, 11, 15].

We have not investigated the conditions for a system under which there exists another system in which every operation admits a generalized definitional tree nor the extent to which the second system can be automatically obtained from the first one.

9 Concluding Remarks

We have described a simple and general transformation scheme of rewrite systems in logic programs. Our transformation starts from an organization of rewrite rules which generalizes a previously proposed notion of definitional tree and significantly extends the class of system which can be transformed. Our approach is based on two relations only: $\Rightarrow$, which extends a previously proposed notion of useful simplification, and $\twoheadrightarrow$ which drives the application of $\Rightarrow$ to the appropriate subterms of a term. The code produced by our transformation is efficient and coexists with handwritten code, thus offering the possibility of combining lazy with eager evaluation. We have characterized two situations in which Prolog adequately interprets the programs generated by our transformation scheme and we have discussed some code optimizations in these situations.

We offer a solution to two problems left open in [12]: to formalize lazy evaluation to general data structures and to integrate it with non-determinism. The solution to the first problem is comprehensive and satisfactory. However, the example of display (7) seems to indicate that non-determinism and lazy evaluation do not mix well in systems lacking right linearity. This is not a specific problem of our transformation scheme. The programs of the benchmark solve the problem by keeping non-linear variables in normal form. We believe that programmers should not be concerned about the evaluation strategy of a logic programming system and a more general solution is needed. A possibility lies in "identifying" all the descendants of a variable so that, for example, *double*(*flip*) evaluates only to either 0 or 2, whereas *flip* + *flip* can still yield 1 too. The effectiveness of this approach needs further investigation. ¿From an implementation point of view the approach seems practical and convenient. Multiple descendants of the same variable share the same content with the advantage of preventing the repeated evaluation of the expression instantiating the variable.

References

[1] Sergio Antoy. Design strategies for rewrite rules. In *CTRS'90*, Montreal, Canada, June 1990. LNCS 516.

[2] Sergio Antoy. Lazy evaluation in logic. In *PLILP'91*, Passau, Germany, August 1991, 371-382. LNCS 528.

[3] L. G. Bouma and H. R. Walters. Implementing algebraic specifications. In J. A. Bergstra, J. Heering, and P. Klint, editors, *Algebraic Specification*, chapter 5. Addison-Wesley, Wokingham, England, 1989.

[4] W. F. Clocksin and C. S. Mellish. *Programming in Prolog*. Springer-Verlag, Berlin, second edition, 1984.

[5] Doug DeGroot and Gary Lindstrom, editors. *Logic Programming: Functions, Relations, and Equations*, Englewood Cliffs, NJ, 1986. Prentice-Hall.

[6] S. Hölldobler. *Foundation of Equational Logic Programming*. Springer-Verlag, Berlin, 1989. Lect. Notes in Artificial Intelligence, Vol. 353.

[7] Paul Hudak. Conception, evolution, and application of functional programming languages. *Computing Surveys*, 21:359–411, 1989.

[8] Gérard Huet. Confluent reductions: Abstract properties and applications to term-rewriting systems. *JACM*, 27:797–821, 1980.

[9] Gérard Huet and Jean-Jacques Lévy. Call by need computations in non-ambiguous linear term rewriting systems. Technical Report 359, INRIA, Le Chesnay, France, 1979.

[10] J. R. Kenneway. Sequential evaluation strategies for parallel-or and related reduction systems. *Annals of Pure and Applied Logics*, 43:31–56, 1989.

[11] Jan Willem Klop. Term rewriting systems. Technical Report CS-R9073, Stichting Mathematisch Centrum, Amsterdam, The Netherlands, 1990.

[12] Sanjai Narain. A technique for doing lazy evaluation in logic. *The Journal of Logic Programming*, 3:259–276, 1986.

[13] Michael J. O'Donnell. *Equational Logic as a Programming Language*. MIT Press, 1985.

[14] H. Petzsch. Automatic prototyping of algebraic specifications using Prolog. In *Recent Trends in Data Type Specification*, pages 207–223. 3rd Workshop on Theory and Applications of Abstract Data Types, Springer-Verlag, 1985.

[15] R. C. Sekar and I. V. Ramakrishnan. Programming in equational logic: Beyond strong sequentiality. In *Proceedings of the Fifth Annual IEEE Symposium on Logic in Computer Science*, pages 230–241, Philadelphia, PA, June 1990.

[16] Leon Sterling and Ehud Shapiro. *The Art of Prolog*. The MIT Press, Cambridge, MA, 1986.

[17] Satish Thatte. On the correspondence between two classes of reduction systems. *Information Processing Letters*, 20:83–85, 1985.

[18] Maarten H. van Emden and Keitaro Yukawa. Logic programming with equations. *The Journal of Logic Programming*, 4:265–288, 1987.

[19] Nicklaus Wirth. *Systematic Programming: An Introduction*. Prentice-Hall, Englewood Cliffs, NJ, 1973.

Appendix

No Equal Subsequence Problem

The problem is to construct a sequence of some given length ¿from the alphabet $\{\clubsuit, \diamondsuit, \heartsuit\}$ such that it contains no adjacent equal subsequences [19]. Examples of such sequences are the null sequence, $\clubsuit$, $\clubsuit\diamondsuit$, $\clubsuit\diamondsuit\clubsuit$, and so on. Some invalid sequences are $\clubsuit\clubsuit$, $\clubsuit\diamondsuit\clubsuit\clubsuit$, $\clubsuit\diamondsuit\clubsuit\diamondsuit$, and $\clubsuit\diamondsuit\diamondsuit$. A rewrite system to compute valid sequences is proposed below.

$$
\begin{aligned}
sequence(0) &\rightarrow [\,] \\
sequence(succ(A)) &\rightarrow valid([pick|sequence(A)]) \\
valid(A) &\rightarrow if\_then(ness(succ(0), \\
&\qquad\qquad length(A)/2, A, tail(A)), A) \\
tail([\_|A]) &\rightarrow A \\
if\_then(true, A) &\rightarrow A \\
ness(A, B, C, D) &\rightarrow A > B \vee no\_prefix(A, C, D) \wedge \\
&\qquad\qquad ness(succ(A), B, C, tail(D)) \\
no\_prefix(succ(A), [B|C], [D|E]) &\rightarrow B \neq D \vee no\_prefix(A, C, E) \\
pick &\rightarrow \clubsuit \\
pick &\rightarrow \diamondsuit \\
pick &\rightarrow \heartsuit
\end{aligned}
$$

The operation *sequence* applied to argument l returns a valid sequence of length l. On positive arguments *sequence* extends a valid sequence by non-deterministically choosing the first symbol and ensuring the validity of the choice. The validity test is controlled by the operation *valid*. The rule defining *valid* has a non-linear variable, A, with a non-deterministic value. The clause generated by this rule is patched to ensure that all the occurrences of A share the same value. The operation *if_then* applied to b and s returns (a reduct of) s if and only if b evaluates to *true*. The operation is incomplete, if b does not evaluate to *true*, then $if\_then(b, s)$ is not reducible to any head normal form term. We take advantage of this incompleteness, through our definition of completeness of $\twoheadrightarrow$, to reject invalid sequences. The operation *ness* applied to a, b, c, and d returns *true* if and only if in c any prefix of length up to b is not immediately followed by itself. b is one half of the length of c. a is the length of the prefix, it ranges from 1 to b. d is the subsequence of c starting at the $a+1$-th position. The operation *no_prefix* applied to arguments l, m, and n, returns *true* if and only if $l > 0$ and the prefix of m of length l is not a prefix of n, otherwise it fails to return a head normal form term. The operation *pick* non-deterministically selects a character of the alphabet.

The remaining operations, i.e. length of a list, integer division by 2, and boolean and relational operators have complete, linear rules. Boolean operators evaluate first their right operands. Each operation in the system has a generalized definitional tree. The system is terminating, hence its translation is a logic program interpretable by Prolog. The execution of the goal

```
sequence(4) ->> T , write(T) , fail .
```

generates all the valid sequences of length 4, i.e.:

$[\heartsuit, \clubsuit, \diamondsuit, \clubsuit]$ $[\clubsuit, \heartsuit, \diamondsuit, \clubsuit]$ $[\diamondsuit, \heartsuit, \diamondsuit, \clubsuit]$ $[\diamondsuit, \clubsuit, \heartsuit, \clubsuit]$ $[\clubsuit, \diamondsuit, \heartsuit, \clubsuit]$ $[\heartsuit, \diamondsuit, \heartsuit, \clubsuit]$
$[\heartsuit, \diamondsuit, \clubsuit, \diamondsuit]$ $[\clubsuit, \heartsuit, \clubsuit, \diamondsuit]$ $[\diamondsuit, \heartsuit, \clubsuit, \diamondsuit]$ $[\diamondsuit, \clubsuit, \heartsuit, \diamondsuit]$ $[\heartsuit, \clubsuit, \heartsuit, \diamondsuit]$ $[\clubsuit, \diamondsuit, \heartsuit, \diamondsuit]$
$[\clubsuit, \diamondsuit, \clubsuit, \heartsuit]$ $[\heartsuit, \diamondsuit, \clubsuit, \heartsuit]$ $[\diamondsuit, \heartsuit, \clubsuit, \heartsuit]$ $[\diamondsuit, \clubsuit, \diamondsuit, \heartsuit]$ $[\heartsuit, \clubsuit, \diamondsuit, \heartsuit]$ $[\clubsuit, \heartsuit, \diamondsuit, \heartsuit]$

Query Optimisation In An Object-Oriented Database Using Prolog

Zhuoan Jiao and Peter M. D. Gray
Dept. of Computing Science
University of Aberdeen, AB9 2UE
Scotland, UK
E-mail: {jiao, pgray}@csd.abdn.ac.uk

— Extended Abstract —

This abstract describes the design of a query optimiser for the object-oriented database P/FDM using Prolog. The translation of a database query into an efficient executable program in many ways resembles a specialised program transformation problem [Fr87]. From a user's point of view, it is obviously desirable that they can write queries against a database clearly and naturally without concern for efficiency issues. However, queries written in this declarative manner are usually not efficient for execution, therefore a query optimiser becomes necessary in a database system to improve the performance.

P/FDM is an object-oriented database system developed at Aberdeen University, and is in use with a database of 40Mb of three-dimensional protein data. In P/FDM, user-submitted queries are expressed declaratively in a language based on Shipman's Daplex language [Sh81]. Although a query expressed in Daplex appears to use nested loops from an imperative language, it can be expressed declaratively in *ZF expression*, and the optimisation is based on the equivalence of most Daplex queries to ZF expressions using objects [PG90]. The optimiser incorporates heuristics and uses rewrite rules to transform the ZF expression of a query into a more efficient query execution strategy expressed in Prolog goals.

Translating a Daplex query into Prolog code proceeds in three stages: (a) the query is parsed into ZF expression; (b) the ZF expression is passed to the P/FDM optimiser to be optimised; (c) the Prolog code is generated based on the result of the optimiser. During the optimisation stage, information on the *key* values of an entity and *inverse* functions are used in deciding access path. Heuristics are also incorporated to reduce the search space. Readers are referred to [JG91] for more details.

Prolog as a language has certain features which recommend it as our implementation language and the target language of the optimiser. It is well suited to query parsing and optimisation [Wa81, Gray85]. A very important feature of Prolog is that data and programs are treated uniformly. We can write rules in Prolog which inspect a query, treating it as a data structure, and rebuild the query in the re-ordered form so that it runs faster [Gray87]. It is interesting to note that although Prolog is generally considered to be a high-level language, in the context of database work it can behave like a navigational query language as noted by [Za84]. Typical optimisation strategies can be expressed easily as rewrite rules in Prolog, for example:

rewrite(generate(ClassName,OidVar),
    getfnval(FuncName, ArgOidList, OidVar)):-
    generate(FuncName, ArgClassNameList, ArgOidList, ClassName, Var),
    Var = OidVar.

Here, expressions in *italic* are P/FDM Prolog primitives generated as the results of rewrite rules. The rule means "if an entity instance can be retrieved by following a function, then do not retrieve it by doing enumeration". The firing of the rewrite rules are decided by pattern matching. Using Prolog enables us to have more control over the rule base and organise rule firings in a more efficient manner.

Our goal is to implement an optimiser which can generate a good query evaluation plan for most queries within a satisfactory response time and avoid producing bad plans.

References

[Fr87] J.C. Freytag, "A Rule-Based View of Query Optimisation", pp173-180, *ACM SIGMOD 1987.*

[Gray85] P.M.D Gray, "Efficient Prolog Access to Codasyl and FDM Databases", pp 437-443, *ACM SIGMOD 1985*, S. Navathe (ed.).

[Gray87] P.M.D Gray, "Integration of Databases and Expert Systems Through Prolog", *Proc. Artificial Intelligence Conference*, San Sebastian (Spain), Sept. 1987, II World Basque Congress Secretariat, Vitoria-Gasteiz.

[JG91] Zhuoan Jiao and P.M.D Gray, "Optimisation Of Methods In A Navigational Query Language", to appear in the *Proc. 2nd International Conference on Deductive and Object-Oriented Database Systems*, December 1991, Munich, Germany.

[PG90] N.W. Paton and P.M.D. Gray, "Optimising and Executing Daplex Queries Using Prolog", *The Computer Journal*, pp547-556, Vol.33, No.6, 1990.

[Sh81] D. Shipman, "The Functional Data Model and the Data Language Daplex", *ACM Transactions on DB Systems*, 6, 1(March 1981).

[Wa81] D.H. Warren, "Efficient Processing of Interactive Relational Database Queries Expressed in Logic", *Proc. 7th VLDB*, 1981.

[Za84] Carlo Zaniolo, "Prolog: a Database Query Language for All Seasons", *Proc. 1st International Workshop on Expert Database Systems*, 1984.

Author Index

Published in 1990

AI and Cognitive Science '89, Dublin City University, Eire, 14–15 September 1989
A. F. Smeaton and G. McDermott (Eds.)

Specification and Verification of Concurrent Systems, University of Stirling, Scotland, 6–8 July 1988
C. Rattray (Ed.)

Semantics for Concurrency, Proceedings of the International BCS-FACS Workshop, Sponsored by Logic for IT (S.E.R.C.), University of Leicester, UK, 23–25 July 1990
M. Z. Kwiatkowska, M. W. Shields and R. M. Thomas (Eds.)

Functional Programming, Glasgow 1989, Proceedings of the 1989 Glasgow Workshop, Fraserburgh, Scotland, 21–23 August 1989
K. Davis and J. Hughes (Eds.)

Persistent Object Systems, Proceedings of the Third International Workshop, Newcastle, Australia, 10–13 January 1989
J. Rosenberg and D. Koch (Eds.)

Z User Workshop, Oxford, 1989, Proceedings of the Fourth Annual Z User Meeting, Oxford, 15 December 1989
J. E. Nicholls (Ed.)

Formal Methods for Trustworthy Computer Systems (FM89), Halifax, Canada, 23–27 July 1989
Dan Craigen (Editor) and Karen Summerskill (Assistant Editor)

Security and Persistence, Proceedings of the International Workshop on Computer Architecture to Support Security and Persistence of Information, Bremen, West Germany, 8–11 May 1990
John Rosenberg and J. Leslie Keedy (Eds.)